P9-AGQ-997

4.50

SCHAUM'S OUTLINE OF

THEORY AND PROBLEMS

OF

GENETICS

•

BY

WILLIAM D. STANSFIELD, Ph.D.

Department of Biological Sciences
California Polytechnic State University

•

SCHAUM'S OUTLINE SERIES

McGRAW-HILL BOOK COMPANY

New York, St. Louis, San Francisco, Düsseldorf, Johannesburg, Kuala Lumpur, London, Mexico,
Montreal, New Delhi, Panama, São Paulo, Singapore, Sydney, and Toronto

Copyright © 1969 by McGraw-Hill, Inc. All Rights Reserved. Printed in the United States of America. No part of this publication may be reproduced. stored in a retrieval system, or transmitted, in any form or by any means, electronic, mechanical, photocopying, recording, or otherwise, without the prior written permission of the publisher.

ISBN 07-060842-3

10 11 12 13 14 15   SH SH   7 5 4 3 2 1 0 6

Preface

Genetics, the science of heredity, is a core subject among the biological sciences. All living things are the products of both "nature and nurture". The hereditary material provides the organism with its "nature" (or biological potentialities and limitations), while the environment provides the "nurture" which interacts with the genes to give the organism its distinctive anatomical, biochemical, physiological and behavioral characteristics. Because of the pervasive influence of genetics in every sphere of life, it has become a required subject in a wide range of college curricula.

The fact that most genetic principles can be precisely expressed in mathematical terms is a rather unique feature among biological disciplines. The mathematics of elementary genetics is not difficult, but genetics does require a degree of logic which some beginning students have not had the opportunity to develop. It is the purpose of this book to aid the beginner in the development of this faculty through the presentation of numerous typical problems and their detailed solutions. While primarily intended as a supplement to any standard genetics textbook, the statements of theory and principle are sufficiently complete that it could be used as a text by itself.

Each chapter begins with a clear statement of pertinent definitions, principles and background information, fully illustrated by examples. This is followed by sets of solved and supplementary problems. Answers to the supplementary problems are given at the end of each chapter. The solved problems serve to illustrate and amplify the theory, bring into sharp focus those fine points without which the student continually feels himself on unsafe ground, and provide the repetition of basic principles so vital to effective learning. The supplementary problems serve as a complete review of the material of each chapter.

Chapter topics correspond to material usually covered in elementary genetics courses, with the exclusion of largely descriptive subjects such as developmental genetics which do not lend themselves readily to problems requiring mathematical solutions. The only mathematical background needed for an understanding of the entire book is arithmetic and the elements of algebra. At least some exposure to college biology is assumed, but not absolutely necessary because important biological principles are reviewed as background information.

It would be desirable to study the material approximately in the order presented, because the vocabulary and principles introduced in earlier chapters are utilized in some of the theory and problems of later chapters. The chapter on Genetics of Microorganisms could be omitted entirely for a course built around the genetics of diploids (higher organisms). Considerably more material has been included here than can be covered in most beginning courses. This has been done to make the book more flexible, to provide a more useful source of reference and to stimulate further interest in the topics.

I am indebted to the Literary Executor of the late Sir Ronald A. Fisher, to Dr. Frank Yates, and to Oliver & Boyd Ltd., Edinburgh, for permission to publish a portion of Table IV from the 6th edition of *Statistical Tables for Biological, Agricultural, and Medical Research*. I am also grateful to Daniel Schaum and Nicola Monti for their splendid editorial cooperation, to Karen Dorr for most of the illustrations, and to Henry Hayden for typographical arrangement and art work.

WILLIAM D. STANSFIELD

California Polytechnic State University
June 1969

CONTENTS

CONTENTS

Chapter 1

The Physical Basis of Heredity

GENETICS

Genetics is that branch of biology concerned with heredity and variation. The hereditary units which are transmitted from one generation to the next (inherited) are called *genes*. The genes reside in a long molecule called deoxyribonucleic acid (DNA). The DNA, in conjunction with a protein matrix, forms nucleoprotein and becomes organized into structures with distinctive staining properties called *chromosomes* found in the nucleus of the cell. The behavior of genes is thus paralleled in many ways by the behavior of the chromosomes of which they are a part. A gene contains coded information for the production of proteins. DNA is normally a stable molecule with the capacity for self-replication. On rare occasions a change may occur spontaneously in some part of DNA. This change, called a *mutation*, alters the coded instructions and may result in a defective protein or in the cessation of protein synthesis. The net result of a mutation is often seen as a change in the physical appearance of the individual or a change in some other measurable attribute of the organism called a *character* or *trait*. Through the process of mutation a gene may be changed into two or more alternative forms called *allelomorphs* or *alleles*.

> **Example:** Healthy people have a gene which specifies the normal protein structure of the red blood cell pigment called hemoglobin. Some anemic individuals have an altered form of this gene, i.e. an allele, which makes a defective hemoglobin protein unable to carry the normal amount of oxygen to the body cells.

Each gene occupies a specific position on a chromosome, called the gene *locus* (*loci*, plural). All allelic forms of a gene therefore are found at corresponding positions on genetically similar (*homologous*) chromosomes. The word "locus" is sometimes used interchangeably for "gene". When the science of genetics was in its infancy the gene was thought to behave as a unit particle. These particles were believed to be arranged on the chromosome like beads on a string. This is still a useful concept for beginning students to adopt, but will require considerable modification when we study the chemical basis of heredity in Chapter 9. All the genes on a chromosome are said to be *linked* to one another and belong to the same *linkage group*. Wherever the chromosome goes it carries all of the genes in its linkage group with it. As we shall see later in this chapter, linked genes are not transmitted independently of one another, but genes in different linkage groups (on different chromosomes) are transmitted independently of one another.

CELLS

The smallest unit of life is the *cell*. All living things are composed of these basic units, from the simple unicellular structures of bacteria and protozoa to the complex structures of trees and man. Even within an individual all of the cells do not look alike. A muscle cell is obviously different from a nerve cell which in turn is different from a blood cell, etc. Thus there is no such thing as a typical cell type. Fig. 1-1 below is a composite diagram of an animal cell showing subcellular structures called *organelles* which many types of cells share in common. Most organelles are too small to be seen with the light microscope, but their structure can be studied with the electron microscope. These organelles perform distinctive functions which in total produce the characteristics of life associated with the cell (Table 1.1).

Fig. 1-1. Diagram of an animal cell.

Table 1.1

Functions of Cellular Organelles	
Cell Organelle	*Functions*
Cell or plasma membrane	Differentially permeable membrane through which extra-cellular substances may be selectively sampled and cell products may be liberated.
Cell wall (plants only)	Thick cellulose wall surrounding the cell membrane giving strength and rigidity to the cell.
Nucleus:	Regulates growth and reproduction of the cell.
Chromosomes	Bearers of hereditary instructions; regulation of cellular processes (seen clearly only during nuclear division).
Nucleolus	Function uncertain; may synthesize ribosomes; disappears during cellular replication.
Nucleoplasm (nuclear sap)	Contains materials for building DNA and messenger molecules which act as intermediates between nucleus and cytoplasm.
Nuclear membrane	Provides selective continuity between nuclear and cytoplasmic materials.
Cytoplasm:	Contains machinery for carrying out the instructions sent from the nucleus.
Endoplasmic reticulum	Greatly expanded surface area for biochemical reactions which normally occur at or across membrane surfaces.
Ribosomes	Sites of protein synthesis (shown as black dots lining the endoplasmic reticulum in Fig. 1-1).
Centrioles	Form poles for the divisional processes; capable of replication; usually not seen in plant cells.
Mitochondria	Energy production (Kreb's cycle, electron transport chain, beta oxidation of fatty acids, etc.).
Plastids (plants only)	Structures for storage of starch, pigments, and other cellular products. Photosynthesis occurs in chloroplasts.
Golgi body or apparatus	Production of cellular secretions; sometimes called dictyosomes in plants.
Lysosome (animals only)	Production of intracellular digestive enzymes which aid in disposal of bacteria and other foreign bodies; may cause cell destruction if ruptured.
Vacuoles	Storage depots for excess water, waste products, soluble pigments, etc.
Hyaloplasm	Contains enzymes for glycolysis and structural materials such as sugars, amino acids, water, vitamins, nucleotides, etc. (nutrient soup or cell sap).

CHROMOSOMES
1. Chromosome Number.

In higher organisms, each *somatic* cell (any body cell exclusive of sex cells) contains one set of chromosomes inherited from the *maternal* (female) parent and a comparable set of chromosomes (*homologous* chromosomes or *homologues*) from the *paternal* (male) parent. The number of chromosomes in this dual set is called the *diploid* (2n) number. The suffix "-ploid" refers to chromosome "sets". The prefix indicates the degree of ploidy. Sex cells or *gametes,* which contain half the number of chromosome sets found in somatic cells, are referred to as *haploid* cells (n). A *genome* is a set of chromosomes corresponding to the haploid set of a species. The number of chromosomes in each somatic cell is the same for all members of a given species. For example, human somatic cells contain 46 chromosomes, tobacco has 48, cattle 60, the garden pea 14, the fruit fly 8, etc. The diploid number of a species bears no direct relationship to the species position in the phylogenetic scheme of classification.

2. Chromosome Morphology.

The structure of chromosomes becomes most easily visible during certain phases of nuclear division when they are highly coiled. Each chromosome in the genome can usually be distinguished from all others by several criteria, including the relative lengths of the chromosomes, the position of a structure called the *centromere* which divides the chromosome into two arms of varying length, the presence and position of enlarged areas called knobs or chromomeres, the presence of tiny terminal extensions of chromatin material called satellites, etc. A chromosome with a median centromere (*metacentric*) will have arms of approximately equal size. A *submetacentric* or *acrocentric* chromosome has arms of distinctly unequal size. If a chromosome has its centromere at or very near one end of the chromosome it is called *telocentric*. Each chromosome of the genome (with the exception of sex chromosomes) is numbered consecutively according to length, beginning with the longest chromosome first.

3. Autosomes vs. Sex Chromosomes.

In the males of some species, including man, sex is associated with a morphologically dissimilar (*heteromorphic*) pair of chromosomes called *sex chromosomes*. Such a chromosome pair is usually labeled X and Y. Genetic factors on the Y chromosome determine maleness. Females have two morphologically identical X chromosomes. The members of any other homologous pairs of chromosomes (homologues) are morphologically indistinguishable, but usually are visibly different from other pairs (non-homologous chromosomes). All chromosomes exclusive of the sex chromosomes are called *autosomes*. Fig. 1-2 shows the chromosomal complement of the fruit fly *Drosophila melanogaster* (2n = 8) with three pairs of autosomes (2, 3, 4) and one pair of sex chromosomes.

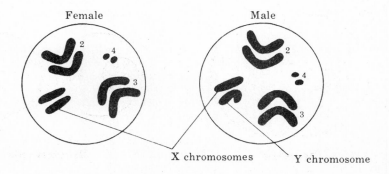

Fig. 1-2. Diagram of diploid cells in *Drosophila melanogaster*.

CELL DIVISION

1. Mitosis.

All somatic cells in a multicellular organism are descendants of one original cell, the *zygote,* through a divisional process called *mitosis* (Fig. 1-3). The function of mitosis is first to construct an exact copy of each chromosome and then to distribute, through division of the original (mother) cell, an identical set of chromosomes to each of the two daughter cells. *Interphase* is the period between division cycles. When the cell is ready to begin mitosis each DNA molecule (which is an integral part of the chromosome) *replicates* or makes an exact copy of itself. This copying process produces a chromosome with two identical functional strands called *chromatids,* both attached to a common centromere. At this stage the chromosomes are in a very long attenuated condition and appear only as chromatin granules under the light microscope. A mitotic division has four major stages: prophase,

Interphase   Prophase (early)   Prophase (middle)

Prophase (late)   Metaphase   Anaphase

Telophase   Daughter cells

Fig. 1-3. Mitosis in animal cells.

metaphase, anaphase and telophase. In *prophase,* the chromosomes become visible in the light microscope presumably due to coiling, shortening and thickening, and adding protein matrix to their mass as the process continues. By late prophase, the two identical or "sister" chromatids may be seen. The centrioles migrate to opposite ends of the cell and there establish mitotic centers (poles) from which spindle fibers organize and extend to the centromeres. The nuclear membrane begins to degenerate and by *metaphase* is completely gone. Now the centromeres move to the center of the cell, a position designated the equatorial or metaphase plate, and the spindle fibers, collectively known as the spindle apparatus, become fully formed. *Anaphase* begins when the centromere splits in two, allowing sister chromatids to separate and move towards opposite poles led by their centromeres. At this stage we may arbitrarily designate the separated sisters as new chromosomes. The arms of each chromosome drag behind their centromeres, giving them characteristic shapes depending upon the location of the centromere. Metacentric chromosomes appear V-shaped, submetacentric chromosomes appear J-shaped, and telocentric chromosomes appear rod shaped. In *telophase,* an identical set of chromosomes is assembled at each pole of the cell. The chromosomes begin to uncoil and return to an interphase condition. The spindle degenerates, the nuclear membrane reforms, and the cytoplasm divides in a process called *cytokinesis.* In animals, cytokinesis is accomplished by the formation of a cleavage furrow which deepens and eventually "pinches" the cell in two as shown in Fig. 1-3. Cytokinesis in most plants involves the construction of a *cell plate* of pectin originating in the center of the cell and spreading laterally to the cell wall. Later, cellulose and other strengthening materials are added to the cell plate, converting it into a new cell wall. The two products of mitosis are called *daughter cells* and may or may not be of equal size depending upon where the plane of cytokinesis sections the cell. Thus while there is no assurance of equal distribution of cytoplasmic components to daughter cells, they do contain exactly the same type and number of chromosomes and hence possess exactly the same genetic constitution.

2. Meiosis.

Sexual reproduction involves the manufacture of gametes (*gametogenesis*) and their union (*fertilization*). Gametogenesis occurs only in specialized cells (*germ line*) of the reproductive organs. Gametes contain the haploid (n) number of chromosomes, but originate from diploid (2n) cells of the germ line. Obviously the number of chromosomes must be reduced by half during gametogenesis. The reductional process is called *meiosis* (Fig. 1-4). Meiosis actually involves two divisions. The first meiotic division (meiosis I) is a reductional division producing two haploid cells from a single diploid cell. The second meiotic division (meiosis II) is an equational division which separates the sister chromatids of the haploid cells. The prophase of meiosis I differs from the prophase of a mitotic division in that homologous chromosomes come to lie side by side in a pairing process called *synapsis.* Each pair of synapsed homologues is called a *bivalent*; since it consists of four chromid strands, a bivalent is also called a *tetrad.* During synapsis non-sister chromatids may break and reunite with one another in a process called *crossing over.* The point of exchange appears in the microscope as an overlapping region called a *chiasma* (chiasmata, plural). During metaphase I, the bivalents orient themselves at random on the equatorial plate. At first anaphase the centromeres do not divide, but continue to hold sister chromatids together. The homologues separate and move to opposite poles. That is, whole chromosomes (each consisting of two chromatids) move apart. This in effect is the movement which reduces the chromosome number from the diploid (2n) condition to the haploid (n) state. Cytokinesis in telophase I divides the diploid mother cell into two haploid daughter cells. This ends the first meiotic division. The brief period between the first and second meiotic divisions is called *interkinesis.* In prophase II, the spindle apparatus reforms. By metaphase II, the centromeres have lined up on the equatorial plate. During anaphase

II the centromeres of each chromosome divide, allowing sister chromatids to separate. Cytokinesis in telophase II divides the two cells into four meiotic products.

| Interphase | Early Prophase I | Synapsis | Crossing Over |

| Metaphase I | Anaphase I | Telophase I | Prophase II |

End Meiosis I
Beginning Meiosis II

| Metaphase II | Anaphase II | Telophase II | Meoitic Products |

Fig. 1-4. Meiosis in plant cells.

The distinguishing characteristics of mitosis and meiosis are summarized in Table 1.2 below.

Table 1.2

Characteristics of Mitosis and Meiosis	
Mitosis	*Meiosis*
(1) An equational division which separates sister chromatids.	(1) The first stage is a reductional division which separates homologous chromosomes at first anaphase; sister chromatids separate in an equational division at second anaphase.
(2) One division per cycle, i.e. one cytoplasmic division (cytokinesis) per equational chromosomal division.	(2) Two divisions per cycle, i.e. two cytoplasmic divisions, one following reductional chromosomal division and one following equational chromosomal division.
(3) Chromosomes fail to synapse; no chiasmata form; genetic exchange between homologous chromosomes does not occur.	(3) Chromosomes synapse and form chiasmata; genetic exchange occurs between homologues.
(4) Two products (daughter cells) produced per cycle.	(4) Four cellular products (gametes or spores) produced per cycle.
(5) Genetic content of mitotic products are identical.	(5) Genetic content of meiotic products different; centromeres may be replicas of either maternal or paternal centromeres in varying combinations.
(6) Chromosome number of daughter cells is the same as that of mother cell.	(6) Chromosome number of meiotic products is half that of the mother cell.
(7) Mitotic products are usually capable of undergoing additional mitotic divisions.	(7) Meiotic products cannot undergo another meiotic division although they may undergo mitotic division.
(8) Normally occurs in most all somatic cells.	(8) Occurs only in specialized cells of the germ line.
(9) Begins at the zygote stage and continues through the life of the organism.	(9) Occurs only after a higher organism has begun to mature; occurs in the zygote of many algae and fungi.

MENDEL'S LAWS

Gregor Mendel published the results of his genetic studies on the garden pea in 1866 and thereby laid the foundation of modern genetics. In this paper Mendel proposed some basic genetic principles. One of these is known as the *principle of segregation*. He found that from any one parent, only one allelic form of a gene is transmitted through a gamete to the offspring. For example, a plant which had a factor (or gene) for round shaped seed and also an allele for wrinkled shaped seed would transmit only one of these two alleles through a gamete to its offspring. Mendel knew nothing of chromosomes or meiosis, as they had not yet been discovered. We now know that the physical basis for this principle is in first meiotic anaphase where homologous chromosomes segregate or separate from each other. If the gene for round seed is on one chromosome and its allelic form for wrinkled seed is on the homologous chromosome, then it becomes clear that alleles normally will not be found in the same gamete.

Mendel's *principle of independent assortment* states that the segregation of one factor pair occurs independently of any other factor pair. We know that this is true only for loci on non-homologous chromosomes. For example, on one homologous pair of chromosomes are the seed shape alleles and on another pair of homologues are the alleles for green and yellow seed color. The segregation of the seed shape alleles occurs independently of the segregation of the seed color alleles because each pair of homologues behaves as an independent unit during meiosis. Furthermore, because the orientation of bivalents on the first meiotic metaphase plate is completely at random, four combinations of factors could be found in the meiotic products: (1) round-yellow, (2) wrinkled-green, (3) round-green, (4) wrinkled-yellow.

GAMETOGENESIS

Usually the immediate end products of meiosis are not fully developed gametes or spores. A period of *maturation* commonly follows meiosis. In plants, one or more mitotic divisions are required to produce reproductive spores, whereas in animals the meiotic products develop directly into gametes through growth and/or differentiation. The entire process of producing mature gametes or spores, of which meiotic division is the most important part, is called *gametogenesis*.

1. Animal Gametogenesis (*as represented in mammals*)

Gametogenesis in the male animal is called *spermatogenesis* (Fig. 1-5(*a*)). Mammalian spermatogenesis originates in the germinal epithelium of the seminiferous tubules of the male gonads (testes) from diploid primordial cells. These cells undergo repeated mitotic divisions to form a population of *spermatogonia*. By growth, a spermatogonium may differentiate into a diploid *primary spermatocyte* with the capacity to undergo meiosis. The first meiotic division occurs in these primary spermatocytes, producing haploid *secondary spermatocytes*. From these cells the second meiotic division produces four haploid meiotic products called *spermatids*. Almost the entire amount of cytoplasm then extrudes into a long whiplike tail during maturation and the cell becomes transformed into a mature male gamete called a *sperm cell* or *spermatozoan* (-zoa, plural).

(*a*) Spermatogenesis   (*b*) Oögenesis

Fig. 1-5. Animal gametogenesis.

Gametogenesis in the female animal is called *oögenesis* (Fig. 1-5(*b*)). Mammalian oögenesis originates in the germinal epithelium of the female gonads (ovaries) in diploid primordial cells called *oögonia*. By growth and storage of much cytoplasm or yolk (to be used as food by the early embryo), the oögonium is transformed into a diploid *primary oöcyte* with the capacity to undergo meiosis. The first meiotic division reduces the chromosome number by half and also distributes vastly different amounts of cytoplasm to the two products by a grossly unequal cytokinesis. The larger cell thus produced is called a *secondary oöcyte* and the smaller is a primary *polar body*. In some cases the first polar body may undergo the second meiotic division, producing two secondary polar bodies. All polar bodies degenerate, however, and take no part in fertilization. The second meiotic division of the oöcyte again involves an unequal cytokinesis, producing a large yolky *oötid* and a secondary polar body. By additional growth and differentiation the oötid becomes a mature female gamete called an *ovum* or *egg cell*.

The union of male and female gametes (sperm and egg) is called *fertilization* and reestablishes the diploid number in the resulting cell called a *zygote*. The head of the sperm enters the egg, but the tail piece (the bulk of the cytoplasm of the male gamete) remains outside and degenerates. Subsequent mitotic divisions produce the numerous cells of the embryo which become organized into the tissues and organs of the new individual.

2. Plant Gametogenesis (*as represented in angiosperms*)

Gametogenesis in the plant kingdom varies considerably between major groups of plants. The process as described below is that typical of many flowering plants (*angiosperms*). *Microsporogenesis* (Fig. 1-6) is the process of gametogenesis in the male part of the flower (*anther*, Fig. 1-7) resulting in reproductive spores called *pollen grains*. A diploid

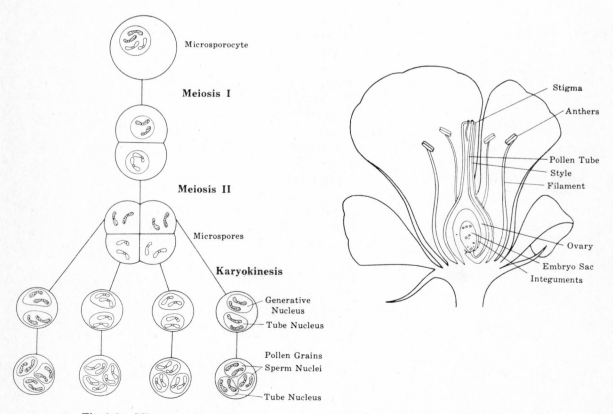

Fig. 1-6. Microsporogenesis.

Fig. 1-7. Diagram of a flower.

microspore mother cell (*microsporocyte*) in the anther divides by meiosis, forming at the first division a pair of haploid cells. The second meiotic division produces a cluster of four haploid *microspores*. Following meiosis, each microspore undergoes a mitotic division of the chromosomes without a cytoplasmic division (*karyokinesis*), producing a cell containing two haploid nuclei. Pollen grains are usually shed at this stage. Upon germination of the pollen tube, one of these nuclei (or haploid sets of chromosomes) becomes a *generative nucleus* and divides again by mitosis without cytokinesis to form two *sperm nuclei*. The other nucleus, which does not divide, becomes the *tube nucleus*.

Megasporogenesis (Fig. 1-8) is the process of gametogenesis in the female part of the flower (*ovary*, Fig. 1-7) resulting in reproductive cells called *embryo sacs*. A diploid megaspore mother cell (*megasporocyte*) in the ovary divides by meiosis, forming in the first division a pair of haploid cells. The second meiotic division produces a linear group of four haploid *megaspores*. Following meiosis, three of the megaspores degenerate. The remaining megaspore undergoes three mitotic divisions of the chromosomes without intervening cytokineses (*karyokineses*), producing a large cell with eight haploid nuclei (immature embryo sac). The sac is surrounded by maternal tissues of the ovary called *integuments* and by the megasporangium (nucellus). At one end of the sac there is an opening in the integuments (*micropyle*) through which the pollen tube will penetrate. Three nuclei of the sac orient themselves near the micropylar end and two of the three (*synergids*) degenerate. The third nucleus develops into an *egg nucleus*. Another group of three nuclei moves to the opposite end of the sac and degenerates (*antipodals*). The two remaining nuclei (*polar nuclei*) unite near the center of the sac, forming a single diploid *fusion nucleus*. The mature embryo sac (*megagametophyte*) is now ready for fertilization.

Fig. 1-8. Megasporogenesis.

Pollen grains from the anthers are carried by wind or insects to the *stigma*. The pollen grain germinates into a pollen tube which grows down the *style,* presumably under the direction of the tube nucleus. The pollen tube enters the ovary and makes its way through the micropyle of the ovule into the embryo sac (Fig. 1-9). Both sperm nuclei are released into the embryo sac. The pollen tube and the tube nucleus, having served their function, degenerate. One sperm nucleus fuses with the egg nucleus to form a diploid zygote which will then develop into the embryo. The other sperm nucleus unites with the fusion nucleus to form a triploid (3n) nucleus which, by subsequent mitotic divisions, forms a starchy nutritive tissue called *endosperm*. The outermost layer of endosperm cells is called *aleurone*. The embryo, surrounded by endosperm tissue, and in some cases such as corn and other grasses where it is also surrounded by a thin outer layer of diploid material tissue called *pericarp,* becomes the familiar seed. Since two sperm nuclei are involved, this process is termed *double fertilization*. Upon germination of the seed, the young seedling (the next sporophytic generation) utilizes the nutrients stored in the endosperm for growth until it emerges from the soil, at which time it becomes capable of manufacturing its own food by photosynthesis.

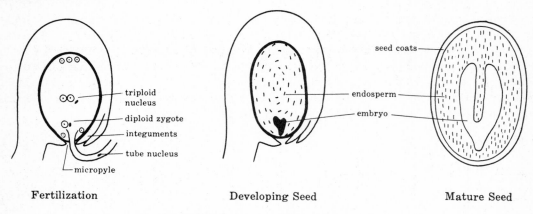

Fertilization   Developing Seed   Mature Seed

Fig. 1-9. Fertilization and development of a seed.

LIFE CYCLES

Life cycles of most plants have two distinctive generations: a haploid *gametophytic* (gamete-bearing plant) generation and a diploid *sporophytic* (spore-bearing plant) generation. Gametophytes produce gametes which unite to form sporophytes which in turn give rise to spores that develop into gametophytes, etc. This process is referred to as the *alternation of generations*. In lower plants, such as mosses and liverworts, the gametophyte is a conspicuous and independently living generation, the sporophyte being small and dependent upon the gametophyte. In higher plants (ferns, gymnosperms and angiosperms), the situation is reversed; the sporophyte is the independent and conspicuous generation and the gametophyte is the less conspicuous and, in the case of gymnosperms (cone bearing plants) and angiosperms (flowering plants), completely dependent generation. We have just seen in angiosperms that the male gametophytic generation is reduced to a pollen tube and three haploid nuclei (*microgametophyte*); the female gametophyte (*megagametophyte*) is a single multinucleated cell called the embryo sac surrounded and nourished by ovarian tissue.

Many simpler organisms such as one-celled animals (protozoa), algae, yeast, and other fungi are useful in genetic studies and have interesting life cycles that exhibit considerable variation. Some of these are discussed below. The life cycles of bacteria and viruses will be presented in Chapter 10.

1. Life Cycle of *Paramecium aurelia*.

This microscopic ciliated protozoan possesses a large vegetative or somatic *macronucleus* consisting of many sets of chromosomes (polyploid) which regulates the physiological processes of the cell. Two smaller diploid *micronuclei* function in fertilization. Paramecia reproduce asexually (mitotically) in a process called *binary fission* (Fig. 1-10(*a*)). All of the cells derived from one ancestral cell by fission are genetically identical and collectively referred to as a *clone*.

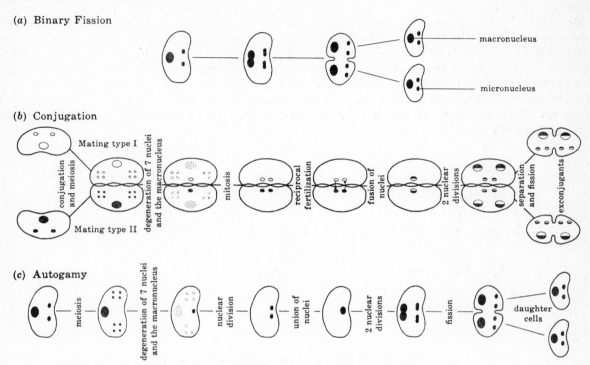

Fig. 1-10. Life cycle of *Paramecium aurelia.*

Sexual reproduction is accomplished by *conjugation* between cells of different mating types (Fig. 1-10(*b*)). During conjugation the macronucleus degenerates and reforms in the cell following mating (exconjugant). After pairing, each of the two micronuclei in both conjugating cells undergoes meiosis forming eight haploid nuclei per cell, seven of which degenerate. The one remaining nucleus in each cell doubles by mitosis, producing two identical gametic nuclei, one being stationary, the other being mobile and migrating into the opposite cell. A fusion nucleus is formed by union of the stationary nucleus and the migratory nucleus from the opposite cell. Each fusion nucleus divides twice by mitosis; two of the products become micronuclei, two become new macronuclei. At the first fission following conjugation, each daughter cell receives one of the two macronuclei, restoring the normal complement of one macronucleus and two micronuclei. Normally, during reciprocal exchange of haploid nuclei, little if any cytoplasm is exchanged. Under certain conditions, however, the bridge connecting the conjugants persists after fertilization, allowing cytoplasmic exchange to occur.

Occasionally an individual *Paramecium* may reorganize its genetic endowment by a process of self-fertilization called *autogamy* (Fig. 1-10(*c*)). An isolated cell will follow the same sequence of events as in conjugation to the point where reciprocal fertilization would be possible. Having no pairing partner with which to exchange nuclei, the two haploid products unite forming a diploid fusion nucleus. The rest of the cycle is analogous to the corresponding steps in conjugation.

2. Life Cycle of *Chlamydomonas reinhardi*.

Asexual reproduction in the single celled motile alga *Chlamydomonas reinhardi* usually involves two mitotic divisions within the old cell wall (Fig. 1-11). Rupture of the sporangium releases the new generation of haploid *zoospores*. If nutritional requirements are satisfied, asexual reproduction may go on indefinitely. In unfavorable conditions where nitrogen balance is upset, daughter cells may be changed to gametes. Genetically there are two mating types, plus (+) and minus (−), which are morphologically indistinguishable and therefore called *isogametes*. Fusion of gametes unites two entire cells into a diploid nonmotile zygote which is relatively resistant to unfavorable growth conditions. With the return of conditions favoring growth, the zygote experiences meiosis and forms four motile haploid daughter cells (zoospores), two of plus and two of minus mating type.

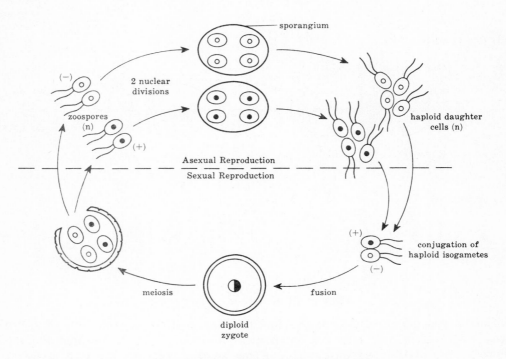

Fig. 1-11.   Life cycle of *Chlamydomonas reinhardi*.

3. Life Cycle of *Saccharomyces cerevisiae*.

Fungi which produce sexual spores (*ascospores*) housed in a common sac (*ascus*) are called *ascomycetes*. One of the simplest ascomycetes is the unicellular baker's yeast *Saccharomyces cerevisiae* (Fig. 1-12 below). Asexual reproduction is by budding, a mitotic process usually with unequal cytokinesis. The sexual cycle involves the union of entire cells of opposite mating type, forming a diploid zygote. The diploid cell may reproduce diploid progeny asexually by budding or haploid progeny by meiosis. The four haploid nuclei form ascospores enclosed by the ascus. Rupture of the ascus releases the haploid spores which then germinate into new yeast cells.

4. Life Cycle of *Neurospora crassa*.

Another ascomycete of interest to geneticists is the bread mold *Neurospora crassa* (Fig. 1-13 below). The fungal mat or *mycelium* is composed of intertwined filaments called *hyphae*. The tips of hyphae may pinch off asexual spores called *conidia*, which germinate

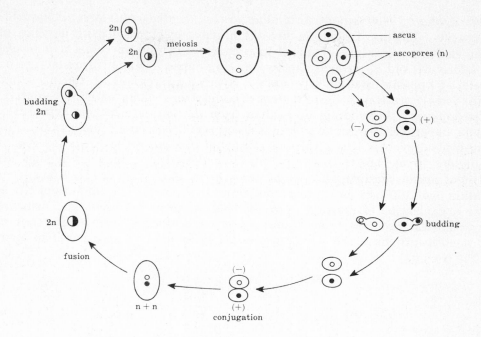

Fig. 1-12.   Life cycle of *Saccharomyces cerevisiae*.

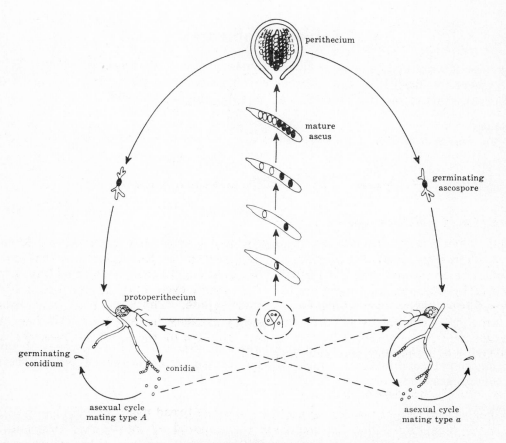

Fig. 1-13.   Life cycle of *Neurospora crassa*.

into more hyphae. The vegetative hyphae are segmented, with several haploid nuclei in each segment. Hyphae from one mycelium may anastomose with hyphae of another mycelium to form a mixture of nuclei in a common cytoplasm called a *heterokaryon*. A pair of alleles, *A* and *a*, governs the two mating types. Sexual reproduction occurs only when cells of opposite mating type unite. Specialized regions of the mycelium produce immature female fruiting bodies (*protoperithecia*) from which extrude receptive filaments called *trichogynes*. A conidium or hyphae from the opposite mating type fuses with the trichogyne, undergoes several karyokineses, and fertilizes many female nuclei. Each of the resulting diploid zygotes lies within an elongated sac called the *ascus* (*asci*, plural). The zygote divides by meiosis to form four nuclei, followed by a mitotic division which yields four pairs of nuclei, maturing into eight *ascospores*. A mature fruiting body (*perithecium*) may contain over 100 asci, each containing eight ascospores. The confines of the ascus force the polar organization of division to orient lengthwise in the ascus and also prevents the meiotic or mitotic products from slipping past each other. Each of the four chromatids of first meiotic prophase are now represented by a pair of ascospores in tandem order within the ascus.

Solved Problems

1.1. Consider 3 pairs of homologous chromosomes with centromeres labeled A/a, B/b and C/c where the slash line separates one chromosome from its homologue. How many different kinds of meiotic products can this individual produce?

Solution:

For ease in determining all possible combinations, we can use a dichotomous branching system.

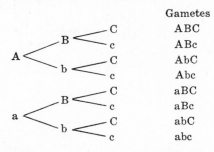

Eight different chromosomal combinations are expected in the gametes.

1.2. Develop a general formula which expresses the number of different types of gametic chromosomal combinations which can be formed in an organism with k pairs of chromosomes.

Solution:

It is obvious from the solution of the preceding problem that 1 pair of chromosomes gives two types of gametes, 2 pairs give 4 types of gametes, 3 pairs give 8 types, etc. The progression 2, 4, 8, ... can be expressed by the formula 2^k where k is the number of chromosome pairs.

1.3.   The horse (*Equus caballus*) has a diploid complement of 64 chromosomes including 36 acrocentric autosomes; the ass (*Equus asinus*) has 62 chromosomes including 22 acrocentric autosomes.   (*a*) Predict the number of chromosomes to be found in the hybrid offspring (mule) produced by mating a male ass (jack) to a female horse (mare).   (*b*) Why are mules usually sterile (incapable of producing viable gametes)?

Solution:

(*a*)   The sperm of the jack carries the haploid number of chromosomes for its species (62/2 = 31); the egg of the mare carries the haploid number for its species (64/2 = 32); the hybrid mule formed by the union of these gametes would have a diploid number of 31 + 32 = 63.

(*b*)   The haploid set of chromosomes of the horse, which includes 18 acrocentric autosomes, is so dissimilar to that of the ass, which includes only 11 acrocentric autosomes, that meiosis in the mule germ line cannot proceed beyond first prophase where synapsis of homologues occurs.

1.4.   When a plant of chromosomal type *aa* pollinates a plant of type *AA*, what chromosomal type of embryo and endosperm is expected in the resulting seeds?

Solution:

The pollen parent produces two sperm nuclei in each pollen grain of type *a*, one combining with the *A* egg nucleus to produce a diploid zygote (embryo) of type *Aa* and the other combining with the maternal fusion nucleus *AA* to produce a triploid endosperm of type *AAa*.

1.5.   Given the first meiotic metaphase orientation shown on the right, and keeping all products in sequential order as they would be formed from left to right, diagram the embryo sac which develops from the meiotic product at the left and label the chromosomal constitution of all its nuclei.

Solution:

| End Meiosis I | End Meiosis II | Mature Embryo Sac |

Supplementary Problems

1.6.   There are 40 chromosomes in somatic cells of the house mouse. (*a*) How many chromosomes does a mouse receive from its father? (*b*) How many autosomes are present in a mouse gamete? (*c*) How many sex chromosomes are in a mouse ovum? (*d*) How many autosomes are in somatic cells of a female?

1.7.   Name each stage of mitosis described.   (*a*) Chromosomes line up in the equatorial plane. (*b*) Nuclear membrane reforms and cytokinesis occurs.   (*c*) Chromosomes become visible, spindle apparatus forms.   (*d*) Sister chromatids move to opposite poles of the cell.

1.8. Identify the mitotic stage represented in each of the following diagrams of isolated cells from an individual with a genome consisting of one metacentric pair and one acrocentric pair of chromosomes.

(a)   (b)   (c)   (d)

1.9. Identify the meiotic stage represented in each of the following diagrams of isolated cells from the germ line of an individual with one pair of acrocentric and one pair of metacentric chromosomes.

(a)   (b)   (c)

(d)   (e)   (f)

1.10. How many different types of gametic chromosomal combinations can be formed in the garden pea (2n = 14)? *Hint*: See Problem 1.2.

1.11. (a) What type of division (equational or reductional) is exemplified by the anaphase chromosomal movements shown below?

(i)   (ii)

(b) Does the movement shown at (i) occur in mitosis or meiosis?
(c) Does the movement shown at (ii) occur in mitosis or meiosis?

1.12. What animal cells correspond to the three megaspores which degenerate following meiosis in plants?

1.13. What plant cell corresponds functionally to the primary spermatocyte?

1.14. What is the probability of a sperm cell of a man (n = 23) containing only replicas of the centromeres which were received from his mother?

1.15.   How many chromosomes of man (2n = 46) will be found in (*a*) a secondary spermatocyte, (*b*) a spermatid, (*c*) a spermatozoan, (*d*) a spermatogonium, (*e*) a primary spermatocyte?

1.16.   How many spermatozoa are produced by (*a*) a spermatogonium, (*b*) a secondary spermatocyte, (*c*) a spermatid, (*d*) a primary spermatocyte?

1.17.   How many human egg cells (ova) are produced by (*a*) an oögonium, (*b*) a primary oöcyte, (*c*) an oötid, (*d*) a polar body?

1.18.   Corn (*Zea mays*) has a diploid number of 20. How many chromosomes would be expected in (*a*) a meiotic product (microspore or megaspore), (*b*) the cell resulting from the first nuclear division (karyokinesis) of a megaspore, (*c*) a polar nucleus, (*d*) a sperm nucleus, (*e*) a microspore mother cell, (*f*) a leaf cell, (*g*) a mature embryo sac (after degeneration of non-functional nuclei), (*h*) an egg nucleus, (*i*) an endosperm cell, (*j*) a cell of the embryo, (*k*) a cell of the pericarp, (*l*) an aleurone cell?

1.19.   A pollen grain of corn with nuclei labeled A, B and C fertilized an embryo sac with nuclei labeled D, E, F, G, H, I, J and K as shown below.

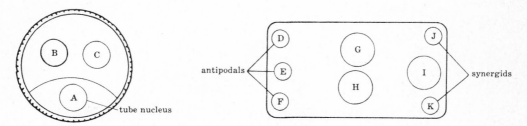

(*a*) Which of the following 5 combinations could be found in the embryo: (1) ABC, (2) BCI, (3) GHC, (4) AI, (5) CI? (*b*) Which of the above 5 combinations could be found in the aleurone layer of the seed? (*c*) Which of the above 5 combinations could be found in the germinating pollen tube? (*d*) Which of the nuclei, if any, in the pollen grain would contain genetically identical sets of chromosomes? (*e*) Which of the nuclei in the embryo sac would be chromosomally and genetically equivalent? (*f*) Which of the nuclei in these two gametophytes will have no descendants in the mature seed?

1.20.   A certain plant has eight chromosomes in its root cells: a long metacentric pair, a short metacentric pair, a long telocentric pair, and a short telocentric pair. If this plant fertilizes itself (self-pollination), what proportion of the offspring would be expected to have (*a*) four pairs of telocentric chromosomes, (*b*) one telocentric pair and three metacentric pairs of chromosomes, (*c*) two metacentric and two telocentric pairs of chromosomes?

1.21.   Referring to the preceding problem, what proportion of the meiotic products from such a plant would be expected to contain (*a*) four metacentric pairs of chromosomes, (*b*) two metacentric and two telocentric pairs of chromosomes, (*c*) one metacentric and one telocentric pair of chromosomes, (*d*) two metacentric and two telocentric chromosomes?

1.22.   How many pollen grains are produced by (*a*) 20 microspore mother cells, (*b*) a cluster of 4 microspores?

1.23.   How many sperm nuclei are produced by (*a*) a dozen microspore mother cells, (*b*) a generative nucleus, (*c*) 100 tube nuclei?

1.24.   (*a*) Diagram the pollen grain responsible for the doubly fertilized embryo sac shown on the right. (*b*) Diagram the first meiotic metaphase (in an organism with two pairs of homologues labeled *A*, *a* and *B*, *b*) which produced the pollen grain in part (*a*).

For Problems 1.25-1.28, diagram the designated stages of gametogenesis in a diploid organism which has one pair of metacentric and one pair of acrocentric chromosomes. Label each of the chromatids assuming that the locus of gene *A* is on the metacentric pair (one of which carries the *A* allele and its homologue carries the *a* allele) and that the locus of gene *B* is on the acrocentric chromosome pair (one of which carries the *B* allele and its homologue carries the *b* allele).

1.25.   *Oögenesis*: (a) first metaphase; (b) first telophase resulting from part (a); (c) second metaphase resulting from part (b); (d) second telophase resulting from part (c).

1.26.   *Spermatogenesis*: (a) anaphase of a dividing spermatogonium; (b) anaphase of a dividing primary spermatocyte; (c) anaphase of a secondary spermatocyte derived from part (b); (d) four sperm cells resulting from part (b).

1.27.   *Microsporogenesis*: (a) synapsis in a microsporocyte; (b) second meiotic metaphase; (c) first meiotic metaphase in the microspore mother cell which produced the cell of part (b); (d) anaphase of the second nuclear division (karyokinesis) following meiosis in a developing microgametophyte derived from part (b).

1.28.   *Megasporogenesis*: (a) second meiotic telophase; (b) first meiotic telophase which produced the cell of part (a); (c) anaphase of the second nuclear division (karyokinesis) in a cell derived from part (a); (d) mature embryo sac produced from part (c).

Answers to Supplementary Problems

1.6.   (a) 20, (b) 19, (c) 1, (d) 38

1.7.   (a) metaphase, (b) telophase, (c) prophase, (d) anaphase

1.8.   (a) metaphase, (b) prophase, (c) telophase, (d) anaphase

1.9.   (a) 1st anaphase, (b) 1st metaphase, (c) 2nd prophase or end of 1st telophase, (d) 2nd anaphase, (e) 1st prophase, (f) 2nd telophase (meiotic product)

1.10.   128

1.11.   (a) (i) is an equational division, (ii) is a reductional division; (b) both; (c) meiosis

1.12.   Polar bodies

1.13.   Microspore mother cell (microsporocyte); both are diploid cells with the capacity to divide meiotically.

1.14. $(\frac{1}{2})^{23}$, less than one chance in 8 million

1.15.   (a) 23, (b) 23, (c) 23, (d) 46, (e) 46

1.16.   (a) 4, (b) 2, (c) 1, (d) 4

1.17.   (a) 1, (b) 1, (c) 1, (d) 0

1.18.   (a) 10, (b) 20, (c) 10, (d) 10, (e) 20, (f) 20, (g) 30, (h) 10, (i) 30, (j) 20, (k) 20, (l) 30

1.19.   (a) 5; (b) 3; (c) 1; (d) A, B, C; (e) D, E, F, G, H, I, J, K; (f) A, D, E, F, J, K

1.20.   (a) 0, (b) 0, (c) all

1.21.   (a) 0, (b) 0, (c) 0, (d) all

1.22.   (a) 80, (b) 4

1.23.   (a) 96, (b) 2, (c) 0

1.24. (*a*)   (*b*)

Only one of several possible solutions is shown for each of Problems 1.25-1.28.

1.25. (*a*)   (*b*)   (*c*)   (*d*)

1.26. (*a*)   (*b*)   (*c*)   (*d*)

1.27. (*a*)   (*b*)   (*c*)   (*d*)

1.28. (*a*)   (*b*)   (*c*)   (*d*)

Chapter 2

Single Gene Inheritance

TERMINOLOGY

1. Phenotype.

A *phenotype* may be any measurable characteristic or distinctive trait possessed by an organism. The trait may be visible to the eye, such as the color of a flower or the texture of hair, or it may require special tests for its identification, as in the determination of the respiratory quotient or the serological test for blood type. The phenotype is the result of gene products brought to expression in a given environment.

> **Example 2.1.** Rabbits of the Himalayan breed in the usual range of environments develop black pigment at the tips of the nose, tail, feet and ears. If raised at very high temperatures, an all white rabbit is produced. The gene for Himalayan color pattern specifies a temperature sensitive enzyme which is inactivated at high temperature, resulting in a loss of pigmentation.

> **Example 2.2.** The flowers of hydrangea may be blue if grown in acid soil or pinkish if grown in alkaline soil, due to an interaction of gene products with the hydrogen ion concentration of their environment.

The kinds of traits which we shall encounter in the study of simple Mendelian inheritance will be considered to be relatively unaffected by the normal range of environmental conditions in which the organism is found. It is important, however, to remember that genes establish boundaries within which the environment may modify the phenotype.

2. Genotype.

All of the genes possessed by an individual constitute its *genotype*. In this chapter, we shall be concerned only with that portion of the genotype involving alleles at a single locus.

(a) ***Homozygous.*** The union of gametes carrying identical alleles produces a *homozygous* genotype. A homozygote produces only one kind of gamete.

(b) ***Pure Line.*** A group of individuals with similar genetic background (breeding) is often referred to as a line or strain or variety or breed. Self-fertilization or mating closely related individuals for many generations (inbreeding) usually produces a population which is homozygous at nearly all loci. Matings between the homozygous individuals of a *pure line* produce only homozygous offspring like the parents. Thus we say that a pure line "breeds true".

Example 2.4.   Pure line parents: AA × AA

Gametes:

Offspring:

(c) **Heterozygous.** The union of gametes carrying different alleles produces a *heterozygous* genotype. Different kinds of gametes are produced by a heterozygote.

Example 2.5.   Uniting gametes:

Zygote
(heterozygous genotype):

Gametes:

(d) **Hybrid.** The term *hybrid* as used in the problems of this book is synonymous with the heterozygous condition. Problems in this chapter may involve a single factor hybrid (monohybrid). Problems in the next chapter will consider heterozygosity at two or more loci (polyhybrids).

ALLELIC RELATIONSHIPS

1. Dominant and Recessive Alleles.

Whenever one of a pair of alleles can come to phenotypic expression only in a homozygous genotype, we call that allele a *recessive* factor. The allele which can phenotypically express itself in the heterozygote as well as in the homozygote is called a *dominant* factor. Upper and lower case letters are commonly used to designate dominant and recessive alleles respectively. Usually the genetic symbol corresponds to the first letter in the name of the abnormal (or mutant) trait.

Example 2.6.   Lack of pigment deposition in the human body is an abnormal recessive trait called "albinism". Using A and a to represent the dominant (normal) allele and the recessive (albino) allele respectively, three genotypes and two phenotypes are possible:

Genotypes	Phenotypes
AA (homozygous dominant)	Normal (pigment)
Aa (heterozygote)	Normal (pigment)
aa (homozygous recessive)	Albino (no pigment)

(a) **Carriers.** Recessive alleles (such as the one for albinism) are often deleterious to those who possess them in duplicate (homozygous recessive genotype). A heterozygote may appear just as normal as the homozygous dominant genotype. A heterozygous individual which possesses a deleterious recessive allele hidden from phenotypic expression by the dominant normal allele is called a *carrier*. Most of the deleterious alleles harbored by a population are found in carrier individuals.

(b) **Wild Type Symbolism.** A different system for symbolizing dominant and recessive alleles is widely used in numerous organisms from higher plants and animals to the bacteria and viruses. Different genetics texts favor either one or the other system. In the author's opinion, every student should become familiar with both kinds of allelic representation and be able to work genetic problems regardless of the symbolic system

used. Throughout the remainder of this book the student will find both systems used extensively. Where one phenotype is obviously of much more common occurrence in the population than its alternative phenotype, the former is usually referred to as *wild type*. The phenotype which is rarely observed is called the *mutant type*. In this system, the symbol + is used to indicate the normal allele for wild type. The base letter for the gene usually is taken from the name of the mutant or abnormal trait. If the mutant gene is recessive the symbol would be a lower case letter(s) corresponding to the initial letter(s) in the name of the trait. Its normal (wild type) dominant allele would have the same lower case letter but with a + as a superscript.

> **Example 2.7.**   Black body color in *Drosophila* is governed by a recessive gene b, and wild type (gray body) by its dominant allele b^+.

If the mutant trait is dominant, the base symbol would be an upper case letter without a superscript, and its recessive wild type allele would have the same upper case symbol with a + as a superscript.

> **Example 2.8.**   Lobe shaped eyes in *Drosophila* are governed by a dominant gene L, and wild type (oval eye) by its recessive allele L^+.

Remember that the case of the symbol indicates the dominance or recessiveness of the *mutant* allele to which the superscript + for wild type must be referred. After the allelic relationships have been defined, the symbol + by itself may be used for wild type and the letter alone may designate the mutant type.

2. Codominant Alleles.

Alleles which lack dominant and recessive relationships may be called intermediate alleles or *codominant* alleles. This means that each allele is capable of some degree of expression when in the heterozygous condition. Hence the heterozygous genotype gives rise to a phenotype distinctly different from either of the homozygous genotypes. Usually the heterozygous phenotype resulting from codominance is intermediate in character between those produced by the homozygous genotypes, hence the erroneous concept of "blending". The phenotype may appear to be a "blend" in heterozygotes but the alleles maintain their individual identities and will segregate from each other in the formation of gametes.

(a) *Symbolism for Codominant Alleles.* For codominant (or intermediate) alleles, all upper case base symbols with different superscripts should be used. The upper case letters call attention to the fact that each allele can express itself to some degree even when in the presence of its alternative allele (heterozygous).

> **Example 2.9.**   The alleles governing the M-N blood group system in man are codominants and may be represented by the symbols L^M and L^N, the base letter (L) being assigned in honor of its discoverers (Landsteiner and Levine). Two antisera (anti-M and anti-N) are used to distinguish three genotypes and their corresponding phenotypes (blood groups). Agglutination is represented by + and non-agglutination by −.

Genotype	Reaction with:		Blood Group
	Anti-M	Anti-N	(Phenotype)
$L^M L^M$	+	−	M
$L^M L^N$	+	+	MN
$L^N L^N$	−	+	N

3. Lethal Alleles.

The phenotypic manifestation of some genes is the death of the individual either in the prenatal or postnatal period prior to maturity. Such factors are called *lethal genes*. A fully dominant lethal allele (i.e. one which kills in both the homozygous and heterozygous conditions) occasionally arises by mutation from a normal allele. Individuals with a dominant lethal die before they can leave progeny. Therefore the mutant dominant lethal is removed from the population in the same generation in which it arose. Recessive lethals kill only when homozygous and may be of two kinds: (1) one which has no obvious phenotypic effect in heterozygotes, and (2) one which exhibits a distinctive phenotype when heterozygous.

Example 2.10. By special techniques, a completely recessive lethal (l) can sometimes be identified in certain families.

Genotype	Phenotype
LL, Ll	normal viability
ll	lethal

Example 2.11. The amount of chlorophyll in snapdragons (*Antirrhinum*) is controlled by an incompletely recessive gene which exhibits a lethal effect when homozygous, and a distinctive phenotypic effect when heterozygous.

Genotype	Phenotype
CC	green (normal)
Cc	pale green (aurea)
cc	white (lethal)

4. Penetrance and Expressivity.

Differences in environmental conditions or in genetic backgrounds may cause individuals which are genetically identical at a particular locus to exhibit different phenotypes. The percentage of individuals with a particular gene combination which exhibits the corresponding character to any degree represents the penetrance of the trait.

Example 2.12. Extra fingers and/or toes (polydactyly) in man is thought to be produced by a dominant gene (P). The normal condition with five digits on each limb is produced by the recessive genotype (pp). Some individuals of genotype Pp are not polydactylous, and therefore the gene has a penetrance of less than 100%.

A trait, though penetrant, may be quite variable in its expression. The degree of effect produced by a penetrant genotype is termed *expressivity*.

Example 2.13. The polydactylous condition may be penetrant in the left hand (6 fingers) and not in the right (5 fingers), or it may be penetrant in the feet and not in the hands.

A recessive lethal gene which lacks complete penetrance and expressivity will kill less than 100% of the homozygotes before sexual maturity. The terms *semilethal* or *subvital* apply to such genes. The effects which various kinds of lethals have on the reproduction of the next generation form a broad spectrum from complete lethality to sterility in completely viable genotypes. Problems in this book, however, will consider only those lethals which become completely penetrant, usually during the embryonic stage. Genes other than lethals will likewise be assumed completely penetrant.

5. Multiple Alleles.

The genetic systems proposed thus far have been limited to a single pair of alleles. The maximum number of alleles at a gene locus which any individual possesses is two, one on each of the homologous chromosomes. But since a gene can be changed to alternative forms by the process of mutation, a large number of alleles is theoretically possible in a population of individuals. Whenever more than two alleles are identified at a gene locus, we have a *multiple allelic series*.

(a) *Symbolism for Multiple Alleles.* The dominance hierarchy should be defined at the beginning of each problem involving multiple alleles. A capital letter is commonly used to designate the allele which is dominant to all others in the series. The corresponding lower case letter designates the allele which is recessive to all others in the series. Other alleles, intermediate in their degree of dominance between these two extremes, are usually assigned the lower case letter with some suitable superscript.

> **Example 2.14.** The color of *Drosophila* eyes is governed by a series of alleles which cause the hue to vary from red or wild type (w^+ or W) through coral (w^{co}), blood (w^{bl}), eosin (w^e), cherry (w^{ch}), apricot (w^a), honey (w^h), buff (w^{bf}), tinged (w^t), pearl (w^p) and ivory (w^i) to white (w). Each allele in the system except w can be considered to produce pigment, but successively less is produced by alleles as we proceed down the hierarchy: $w^+ > w^{co} > w^{bl} > w^e > w^{ch} > w^a > w^h > w^{bf} > w^t > w^p > w^i > w$. The wild type allele ($w^+$) is completely dominant and w is completely recessive to all other alleles in the series. *Compounds* are heterozygotes which contain unlike members of an allelic series. The compounds of this series which involve alleles other than w^+ tend to be phenotypically intermediate between the eye colors of the parental homozygotes.

> **Example 2.15.** A classical example of multiple alleles is found in the ABO blood group system of man, where the allele I^A for the A antigen is codominant with the allele I^B for the B antigen. Both I^A and I^B are completely dominant to the allele i which fails to specify any detectable antigenic structure. The hierarchy of dominance relationships is symbolized as $(I^A = I^B) > i$. Two antisera (anti-A and anti-B) are required for the detection of four phenotypes.

Genotypes	Reaction with:		Phenotype
	Anti-A	Anti-B	(Blood Groups)
$I^A I^A$, $I^A i$	+	−	A
$I^B I^B$, $I^B i$	−	+	B
$I^A I^B$	+	+	AB
ii	−	−	O

> **Example 2.16.** A slightly different kind of multiple allelic system is encountered in the coat colors of rabbits: C allows full color to be produced (typical gray rabbit); c^{ch}, when homozygous, removes yellow pigment from the fur, making a silver-gray color called chinchilla; c^{ch}, when heterozygous with alleles lower in the dominance hierarchy, produces light gray fur; c^h produces a white rabbit with black extremities called Himalayan; c fails to produce pigment, resulting in albino. The dominance hierarchy may be symbolized as follows: $C > c^{ch} > c^h > c$.

Phenotypes	Possible Genotypes
full color	CC, Cc^{ch}, Cc^h, Cc
chinchilla	$c^{ch}c^{ch}$
light gray	$c^{ch}c^h$, $c^{ch}c$
Himalayan	$c^h c^h$, $c^h c$
albino	cc

SINGLE GENE (MONOFACTORIAL) CROSSES

1. The Six Basic Types of Matings.

A pair of alleles governs pelage color in the guinea pig; a dominant allele *B* produces black and its recessive allele *b* produces white. There are six types of matings possible among the three genotypes. The parental generation is symbolized P and the first filial generation of offspring is symbolized F_1.

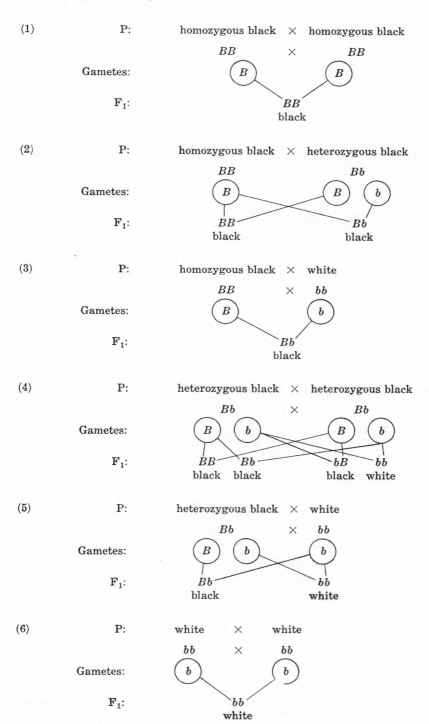

Summary of the six types of matings:

No.	Matings	Expected F_1 Ratios	
		Genotypes	Phenotypes
(1)	$BB \times BB$	all BB	all black
(2)	$BB \times Bb$	$\frac{1}{2}BB : \frac{1}{2}Bb$	all black
(3)	$BB \times bb$	all Bb	all black
(4)	$Bb \times Bb$	$\frac{1}{4}BB : \frac{1}{2}Bb : \frac{1}{4}bb$	$\frac{3}{4}$ black : $\frac{1}{4}$ white
(5)	$Bb \times bb$	$\frac{1}{2}Bb : \frac{1}{2}bb$	$\frac{1}{2}$ black : $\frac{1}{2}$ white
(6)	$bb \times bb$	all bb	all white

2. Conventional Production of the F_2.

Unless otherwise specified in the problem, the second filial generation (F_2) is produced by crossing the F_1 individuals among themselves randomly. Plants which are normally self-fertilized can be artificially cross pollinated in the parental generation and the resulting F_1 progeny are then allowed to pollinate themselves to produce the F_2.

Example 2.17.   P: BB $\times$ bb
                                                   black   white

                        F_1: Bb
                                                   black

The black F_1 males are mated to the black F_1 females to produce the F_2.

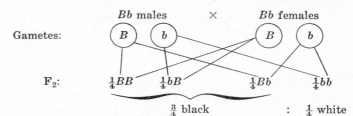

An alternative method for combining the F_1 gametes is to place the female gametes along one side of a "checkerboard" (Punnett square) and the male gametes along the other side and then combine them to form zygotes as shown below.

	B	b
B	BB black	Bb black
b	Bb black	bb white

3. Testcross.

Because a homozygous dominant genotype has the same phenotype as the heterozygous genotype, a *testcross* is required to distinguish between them. The testcross parent is always homozygous recessive for all of the genes under consideration. The purpose of a testcross is to discover how many different kinds of gametes are being produced by the individual whose genotype is in question. A homozygous dominant individual will produce only one kind of gamete; a *monohybrid* individual (heterozygous at one locus) produces two kinds of gametes with equal frequency.

Example 2.18. Consider the case in which testcrossing a black female produced only black offspring.

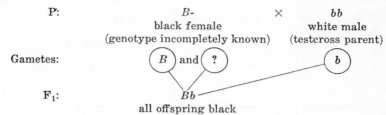

P: *B-*   ×   *bb*
                            black female   white male
                    (genotype incompletely known)   (testcross parent)

Gametes: (*B*) and (*?*)   (*b*)

F₁: *Bb*
                            all offspring black

Conclusion: The female parent must be producing only one kind of gamete and therefore she is homozygous dominant *BB*.

Example 2.19. Consider the case in which testcrossing a black male produced black and white offspring in approximately equal numbers.

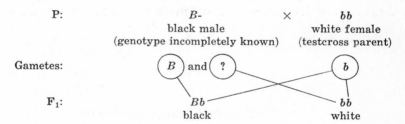

P: *B-*   ×   *bb*
                             black male   white female
                    (genotype incompletely known)   (testcross parent)

Gametes: (*B*) and (*?*)   (*b*)

F₁: *Bb*   *bb*
                           black   white

Conclusion: The male parent must be producing two kinds of gametes and therefore he is heterozygous *Bb*.

4. Backcross.

If the F₁ progeny are mated back to one of their parents (or to individuals with a genotype identical to that of their parents) the mating is termed *backcross*. Sometimes "backcross" is used synonymously with "testcross" in genetic literature, but it will be used exclusively in the former sense in this book.

Example 2.20. A homozygous black female guinea pig is crossed to a white male. An F₁ son is backcrossed to his mother. Using the symbol ♀ for female and ♂ for male (♀♀ = females, ♂♂ = males), we diagram this backcross as follows:

P: *BB* ♀   ×   *bb* ♂
                    black female   white male

F₁: *Bb* ♂♂ and ♀♀
                      black males and females

F₁ backcross: *Bb* ♂   ×   *BB* ♀
                    black son   black mother

Backcross progeny: $\frac{1}{2}BB$ ⎫
                                       ⎬ all black offspring
                       $\frac{1}{2}Bb$ ⎭

PEDIGREE ANALYSIS

A pedigree is a systematic listing (either as words or as symbols) of the ancestors of a given individual, or it may be the "family tree" for a large number of individuals. It is customary to represent females as circles and males as squares. Matings are shown as horizontal lines between two individuals. The offspring of a mating are connected by a vertical line to the mating line. Different shades or colors added to the symbols can represent various phenotypes. Each generation is listed on a separate row labeled with Roman numerals. Individuals within a generation receive Arabic numerals.

Example 2.21.   Let solid symbols represent black guinea pigs and open symbols represent white guinea pigs.

Individuals	Phenotype	Genotype
I 1	black ♀	Bb
I 2	white ♂	bb
II 1	white ♀	bb
II 2	black ♂	Bb
II 3	black ♀	Bb
III 1	black ♀	$B\text{-}*$

*The dash indicates that the genotype could be either homozygous or heterozygous.

PROBABILITY THEORY

1. Observed vs. Expected Results.

Experimental results seldom conform exactly to the expected ratios. Genetic probabilities derive from the operation of chance events in the meiotic production of gametes and the random union of these gametes in fertilization. Samples from a population of individuals often deviate from the expected ratios, rather widely in very small samples, but usually approaching the expectations more closely with increasing sample size.

Example 2.22.   Suppose that a testcross of heterozygous black guinea pigs ($Bb \times bb$) produces 5 offspring: 3 black (Bb) and 2 white (bb). Theoretically we expect half of the total number of offspring to be black and half to be white $= \frac{1}{2}(5) = 2\frac{1}{2}$. Obviously we cannot observe half of an individual, and the results conform as closely to the theoretical expectations as is biologically possible.

Example 2.23.   Numerous testcrosses of a black guinea pig produced a total of 10 offspring, 8 of which were black and 2 were white. We theoretically expected 5 black and 5 white, but the deviation from the expected numbers which we observed in our small sample of 10 offspring should not be any more surprising than the results of tossing a coin 10 times and observing 8 heads and 2 tails. The fact that at least one white offspring appeared is sufficient to classify the black parent as genetically heterozygous (Bb).

2. Combining Probabilities.

Two or more events are said to be *independent* if the occurrence or non-occurrence of any one of them does not effect the probabilities of occurrence of any of the others. When two independent events occur with the probabilities p and q respectively, then the probability of their joint occurrence is pq. That is, the combined probability is the product of the probabilities of the independent events. If the word "and" is used or implied in the phrasing of a problem solution, a *multiplication* of independent probabilities is usually required.

Example 2.24. Theoretically there is an equal opportunity for a tossed coin to land on either heads or tails. Let p = probability of heads = $\frac{1}{2}$, and q = probability of tails = $\frac{1}{2}$. In two tosses of a coin the probability of two heads appearing (i.e. a head on the first toss *and* a head on the second toss) is $p \times p = p^2 = (\frac{1}{2})^2 = \frac{1}{4}$.

Example 2.25. In testcrossing a heterozygous black guinea pig ($Bb \times bb$), let the probability of a black (Bb) offspring be $p = \frac{1}{2}$ and of a white (bb) offspring be $q = \frac{1}{2}$. The combined probability of the first two offspring being white (i.e. the first offspring is white *and* the second offspring is white) $= q \times q = q^2 = (\frac{1}{2})^2 = \frac{1}{4}$.

There is only one way in which two heads may appear in two tosses of a coin, i.e. heads on the first toss and heads on the second toss. The same is true for two tails. There are two ways, however, to obtain one head and one tail in two tosses of a coin. The head may appear on the first toss and the tail on the second *or* the tail may appear on the first toss and the head on the second. *Mutually exclusive events* are those in which the occurrence of any one of them excludes the occurrence of the others. The word "or" is usually required or implied in the phrasing of problem solutions involving mutually exclusive events, signaling that an *addition* of probabilities is to be performed. That is, whenever alternative possibilities exist for the satisfaction of the conditions of a problem, the individual probabilities are combined by addition.

Example 2.26. In two tosses of a coin, there are two ways to obtain a head and a tail.

	First Toss		Second Toss		Probability
First Alternative:	Head (p)	(and)	Tail (q)	=	pq
					(or)
Second Alternative:	Tail (q)	(and)	Head (p)	=	qp
			Combined probability	=	$2pq$

$p = q = \frac{1}{2}$; hence the combined probability $= 2(\frac{1}{2})(\frac{1}{2}) = \frac{1}{2}$.

Example 2.27. In testcrossing heterozygous black guinea pigs ($Bb \times bb$), there are two ways to obtain one black (Bb) and one white (bb) offspring in a litter of two animals. Let p = probability of black = $\frac{1}{2}$ and q = probability of white = $\frac{1}{2}$.

	First Offspring		Second Offspring		Probability
First Alternative:	Black (p)	(and)	White (q)	=	pq
					(or)
Second Alternative:	White (q)	(and)	Black (p)	=	qp
			Combined probability	=	$2pq$

$p = q = \frac{1}{2}$; hence the combined probability $= 2(\frac{1}{2})(\frac{1}{2}) = \frac{1}{2}$.

Many readers will recognize that the application of the above two rules for combining probabilities (independent and mutually exclusive events) is the basis of the binomial distribution, which will be considered in detail in Chapter 7.

Solved Problems

DOMINANT AND RECESSIVE ALLELES

2.1. Black pelage of guinea pigs is a dominant trait, white is the alternative recessive trait. When a pure black guinea pig is crossed to a white one, what fraction of the black F_2 is expected to be heterozygous?

Solution:

As shown in Example 2.17, the F_2 genotypic ratio is $1BB : 2Bb : 1bb$. Considering only the black F_2, we expect $1BB : 2Bb$ or 2 out of every 3 black pigs are expected to be heterozygous; the fraction is $\frac{2}{3}$.

2.2. If a black female guinea pig is testcrossed and produces two offspring in each of three litters, all of which are black, what is her probable genotype? With what degree of confidence may her genotype be specified?

Solution:

$$P: \quad \underset{\text{black female}}{B\text{-}} \quad \times \quad \underset{\text{white male}}{bb}$$

$$F_1: \quad \text{all } Bb \; = \; \text{all black}$$

The female parent could be homozygous BB or heterozygous Bb and still be phenotypically black, hence the symbol $B\text{-}$. If she is heterozygous, each offspring from this testcross has a 50% chance of being black. The probability of 6 offspring being produced, all of which are black, is $(\frac{1}{2})^6 = \frac{1}{64} = 0.0156 = 1.56\%$. In other words, we expect such results to occur by chance less than 2% of the time. Since it is chance that operates in the union of gametes, she might actually be heterozygous and thus far only her B gametes have been the "lucky ones" to unite with the b gametes from the white parent. Since no white offspring have appeared in six of these chance unions we may be approximately 98% confident $(1 - 0.0156 = 0.9844$ or $98.44\%)$ on the basis of chance, that she is of homozygous genotype (BB). It is possible, however, for her very next testcross offspring to be white, in which case we would then become certain that her genotype was heterozygous Bb and not BB.

2.3. Heterozygous black guinea pigs (Bb) are crossed among themselves. (a) What is the probability of the first three offspring being alternately black-white-black or white-black-white? (b) What is the probability among 3 offspring of producing 2 black and 1 white in any order?

Solution:

$(a) \qquad P: \qquad \underset{\text{black}}{Bb} \quad \times \quad \underset{\text{black}}{Bb}$

$$F_1: \qquad \tfrac{3}{4} \text{ black} : \tfrac{1}{4} \text{ white}$$

Let p = probability of black = $\frac{3}{4}$, q = probability of white = $\frac{1}{4}$.

$$\text{Probability of black } and \text{ white } and \text{ black} \; = \; p \times q \times p \; = \; p^2q, \quad or$$
$$\text{Probability of white } and \text{ black } and \text{ white} \; = \; q \times p \times q \; = \; \underline{pq^2}$$
$$\text{Combined probability} \; = \; p^2q + pq^2 \; = \; \tfrac{3}{16}$$

(b) Consider the number of ways that 2 black and 1 white offspring could be produced.

Offspring Order			Probability
1st	2nd	3rd	
black and	black and	white	$= (\frac{3}{4})(\frac{3}{4})(\frac{1}{4}) = \frac{9}{64}, \quad or$
black and	white and	black	$= (\frac{3}{4})(\frac{1}{4})(\frac{3}{4}) = \frac{9}{64}, \quad or$
white and	black and	black	$= (\frac{1}{4})(\frac{3}{4})(\frac{3}{4}) = \frac{9}{64}$
		Combined probability	$= \frac{27}{64}$

Once we have ascertained that there are three ways to obtain 2 black and 1 white, the total probability becomes $3(\frac{3}{4})^2(\frac{1}{4}) = \frac{27}{64}$.

2.4. A dominant gene b^+ is responsible for the wild type body color of *Drosophila*; its recessive allele b produces black body color. A testcross of a wild type female gave 52 black and 58 wild type in the F_1. If the wild type F_1 females are crossed to their black F_1 brothers, what genotypic and phenotypic ratios would be expected in the F_2? Diagram the results using the appropriate genetic symbols.

Solution:

$$P: \qquad \underset{\text{wild type female}}{b^+\text{- } ♀} \qquad \times \qquad \underset{\text{black male}}{bb \, ♂}$$

$$F_1: \qquad 52bb \text{ (black)} : 58b^+b \text{ (wild type)}$$

Since the recessive black phenotype appears in the F_1 in approximately a $1:1$ ratio, we know that the female parent must be heterozygous b^+b. Furthermore, we know that the wild type F_1 progeny must also be heterozygous. The wild type F_1 females are then crossed with their black brothers:

$$F_1 \text{ cross}: \qquad \underset{\text{wild type females}}{b^+b \, ♀♀} \qquad \times \qquad \underset{\text{black males}}{bb \, ♂♂}$$

$$F_2: \qquad \tfrac{1}{2}b^+b \text{ wild type} : \tfrac{1}{2}bb \text{ black}$$

The expected F_2 ratio is therefore the same as that observed in the F_1, namely 1 wild type : 1 black.

CODOMINANT ALLELES

2.5. Coat colors of the Shorthorn breed of cattle represent a classical example of codominant alleles. Red is governed by the genotype C^RC^R, roan (mixture of red and white) by C^RC^W, and white by C^WC^W. (*a*) When roan Shorthorns are crossed among themselves, what genotypic and phenotypic ratios are expected among their progeny? (*b*) If red Shorthorns are crossed with roans, and the F_1 progeny are crossed among themselves to produce the F_2, what percentage of the F_2 will probably be roan?

Solution:

(*a*)
$$P: \qquad \underset{\text{roan}}{C^RC^W} \quad \times \quad \underset{\text{roan}}{C^RC^W}$$

$$F_1: \qquad \tfrac{1}{4}C^RC^R \text{ red} : \tfrac{1}{2}C^RC^W \text{ roan} : \tfrac{1}{4}C^WC^W \text{ white}$$

Since each genotype produces a unique phenotype, the phenotypic ratio $1:2:1$ corresponds to the same genotypic ratio.

(*b*)
$$P: \qquad \underset{\text{red}}{C^RC^R} \quad \times \quad \underset{\text{roan}}{C^RC^W}$$

$$F_1: \qquad \tfrac{1}{2}C^RC^R \text{ red} : \tfrac{1}{2}C^RC^W \text{ roan}$$

There are three types of matings possible for the production of the F_2. Their relative frequencies of occurrence may be calculated by preparing a mating table.

	$\tfrac{1}{2}C^RC^R \, ♂$	$\tfrac{1}{2}C^RC^W \, ♂$
$\tfrac{1}{2}C^RC^R \, ♀$	(1) $\tfrac{1}{4}C^RC^R \, ♀ \times C^RC^R \, ♂$	(2) $\tfrac{1}{4}C^RC^R \, ♀ \times C^RC^W \, ♂$
$\tfrac{1}{2}C^RC^W \, ♀$	(2) $\tfrac{1}{4}C^RC^W \, ♀ \times C^RC^R \, ♂$	(3) $\tfrac{1}{4}C^RC^W \, ♀ \times C^RC^W \, ♂$

(1) The mating $C^RC^R \, ♀ \times C^RC^R \, ♂$ (red × red) produces only red (C^RC^R) progeny. But only one-quarter of all matings are of this type. Therefore $\tfrac{1}{4}$ of all the F_2 should be red from this source.

(2) The matings $C^RC^W \times C^RC^R$ (roan female × red male or roan male × red female) are expected to produce $\tfrac{1}{2}C^RC^R$ (red) and $\tfrac{1}{2}C^RC^W$ (roan) progeny. Half of all matings are of this kind. Therefore $(\tfrac{1}{2})(\tfrac{1}{2}) = \tfrac{1}{4}$ of all the F_2 progeny should be red and $\tfrac{1}{4}$ should be roan from this source.

(3) The mating $C^RC^W \, ♀ \times C^RC^W \, ♂$ (roan × roan) is expected to produce $\tfrac{1}{4}C^RC^R$ (red), $\tfrac{1}{2}C^RC^W$ (roan), and $\tfrac{1}{4}C^WC^W$ (white) progeny. This mating type constitutes $\tfrac{1}{4}$ of all crosses. Therefore the fraction of all F_2 progeny contributed from this source is $(\tfrac{1}{4})(\tfrac{1}{4}) = \tfrac{1}{16}C^RC^R$, $(\tfrac{1}{4})(\tfrac{1}{2}) = \tfrac{1}{8}C^RC^W$, $(\tfrac{1}{4})(\tfrac{1}{4}) = \tfrac{1}{16}C^WC^W$.

The expected F_2 contributions from all three types of matings are summarized in the following table.

Type of Mating	Frequency of Mating	F$_2$ Progeny		
		Red	Roan	White
(1) red $\times$ red	$\frac{1}{4}$	$\frac{1}{4}$	0	0
(2) red $\times$ roan	$\frac{1}{2}$	$\frac{1}{4}$	$\frac{1}{4}$	0
(3) roan $\times$ roan	$\frac{1}{4}$	$\frac{1}{16}$	$\frac{1}{8}$	$\frac{1}{16}$
Totals		$\frac{9}{16}$	$\frac{6}{16}$	$\frac{1}{16}$

The fraction of roan progeny in the F_2 is $\frac{3}{8}$ or approximately 38%.

LETHAL ALLELES

2.6. The absence of legs in cattle ("amputated") has been attributed to a completely recessive lethal gene. A normal bull is mated with a normal cow and they produce an amputated calf (usually dead at birth). The same parents are mated again.

(a) What is the chance of the next calf being amputated?

(b) What is the chance of these parents having two calves, both of which are amputated?

(c) Bulls carrying the amputated allele (heterozygous) are mated to non-carrier cows. The F_1 is allowed to mate at random to produce the F_2. What genotypic ratio is expected in the adult F_2?

(d) Suppose that each F_1 female in part (c) rears one viable calf, i.e. each of the cows which throws an amputated calf is allowed to remate to a carrier sire until she produces a viable offspring. What genotypic ratio is expected in the adult F_2?

Solution:

(a) If phenotypically normal parents produce an amputated calf, they must both be genetically heterozygous.

P: Aa $\times$ Aa
              normal   normal

F_1:   **Genotypes**   **Phenotypes**

$\left. \begin{array}{l} \frac{1}{4}AA \\ \frac{1}{2}Aa \end{array} \right\}$ $\frac{3}{4}$ normal

$\frac{1}{4}aa \; = \; \frac{1}{4}$ amputated (dies)

Thus there is a 25% chance of the next offspring being amputated.

(b) The chance of the first calf being amputated *and* the second calf also being amputated is the product of the separate probabilities: $(\frac{1}{4})(\frac{1}{4}) = \frac{1}{16}$.

(c) The solution to part (c) is analogous to that of Problem 2.5(b). A summary of the expected F_2 follows:

Type of Mating	F$_2$ Genotypes		
	AA	Aa	aa
$AA \times AA$	$\frac{4}{16}$		
$AA \times Aa$	$\frac{4}{16}$	$\frac{4}{16}$	
$Aa \times Aa$	$\frac{1}{16}$	$\frac{2}{16}$	$\frac{1}{16}$
Totals	$\frac{9}{16}$	$\frac{6}{16}$	$\frac{1}{16}$

All aa genotypes die and fail to appear in the adult progeny. Therefore the adult progeny has the genotypic ratio $9AA : 6Aa$ or $3AA : 2Aa$.

(d) The results of matings $AA \times AA$ and $AA \times Aa$ remain the same as in part (c). The mating of Aa by Aa now is expected to produce $\frac{1}{3}AA$ and $\frac{2}{3}Aa$ adult progeny. Correcting for the frequency of occurrence of this mating, we have $(\frac{1}{4})(\frac{1}{3}) = \frac{1}{12}AA$ and $(\frac{1}{4})(\frac{2}{3}) = \frac{2}{12}Aa$.

Summary of the F_2:

Type of Mating	F_2 Genotypes	
	AA	Aa
$AA \times AA$	$\frac{3}{12}$	
$AA \times Aa$	$\frac{3}{12}$	$\frac{3}{12}$
$Aa \times Aa$	$\frac{1}{12}$	$\frac{2}{12}$
Totals	$\frac{7}{12}$	$\frac{5}{12}$

The adult F_2 genotypic ratio is expected to be $7AA$ to $5Aa$.

2.7. A bull, heterozygous for a completely recessive lethal gene, sires 3 calves each out of 32 cows. Twelve of the cows have one or more stillborn calves and therefore must be carriers of this lethal. How many more carrier cows probably exist in this herd undetected?

Solution:

The probability that a heterozygous cow will not have a stillborn calf in 3 matings to a heterozygous male is calculated as follows: each calf has a $\frac{3}{4}$ chance of being normal; therefore the probability of 3 calves being normal is $(\frac{3}{4})^3 = \frac{27}{64}$. That is, the probability that we will fail to detect a heterozygous (carrier) cow with 3 calves is $\frac{27}{64}$. The probability that we will detect a carrier cow with 3 calves is $\frac{37}{64}$. Let $x =$ number of heterozygous cows in the herd; then $(\frac{37}{64})x = 12$ or $x = 21$ (to the nearest integer). 21 carrier cows probably exist; since we have detected 12 of them, there are probably 9 carrier cows undetected in this herd.

MULTIPLE ALLELES

2.8. The genetics of rabbit coat colors is given in Example 2.16, page 26. Determine the genotypic and phenotypic ratios expected from mating full colored males of genotype Cc^{ch} to light gray females of genotype $c^{ch}c$.

Solution:

P: $Cc^{ch} \male\male$ $\times$ $c^{ch}c \female\female$
            full color   light gray

F_1:

	C	c^{ch}
c^{ch}	Cc^{ch} full color	$c^{ch}c^{ch}$ chinchilla
c	Cc full color	$c^{ch}c$ light gray

Thus we have a $1:1:1:1$ genotypic ratio, but a phenotypic ratio of 2 full color : 1 chinchilla : 1 light gray.

2.9. The coat colors of mice are known to be governed by a multiple allelic series in which the allele A^y, when homozygous, is lethal early in embryonic development but produces yellow color when in heterozygous condition with other alleles. Agouti (mousy color) is governed by the A allele, and black by the recessive a. The dominance hierarchy is as follows: $A^y > A > a$. What phenotypic and genotypic ratios are expected in the viable F_1 from the cross $A^yA \times A^ya$?

Solution:

P: A^yA $\times$ A^ya
            yellow   yellow

F_1:

	A^y	a
A^y	A^yA^y dies	A^ya yellow
A	A^yA yellow	Aa agouti

Since $\frac{1}{4}$ of the progeny dies before birth, we should observe two yellow offspring for every one agouti (phenotypic ratio of 2:1). However, the genotypic ratio is a 1:1:1 relationship. That is, $\frac{1}{3}$ of the viable genotypes should be A^yA, $\frac{1}{3}A^ya$, and $\frac{1}{3}Aa$.

2.10. A man is suing his wife for divorce on the grounds of infidelity. Their first and second child, whom they both claim, are blood groups O and AB respectively. The third child, whom the man disclaims, is blood type B. (*a*) Can this information be used to support the man's case? (*b*) Another test was made in the M-N blood group system. The third child was group M, the man was group N. Can this information be used to support the man's case?

Solution:

(*a*) The genetics of the ABO blood group system was presented in Example 2.15, page 26. Because the group O baby has the genotype ii, each of the parents must have been carrying the recessive allele. The AB baby indicates that one of his parents had the dominant I^A allele and the other had the codominant allele I^B. Any of the four bloodgroups can appear among the children whose parents are $I^Ai \times I^Bi$. The information given on ABO blood groups is of no use in supporting the man's claim.

(*b*) The genetics of the M-N blood group system was presented in Example 2.9, page 24. The M-N blood groups are governed by a pair of codominant alleles, where groups M and N are produced by homozygous genotypes. A group N father must pass the L^N allele to his offspring; they all would have the N antigen on their red blood cells, and would all be classified serologically as either group MN or N depending upon the genotype of the mother. This man could not be the father of a group M child.

PEDIGREE ANALYSIS

2.11. The black hair of guinea pigs is produced by a dominant gene B and white by its recessive allele b. Unless there is evidence to the contrary, assume that II1 and II4 do not carry the recessive allele. Calculate the probability that an offspring of III1 × III2 will have white hair.

Solution:

Both I1 and I2 must be heterozygous (Bb) in order to have the white (bb) offspring II2. If III1 or III2 had been white, this would constitute evidence that II1 or II4 were heterozygous. In the absence of this evidence the problem tells us to assume that II1 and II4 are homozygous (BB). If the offspring of III1 $\times$ III2 is to be white, then both III1 and III2 would have to be heterozygous (Bb). In this case, II3 would also have to be heterozygous in order to pass the recessive allele on to III2. Under the conditions of the problem, we are certain that III1 is heterozygous because his parents (II1 $\times$ II2) are $BB \times bb$. We notice that II3 is black. The probability that *black* progeny from I1 $\times$ I2 are heterozygous is $\frac{2}{3}$. If II3 is heterozygous, the probability that III2 is heterozygous is $\frac{1}{2}$. If III2 is heterozygous, there is a 25% chance that the offspring of III1 $\times$ III2 will be white (bb). Thus the combined probability that II3 is heterozygous *and* III2 is heterozygous *and* producing a white offspring is the product of the independent probabilities = $(\frac{2}{3})(\frac{1}{2})(\frac{1}{4}) = \frac{2}{24} = \frac{1}{12}$.

Supplementary Problems

DOMINANT AND RECESSIVE ALLELES

2.12. Several black guinea pigs of the same genotype were mated and produced 29 black and 9 white offspring. What would you predict the genotypes of the parents to be?

2.13 If a black female guinea pig is testcrossed and produces at least one white offspring, determine (*a*) the genotype and phenotype of the sire (male parent) which produced the white offspring, (*b*) the genotype of this female.

2.14. Heterozygous black (Bb) guinea pigs are mated to homozygous recessive (bb) whites. Predict the genotypic and phenotypic ratios expected from backcrossing the black F_1 progeny to (*a*) the black parent, (*b*) the white parent.

2.15. In *Drosophila*, sepia colored eyes are due to a recessive allele s and wild type (red eye color) to its dominant allele s^+. If sepia eyed females are crossed to pure wild type males, what phenotypic and genotypic ratios are expected if the F_2 males are backcrossed to the sepia eyed parental females?

2.16. The lack of pigmentation, called albinism, in man is the result of a recessive allele (a) and normal pigmentation is the result of its dominant allele (A). Two normal parents have an albino child. Determine the probability that (*a*) the next child is albino, (*b*) the next two children are albinos. (*c*) What is the chance of these parents producing two children, one albino and the other normal?

2.17. Short hair is due to a dominant gene L in rabbits, and long hair to its recessive allele l. A cross between a short haired female and a long haired male produced a litter of 1 long haired and 7 short haired bunnies. (*a*) What are the genotypes of the parents? (*b*) What phenotypic ratio was expected in the offspring generation? (*c*) How many of the eight bunnies were expected to be long haired?

2.18. A dominant gene W produces wire-haired texture in dogs; its recessive allele w produces smooth hair. A group of heterozygous wire-haired individuals are crossed and their F_1 progeny are then testcrossed. Determine the expected genotypic and phenotypic ratios among the testcross progeny.

2.19. Black wool of sheep is due to a recessive allele b and white wool to its dominant allele B. A white buck (male) is crossed to a white ewe (female), both animals carrying the allele for black. They produce a white buck lamb which is then backcrossed to the female parent. What is the probability of the backcross offspring being black?

2.20. In foxes, silver-black coat color is governed by a recessive allele b and red color by its dominant allele B. Determine the genotypic and phenotypic ratios expected from the following matings: (*a*) pure red $\times$ carrier red, (*b*) carrier red $\times$ silver-black, (*c*) pure red $\times$ silver-black.

2.21. In the Holstein-Friesian breed of dairy cattle, a recessive allele r is known to produce red and white; the dominant allele R is known to produce black and white. If a carrier bull is mated to carrier cows, determine the probability (*a*) of the first offspring being born red and white, (*b*) of the first four offspring born being black and white. (*c*) What is the expected phenotypic ratio among offspring resulting from backcrossing black and white F_1 cows to the carrier bull? (*d*) If the carrier bull was mated to homozygous black and white cows, what phenotypic ratio would be expected among the backcross progeny from F_1 cows $\times$ carrier bull?

2.22. Consider a cross between two heterozygous black guinea pigs (*Bb*). (*a*) In how many ways can three black and two white offspring be produced? (*b*) What is the probability from such a cross of three black and two white offspring appearing in any order?

CODOMINANT ALLELES

2.23. When chickens with splashed white feathers are crossed with black feathered birds, their offspring are all slate blue (Blue Andalusian). When Blue Andalusians are crossed among themselves, they produce splashed white, blue, and black offspring in the ratio of $1:2:1$ respectively. (*a*) How are these feather traits inherited? (*b*) Using any appropriate symbols, indicate the genotypes for each phenotype.

2.24. Yellow coat color in guinea pigs is produced by the homozygous genotype $C^Y C^Y$, cream color by the heterozygous genotype $C^Y C^W$, and white by the homozygous genotype $C^W C^W$. What genotypic and phenotypic ratios are matings between cream colored individuals likely to produce?

2.25. The shape of radishes may be long ($S^L S^L$), round ($S^R S^R$), or oval ($S^L S^R$). If long radishes are crossed to oval radishes and the F_1 then allowed to cross at random among themselves, what phenotypic ratio is expected in the F_2?

2.26. The Palomino horse is a hybrid exhibiting a golden color with lighter mane and tail. A pair of codominant alleles (D^1 and D^2) is known to be involved in the inheritance of these coat colors. Genotypes homozygous for the D^1 allele are chestnut colored (reddish), heterozygous genotypes are Palomino colored, and genotypes homozygous for the D^2 allele are almost white and called *cremello*. (*a*) From matings between Palominos, determine the expected Palomino : non-Palomino ratio among the offspring. (*b*) What percentage of the non-Palomino offspring in part (*a*) will breed true? (*c*) What kind of mating will produce only Palominos?

LETHAL ALLELES

2.27. Chickens with shortened wings and legs are called creepers. When creepers are mated to normal birds they produce creepers and normals with equal frequency. When creepers are mated to creepers they produce 2 creepers to 1 normal. Crosses between normal birds produce only normal progeny. How can these results be explained?

2.28. In the Mexican Hairless breed of dogs, the hairless condition is produced by the heterozygous genotype (*Hh*). Normal dogs are homozygous recessive (*hh*). Puppies homozygous for the H allele are usually born dead with abnormalities of the mouth and absence of external ears. If the average litter size at weaning is 6 in matings between hairless dogs, what would be the average expected *number* of hairless and normal offspring at weaning from matings between hairless and normal dogs?

2.29. A pair of codominant alleles is known to govern cotyledon leaf color in soybeans. The homozygous genotype $C^G C^G$ produces dark green, the heterozygous genotype $C^G C^Y$ produces light green, and the other homozygous genotype $C^Y C^Y$ produces yellow leaves so deficient in chloroplasts that seedlings do not grow to maturity. If dark green plants are pollinated only by light green plants and the F_1 crosses are made at random to produce an F_2, what phenotypic and genotypic ratios would be expected in the mature F_2 plants?

2.30. Thalassemia is a hereditary disease of the blood of man resulting in anemia. Severe anemia (thalassemia major) is found in homozygotes ($T^M T^M$) and a milder form of anemia (thalassemia minor) is found in heterozygotes ($T^M T^N$). Normal individuals are homozygous $T^N T^N$. If all individuals with thalassemia major die before sexual maturity, (*a*) what proportion of the adult F_1 from marriages of thalassemia minors by normals would be expected to be normal, (*b*) what fraction of the adult F_1 from marriages of minors by minors would be expected to be anemic?

2.31. The Pelger anomaly of rabbits involves abnormal white blood cell nuclear segmentation. Pelgers are heterozygous (Pp), normal individuals are homozygous (PP). The homozygous recessive genotypes (pp) have grossly deformed skeletons and usually die before or soon after birth. If Pelgers are mated together, what phenotypic ratio is expected in the adult F_2?

MULTIPLE ALLELES

2.32. A multiple allelic series is known in the Chinese primrose where A (Alexandria type = white eye) $> a^n$ (normal type = yellow eye) $> a$ (Primrose Queen type = large yellow eye). List all of the genotypes possible for each of the phenotypes in this series.

2.33. Plumage color in mallard ducks is dependent upon a set of three alleles: M^R for restricted mallard pattern, M for mallard, and m for dusky mallard. The dominance hierarchy is $M^R > M > m$. Determine the genotypic and phenotypic ratios expected in the F_1 from the following crosses (a) $M^R M^R \times M^R M$, (b) $M^R M^R \times M^R m$, (c) $M^R M \times M^R m$, (d) $M^R m \times Mm$, (e) $Mm \times mm$.

2.34. A number of self-incompatibility alleles is known in clover such that the growth of a pollen tube down the style of a diploid plant is inhibited when the latter contains the same self-incompatibility allele as that in the pollen tube. Given a series of self-incompatibility alleles S^1, S^2, S^3, S^4, what genotypic ratios would be expected in embryos and in endosperms of seeds from the following crosses?

	Seed Parent	Pollen Parent
(a)	$S^1 S^4$	$S^3 S^4$
(b)	$S^1 S^2$	$S^1 S^2$
(c)	$S^1 S^3$	$S^2 S^4$
(d)	$S^2 S^3$	$S^3 S^4$

2.35. The coat colors of many animals exhibit the "agouti" pattern which is characterized by a yellow band of pigment near the tip of the hair. In rabbits, a multiple allelic series is known where the genotypes $E^D E^D$ and $E^D e$ produce only black (non-agouti), but the heterozygous genotype $E^D E$ produces black with a trace of agouti. The genotypes EE or Ee produce full color, and the recessive genotype ee produces reddish-yellow. What phenotypic and genotypic ratios would be expected in the F_1 and F_2 from the cross (a) $E^D E^D \times Ee$, (b) $E^D e \times ee$?

2.36. The inheritance of coat colors of cattle involves a multiple allelic series with a dominance hierarchy as follows: $S > s^h > s^c > s$. The S allele puts a band of white color around the middle of the animal and is referred to as a Dutch belt; the s^h allele produces Hereford-type spotting; solid color is a result of the s^c allele; and Holstein-type spotting is due to the s allele. Homozygous Dutch-belted males are crossed to Holstein-type spotted females. The F_1 females are crossed to a Hereford-type spotted male of genotype $s^h s^c$. Predict the genotypic and phenotypic frequencies in the progeny.

2.37. The genetics of the ABO human blood groups was presented in Example 2.15, page 26. A man of blood group B is being sued by a woman of blood group A for paternity. The woman's child is blood group O. (a) Is this man the father of this child? Explain. (b) If this man actually is the father of this child, specify the genotypes of both parents. (c) If it was impossible for this group B man to be the father of a type O child, regardless of the mother's genotype, specify his genotype. (d) If a man was blood group AB, could he be the father of a group O child?

2.38. A multiple allelic series is known to govern the intensity of pigmentation in the mouse such that D = full color, d = dilute color, and d^l is lethal when homozygous. The dominance order is $D > d > d^l$. A full colored mouse carrying the lethal is mated to a dilute colored mouse also carrying the lethal. The F_1 is backcrossed to the dilute parent. (a) What phenotypic ratio is expected in the viable backcross progeny? (b) What percentage of the full colored backcross progeny carry the lethal? (c) What fraction of the dilute colored progeny carry the lethal?

PEDIGREE ANALYSIS

2.39. The phenotypic expression of a dominant gene in Ayrshire cattle is a notch in the tips of the ears. In the pedigree below, where solid symbols represent notched individuals, determine the probability of notched progeny being produced from the matings (a) III1 × III3, (b) III2 × III3, (c) III3 × III4, (d) III1 × III5, (e) III2 × III5.

2.40. A single recessive gene r is largely responsible for the development of red hair in man. Dark hair is largely due to its dominant allele R. In the family pedigree shown below, unless there is evidence to the contrary, assume that individuals who marry into this family do not carry the r allele. Calculate the maximum probability of red hair appearing in children from the marriages (a) III3 × III9, (b) III4 × III10, (c) IV1 × IV2, (d) IV1 × IV3. Solid symbols represent red hair; open symbols represent dark hair.

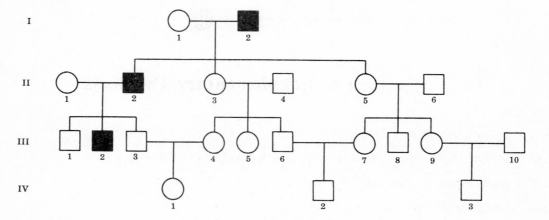

2.41. The gene for spotted coat color in rabbits (S) is dominant to its allele for solid color (s). In the following pedigree assume that those individuals brought into the family from outside do not carry the gene for solid color, unless there is evidence to the contrary. Calculate the probability of solid colored bunnies being produced from the matings (a) III1 × III9, (b) III1 × III5, (c) III3 × III5, (d) III4 × III6, (e) III6 × III9, (f) IV1 × IV2, (g) III9 × IV2, (h) III5 × IV2, (i) III6 × IV1. Solid symbols represent solid colored animals, open symbols represent spotted animals.

2.42. A multiple allelic series in dogs governs the distribution of coat color pigments. The allele A^s produces an even distribution of dark pigment over the body; the allele a^y reduces the intensity of pigmentation and produces sable or tan colored dogs; the allele a^t produces spotted patterns such as tan and black, tan and brown, etc. The dominance hierarchy is $A^s > a^y > a^t$. Given the following family pedigree, (a) determine the genotypes of all the individuals insofar as possible, (b) calculate the probability of spotted offspring being produced by mating III1 by III2, (c) find the fraction of the dark pigmented offspring from I1 × II3 that is expected to be heterozygous.

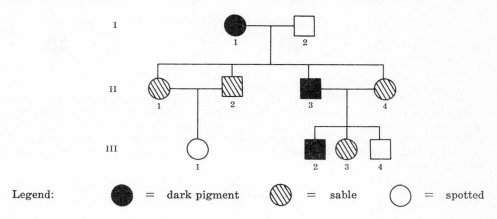

Legend: ● = dark pigment   ▨ = sable   ○ = spotted

Answers to Supplementary Problems

2.12. $Bb \times Bb$

2.13. (a) bb = white, (b) Bb

2.14. (a) $\frac{1}{4}BB : \frac{1}{2}Bb : \frac{1}{4}bb$; $\frac{3}{4}$ black : $\frac{1}{4}$ white.   (b) $\frac{1}{2}Bb$ = black : $\frac{1}{2}bb$ = white

2.15. $\frac{1}{2}$ wild type s^+s : $\frac{1}{2}$ sepia ss

2.16. (a) $\frac{1}{4}$, (b) $\frac{1}{16}$, (c) $\frac{3}{8}$

2.17. (a) Ll female × ll male, (b) 1 short : 1 long, (c) 4

2.18. $\frac{1}{2}Ww$ = wire-haired : $\frac{1}{2}ww$ = smooth

2.19. $\frac{1}{6}$

2.20. (a) $\frac{1}{2}BB : \frac{1}{2}Bb$; all red.   (b) $\frac{1}{2}Bb$ = red : $\frac{1}{2}bb$ = silver-black.   (c) all Bb = red.

2.21. (a) $\frac{1}{4}$, (b) $\frac{81}{256}$, (c) $\frac{5}{6}$ black and white : $\frac{1}{6}$ red and white, (d) 7 black and white : 1 red and white

2.22. (a) 10, (b) $10(\frac{3}{4})^3(\frac{1}{4})^2 = \frac{135}{512}$

2.23. (a) Single pair of codominant alleles
(b) F^SF^S = splashed-white : F^SF^B = Blue Andalusian : F^BF^B = black

2.24. $\frac{1}{4}C^YC^Y$ = yellow : $\frac{1}{2}C^YC^W$ = cream : $\frac{1}{4}C^WC^W$ = white

2.25. $\frac{9}{16}$ long : $\frac{6}{16}$ oval : $\frac{1}{16}$ round

2.26. (a) 1 Palomino : 1 non-Palomino
(b) 100%, $D^1D^1 \times D^1D^1$ = all D^1D^1 (chestnut); similarly $D^2D^2 \times D^2D^2$ = all D^2D^2 (cremello)
(c) D^1D^1 (chestnut) × D^2D^2 (cremello)

2.27. Creepers are heterozygous Cc; normal birds are homozygous dominant CC; the homozygous recessive genotype cc is lethal.

2.28. 4 normal : 4 hairless

2.29. $\frac{9}{15}$ dark green $C^G C^G : \frac{6}{15}$ light green $C^G C^Y$

2.30. (a) $\frac{1}{2}$, (b) $\frac{2}{3}$

2.31. $\frac{1}{2}$ Pelger : $\frac{1}{2}$ normal

2.32. Alexandria type (white eye) = AA, Aa^n, Aa; normal type (yellow eye) = $a^n a^n$, $a^n a$; Primrose Queen type (large yellow eye) = aa

2.33. (a) $\frac{1}{2}M^R M^R : \frac{1}{2}M^R M$; all restricted

    (b) $\frac{1}{2}M^R M^R : \frac{1}{2}M^R m$; all restricted

    (c) $\frac{1}{4}M^R M^R : \frac{1}{4}M^R m : \frac{1}{4}M^R M : \frac{1}{4}Mm$; $\frac{3}{4}$ restricted : $\frac{1}{4}$ mallard

    (d) $\frac{1}{4}M^R M : \frac{1}{4}M^R m : \frac{1}{4}Mm : \frac{1}{4}mm$; $\frac{1}{2}$ restricted : $\frac{1}{4}$ mallard : $\frac{1}{4}$ dusky

    (e) $\frac{1}{2}Mm$ = mallard : $\frac{1}{2}mm$ = dusky

2.34. (a) embryos = $\frac{1}{2}S^1 S^3 : \frac{1}{2}S^3 S^4$ endosperms = $\frac{1}{2}S^1 S^1 S^3 : \frac{1}{2}S^4 S^4 S^3$

    (b) none

    (c) embryos = $\frac{1}{4}S^1 S^2 : \frac{1}{4}S^1 S^4 : \frac{1}{4}S^3 S^2 : \frac{1}{4}S^3 S^4$; endosperms = $\frac{1}{4}S^1 S^1 S^2 : \frac{1}{4}S^1 S^1 S^4 : \frac{1}{4}S^3 S^3 S^2 : \frac{1}{4}S^3 S^3 S^4$

    (d) embryos = $\frac{1}{2}S^2 S^4 : \frac{1}{2}S^3 S^4$, endosperms = $\frac{1}{2}S^2 S^2 S^4 : \frac{1}{2}S^3 S^3 S^4$

2.35. (a) $F_1 = \frac{1}{2}E^D E$ (black with trace of agouti) : $\frac{1}{2}E^D e$ (non-agouti black); $F_2 = \frac{1}{4}E^D E^D : \frac{1}{4}E^D e : \frac{1}{4}E^D E : \frac{1}{16}EE : \frac{1}{8}Ee : \frac{1}{16}ee$; $\frac{1}{2}$ non-agouti black : $\frac{1}{4}$ black with trace of agouti : $\frac{3}{16}$ full color : $\frac{1}{16}$ reddish-yellow

    (b) $F_1 = \frac{1}{2}E^D e$ (non-agouti black) : $\frac{1}{2}ee$ (reddish-yellow); $F_2 = \frac{1}{16}E^D E^D : \frac{3}{8}E^D e : \frac{9}{16}ee$; $\frac{7}{16}$ non-agouti black : $\frac{9}{16}$ reddish-yellow

2.36. $\frac{1}{4}Ss^h : \frac{1}{4}Ss^c : \frac{1}{4}s^h s : \frac{1}{4}s^c s$; $\frac{1}{2}$ Dutch-belted : $\frac{1}{4}$ Hereford-type spotting : $\frac{1}{4}$ solid color

2.37. (a) The man could be the father, but paternity cannot be *proved* by blood type. In certain cases, a man may be *excluded* as a father of a child (see part (d)). (b) $I^B i$ man × $I^A i$ woman, (c) $I^B I^B$, (d) No

2.38. (a) $\frac{2}{5}$ full color : $\frac{3}{5}$ dilute, (b) 50%, (c) $\frac{2}{3}$

2.39. (a) 0, (b) $\frac{1}{2}$, (c) 0, (d) $\frac{1}{2}$, (e) $\frac{3}{4}$

2.40. (a) $\frac{1}{8}$, (b) 0, (c) $\frac{35}{576}$, (d) $\frac{7}{192}$

2.41. (a) $\frac{1}{16}$, (b) $\frac{1}{4}$, (c) $\frac{1}{2}$, (d) $\frac{1}{6}$, (e) $\frac{1}{12}$, (f) $\frac{119}{1728}$, (g) $\frac{17}{288}$, (h) $\frac{17}{72}$, (i) $\frac{7}{72}$

2.42. (a) I1 = $A^s a^y$, I2 = $a^t a^t$, II1 = $a^y a^t$, II2 = $a^y a^t$, II3 = $A^s a^t$, II4 = $a^y a^t$, III1 = $a^t a^t$, III2 = A^s-($A^s a^y$ or $A^s a^t$), III3 = $a^y a^t$, III4 = $a^t a^t$, (b) $\frac{1}{4}$, (c) $\frac{2}{3}$

Chapter 3

Two or More Genes

INDEPENDENT ASSORTMENT

In this chapter we shall consider simultaneously two or more traits, each specified by a different pair of independently assorting autosomal genes, i.e., genes on different chromosomes other than the sex chromosomes.

> **Example 3.1:** In addition to the coat color locus of guinea pigs introduced in Chapter 2 (B- = black, bb = white), another locus on a different chromosome (independently assorting) is known to govern length of hair, such that L- = short hair and ll = long hair. Any of 4 different genotypes exist for the black, short-haired phenotype: $BBLL$, $BBLl$, $BbLL$, $BbLl$. Two different genotypes produce a black, long-haired pig: $BBll$ or $Bbll$; likewise 2 genotypes for a white, short-haired pig: $bbLL$ or $bbLl$; and only 1 genotype specifies a white, long-haired pig: $bbll$.

A *dihybrid* genotype is heterozygous at two loci. Dihybrids form four genetically different gametes with approximately equal frequencies because of the random orientation of non-homologous chromosome pairs on the first meiotic metaphase plate (Chapter 1).

> **Example 3.2:** A dihybrid black, short-haired guinea pig ($BbLl$) produces 4 types of gametes in equal frequencies.
>
> | | Gametes | Frequency |
> |---|---|---|
> | B — L = | BL | $\frac{1}{4}$ |
> | B — l = | Bl | $\frac{1}{4}$ |
> | b — L = | bL | $\frac{1}{4}$ |
> | b — l = | bl | $\frac{1}{4}$ |

A summary of the gametic output for all 9 genotypes involving two pairs of independently assorting factors is shown below.

Genotypes	Gametes in Relative Frequencies
$BBLL$	all BL
$BBLl$	$\frac{1}{2}BL : \frac{1}{2}Bl$
$BBll$	all Bl
$BbLL$	$\frac{1}{2}BL : \frac{1}{2}bL$
$BbLl$	$\frac{1}{4}BL : \frac{1}{4}Bl : \frac{1}{4}bL : \frac{1}{4}bl$
$Bbll$	$\frac{1}{2}Bl : \frac{1}{2}bl$
$bbLL$	all bL
$bbLl$	$\frac{1}{2}bL : \frac{1}{2}bl$
$bbll$	all bl

A *testcross* is the mating of an incompletely known genotype to a genotype which is homozygous recessive at all of the loci under consideration. The phenotypes of the offspring produced by a testcross reveal the number of different gametes formed by the parental genotype under test. When all of the gametes of an individual are known, the genotype of that individual also becomes known. A monohybrid testcross gives a 1:1 phenotypic ratio, indicating that one pair of factors is segregating. A dihybrid testcross gives a 1:1:1:1 ratio, indicating that two pairs of factors are segregating and assorting independently.

Example 3.3: Testcrossing a dihybrid yields a 1 : 1 : 1 : 1 genotypic and phenotypic ratio among the progeny.

Parents: $BbLl$ $\times$ $bbll$
                  black, short-haired   white, long-haired

F$_1$: $\frac{1}{4}BbLl$ black, short-haired
                  $\frac{1}{4}Bbll$ black, long-haired
                  $\frac{1}{4}bbLl$ white, short-haired
                  $\frac{1}{4}bbll$ white, long-haired

SYSTEMS FOR SOLVING DIHYBRID CROSSES

1. Gametic Checkerboard Method.

When two dihybrids are crossed, four kinds of gametes are produced in equal frequencies in both the male and female. A 4 × 4 gametic checkerboard can be used to show all 16 possible combinations of these gametes. This method is laborious, time-consuming, and offers more opportunities for error than the other methods which follow.

Example 3.4:   P: $BBLL$ $\times$ $bbll$
                               black, short   white, long

F$_1$: $BbLl$ = black, short

F$_2$:

		Male Gametes			
		BL	Bl	bL	bl
Female Gametes	BL	$BBLL$ black short	$BBLl$ black short	$BbLL$ black short	$BbLl$ black short
	Bl	$BBLl$ black short	$BBll$ black long	$BbLl$ black short	$Bbll$ black long
	bL	$BbLL$ black short	$BbLl$ black short	$bbLL$ white short	$bbLl$ white short
	bl	$BbLl$ black short	$Bbll$ black long	$bbLl$ white short	$bbll$ white long

F$_2$ Summary:

Proportions	Genotypes	Proportions	Phenotypes
$\frac{1}{16}$	$BB\ LL$	$\frac{9}{16}$	black, short
$\frac{1}{8}$	$BB\ Ll$	$\frac{3}{16}$	black, long
$\frac{1}{16}$	$BB\ ll$	$\frac{3}{16}$	white, short
$\frac{1}{8}$	$Bb\ LL$	$\frac{1}{16}$	white, long
$\frac{1}{4}$	$Bb\ Ll$		
$\frac{1}{8}$	$Bb\ ll$		
$\frac{1}{16}$	$bb\ LL$		
$\frac{1}{8}$	$bb\ Ll$		
$\frac{1}{16}$	$bb\ ll$		

2. Genotypic and Phenotypic Checkerboard Methods.

A knowledge of the monohybrid probabilities presented in Chapter 2 may be applied in a simplified genotypic or phenotypic checkerboard.

Example 3.5:   Genotypic checkerboard.

F_1: $BbLl$ $\times$ $BbLl$

black, short   black, short

Considering only the B locus, $Bb \times Bb$ produces $\frac{1}{4}BB$, $\frac{1}{2}Bb$ and $\frac{1}{4}bb$. Likewise for the L locus, $Ll \times Ll$ produces $\frac{1}{4}LL$, $\frac{1}{2}Ll$ and $\frac{1}{4}ll$. Let us place these genotypic probabilities in a checkerboard and combine independent probabilities by multiplication.

F_2:

	$\frac{1}{4}LL$	$\frac{1}{2}Ll$	$\frac{1}{4}ll$
$\frac{1}{4}BB$	$\frac{1}{16}BBLL$	$\frac{1}{8}BBLl$	$\frac{1}{16}BBll$
$\frac{1}{2}Bb$	$\frac{1}{8}BbLL$	$\frac{1}{4}BbLl$	$\frac{1}{8}Bbll$
$\frac{1}{4}bb$	$\frac{1}{16}bbLL$	$\frac{1}{8}bbLl$	$\frac{1}{16}bbll$

Example 3.6:   Phenotypic checkerboard.

F_1: $BbLl$ $\times$ $BbLl$

black, short   black, short

Considering the B locus, $Bb \times Bb$ produces $\frac{3}{4}$ black and $\frac{1}{4}$ white. Likewise at the L locus, $Ll \times Ll$ produces $\frac{3}{4}$ short and $\frac{1}{4}$ long. Let us place these independent phenotypic probabilities in a checkerboard and combine them by multiplication.

F_2:

	$\frac{3}{4}$ black	$\frac{1}{4}$ white
$\frac{3}{4}$ short	$\frac{9}{16}$ black, short	$\frac{3}{16}$ white, short
$\frac{1}{4}$ long	$\frac{3}{16}$ black, long	$\frac{1}{16}$ white, long

3. Branching Systems.

This procedure was introduced in Chapter 1 as a means for determining all possible ways in which any number of chromosome pairs could orient themselves on the first meiotic metaphase plate. It can also be used to find all possible genotypic or phenotypic combinations. It will be the method of choice for solving most examples in this and subsequent chapters.

Example 3.7:   Genotypic trichotomy.

		Ratio	Genotypes

$\frac{1}{4}BB$ — $\frac{1}{4}LL$ = $\frac{1}{16}$ $BB\ LL$
         — $\frac{1}{2}Ll$ = $\frac{1}{8}$ $BB\ Ll$
         — $\frac{1}{4}ll$ = $\frac{1}{16}$ $BB\ ll$

$\frac{1}{2}Bb$ — $\frac{1}{4}LL$ = $\frac{1}{8}$ $Bb\ LL$
         — $\frac{1}{2}Ll$ = $\frac{1}{4}$ $Bb\ Ll$
         — $\frac{1}{4}ll$ = $\frac{1}{8}$ $Bb\ ll$

$\frac{1}{4}bb$ — $\frac{1}{4}LL$ = $\frac{1}{16}$ $bb\ LL$
         — $\frac{1}{2}Ll$ = $\frac{1}{8}$ $bb\ Ll$
         — $\frac{1}{4}ll$ = $\frac{1}{16}$ $bb\ ll$

Example 3.8:   Phenotypic dichotomy.

		Ratio	Phenotypes

$\frac{3}{4}$ black — $\frac{3}{4}$ short = $\frac{9}{16}$ black, short
          — $\frac{1}{4}$ long = $\frac{3}{16}$ black, long

$\frac{1}{4}$ white — $\frac{3}{4}$ short = $\frac{3}{16}$ white, short
          — $\frac{1}{4}$ long = $\frac{1}{16}$ white, long

If only one of the genotypic frequencies or phenotypic frequencies is required, there is no need to be concerned with any other genotypes or phenotypes. A mathematical solution can be readily obtained by combining independent probabilities.

Example 3.9: To find the frequency of genotype $BBLl$ in the offspring of dihybrid parents, first consider each locus separately: $Bb \times Bb = \frac{1}{4}BB$; $Ll \times Ll = \frac{1}{2}Ll$. Combining these independent probabilities, $\frac{1}{4} \times \frac{1}{2} = \frac{1}{8}BBLl$.

Example 3.10: To find the frequency of white, short pigs in the offspring of dihybrid parents, first consider each trait separately: $Bb \times Bb = \frac{1}{4}$ white (bb); $Ll \times Ll = \frac{3}{4}$ short $(L\text{-})$. Combining these independent probabilities, $\frac{1}{4} \times \frac{3}{4} = \frac{3}{16}$ white, short.

MODIFIED DIHYBRID RATIOS

The classical phenotypic ratio resulting from the mating of dihybrid genotypes is $9:3:3:1$. This ratio appears whenever the alleles at both loci display dominant and recessive relationships. The classical dihybrid ratio may be modified if one or both loci have codominant alleles or lethal alleles. A summary of these modified phenotypic ratios in adult progeny is shown below.

Allelic Relationships in Dihybrid Parents		Expected Adult Phenotypic Ratio
First Locus	Second Locus	
dominant-recessive	codominants	$3:6:3:1:2:1$
codominants	codominants	$1:2:1:2:4:2:1:2:1$
dominant-recessive	lethal*	$3:1:6:2$
codominant	lethal*	$1:2:1:2:4:2$
lethal*	lethal*	$4:2:2:1$

*lethal gene is incompletely recessive (see Example 2.11)

HIGHER COMBINATIONS

The methods for solving two factor crosses may easily be extended to solve problems involving three or more pairs of independently assorting autosomal factors. Given any number of heterozygous pairs of factors (n) in the F_1, the following general formulas apply.

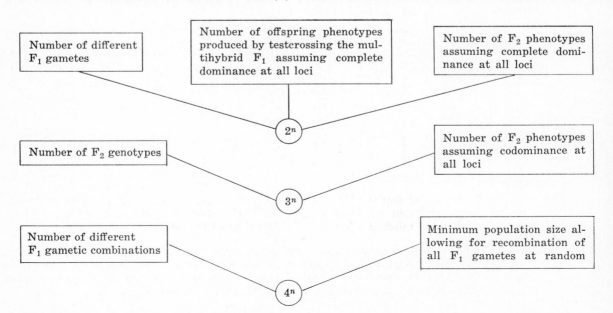

Solved Problems

3.1. Black coat color in Cocker Spaniels is governed by a dominant allele B and red coat color by its recessive allele b; solid pattern is governed by the dominant allele of an independently assorting locus S, and spotted pattern by its recessive allele s. A solid black male is mated to a solid red female and produces a litter of six pups: two solid black, two solid red, one black and white, and one red and white. Determine the genotypes of the parents.

Solution:

An unknown portion of a genotype will be indicated by a dash (-).

P: solid black male $\times$ solid red female
                                                $B\text{-}S\text{-}$ $bb\ S\text{-}$

F₁: $B\text{-}S\text{-}$ $bb\ S\text{-}$ $B\text{-}ss$ $bb\ ss$
          2 solid black : 2 solid red : 1 black and white : 1 red and white

Whenever a homozygous double recessive progeny appears (red and white in this case), each of the parents must have possessed at least one recessive allele at each locus. The black and white pup also indicates that both parents were heterozygous at the S-locus. The solid red pups likewise indicate that the male parent must have been heterozygous at the B-locus. The solid black pups fail to be of any help in determining the genotypes of these parents. Complete genotypes may now be written for both parents and for two of the pups.

P: solid black male $\times$ solid red female
                        $BbSs$ $bbSs$

F₁: $BbS\text{-}$ $bbS\text{-}$ $Bbss$ $bbss$
          2 solid black : 2 solid red : 1 black and white : 1 red and white

3.2. How many different crosses may be made (*a*) from a single pair of factors, (*b*) from two pairs of factors, and (*c*) from any given number n of pairs of factors?

Solution:

(*a*) All possible matings of the three genotypes produced by a single pair of factors may be represented in a genotypic checkerboard.

	AA	Aa	aa
AA	$AA \times AA$ (1)	$AA \times Aa$ (2)	$AA \times aa$ (3)
Aa	$Aa \times AA$ (2)	$Aa \times Aa$ (4)	$Aa \times aa$ (5)
aa	$aa \times AA$ (3)	$aa \times Aa$ (5)	$aa \times aa$ (6)

The symmetry of matings above and below the squares on the diagonal becomes obvious. The number of different crosses may be counted as follows: 3 in the first column, 2 in the second, and 1 in the third: $3 + 2 + 1 = 6$ different types of matings.

(*b*) There are $3^2 = 9$ different genotypes possible with two pairs of factors. If a nine by nine checkerboard were constructed, the same symmetry would exist above and below the squares on the diagonal as was shown in part (*a*). Again, we may count the different types of matings as an arithmetic progression from 9 to 1; $9 + 8 + 7 + 6 + 5 + 4 + 3 + 2 + 1 = 45$.

(c) The sum of any arithmetic progression of this particular type may be found by the formula $M = \frac{1}{2}(g^2 + g)$ where M = number of different types of matings, and g = number of genotypes possible with n pairs of factors.

3.3. In the garden pea, Mendel found that yellow seed color was dominant to green ($Y > y$) and round seed shape was dominant to shrunken ($S > s$). (a) What phenotypic ratio would be expected in the F_2 from a cross of a pure yellow, round × green, shrunken? (b) What is the F_2 ratio of yellow : green and of round : shrunken?

Solution:

(a)   P: $YY\,SS$ × $yy\,ss$
                       yellow, round   green, shrunken

         F_1: $Yy\,Ss$
                          yellow, round

         F_2: $\frac{9}{16}Y\text{-}S\text{-}$ yellow, round
                    $\frac{3}{16}Y\text{-}ss$ yellow, shrunken
                    $\frac{3}{16}yyS\text{-}$ green, round
                    $\frac{1}{16}yy\,ss$ green, shrunken

(b) The ratio of yellow : green $= (\frac{9}{16}$ yellow, round $+ \frac{3}{16}$ yellow, shrunken) : $(\frac{3}{16}$ green, round $+ \frac{1}{16}$ green, shrunken) $= 12 : 4 = 3 : 1$. The ratio of round : shrunken $= (\frac{9}{16}$ yellow, round $+ \frac{3}{16}$ green, round) : $(\frac{3}{16}$ yellow, shrunken $+ \frac{1}{16}$ green, shrunken) $= 12 : 4 = 3 : 1$. Thus at each of the individual loci a $3 : 1$ F_2 phenotypic ratio is observed, just as would be expected for a monohybrid cross.

3.4. Tall tomato plants are produced by the action of a dominant allele D, and dwarf plants by its recessive allele d. Hairy stems are produced by a dominant gene H, and hairless stems by its recessive allele h. A dihybrid tall, hairy plant is testcrossed. The F_1 progeny were observed to be 118 tall, hairy : 121 dwarf, hairless : 112 tall, hairless : 109 dwarf, hairy. (a) Diagram this cross. (b) What is the ratio of tall : dwarf; of hairy : hairless? (c) Are these two loci assorting independently of one another?

Solution:

(a)   Parents: $Dd\,Hh$ × $dd\,hh$
                      tall, hairy   dwarf, hairless

     Gametes: ⒟Ⓗ   Ⓓⓗ   ⓓⒽ   ⓓⓗ   ⓓⓗ

     F_1:

Genotypes	Number	Phenotypes
$Dd\,Hh$	118	tall, hairy
$Dd\,hh$	112	tall, hairless
$dd\,Hh$	109	dwarf, hairy
$dd\,hh$	121	dwarf, hairless

Note that the observed numbers approximate a $1 : 1 : 1 : 1$ phenotypic ratio.

(b) The ratio of tall : dwarf $= (118 + 112) : (109 + 121) = 230 : 230$ or $1 : 1$ ratio. The ratio of hairy : hairless $= (118 + 109) : (112 + 121) = 227 : 233$ or approximately $1 : 1$ ratio. Thus the testcross results for each locus individually approximate a $1 : 1$ phenotypic ratio.

(c) Whenever the results of a testcross approximate a $1 : 1 : 1 : 1$ ratio, it indicates that the two gene loci are assorting independently of each other in the formation of gametes. That is to say, all four types of gametes have an equal opportunity of being produced through the random orientation which non-homologous chromosomes assume on the first meiotic metaphase plate.

3.5. A dominant allele L governs short hair in guinea pigs and its recessive allele l governs long hair. Codominant alleles at an independently assorting locus specify hair color, such that $C^Y C^Y$ = yellow, $C^Y C^W$ = cream, and $C^W C^W$ = white. From matings between dihybrid short, cream pigs ($LlC^Y C^W$), predict the phenotypic ratio expected in the progeny.

Solution:

$$\frac{3}{4}L\text{-} \begin{cases} \frac{1}{4}C^Y C^Y & = & \frac{3}{16}L\text{-}C^Y C^Y & \text{short, yellow} \\ \frac{1}{2}C^Y C^W & = & \frac{6}{16}L\text{-}C^Y C^W & \text{short, cream} \\ \frac{1}{4}C^W C^W & = & \frac{3}{16}L\text{-}C^W C^W & \text{short, white} \end{cases}$$

$$\frac{1}{4}ll \begin{cases} \frac{1}{4}C^Y C^Y & = & \frac{1}{16}llC^Y C^Y & \text{long, yellow} \\ \frac{1}{2}C^Y C^W & = & \frac{2}{16}llC^Y C^W & \text{long, cream} \\ \frac{1}{4}C^W C^W & = & \frac{1}{16}llC^W C^W & \text{long, white} \end{cases}$$

Thus six phenotypes appear in the offspring in the ratio $3:6:3:1:2:1$. The dash (-) in the genotypes L- indicates that either allele L or l may be present, both combinations resulting in a short-haired phenotype.

3.6. Normal leg size, characteristic of the Kerry type of cattle, is produced by the homozygous genotype DD. Short legged Dexter type cattle possess the heterozygous genotype Dd. The homozygous genotype dd is lethal, producing grossly deformed stillbirths called "bulldog calves". The presence of horns in cattle is governed by the recessive allele of another gene locus p, the polled condition (absence of horns) being produced by its dominant allele P. In matings between polled Dexter cattle of genotype $DdPp$, what phenotypic ratio is expected in the adult progeny?

Solution:

P: $DdPp$ $\times$ $DdPp$

      Dexter, polled   Dexter, polled

F_1:

$$\frac{1}{4}DD \begin{cases} \frac{3}{4}P\text{-} & = & \frac{3}{16}DD\ P\text{-} & \text{polled, Kerry} \\ \frac{1}{4}pp & = & \frac{1}{16}DD\ pp & \text{horned, Kerry} \end{cases}$$

$$\frac{1}{2}Dd \begin{cases} \frac{3}{4}P\text{-} & = & \frac{6}{16}Dd\ P\text{-} & \text{polled, Dexter} \\ \frac{1}{4}pp & = & \frac{2}{16}Dd\ pp & \text{horned, Dexter} \end{cases}$$

$$\frac{1}{4}dd \begin{cases} \frac{3}{4}P\text{-} & = & \frac{3}{16}dd\ P\text{-} & \text{lethal} \\ \frac{1}{4}pp & = & \frac{1}{16}dd\ pp & \text{lethal} \end{cases}$$

The phenotypic ratio of viable offspring thus becomes: $\frac{3}{12}$ polled, Kerry; $\frac{1}{12}$ horned, Kerry; $\frac{6}{12}$ polled, Dexter; $\frac{2}{12}$ horned, Dexter.

3.7. Stem color of tomato plants is known to be under the genetic control of at least one pair of alleles such that A- results in the production of anthocyanin pigment (purple stem). The recessive genotype aa lacks this pigment and hence is green. The edge of the tomato leaf may be deeply cut under the influence of a dominant allele C. The recessive genotype cc produces smooth edged leaves called "potato leaf". The production of two locules in the tomato fruit is a characteristic of the dominant allele M; multiple locules are produced by the recessive genotype mm. A cross is made between two pure lines: purple, potato, biloculed × green, cut, multiloculed. What phenotypic ratio is expected in the F_2?

Solution:

P: $AA\ cc\ MM$ $\times$ $aa\ CC\ mm$

     purple, potato, biloculed   green, cut, multiloculed

F$_1$: $Aa\,Cc\,Mm$
         purple, cut, biloculed

F$_2$:

$\frac{3}{4}A\text{-}$

   $\frac{3}{4}C\text{-}$

     $\frac{3}{4}M\text{-}$ = $\frac{27}{64}A\text{-}\,C\text{-}\,M\text{-}$ purple, cut, biloculed

     $\frac{1}{4}mm$ = $\frac{9}{64}A\text{-}\,C\text{-}\,mm$ purple, cut, multiloculed

   $\frac{1}{4}cc$

     $\frac{3}{4}M\text{-}$ = $\frac{9}{64}A\text{-}\,cc\,M\text{-}$ purple, potato, biloculed

     $\frac{1}{4}mm$ = $\frac{3}{64}A\text{-}\,cc\,mm$ purple, potato, multiloculed

$\frac{1}{4}aa$

   $\frac{3}{4}C\text{-}$

     $\frac{3}{4}M\text{-}$ = $\frac{9}{64}aa\,C\text{-}\,M\text{-}$ green, cut, biloculed

     $\frac{1}{4}mm$ = $\frac{3}{64}aa\,C\text{-}\,mm$ green, cut, multiloculed

   $\frac{1}{4}cc$

     $\frac{3}{4}M\text{-}$ = $\frac{3}{64}aa\,cc\,M\text{-}$ green, potato, biloculed

     $\frac{1}{4}mm$ = $\frac{1}{64}aa\,cc\,mm$ green, potato, multiloculed

Supplementary Problems

DIHYBRID CROSSES WITH DOMINANT AND RECESSIVE ALLELES

3.8. The position of the flower on the stem of the garden pea is governed by a pair of alleles. Flowers growing in the axils (upper angle between petiole and stem) are produced by the action of a dominant allele T, those growing only at the tip of the stem by its recessive allele t. Colored flowers are produced by a dominant gene C, and white flowers by its recessive allele c. A dihybrid plant with colored flowers in the leaf axils is crossed to a pure strain of the same phenotype. What genotypic and phenotypic ratios are expected in the F$_1$ progeny?

3.9. In summer squash, white fruit color is governed by a dominant allele (W) and yellow fruit color by the recessive (w). A dominant allele at another locus (S) produces disc shaped fruit and its recessive allele (s) yields sphere-shaped fruit. If a homozygous white disc variety of genotype $WWSS$ is crossed with a homozygous yellow sphere variety ($wwss$), the F$_1$ are all white disc dihybrids of genotype $WwSs$. If the F$_1$ is allowed to mate at random, what would be the phenotypic ratio expected in the F$_2$ generation?

3.10. In *Drosophila*, ebony body color is produced by a recessive gene e and wild type (gray) body color by its dominant allele e^+. Vestigial wings are governed by a recessive gene vg, and normal wing size (wild type) by its dominant allele vg^+. If wild type dihybrid flies are crossed and produce 256 progeny, how many of these progeny flies are expected in each phenotypic class?

3.11. Short hair in rabbits is governed by a dominant gene (L) and long hair by its recessive allele (l). Black hair results from the action of the dominant genotype ($B\text{-}$) and brown from the recessive genotype (bb). (*a*) In crosses between dihybrid short, black and homozygous short, brown rabbits, what genotypic and phenotypic ratios are expected among their progeny? (*b*) Determine the expected genotypic and phenotypic ratios in progeny from the cross $LlBb \times Llbb$.

3.12. The genetic information for the following eight parts is found in Problem 3.11. (*a*) What phenotypic ratio is expected among progeny from crosses of $LlBb \times LlBb$? (*b*) What percentage of the F$_1$ genotypes in part (*a*) breeds true (i.e. what percentage is of homozygous genotypes)? (*c*) What percentage of the F$_1$ genotypes is heterozygous for only one pair of genes? (*d*) What percentage of the F$_1$ genotypes is heterozygous at both loci? (*e*) What percentage of the F$_1$ genotypes could be used for testcross purposes (i.e. homozygous double recessive)? (*f*) What percentage of the F$_1$ progeny could be used for testcross purposes at the B locus (i.e. homozygous recessive bb)? (*g*) What percentage of all short haired F$_1$ individuals is expected to be brown? (*h*) What percentage of all black F$_1$ individuals will breed true for both black and short hair?

3.13. How many different matings are possible (a) when three pairs of factors are considered simultaneously, (b) when four pairs of factors are considered simultaneously? *Hint.* See Problem 3.2(c).

3.14. (a) What percentage of all possible types of matings with two pairs of factors would be represented by matings between identical genotypes? (b) What percentage of all the matings possible with three pairs of factors would be represented by matings between non-identical genotypes?

3.15. The presence of feathers on the legs of chickens is due to a dominant allele (F) and clean legs to its recessive allele (f). Pea comb shape is produced by another dominant allele (P) and single comb by its recessive allele (p). In crosses between pure feathered leg, single-combed individuals and pure pea-combed, clean leg individuals, suppose that only the single-combed, feathered leg F_2 progeny are saved and allowed to mate at random. What genotypic and phenotypic ratios would be expected among the progeny (F_3)?

3.16. List all the different gametes produced by the following individuals: (a) $AA\,BB\,Cc$, (b) $aa\,Bb\,Cc$, (c) $Aa\,Bb\,cc\,Dd$, (d) $AA\,Bb\,Cc\,dd\,Ee\,Ff$.

3.17. The normal cloven-footed condition in swine is produced by the homozygous recessive genotype mm. A mule-footed condition is produced by the dominant genotype M-. White coat color is governed by the dominant allele of another locus B and black by its recessive allele b. A white, mule-footed sow (female) is mated to a black, cloven-footed boar (male) and produces several litters. Among 26 offspring produced by this mating, all were found to be white with mule feet. (a) What is the most probable genotype of the sow? (b) The next litter produced 8 white, mule-footed offspring and one white cloven-footed pig. Now, what is the most probable genotype of the sow?

3.18. A white, mule-footed boar (see Problem 3.17) is crossed to a sow of the same phenotype. Among the F_1 offspring there were found 6 white, cloven-footed : 7 black, mule-footed : 15 white, mule-footed : 3 black, cloven-footed pigs. (a) If all the black mule-footed F_1 offspring from this type of mating were to be testcrossed, what phenotypic ratio would be expected among the testcross progeny? (b) If the sow was to be testcrossed, what phenotypic ratio of progeny is expected?

3.19. In poultry, a crested head is produced by a dominant gene C and plain head by its recessive allele c. Black feather color R- is dominant to red rr. A homozygous black-feathered, plain-headed bird is crossed to a homozygous red-feathered, crested-headed bird. What phenotypic and genotypic ratios are expected from testcrossing only the F_2 black-crested birds? *Hint.* Remember to account for the relative frequencies of the different genotypes in this one phenotypic class.

3.20. Bronze turkeys have at least one dominant allele R. Red turkeys are homozygous for its recessive allele rr. Another dominant gene H produces normal feathers, and the recessive genotype hh produces feathers lacking webbing, a condition termed "hairy". In crosses between homozygous bronze, hairy birds and homozygous red, normal-feathered birds, what proportion of the F_2 progeny will be (a) genotype $Rrhh$, (b) phenotype bronze, hairy, (c) genotype $rrHH$, (d) phenotype red, normal-feathered, (e) genotype $RrHh$, (f) phenotype bronze, normal feathered, (g) genotype $rrhh$, (h) phenotype red, normal-feathered, (i) genotype $RRHh$?

MODIFIED DIHYBRID RATIOS

3.21. In peaches, the homozygous genotype G^oG^o produces oval glands at the base of the leaves, the heterozygous genotype G^oG^a produces round glands, and the homozygous genotype G^aG^a results in the absence of glands. At another locus, a dominant gene S produces fuzzy peach skin and its recessive allele s produces smooth (nectarine) skin. A homozygous variety with oval glands and smooth skin is crossed to a homozygous variety with fuzzy skin lacking glands at the base of its leaves. What genotypic and phenotypic proportions are expected in the F_2?

3.22. In Shorthorn cattle, coat colors are governed by a codominant pair of alleles C^R and C^W. The homozygous genotype C^RC^R produces red, the other homozygote produces white and the heterozygote produces roan (a mixture of red and white). The presence of horns is produced by the homozygous recessive genotype pp and the polled condition by its dominant allele P. If roan cows heterozygous for the horned gene are mated to a horned, roan bull, what phenotypic ratio is expected in the offspring?

3.23. A gene locus with codominant alleles is known to govern feather color in chickens such that the genotype F^BF^B = black, F^WF^W = splashed white and F^BF^W = blue. Another locus with codominant alleles governs feather morphology such that M^NM^N = normal feather shape, M^NM^F = slightly abnormal feathers called "mild frizzle", and M^FM^F = grossly abnormal feathers called "extreme frizzle". If blue, mildly-frizzled birds are crossed among themselves, what phenotypic proportions are expected among their offspring?

3.24. In the above problem, if all the blue offspring with normal feathers and all the splashed-white, extremely-frizzled offspring are isolated and allowed to mate at random, what phenotypic ratio would be expected among their progeny?

3.25. The shape of radishes may be long (LL), round ($L'L'$) or oval (LL'). Color may be red (RR), white ($R'R'$) or purple (RR'). If a long, white strain is crossed with a round, red strain, what phenotypic proportions are expected in the F_1 and F_2?

3.26. Suppose that two strains of radishes are crossed (see above problem) and produce a progeny consisting of 16 long white, 31 oval purple, 16 oval white, 15 long red, 17 oval red and 32 long purple. What would be the phenotypes of the parental strains?

3.27. A dominant gene in mice, K, produces a kinked tail; recessive genotypes at this locus, kk, have normal tails. The homozygous condition of another locus, AA, produces a gray color called agouti; the heterozygous condition A^yA produces yellow color; the homozygous genotype A^yA^y is lethal. (a) If yellow mice, heterozygous for kinky tail, are crossed together, what phenotypic proportions are expected in their offspring? (b) What proportion of the offspring is expected to be of genotype A^yAKk? (c) If all the yellow offspring were allowed to mate at random, what would be the genotypic and phenotypic ratios among their adult progeny?

3.28. An incompletely dominant gene N in the Romney Marsh breed of sheep causes the fleece of homozygotes to be "hairy", i.e. containing fibers which lack the normal amount of crimp. Normal wool is produced by the homozygous genotype $N'N'$. Heterozygotes, NN', can be distinguished at birth by the presence of large, medulated fibers called "halo-hairs" scattered over the body. A gene known as "lethal gray" causes homozygous gray fetuses (G^lG^l) to die before 15 weeks in gestation. The heterozygous genotype G^lG produces gray fleece, and the homozygous genotype GG produces black. If heterozygous halo, gray individuals are mated together, (a) what would be the phenotypic proportions expected in the live progeny, (b) what proportion of the live progeny would carry the lethal gene, (c) what proportion of the live progeny with halo-hairs would carry the lethal gene, (d) what proportion of all the zygotes would be expected to be of genotype $NN'G^lG^l$?

3.29. Infantile amaurotic idiocy (Tay Sachs disease) is a recessive hereditary abnormality causing death within the first few years of life only when homozygous (ii). The dominant condition at this locus produces a normal phenotype (I-). Abnormally shortened fingers (brachyphalangy) is thought to be due to a genotype heterozygous for a lethal gene (BB^L), the homozygote (BB) being normal, and the other homozygote (B^LB^L) being lethal. What are the phenotypic expectations among teen-age children from parents who are both brachyphalangic and heterozygous for infantile amaurotic idiocy?

3.30. In addition to the gene governing infantile amaurotic idiocy in the above problem, the recessive genotype of another locus (jj) results in death before age 18 due to a condition called "juvenile amaurotic idiocy". Only individuals of genotype I-J- will survive to adulthood. (a) What proportion of the children from parents of genotype ($IiJj$) would probably not survive to adulthood? (b) What proportion of the adult survivors in part (a) would not be carriers of either hereditary abnormality?

3.31. A genetic condition on chromosome 2 in the fruit fly *Drosophila melanogaster* is lethal when homozygous (Pm/Pm), but when heterozygous (Pm/Pm^+) produces a purplish eye color called "plum". The other homozygous condition (Pm^+/Pm^+) produces wild type eye color. On chromosome 3, a gene called "stubble" produces short, thick bristles when heterozygous (Sb/Sb^+), but is lethal when homozygous (Sb/Sb). The homozygous condition of its alternative allele (Sb^+/Sb^+), produces bristles of normal size (wild type). (a) What phenotypic ratio is expected among progeny from crosses between plum, stubble parents? (b) If the offspring of part (a) are allowed to mate at random to produce an F_2, what phenotypic ratio is expected?

3.32. Feather color in chickens is governed by a pair of codominant alleles such that F^BF^B produces black, F^WF^W produces splashed white and F^BF^W produces blue. An independently segregating locus governs the length of leg; CC genotypes possess normal leg length, CC^L genotypes produce squatty, shortlegged types called "creepers", but homozygous C^LC^L genotypes are lethal. Determine the kinds of progeny phenotypes and their expected ratios which crosses between dihybrid blue creepers are likely to produce.

3.33. Fat mice can be produced by two independently assorting genes. The recessive genotype ob/ob produces a fat, sterile mouse called "obese". Its dominant allele Ob produces normal growth. The recessive genotype ad/ad also produces a fat, sterile mouse called "adipose" and its dominant allele Ad produces normal growth. What phenotypic proportions of fat versus normal would be expected among the F_1 and F_2 from parents of genotype $Ob/ob, Ad/ad$?

HIGHER COMBINATIONS

3.34. The seeds from Mendel's tall plants were round and yellow, all three characters due to a dominant gene at each of three independently assorting loci. The recessive genotypes dd, ww and gg produce dwarf plants with wrinkled and green seeds respectively. (a) If a pure tall, wrinkled, yellow variety is crossed with a pure dwarf, round, green variety, what phenotypic ratio is expected in the F_1 and F_2? (b) What percentage of the F_2 is expected to be of genotype $Dd\,WW\,gg$? (c) If all the dwarf, round, green individuals in the F_2 are isolated and artificially crossed at random, what phenotypic ratio of offspring is expected?

3.35. The coat colors of mice are known to be governed by several genes. The presence of a yellow band of pigment near the tip of the hair is called "agouti" pattern and is produced by the dominant allele A. The recessive condition at this locus (aa) does not have this subapical band and is termed non-agouti. The dominant allele of another locus, B, produces black and the recessive genotype bb produces brown. The homozygous genotype c^hc^h restricts pigment production to the extremities in a pattern called Himalayan, whereas the genotype C- allows pigment to be distributed over the entire body. (a) In crosses between pure brown, agouti, Himalayan and pure black mice, what are the phenotypic expectations of the F_1 and F_2? (b) What proportion of the black-agouti, full colored F_2 would be expected to be of genotype $AaBBCc$? (c) What percentage of all the Himalayans in the F_2 would be expected to show brown pigment? (d) What percentage of all the agoutis in the F_2 would be expected to exhibit black pigment?

3.36. In addition to the information given in the problem above, a fourth locus in mice is known to govern the density of pigment deposition. The genotype D- produces full color, but the recessive genotype dd produces a dilution of pigment. Another allele at this locus, d^l, is lethal when homozygous, produces a dilution of pigment in the genotype dd^l, and produces full color when in heterozygous condition with the dominant allele Dd^l. (a) What phenotypic ratio would be expected among the live F_2 progeny if the F_1 from the cross $aabbCCDd \times AABBccdd^l$ were allowed to mate at random? (b) What proportion of the live F_2 would be expected to be of genotype $AABbccdd^l$?

3.37. In the parental cross $AABBCCDDEE \times aabbccddee$, (a) how many different F_1 gametes can be formed, (b) how many different genotypes are expected in the F_2, (c) how many squares would be necessary in a gametic checkerboard to accommodate the F_2?

3.38. A pure strain of Mendel's peas, dominant for all seven of his independently assorting genes, was testcrossed. (a) How many different kinds of gametes could each of the parents produce? (b) How many different gametes could the F_1 produce? (c) If the F_1 was testcrossed, how many phenotypes would be expected in the offspring and in what proportions? (d) How many genotypes would be expected in the F_2? (e) How many combinations of F_1 gametes are theoretically possible (considering, e.g., $AABBCCDDEEFFGG$ sperm nucleus $\times$ $aabbccddeeffgg$ egg nucleus a different combination than $AABBCCDDEEFFGG$ egg nucleus $\times$ $aabbccddeeffgg$ sperm nucleus)? (f) How many different kinds of matings could theoretically be made among the F_2? *Hint.* See solution to Problem 3.2(c).

Answers to Supplementary Problems

3.8. $\frac{1}{4}CCTT : \frac{1}{4}CCTt : \frac{1}{4}CcTT : \frac{1}{4}CcTt$; all axial, colored

3.9. $\frac{9}{16}$ white, disc : $\frac{3}{16}$ white, sphere : $\frac{3}{16}$ yellow, disc : $\frac{1}{16}$ yellow, sphere

3.10. 144 wild type : 48 vestigial : 48 ebony : 16 ebony, vestigial

3.11.   (a) $\frac{1}{4}LLBb:\frac{1}{4}LlBb:\frac{1}{4}LLbb:\frac{1}{4}Llbb$; $\frac{1}{2}$ short, black : $\frac{1}{2}$ short, brown

      (b) $\frac{1}{8}LLBb:\frac{1}{4}LlBb:\frac{1}{8}LLbb:\frac{1}{4}Llbb:\frac{1}{8}llBb:\frac{1}{8}llbb$;

        $\frac{3}{8}$ short, black : $\frac{3}{8}$ short, brown : $\frac{1}{8}$ long, black : $\frac{1}{8}$ long, brown

3.12.   (a) $\frac{9}{16}$ short, black : $\frac{3}{16}$ short, brown : $\frac{3}{16}$ long, black : $\frac{1}{16}$ long, brown, (b) 25%, (c) 50%, (d) 25%, (e) 6.25%, (f) 25%, (g) 25%, (h) 8.33%

3.13.   (a) 378, (b) 3321   **3.14.**   (a) 20%, (b) 92.86%

3.15. $4FFpp:4Ffpp:1ffpp$; 8 feathered leg, single comb : 1 clean leg, single comb

3.16.   (a) ABC, ABc, (b) aBC, aBc, abC, abc, (c) $ABcD, ABcd, AbcD, Abcd, aBcD, aBcd, abcD, abcd$, (d) $ABCdEF, ABCdEf, ABCdeF, ABCdef, ABcdEF, ABcdEf, ABcdeF, ABcdef, AbCdEF, AbCdEf, AbCdeF, AbCdef, AbcdEF, AbcdEf, AbcdeF, Abcdef$

3.17.   (a) $BBMM$, (b) $BBMm$

3.18.   (a) 2 black, mule-foot : 1 black, cloven foot, (b) $\frac{1}{4}$ white, mule-foot : $\frac{1}{4}$ white, cloven-foot : $\frac{1}{4}$ black, mule foot : $\frac{1}{4}$ black, cloven-foot

3.19. $4RrCc$ = black, crested : $2Rrcc$ = black, plain : $2rrCc$ = red, crested : $1rrcc$ = red, plain

3.20.   (a) $\frac{1}{8}$, (b) $\frac{3}{16}$, (c) $\frac{1}{16}$, (d) $\frac{3}{16}$, (e) $\frac{1}{4}$, (f) $\frac{9}{16}$, (g) $\frac{1}{16}$, (h) $\frac{3}{16}$, (i) $\frac{1}{8}$

3.21. $\frac{1}{16}G^AG^ASS:\frac{2}{16}G^AG^ASs:\frac{1}{16}G^AG^Ass:\frac{2}{16}G^AG^OSS:\frac{4}{16}G^AG^OSs:\frac{2}{16}G^AG^Oss:\frac{1}{16}G^OG^OSS:\frac{2}{16}G^OG^OSs:$ $\frac{1}{16}G^OG^Oss$; $\frac{3}{16}$ fuzzy, glandless : $\frac{1}{16}$ smooth, glandless : $\frac{6}{16}$ round gland, fuzzy : $\frac{2}{16}$ round gland, smooth : $\frac{3}{16}$ oval gland, fuzzy : $\frac{1}{16}$ oval gland, smooth

3.22.   1 red, polled : 1 red, horned : 2 roan, polled : 2 roan, horned : 1 white, polled : 1 white, horned

3.23. $\frac{1}{16}$ black : $\frac{1}{8}$ black, mildly frizzled : $\frac{1}{16}$ black, extremely frizzled : $\frac{1}{8}$ blue : $\frac{1}{4}$ blue, mildly frizzled : $\frac{1}{8}$ blue, extremely frizzled : $\frac{1}{16}$ splashed-white : $\frac{1}{8}$ splashed-white, mildly frizzled : $\frac{1}{16}$ splashed-white, extremely frizzled

3.24.   1 black : 2 blue : 1 splashed-white : 2 blue, mildly frizzled : 2 splashed-white, mildly frizzled : 1 splashed-white, extremely frizzled

3.25. F_1 is all oval, purple; F_2 is $\frac{1}{16}$ long, red : $\frac{1}{8}$ long, purple : $\frac{1}{16}$ long, white : $\frac{1}{8}$ oval, red : $\frac{1}{4}$ oval, purple : $\frac{1}{8}$ oval, white : $\frac{1}{16}$ round, red : $\frac{1}{8}$ round, purple : $\frac{1}{16}$ round, white

3.26.   long, purple $\times$ oval, purple

3.27.   (a) $\frac{1}{2}$ yellow, kinky : $\frac{1}{6}$ yellow : $\frac{1}{4}$ agouti, kinky : $\frac{1}{12}$ agouti, (b) $\frac{1}{3}$, (c) $\frac{1}{6}A^yAKK:\frac{1}{4}A^yAKk:$ $\frac{1}{6}A^yAkk:\frac{1}{12}AAKK:\frac{1}{4}AAKk:\frac{1}{12}AAkk$; $\frac{1}{2}$ yellow, kinky : $\frac{1}{6}$ yellow : $\frac{1}{4}$ agouti, kinky : $\frac{1}{12}$ agouti

3.28.   (a) $\frac{1}{12}$ black, hairy : $\frac{1}{6}$ black, halo-haired : $\frac{1}{12}$ black : $\frac{1}{6}$ gray, hairy : $\frac{1}{3}$ gray, halo-haired : $\frac{1}{6}$ gray, (b) $\frac{2}{3}$, (c) $\frac{2}{3}$, (d) $\frac{1}{8}$

3.29. $\frac{1}{3}$ normal : $\frac{2}{3}$ brachyphalangic   **3.30.**   (a) $\frac{7}{16}$, (b) $\frac{1}{9}$

3.31.   (a) $\frac{4}{9}$ plum, stubble : $\frac{2}{9}$ plum : $\frac{2}{9}$ stubble : $\frac{1}{9}$ wild type, (b) 1 plum, stubble : 1 plum : 1 stubble : 1 wild type

3.32. $\frac{1}{12}$ black : $\frac{1}{6}$ blue : $\frac{1}{12}$ splashed-white : $\frac{1}{6}$ black, creeper : $\frac{1}{3}$ blue, creeper : $\frac{1}{6}$ splashed-white, creeper

3.33. $F_1 = \frac{9}{16}$ normal : $\frac{7}{16}$ fat; $F_2 = \frac{64}{81}$ normal : $\frac{17}{81}$ fat

3.34.   (a) F_1 is all tall, round, yellow; F_2 is 27 tall, round, yellow : 9 tall, round, green : 9 tall, wrinkled, yellow : 9 dwarf, round, yellow : 3 tall, wrinkled, green : 3 dwarf, round, green : 3 dwarf, wrinkled, yellow : 1 dwarf, wrinkled, green, (b) 3.12%, (c) 8 round : 1 wrinkled

3.35.   (a) F_1 is all agouti, black; F_2 is 27 agouti, black : 9 agouti, black, Himalayan : 9 agouti, brown : 9 black : 3 agouti, brown, Himalayan : 3 black, Himalayan : 3 brown : 1 brown, Himalayan, (b) $\frac{4}{27}$, (c) 25%, (d) 75%

3.36.   (a) 189 agouti, black : 216 agouti, black, dilute : 63 agouti, black, Himalayan : 72 agouti, black, Himalayan, dilute : 63 agouti, brown : 72 agouti, brown, dilute : 63 black : 72 black, dilute : 21 agouti, brown, Himalayan : 24 agouti, brown, Himalayan, dilute : 21 black, Himalayan : 24 black, Himalayan, dilute : 21 brown : 24 brown, dilute : 7 brown, Himalayan : 8 brown, Himalayan, dilute, (b) $\frac{1}{120}$

3.37.   (a) 32, (b) 243, (c) 1024

3.38.   (a) one each, (b) 128, (c) 128, each with equal frequency, (d) 2187, (e) 16,384, (f) 2,392,578

Chapter 4

Genetic Interaction

TWO FACTOR INTERACTIONS

The phenotype is a result of gene products brought to expression in a given environment. The environment includes not only external factors such as temperature and the amount or quality of light, but also internal factors such as hormones and *enzymes*. Genes specify the structure of proteins. All known enzymes are proteins. Enzymes perform catalytic functions, causing the splitting or union of various molecules. All of the chemical reactions which occur in the cell constitute the subject of *intermediary metabolism*. These reactions occur as stepwise conversions of one substance into another, each step being mediated by a specific enzyme. All of the steps which transform a precursor substance to its end product constitute a *biosynthetic pathway*.

Several genes are usually required to specify the enzymes involved in even the simplest pathways. Each metabolite (A, B, C) is produced by the catalytic action of different enzymes (e_x) specified by different wild type genes (g_x^+). *Genetic interaction* occurs whenever two or more genes specify enzymes which catalyze steps in a common pathway. If substance C is essential for the production of a normal phenotype, and the recessive mutant alleles g_1, g_2 and g_3 produce defective enzymes, then a mutant (abnormal) phenotype would result from a genotype homozygous recessive at any of the three loci. If g_3 is mutant, the conversion of B to C does not occur and substance B tends to accumulate in excessive quantity; if g_2 is mutant, substance A will accumulate. Thus mutants are said to produce "metabolic blocks". An organism with a mutation only in g_2 could produce a normal phenotype if it was given either substance B or C, but an organism with a mutation in g_3 has a specific requirement for C. Thus gene g_3^+ becomes dependent upon gene g_2^+ for its expression as a normal phenotype. If the genotype is homozygous for the recessive g_2 allele, then the pathway ends with substance A. Neither g_3^+ nor its recessive allele g_3 has any effect on the phenotype. Thus genotype g_2g_2 can hide or mask the phenotypic expression of alleles at the g_3 locus. Originally a gene or locus which suppressed or masked the action of a gene at another locus was termed *epistatic*. The gene or locus suppressed was *hypostatic*. Later it was found that both loci could be mutually epistatic to one another. Now the term epistasis has come to be synonomous with almost any type of gene interaction. Dominance involves *intra*-allelic gene suppression, or the masking effect which one allele has upon the expression of another allele at the same locus. Epistasis involves *inter*-allelic gene suppression, or the masking effect which one gene locus has upon the expression of another. The classical phenotypic ratio of $9:3:3:1$ observed in the progeny of dihybrid parents becomes modified by epistasis into ratios which are various combinations of the $9:3:3:1$ groupings.

Example 4.1:   A particularly illuminating example of gene interaction occurs in white clover. Some strains have a high cyanide content, others have a low cyanide content. Crosses between two strains with low cyanide have produced an F_1 with a high concentration of cyanide in their leaves. The F_2 shows a ratio of 9 high cyanide : 7 low cyanide. Cyanide is known to be produced from the substrate cyanogenic glucoside by enzymatic catalysis. One strain of clover has the enzyme but not the substrate. The other strain makes substrate but is unable to convert it to cyanide. The pathway may be diagrammed as follows where G^x produces an enzyme and g^x results in a metabolic block.

$$
A \xrightarrow{\quad E_1 \quad} B \xrightarrow{\quad E_2 \quad} C
$$

G^1 ... G^2 ... g^1 ... g^2

(unknown precursor)   (glucoside)   (cyanide)

Tests on leaf extracts have been made for cyanide content before and after the addition of either glucoside or the enzyme E_2.

F_2 Ratio	Genotype	Leaf Extract Alone	Leaf Extract Plus Glucoside	Leaf Extract Plus E_2
9	$G^1\text{-}G^2\text{-}$	+	+	+
3	$G^1\text{-}g^2g^2$	0	0	+
3	$g^1g^1G^2\text{-}$	0	+	0
1	$g^1g^1g^2g^2$	0	0	0

Legend: + = cyanide present,   0 = no cyanide present.

If the leaves are phenotypically classified on the basis of cyanide content of extract alone, a ratio of 9 : 7 results. If the phenotypic classification is based either on extract plus glucoside or on extract plus E_2, a ratio of 12 : 4 is produced. If all of these tests form the basis of phenotypic classification, the classical 9 : 3 : 3 : 1 ratio emerges.

EPISTATIC INTERACTIONS

When epistasis is operative between two gene loci, the number of phenotypes appearing in the offspring from dihybrid parents will be less than four. There are six types of epistatic ratios commonly recognized, three of which have 3 phenotypes and the other three having only 2 phenotypes.

1. Dominant Epistasis (12 : 3 : 1).

When the dominant allele at one locus, for example the *A* allele, produces a certain phenotype regardless of the allelic condition of the other locus, then the A-locus is said to be epistatic to the B-locus. Furthermore, since the dominant allele *A* is able to express itself in the presence of either *B* or *b*, this is a case of dominant epistasis. Only when the genotype of the individual is homozygous recessive at the epistatic locus (*aa*) can the alleles of the hypostatic locus (*B* or *b*) be expressed. Thus the genotypes *A-B-* and *A-bb* produce the same phenotype, whereas *aaB-* and *aabb* produce two additional phenotypes. The classical 9 : 3 : 3 : 1 ratio becomes modified into a 12 : 3 : 1 ratio.

2. Recessive Epistasis (9 : 3 : 4).

If the recessive genotype at one locus (e.g. *aa*) suppresses the expression of alleles at the B-locus, the A-locus is said to exhibit recessive epistasis over the B-locus. Only if the dominant allele is present at the A-locus can the alleles of the hypostatic B-locus be expressed. The genotypes *A-B-* and *A-bb* produce two additional phenotypes. The 9 : 3 : 3 : 1 ratio becomes a 9 : 3 : 4 ratio.

3. Duplicate Genes with Cumulative Effect (9 : 6 : 1).

If the dominant condition (either homozygous or heterozygous) at either locus (but not both) produces the same phenotype, the F_2 ratio becomes 9 : 6 : 1. For example, where the epistasic genes are involved in producing various amounts of a substance such as pigment, the dominant genotypes of each locus may be considered to produce one unit of pigment independently. Thus genotypes *A-bb* and *aaB-* produce one unit of pigment each and therefore have the same phenotype. The genotype *aabb* produces no pigment, but in the genotype *A-B-* the effect is cumulative and two units of pigment are produced.

4. Duplicate Dominant Genes (15 : 1).

The 9 : 3 : 3 : 1 ratio is modified into a 15 : 1 ratio if the dominant alleles of both loci each produce the same phenotype without cumulative effect.

5. Duplicate Recessive Genes (9 : 7).

In the case where identical phenotypes are produced by both homozygous recessive genotypes, the F_2 ratio becomes 9 : 7. The genotypes *aaB-*, *A-bb* and *aabb* produce one phenotype. Both dominant alleles, when present together, complement each other and produce a different phenotype.

6. Dominant and Recessive Interaction (13 : 3).

Only two F_2 phenotypes result when a dominant genotype at one locus (e.g. *A-*) and the recessive genotype at the other (*bb*) produce the same phenotypic effect. Thus *A-B-*, *A-bb* and *aabb* produce one phenotype and *aaB-* produces another in the ratio 13 : 3. A summary of these epistatic ratios appears in the following table.

Genotypes	A-B-	A-bb	aaB-	aabb
Classical ratio	9	3	3	1
Dominant epistasis	12		3	1
Recessive epistasis	9	3	4	
Duplicate genes with cumulative effect	9	6		1
Duplicate dominant genes	15			1
Duplicate recessive genes	9	7		
Dominant and recessive interaction	13		3	

NON-EPISTATIC INTERACTIONS

Genetic interaction may also occur without epistasis if the end products of different pathways each contribute to the same trait.

Example 4.2:   The dull-red eye color characteristic of wild type flies is a mixture of two kinds of pigments (B and D) each produced from non-pigmented compounds (A and C) by the action of different enzymes (e_1 and e_2) specified by different wild type genes (g_1^+ and g_2^+).

$$g_1^+$$
$$\downarrow$$
$$A \longrightarrow e_1 \longrightarrow B$$
$$\left.\begin{array}{c} \\ \\ \end{array}\right\} \text{mixture} = \text{wild type eye color}$$
$$C \longrightarrow e_2 \longrightarrow D$$
$$\uparrow$$
$$g_2^+$$

The recessive alleles at these two loci (g_1 and g_2) specify enzymatically inactive proteins. Thus a genotype without either dominant allele would not produce any pigmented compounds and the eye color would be white.

Phenotypes	Genotypes	End Products
wild type	$g_1^+/-, g_2^+/-$	B and D
color B	$g_1^+/-, g_2/g_2$	B and C
color D	$g_1/g_1, g_2^+/-$	D and A
white	$g_1/g_1, g_2/g_2$	A and C

In the above example, the genes for color B and color D are both dominant to white, but when they occur together they produce a novel phenotype (wild type) by interaction. If the two genes are assorting independently, the classical $9:3:3:1$ ratio will not be disturbed.

Example 4.3: A brown ommochrome pigment is produced in *Drosophila melanogaster* by a dominant gene st^+ on chromosome 3. A scarlet pterin pigment is produced by a dominant gene bw^+ on chromosome 2. The recessive alleles at these two loci produce no pigment. When pure scarlet flies are mated to pure brown flies, a novel phenotype (wild type) appears in the progeny.

P: brown $\times$ scarlet
                 $st^+/st^+, bw/bw$ $st/st, bw^+/bw^+$

F$_1$:   wild type
                              $st^+/st, bw^+/bw$

F$_2$:   9 $st^+/-, bw^+/-$ wild type
            3 $st^+/-, bw/bw$ brown
            3 $st/st, bw^+/-$ scarlet
            1 $st/st, bw/bw$ white

INTERACTIONS WITH THREE OR MORE FACTORS

Recall from Chapter 3 that the progeny from trihybrid parents are expected in the phenotypic ratio $27:9:9:9:3:3:3:1$. This classical ratio can also be modified whenever two or all three of the loci interact. Interactions involving four or more loci are also possible. Most genes probably depend to some extent upon other genes in the total genotype. The total phenotype depends upon interactions of the total genotype with the environment.

PLEIOTROPISM

Many and perhaps most of the biochemical pathways in the living organism are interconnected and often interdependent. Products of one reaction chain may be used in several other metabolic schemes. It is not surprising, therefore, that the phenotypic expression of a gene usually involves more than one trait. Sometimes one trait will be clearly evident (major effect) and other, perhaps seemingly unrelated ramifications (secondary effects) will be less evident to the casual observer. In other cases, a number of related changes may be considered together as a *syndrome*. All of the manifold phenotypic expressions of a single gene are spoken of as *pleiotropic* gene effects.

Example 4.4: The syndrome called "sickle cell anemia" in man is due to an abnormal hemoglobin. This is the primary effect of the mutant gene. Subsidiary effects of the abnormal hemoglobin include the sickle-shape of the cells and their tendency to clump together and clog blood vessels in various organs of the body. As a result, heart, kidney, spleen and brain damage are common elements of the syndrome. Defective corpuscles are readily destroyed in the body, causing severe anemia.

Solved Problems

TWO FACTOR INTERACTIONS

4.1. Coat colors of dogs depend upon the action of at least two genes. At one locus a dominant epistatic inhibitor of coat color pigment (*I*-) prevents the expression of color alleles at another independently assorting locus, producing white coat color. When the recessive condition exists at the inhibitor locus (*ii*), the alleles of the hypostatic locus may be expressed, *iiB*- producing black and *iibb* producing brown. When dihybrid white dogs are mated together, determine (*a*) the phenotypic proportions expected in the progeny, (*b*) the chance of choosing, from among the white progeny, a genotype homozygous at both loci.

Solution:

(*a*)   P: *IiBb*   ×   *IiBb*
                      white   white

F$_1$:   9/16 *I-B-* ⎱
              3/16 *I-bb* ⎰ =   12/16 white
              3/16 *iiB-*   =   3/16 black
              1/16 *iibb*   =   1/16 brown

(*b*) The genotypic proportions among the white progeny are as follows:

		Proportion of Total F$_1$	Proportion of White F$_1$
¼*II*	¼*BB*	1/16 *IIBB*	1/12
	½*Bb*	2/16 *IIBb*	2/12
	¼*bb*	1/16 *IIbb*	1/12
½*Ii*	¼*BB*	2/16 *IiBB*	2/12
	½*Bb*	4/16 *IiBb*	4/12
	¼*bb*	2/16 *Iibb*	2/12
Totals:		12/16	12/12

The only homozygous genotypes at both loci in the above list are $\frac{1}{12}IIBB$ and $\frac{1}{12}IIbb = \frac{2}{12}$ or $\frac{1}{6}$ of all the white progeny. Thus there is one chance in six of choosing a homozygous genotype from among the white progeny.

4.2. Two white flowered strains of the sweet pea (*Lathyrus odoratus*) were crossed, producing an F$_1$ with only purple flowers. Random crossing among the F$_1$ produced 96 progeny plants, 53 exhibiting purple flowers and 43 with white flowers. (*a*) What phenotypic ratio is approximated by the F$_2$? (*b*) What type of interaction is involved? (*c*) What were the probable genotypes of the parental strains?

Solution:

(*a*) To determine the phenotypic ratio in terms of familiar sixteenths, the following proportion for white flowers may be made: $43/96 = x/16$, from which $x = 7.2$. That is, 7.2 white : 8.8 purple, or approximately a 7 : 9 ratio. We might just as well have arrived at the same conclusion by establishing the proportion for purple flowers: $53/96 = x/16$, from which $x = 8.8$ purple.

(*b*) A 7 : 9 ratio is characteristic of duplicate recessive genes where the recessive genotype at either or both of the loci produces the same phenotype.

(*c*) If *aa* or *bb* or both could produce white flowers, then only the genotype *A-B-* could produce purple. For two white parental strains (pure lines) to be able to produce an all purple F$_1$, they must be homozygous for different dominant-recessive combinations. Thus

P: $aaBB$ $\times$ $AAbb$
            white   white

F_1: $AaBb$
                    purple

F_2:   9/16 $A\text{-}B\text{-}$ = 9/16 purple
            3/16 $A\text{-}bb$ ⎤
            3/16 $aaB\text{-}$ ⎬ = 7/16 white
            1/16 $aabb$ ⎦

4.3. Red color in wheat kernels is produced by the genotype $R\text{-}B\text{-}$, white by the double recessive genotype ($rrbb$). The genotypes $R\text{-}bb$ and $rrB\text{-}$ produce brown kernels. A homozygous red variety is crossed to a white variety. (*a*) What phenotypic results are expected in the F_1 and F_2? (*b*) If the brown F_2 is artificially crossed at random (wheat is normally self-fertilized), what phenotypic and genotypic proportions are expected in the offspring?

Solution:

(*a*)   P: $RRBB$ $\times$ $rrbb$
                    red   white

        F_1: $RrBb$
                         red

        F_2:   9/16 $R\text{-}B\text{-}$ = 9/16 red
                3/16 $R\text{-}bb$ ⎤
                3/16 $rrB\text{-}$ ⎬ = 6/16 brown
                1/16 $rrbb$ = 1/16 white

(*b*) The proportion of genotypes represented among the brown F_2 must first be determined.

	Proportion of Total F_2	Proportion of Brown F_2
$(\frac{1}{4}RR)(\frac{1}{4}bb)$	1/16 $RRbb$	1/6
$(\frac{1}{2}Rr)(\frac{1}{4}bb)$	2/16 $Rrbb$	2/6
$(\frac{1}{4}rr)(\frac{1}{4}BB)$	1/16 $rrBB$	1/6
$(\frac{1}{4}rr)(\frac{1}{2}Bb)$	2/16 $rrBb$	2/6
Totals:	6/16	6/6

Next, the relative frequencies of the various matings may be calculated in a checkerboard.

	1/6 $RRbb$	2/6 $Rrbb$	1/6 $rrBB$	2/6 $rrBb$
1/6 $RRbb$	1/36 $RRbb \times RRbb$ (1)	2/36 $RRbb \times Rrbb$ (2)	1/36 $RRbb \times rrBB$ (3)	2/36 $RRbb \times rrBb$ (4)
2/6 $Rrbb$	2/36 $Rrbb \times RRbb$ (2)	4/36 $Rrbb \times Rrbb$ (5)	2/36 $Rrbb \times rrBB$ (6)	4/36 $Rrbb \times rrBb$ (7)
1/6 $rrBB$	1/36 $rrBB \times RRbb$ (3)	2/36 $rrBB \times Rrbb$ (6)	1/36 $rrBB \times rrBB$ (8)	2/36 $rrBB \times rrBb$ (9)
2/6 $rrBb$	2/36 $rrBb \times RRbb$ (4)	4/36 $rrBb \times Rrbb$ (7)	2/36 $rrBb \times rrBB$ (9)	4/36 $rrBb \times rrBb$ (10)

Matings	Progeny	Genotypic Proportions (f)	Mating Frequency (m)	m · f
(1) $RRbb \times RRbb$	$RRbb$	100%	1/36	1/36
(2) $RRbb \times Rrbb$	$RRbb$	1/2	4/36	4/72
	$Rrbb$	1/2		4/72
(3) $RRbb \times rrBB$	$RrBb$	100%	2/36	2/36
(4) $RRbb \times rrBb$	$RrBb$	1/2	4/36	4/72
	$Rrbb$	1/2		4/72
(5) $Rrbb \times Rrbb$	$RRbb$	1/4	4/36	4/144
	$Rrbb$	1/2		4/72
	$rrbb$	1/4		4/144
(6) $Rrbb \times rrBB$	$RrBb$	1/2	4/36	4/72
	$rrBb$	1/2		4/72
(7) $Rrbb \times rrBb$	$RrBb$	1/4	8/36	8/144
	$rrBb$	1/4		8/144
	$Rrbb$	1/4		8/144
	$rrbb$	1/4		8/144
(8) $rrBB \times rrBB$	$rrBB$	100%	1/36	1/36
(9) $rrBb \times rrBB$	$rrBB$	1/2	4/36	4/72
	$rrBb$	1/2		4/72
(10) $rrBb \times rrBb$	$rrBB$	1/4	4/36	4/144
	$rrBb$	1/2		4/72
	$rrbb$	1/4		4/144

Summary of progeny genotypes:

 1/9 $RRbb$
 2/9 $RrBb$
 2/9 $Rrbb$
 1/9 $rrBB$
 2/9 $rrBb$
 1/9 $rrbb$

Summary of progeny phenotypes:

 2/9 $R\text{-}B\text{-}$ = 2/9 red
 1/3 $R\text{-}bb$ $\Big\}$
 1/3 $rrB\text{-}$ $\Big\}$ = 2/3 brown
 1/9 $rrbb$ = 1/9 white

4.4. The following pedigree shows the transmission of swine coat colors through three generations:

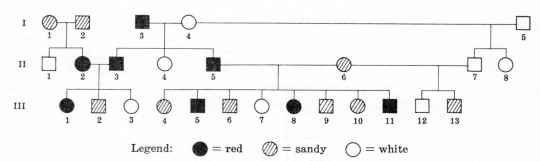

Legend: ● = red ⊘ = sandy ○ = white

Assume the offspring of II5 × II6 shown in this pedigree occur in the ratio expected from the genotypes represented by their parents. How are these colors most likely inherited?

Solution:

 Notice first that three phenotypes are expressed in this pedigree. This rules out epistatic combinations producing only two phenotypes such as those expressed in dominant and recessive interaction (13 : 3), duplicate dominant genes (15 : 1), and duplicate recessive genes (9 : 7). Epistatic gene interactions producing three phenotypes are those expressed in dominant epistasis (12 : 3 : 1), recessive epistasis $(9:3:4)$, and dominant genes with cumulative action $(9:6:1)$. Let us proceed to solve this problem by making an assumption and then applying it to the pedigree to see if the phenotypes shown there can be explained by our hypothesis.

Case 1. Assume dominant epistasis is operative. The genotypes responsible for the three phenotypes may be represented as follows: A-B- and A-bb = 1st phenotype, aaB- = 2nd phenotype, and $aabb$ = 3rd phenotype. We must now determine which of the phenotypes represented in this pedigree corresponds to each of the genotypic classes. Obviously the only pure line phenotype is the third one. Offspring of the mating $aabb \times aabb$ would all be phenotypically identical to the parents. The mating I4 × I5 appears to qualify in this respect and we shall tentatively assume that white coat color is represented by the genotype $aabb$. Certain matings between individuals with the dominant epistatic gene (A) could produce three phenotypically different types of offspring (e.g. $AaBb \times AaBb$). Such a mating is observed between II2 and II3. Therefore we might assume red color to be represented by the genotype A-. Sandy color must then be represented by genotype aaB-. Matings between sandy individuals could produce only sandy (aaB-) or white ($aabb$) progeny. However, sandy parents I1 × I2 produce white and red progeny (II1, II2). Therefore the assumption of dominant interaction must be wrong.

Case 2. Assume recessive epistasis to be operative. The genotypes responsible for the three phenotypes in this case may be represented as follows: A-B- as 1st phenotype, A-bb as 2nd phenotype, and aaB- and $aabb$ as 3rd phenotype. As pointed out in Case 1, matings between individuals of genotype $AaBb$ are the only kind among identical phenotypes capable of producing all three phenotypes in the progeny. Thus A-B- should represent red (e.g. II2 × II3). The aa genotypes breed true, producing only white individuals (I4 × I5). Sandy is produced by genotype A-bb. Sandy × sandy (I1 × I2) could not produce the red offspring (II2). Therefore the assumption of recessive interaction must be wrong.

Case 3. Assume that duplicate genes with cumulative action are interacting. The genotypes responsible for the three phenotypes in this case may be represented as follows: A-B- as 1st phenotype, A-bb and aaB- as 2nd phenotype, and $aabb$ as 3rd phenotype. As explained in the previous two cases, A-B- must be red and $aabb$ must be white. If we assume that any dominant genotype at either the A-locus or B-locus contributes one unit of pigment to the phenotype, then either the genotype aaB- or A-bb could be sandy; we further assume that the presence of both dominant genes (A-B-) would contribute two units of pigment to produce a red phenotype. Thus the mating II5 ($AaBb$) red × II6 ($aaBb$) sandy would be expected to produce offspring phenotypes in the following proportions:

$$
\begin{array}{llll}
\text{red} & A\text{-}B\text{-} & \frac{1}{2} \cdot \frac{3}{4} = & \frac{3}{8} \\
\text{sandy} \left\{ \begin{array}{l} A\text{-}bb \\ aaB\text{-} \end{array} \right. & & \begin{array}{l} \frac{1}{2} \cdot \frac{1}{4} = \frac{1}{8} \\ \frac{1}{2} \cdot \frac{3}{4} = \frac{3}{8} \end{array} \right\} \frac{1}{2} \\
\text{white} & aabb & \frac{1}{2} \cdot \frac{1}{4} = & \frac{1}{8}
\end{array}
$$

These expectations correspond to the ones given in the pedigree (III4 through III11) and therefore the hypothesis of dominant genes with cumulative action is consistent with the data.

INTERACTIONS WITH THREE OR MORE FACTORS

4.5.   At least three loci are known to govern coat colors in mice. The genotype C- will allow pigment to be produced at the other two loci. The recessive genotype cc does not allow pigment production, resulting in "albino". The "agouti" pattern depends upon the genotype A-, and non-agouti upon the recessive aa. The color of the pigment may be black (B-) or chocolate (bb). Five coat colors may be produced by the action of alleles at these three loci:

wild type (agouti, black)	A-B-C-
black (non-agouti)	aaB-C-
chocolate (non-agouti)	$aabbC$-
cinnamon (agouti, chocolate)	A-bbC-
albino	- - - -cc

(a) What phenotypic frequencies are expected in the F_2 from crosses of pure black with albinos of type $AAbbcc$? (b) A cinnamon male is mated to a group of albino females of identical genotype and among their progeny were observed 43 wild type, 40 cinnamon, 39 black, 41 chocolate and 168 albino. What are the most probable genotypes of the parents?

Solution:

(*a*)   P: $aaBBCC$ $\times$ $AAbbcc$ (*b*)   P: $A\text{-}bbC\text{-}\,\delta$ $\times$ $\text{-}\text{-}\text{-}\text{-}cc\,\female\female$
                 pure black   albino   cinnamon male   albino females

F$_1$: $AaBbCc$ F$_1$:   43 wild type $A\text{-}B\text{-}C\text{-}$
                   wild type   40 cinnamon $A\text{-}bbC\text{-}$
                                                                  39 black $aaB\text{-}C\text{-}$
F$_2$:   27 $A\text{-}B\text{-}C\text{-}$ wild type   41 chocolate $aabbC\text{-}$
          9 $A\text{-}B\text{-}cc$ albino   168 albino $\text{-}\text{-}\text{-}\text{-}cc$
          9 $A\text{-}bbC\text{-}$ cinnamon   ――――
          9 $aaB\text{-}C\text{-}$ black   331
          3 $A\text{-}bbcc$ albino
          3 $aaB\text{-}cc$ albino
          3 $aabbC\text{-}$ chocolate
          1 $aabbcc$ albino

Summary: 27/64 wild type
            16/64 albino
            9/64 cinnamon
            9/64 black
            3/64 chocolate

The cinnamon progeny, $A\text{-}bbC\text{-}$, indicate *b* in the female parents of part (*b*). The black progeny, $aaB\text{-}C\text{-}$, indicate *a* in both parents, and *B* in the female parents. The chocolate progeny, $aabbC\text{-}$, indicate *a* in both parents, and *b* in the females. The albinos indicate *c* in the male. The genotype of the male is now known to be $AabbCc$. But the genotype of the albino females is known only to be $a\text{-}Bbcc$. They could be either $AaBbcc$ or $aaBbcc$.

Case 1.   Assume the females to be $AaBbcc$.

Parents: $AabbCc\,\delta$ $\times$ $AaBbcc\,\female\female$

The expected phenotypic frequencies among the progeny would be:

$A\text{-}BbCc$ wild type $\frac{3}{4}\cdot\frac{1}{2}\cdot\frac{1}{2}$ $=$ $\frac{3}{16}(331)$ $=$ approx. 62
$A\text{-}bbCc$ cinnamon $\frac{3}{4}\cdot\frac{1}{2}\cdot\frac{1}{2}$ $=$ $\frac{3}{16}(331)$ $=$ approx. 62
$aaBbCc$ black $\frac{1}{4}\cdot\frac{1}{2}\cdot\frac{1}{2}$ $=$ $\frac{1}{16}(331)$ $=$ approx. 21
$aabbCc$ chocolate $\frac{1}{4}\cdot\frac{1}{2}\cdot\frac{1}{2}$ $=$ $\frac{1}{16}(331)$ $=$ approx. 21
$\text{-}\text{-}\text{-}\text{-}cc$ albino $1\cdot1\cdot\frac{1}{2}$ $=$ $\frac{1}{2}(331)$ $=$ approx. 166

Obviously, the expectations deviate considerably from the observations. Therefore, the females are probably not of genotype $AaBbcc$.

Case 2.   Assume the females to be of genotype $aaBbcc$.

Parents: $AabbCc\,\delta$ $\times$ $aaBbcc\,\female\female$

The expected phenotypic frequencies among the progeny would be:

$AaBbCc$ wild type $\frac{1}{2}\cdot\frac{1}{2}\cdot\frac{1}{2}$ $=$ $\frac{1}{8}(331)$ $=$ approx. 41
$AabbCc$ cinnamon $\frac{1}{2}\cdot\frac{1}{2}\cdot\frac{1}{2}$ $=$ $\frac{1}{8}(331)$ $=$ approx. 41
$aaBbCc$ black $\frac{1}{2}\cdot\frac{1}{2}\cdot\frac{1}{2}$ $=$ $\frac{1}{8}(331)$ $=$ approx. 41
$aabbCc$ chocolate $\frac{1}{2}\cdot\frac{1}{2}\cdot\frac{1}{2}$ $=$ $\frac{1}{8}(331)$ $=$ approx. 41
$\text{-}\text{-}\text{-}\text{-}cc$ albino $1\cdot1\cdot\frac{1}{2}$ $=$ $\frac{1}{2}(331)$ $=$ approx. 166

Now the expectations correspond very closely to the observations. Hence the genotype of the parental albino females is probably $aaBbcc$.

4.6.   Lewis-a blood group substance appears on the human red blood cell when the dominant gene *Le* is present, but is absent if the dominant gene of the "secretor" locus, *Se,* is present. Suppose that from a number of families where both parents are Lewis-a negative of genotype *LeleSese,* we find that most of them have 3 Lewis-a positive : 13 Lewis-a negative children. In a few other families, suppose we find 2 Lewis-a negative : 1 Lewis-a positive. Furthermore, in families where both parents are secretors of genotype *Sese,* we find most of them exhibit a ratio of 3 secretor : 1 non-secretor, but a few of them show 9 secretor : 7 non-secretor. Propose a hypothesis to account for these results.

Solution:

If only two loci are interacting, the dominant *Se* gene can suppress the expression of *Le*, resulting in Lewis-a negative blood type. When both parents are dihybrid, we expect a 13:3 ratio in the progeny characteristic of dominant and recessive interaction.

P: *LeleSese*   ×   *LeleSese*
            Lewis-a neg.   Lewis-a neg.

F$_1$:   9 *Le-Se-* ⎫
            3 *leleSe-* ⎬ = 13 Lewis-a negative
            1 *lelesese* ⎭

            3 *Le-sese* = 3 Lewis-a positive

The 9:7 ratio found in some families for the secretor trait indicates that two factors are again interacting. This is the ratio produced by duplicate recessive interaction; i.e. whenever the recessive alleles at either of two loci are present, a non-secretor phenotype results. Let us symbolize the alleles of the second locus by *X* and *x*.

P: *SeseXx*   ×   *SeseXx*
            secretor   secretor

F$_1$:   9 *Se-X-*   =   9 secretors

            3 *Se-xx* ⎫
            3 *seseX-* ⎬ = 7 non-secretors; the *xx* genotype suppresses the expression of *Se*.
            1 *sesexx* ⎭

If we assume the *x* gene to be relatively rare, then most families will have only the dominant gene *X*, but in a few families both parents will be heterozygous *Xx*. Let us assume that this is the case in those families which produce 2 Lewis-a negative : 1 Lewis-a positive.

P: *LeleSeseXx*   ×   *LeleSeseXx*
            Lewis-a negative   Lewis-a negative

F$_1$:   27 *Le-Se-X-*
            *9 *Le-Se-xx*
            *9 *Le-seseX-*
            9 *leleSe-X-*
            *3 *Le-sesexx*
            3 *leleSe-xx*
            3 *leleseseX-*
            1 *lelesesexx*

If *Se* suppresses *Le*, but *xx* suppresses *Se*, then only the genotypes marked with an asterisk (*) will be Lewis-a positive, giving a ratio of 21 Lewis-a positive : 43 Lewis-a negative. This is very close to a 1:2 ratio and indeed would appear to be such with limited data.

Supplementary Problems

TWO FACTOR INTERACTIONS

4.7. When homozygous yellow rats are crossed to homozygous black rats, the F$_1$ is all gray. Mating the F$_1$ among themselves produced an F$_2$ consisting of 10 yellow, 28 gray, 2 cream-colored and 8 black. (*a*) How are these colors inherited? (*b*) Show, using appropriate genetic symbols, the genotypes for each color. (*c*) How many of the 48 F$_2$ rats were expected to be cream-colored? (*d*) How many of the 48 F$_2$ rats were expected to be homozygous?

4.8. Four comb shapes in poultry are known to be governed by two gene loci. The genotype *R-P-* produces walnut comb, characteristic of the Malay breed; *R-pp* produces rose comb, characteristic of the Wyandotte breed; *rrP-* produces pea comb, characteristic of the Brahma breed; *rrpp* produces single comb, characteristic of the Leghorn breed. (*a*) If pure Wyandottes are crossed with pure Brahmas, what phenotypic ratios are expected in the F$_1$ and F$_2$? (*b*) A Malay hen was crossed to a Leghorn cock and produced a dozen eggs, 3 of which grew into birds with rose combs and 9 with walnut combs. What is the probable genotype of the hen? (*c*) Determine the proportion of comb types that would be expected in offspring from each of the following crosses: (1) *Rrpp* × *RrPP*, (2) *rrPp* × *RrPp*, (3) *rrPP* × *RRPp*, (4) *RrPp* × *rrpp*, (5) *RrPp* × *RRpp*, (6) *RRpp* × *rrpp*, (7) *RRPP* × *rrpp*, (8) *Rrpp* × *Rrpp*, (9) *rrPp* × *Rrpp*, (10) *rrPp* × *rrpp*.

4.9. Listed below are 7 two-factor interaction ratios observed in progeny from various dihybrid parents. Suppose that in each case one of the dihybrid parents is testcrossed (instead of being mated to another dihybrid individual). What phenotypic ratio is expected in the progeny of each testcross? (a) $9:6:1$, (b) $9:3:4$, (c) $9:7$, (d) $15:1$, (e) $12:3:1$, (f) $9:3:3:1$, (g) $13:3$.

4.10. White fruit color in summer squash is governed by a dominant gene (W) and colored fruit by its recessive allele (w). Yellow fruit is governed by an independently assorting hypostatic gene (G) and green by its recessive allele (g). When dihybrid plants are crossed, the offspring appear in the ratio 12 white : 3 yellow : 1 green. What fruit color ratios are expected from the crosses (a) $Wwgg \times WwGG$, (b) $WwGg \times$ green, (c) $Wwgg \times wwGg$, (d) $WwGg \times Wwgg$? (e) If two plants are crossed producing $\frac{1}{2}$ yellow and $\frac{1}{2}$ green progeny, what are the genotypes and phenotypes of the parents?

4.11. Matings between black rats of identical genotype produced offspring as follows: 14 cream-colored, 47 black, and 19 albino. (a) What epistatic ratio is approximated by these offspring? (b) What type of epistasis is operative? (c) What are the genotypes of the parents and the offspring (use your own symbols)?

4.12. A dominant gene S in *Drosophila* produces a peculiar eye condition called "star". Its recessive allele S^+ produces the normal eye of wild type. The expression of S can be suppressed by the dominant allele of another locus, $Su\text{-}S$. The recessive allele of this locus, $Su\text{-}S^+$, has no effect on S^+. (a) What type of interaction is operative? (b) When a normal-eyed male of genotype $Su\text{-}S/Su\text{-}S$, S/S is crossed to a homozygous wild type female of genotype $Su\text{-}S^+/Su\text{-}S^+$, S^+/S^+, what phenotypic ratio is expected in the F_1 and F_2? (c) What percentage of the wild type F_2 is expected to carry the dominant gene for star-eye?

4.13. The Black Langshan breed of chickens has feathered shanks. When Langshans are crossed to the Buff Rock breed with unfeathered shanks, all the F_1 have feathered shanks. Out of 360 F_2 progeny, 24 were found to have non-feathered shanks and 336 had feathered shanks. (a) What is the mode of interaction in this trait? (b) What proportion of the feathered F_2 would be expected to be heterozygous at one locus and homozygous at the other?

4.14. On chromosome three of corn there is a dominant gene (A_1) which, together with the dominant gene (A_2) on chromosome nine, produces colored aleurone. All other genetic combinations produce colorless aleurone. Two pure colorless strains are crossed to produce an all colored F_1. (a) What were the genotypes of the parental strains and the F_1? (b) What phenotypic proportions are expected among the F_2? (c) What genotypic ratio exists among the white F_2?

4.15. Two pairs of alleles govern the color of onion bulbs. A pure red strain crossed to a pure white strain produces an all red F_1. The F_2 was found to consist of 47 white, 38 yellow and 109 red bulbs. (a) What epistatic ratio is approximated by the data? (b) What is the name of this type of gene interaction? (c) If another F_2 is produced by the same kind of a cross, and 8 bulbs of the F_2 are found to be of the double recessive genotype, how many bulbs would be expected in each phenotypic class?

4.16. A plant of the genus *Capsella*, commonly called "shepherd's purse", produces a seed capsule the shape of which is controlled by two independently assorting genes. When dihybrid plants were interpollinated, 6% of the progeny were found to possess ovoid-shaped seed capsules. The other 94% of the progeny had triangular-shaped seed capsules. (a) What two factor epistatic ratio is approximated by the progeny? (b) What type of interaction is operative?

4.17. The color of corn aleurone is known to be controlled by several genes; A, C, and R are all necessary for color to be produced. The locus of a dominant inhibitor of aleurone color, I, is very closely linked to that of C. Thus any one or more of the genotypes $I\text{-}$, $aa\text{-}$, $cc\text{-}$ or $rr\text{-}$ produces colorless aleurone. (a) What would be the colored : colorless ratio among F_2 progeny from the cross $AAIICCRR \times aaiiCCRR$? (b) What proportion of the colorless F_2 is expected to be homozygous?

4.18. A dominant allele C must be present in order for any pigment to be developed in mice. The kind of pigment produced depends upon another locus such that $B\text{-}$ produces black and bb produces brown. Individuals of epistatic genotype cc are incapable of making pigment and are called "albinos". A homozygous black female is testcrossed to an albino male. (a) What phenotypic ratio is expected in the F_1 and F_2? (b) If all the albino F_2 mice are allowed to mate at random, what genotypic ratio is expected in the progeny?

4.19. Suppose that crossing two homozygous lines of white clover, each with a low content of cyanide, produces only progeny with high levels of cyanide. When these F_1 progeny are backcrossed to either parental line, half the progeny has low cyanide content and the other half has high cyanide content. (*a*) What type of interaction may account for these results? (*b*) What phenotypic ratio is expected in the F_2? (*c*) If a 12:4 ratio is observed among progeny from parents with high cyanide content, what are the parental genotypes? (*d*) If the low cyanide F_2, exclusive of the double recessives, are allowed to cross at random among themselves, what proportion of their progeny is expected to contain a high cyanide content?

4.20. In cultivated flowers called "stocks", the recessive genotype of one locus (*aa*) prevents the development of pigment in the flower, thus producing a white color. In the presence of the dominant allele *A*, alleles at another locus may be expressed as follows: C- = red, cc = cream. (*a*) When cream stocks of the genotype *Aacc* are crossed to red stocks of the genotype *AaCc*, what phenotypic and genotypic proportions are expected in the progeny? (*b*) If cream stocks crossed to red stocks produce white progeny, what may be the genotypes of the parents? (*c*) When dihybrid red stocks are crossed together, what phenotypic ratio is expected among the progeny? (*d*) If red stocks crossed to white stocks produce progeny with red, cream and white flowers, what are the genotypes of the parents?

4.21. An inhibitor of pigment production in onion bulbs (*I*-) exhibits dominant epistasis over another locus, the genotype *iiR*- producing red bulbs and *iirr* producing yellow bulbs. (*a*) A pure white strain is crossed to a pure red strain and produces an all white F_1 and an F_2 with $\frac{12}{16}$ white, $\frac{3}{16}$ red and $\frac{1}{16}$ yellow. What were the genotypes of the parents? (*b*) If yellow onions are crossed to a pure white strain of a genotype different from the parental type in part (*a*), what phenotypic ratio is expected in the F_1 and F_2? (*c*) Among the white F_2 of part (*a*), suppose that 32 were found to be of genotype *IiRR*. How many progeny are expected in each of the three F_2 phenotypic classes?

4.22. For color to be produced in corn kernels, the dominant alleles at three loci must be present (*A*, *C*, *R*). Another locus is hypostatic to these three loci; the dominant allele of this locus (*Pr*) yields purple pigment and the recessive allele (*pr*) determines red kernels. (*a*) What phenotypic proportions are expected in the F_1 and F_2 when a red strain of genotype *AACCRRprpr* is crossed to a colorless strain of genotype *AACCrrPrPr*? (*b*) If the red F_2 are crossed among themselves, what genotypic and phenotypic ratios are expected among the progeny?

4.23. Crossing certain genetically identical monohybrid white-bulbed onions produces white and colored progeny in the ratio 3:1 respectively. Crossing certain genetically identical monohybrid colored-bulbed onions produces colored and white progeny in the ratio 3:1 respectively. (*a*) What phenotypic ratio is expected among the F_1 and F_2 progeny produced by testcrossing a white **variety** homozygous for the dominant alleles at two independently assorting loci? (*b*) What type of interaction is operative? (*c*) Suppose that the dominant condition (*I*-) at one locus and/or the recessive condition at the other (*cc*) could both produce white onion bulbs. White onions of genotype *I-C*-, in the presence of ammonia fumes, turn yellow. Onions which are white due to the action of *cc* in their genotype fail to change color in the presence of ammonia fumes. A white plant which turns yellow in ammonia fumes is crossed to a white one which does not change color. The progeny occur in the proportions $\frac{7}{8}$ white : $\frac{1}{8}$ colored. What are the genotypes of the parents? (*d*) A white plant which changes color in ammonia fumes is crossed to a colored plant. The progeny occur in the ratio 3 colored : 5 white. Determine the genotypes of the parents.

4.24. The color of the flower center in the common yellow daisy may be either purple-centered or yellow-centered. Two genes (*P* and *Y*) are known to interact in this trait. The results of two matings are given below:

(1)   P: $PpYY$ $\times$ $PpYY$
                  purple-centered   purple-centered

    F_1:   3/4 P-YY purple-centered
                 1/4 $ppYY$ yellow-centered

(2)   P: $ppYy$ $\times$ $ppYy$
                  yellow-centered   yellow-centered

    F_1:   3/4 ppY-⎫
                 1/4 $ppyy$ ⎭ all yellow-centered

Determine the phenotypic ratios of progeny from the matings (*a*) $PpYy \times PpYy$, (*b*) $PpYy \times ppyy$, (*c*) $PPyy \times ppYY$.

4.25. The aleurone of corn kernels may be either yellow, white or purple. When pollen from a homozygous purple plant is used to fertilize a homozygous white plant, the aleurone of the resulting kernels are all purple. When homozygous yellow plants are crossed to homozygous white plants, only seeds with yellow aleurone are produced. When homozygous purple plants are crossed to homozygous yellow plants, only purple progeny appear. Some crosses between purple plants produce purple, yellow and white progeny. Some crosses between yellow plants produce both yellow and white offspring. Crosses between yellow plants never produce purple progeny. Crosses among plants produced from seeds with white aleurone always produce only white progeny. (*a*) Can these results be explained on the basis of the action of a single gene locus with multiple alleles? (*b*) What is the simplest explanation for the mode of gene action? (*c*) If plants with only dominant alleles at the two loci are crossed to plants grown from white seeds, what phenotypic proportions are expected among their F_2 progeny? (*d*) In part (*c*), how many generations of seeds must be planted in order to obtain an F_2 progeny phenotypically expressing the aleurone genes derived from the adult parent sporophytes? (*e*) What is the advantage of studying the genetics of seed traits rather than traits of the sporophyte?

4.26. Three fruit shapes are recognized in the summer squash (*Cucurbita pepo*): disk-shaped, elongated and sphere shaped. A pure disk-shaped variety was crossed to a pure elongated variety. The F_1 were all disk-shaped. Among 80 F_2, there were 30 sphere-shaped, 5 elongated and 45 disk-shaped. (*a*) Reduce the F_2 numbers to their lowest ratio. (*b*) What type of interaction is operative? (*c*) If the sphere-shaped F_2 cross at random, what phenotypic proportions are expected in the progeny?

4.27. When yellow mice are mated together, $\frac{2}{3}$ of the progeny are yellow and $\frac{1}{3}$ are agouti. Another locus is known to govern pigment production. When parents heterozygous at this locus are mated together, $\frac{3}{4}$ of the offspring are colored and $\frac{1}{4}$ are albino. These albino mice cannot express whatever genes they may have at the agouti locus. Yellow mice are crossed with albinos and produce an F_1 containing $\frac{1}{2}$ albino, $\frac{1}{3}$ yellow and $\frac{1}{6}$ agouti. (*a*) What are the probable genotypes of the parents (use your own symbols)? (*b*) If the yellow F_1 mice are crossed among themselves, what phenotypic ratio is expected among the offspring? (*c*) What proportion of the yellow offspring from part (*b*) would be expected to breed true?

4.28. The pedigree on the right illustrates a case of dominant epistasis. (*a*) What symbol represents the genotype *A-B-*? (*b*) What symbol represents the genotype *aaB-*? (*c*) What symbol represents the genotype *aabb*? (*d*) What type of epistasis would be represented if II2 × II3 produced, in addition to ☐ and ▨, an offspring of type ● ? (*e*) What type of interaction would be represented if III5 × III6 produced, in addition to ▨ and ◯, an offspring of type ● ?

4.29. Given the following pedigree showing three generations of mink breeding, where open symbols represent wild type and solid symbols represent platinum, determine (*a*) the mode of inheritance of these coat colors, (*b*) the most probable genotypes of all individuals in the pedigree (use of familiar symbols such as *A,a* and *B,b* are suitable), (*c*) what phenotypic proportions are expected in progeny from III1 × III2.

4.30. The pedigree in Fig. (*a*) shows the genetic transmission of feather color in chickens. Open symbols represent white feathers, solid symbols represent colored feathers. Under the assumption of dominant and recessive interaction (given *A*- or *bb* or both = white, *aaB*- = color) assign genotypes to each individual in the pedigree. Indicate by (-) whatever genes cannot be determined.

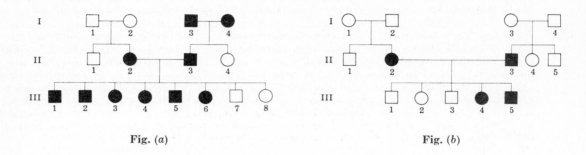

Fig. (*a*)   Fig. (*b*)

4.31. The pedigree in Fig. (*b*) shows the inheritance of deafness in humans. Open symbols represent normal hearing and solid symbols represent deafness. Under the assumption of duplicate recessive interaction (given *A*-*B*- = normal, *aa* or *bb* or both = deaf) assign genotypes to each individual in the pedigree. Indicate by (-) whatever genes cannot be determined.

INTERACTIONS WITH THREE OR MORE FACTORS

4.32. A wheat variety with colored seeds is crossed to a colorless strain producing an all colored F_1. In the F_2, $\frac{1}{64}$ of the progeny has colorless seeds. (*a*) How many pairs of genes control seed color? (*b*) What were the genotypes of the parents and the F_1 (use your own symbols)?

4.33. In mice, spotted coat color is due to a recessive gene *s* and solid coat color to its dominant allele *S*. Colored mice possess a dominant allele *C* whereas albinos are homozygous recessive *cc*. Black is produced by a dominant allele *B* and brown by its recessive allele *b*. The *cc* genotype is epistatic to both the B and S loci. What phenotypic ratio is expected among the progeny of trihybrid parents?

4.34. A pure line of corn (*CCRR*) exhibiting colored aleurone is testcrossed to a colorless aleurone strain. Approximately 56% of the F_2 has colored aleurone, the other 44% being colorless. A pure line (*AARR*) with colored aleurone, when testcrossed, also produces the same phenotypic ratio in the F_2. (*a*) What phenotypic ratio is expected in the F_2 when a pure colored line of genotype *AACCRR* is testcrossed? (*b*) What proportion of the colorless F_2 is *aaccrr*? (*c*) What genotypic ratio exists among the colored F_2?

4.35. If a pure white onion strain is crossed to a pure yellow strain, the F_2 ratio is 12 white : 3 red : 1 yellow. If another pure white onion is crossed to a pure red onion, the F_2 ratio is 9 red : 3 yellow : 4 white. (*a*) What percentage of the white F_2 from the second mating would be homozygous for the yellow allele? (*b*) If the white F_2 (homozygous for the yellow allele) of part (*a*) is crossed to the pure white parent of the first mating mentioned at the beginning of this problem, determine the F_1 and F_2 phenotypic expectations.

4.36. For any color to be developed in the aleurone layer of corn kernels, the dominant alleles at two loci plus the recessive condition at a third locus (*A*-*R*-*ii*) must be present. Any other genotypes produce colorless aleurone. (*a*) What phenotypic ratio of colored : colorless would be expected in progeny from matings between parental plants of genotype *AaRrIi*? (*b*) What proportion of the colorless progeny in part (*a*) would be expected to be heterozygous at one or more of the three loci? (*c*) What is the probability of picking from among the colored seeds in part (*a*) two which, when grown into adult sporophytes and artificially crossed, would produce some colorless progeny with the triple recessive genotype?

4.37. A dominant gene *V* is known in man which causes certain areas of the skin to become depigmented, a condition called "viteligo". Albinism is the complete lack of pigment production and is produced by the recessive genotype *aa*. The albino locus is epistatic to the viteligo locus. Another gene locus, the action of which is independent of the previously mentioned loci, is known to be involved in a mildly anemic condition called "thalassemia". (a) When adult progeny from parents both of which exhibit viteligo and a mild anemia is examined, the following phenotypic proportions are observed: $\frac{1}{16}$ normal : $\frac{3}{16}$ viteligo : $\frac{1}{8}$ mildly anemic : $\frac{1}{12}$ albino : $\frac{3}{8}$ viteligo and mildly anemic : $\frac{1}{6}$ albino and mildly anemic. What is the mode of genetic action of the gene for thalassemia? (b) What percentage of the viable albino offspring in part (a) would carry the gene for viteligo? (c) What percentage of viable offspring with symptoms of mild anemia also shows viteligo?

4.38. When the White Leghorn breed of chickens is crossed to the White Wyandotte breed, all the F_1 birds have white feathers. The F_2 birds appear in the ratio 13 white : 3 colored. When the White Leghorn breed is crossed to the White Silkie breed, the F_1 is white and the F_2 is also 13 white : 3 colored. But when White Wyandottes are crossed to White Silkies, the F_1 is all colored and the F_2 appears in the ratio 9 colored : 7 white. (a) How are feather colors inherited in these breeds (use appropriate symbols in your explanation)? (b) Show, by use of your own symbols, the genotypes of each of the three breeds (assume the breed is homozygous for all loci under consideration). (c) What phenotypic ratio is expected among progeny from trihybrid parents? (d) What proportion of the white offspring of part (c) is expected to be dihybrid?

4.39. A corn plant which grew from a seed with purple aleurone is self-pollinated. The F_1 produces $\frac{9}{16}$ purple aleurone, $\frac{3}{16}$ red, $\frac{3}{16}$ yellow and $\frac{1}{16}$ white. Some of the red F_1, when selfed, produce progeny in the ratio 12 red : 3 yellow : 1 white. Some of the purple F_1, when selfed, produce progeny in the ratio of 9 purple : 3 red : 4 white. (a) How can these results be explained? Using any appropriate symbols, diagram all three of the crosses mentioned above. (b) If, instead of being selfed, each of the above three parental types had been testcrossed, what phenotypic results would be expected? (c) What phenotypic proportions are observed in progeny from mating trihybrid purple × dihybrid purple (with the third locus homozygous recessive)?

4.40. For color to be developed in the aleurone layer of corn, the dominant alleles at four loci must be present (A_1, A_2, C and R). If a line pure for colored aleurone is testcrossed to a non-colored line, find (a) the phenotypic ratio expected in the F_1 and F_2, (b) the percentage of the colored F_2 expected to be genetically like the F_1, (c) the percentage of the colorless F_2 expected to be homozygous for both the A_1 and A_2 alleles. (d) If a colored line is testcrossed and 25% of the offspring are colored, how many loci are heterozygous? (e) If the colored line in part (d) produces $12\frac{1}{2}\%$ colored offspring, how many loci are heterozygous? (f) If all four loci of the colored line in part (d) are heterozygous, what percentage of the offspring are expected to be colorless?

Answers to Supplementary Problems

4.7. (a) Two pairs of non-epistatic genes interact to produce these coat colors.

(b) A-B- (gray), A-bb (yellow), aaB- (black), aabb (cream)   (c) 3   (d) 12

4.8. (a) F_1 : all walnut comb; F_2 : $\frac{9}{16}$ walnut : $\frac{3}{16}$ rose : $\frac{3}{16}$ pea : $\frac{1}{16}$ single   (b) RRPp

(c)

	R-P- walnut	R-pp rose	rrP- pea	rrpp single
(1)	3/4		1/4	
(2)	3/8	1/8	3/8	1/8
(3)	all			
(4)	1/4	1/4	1/4	1/4
(5)	1/2	1/2		
(6)		all		
(7)	all			
(8)		3/4		1/4
(9)	1/4	1/4	1/4	1/4
(10)			1/2	1/2

4.9. (a) $1:2:1$ (c) $1:3$ (e) $2:1:1$ (g) $3:1$
          (b) $1:1:2$ (d) $3:1$ (f) $1:1:1:1$

4.10. (a) $\frac{3}{4}$ white : $\frac{1}{4}$ yellow (d) $\frac{3}{4}$ white : $\frac{1}{8}$ yellow : $\frac{1}{8}$ green
          (b) and (c) $\frac{1}{2}$ white : $\frac{1}{4}$ yellow : $\frac{1}{4}$ green (e) yellow $(wwGg) \times$ green $(wwgg)$

4.11. (a) $9:3:4$ (c) P: $BbCc$ (black); F_1: $B\text{-}C\text{-}$ (black), $bbC\text{-}$ (cream), $B\text{-}cc$ and $bbcc$ (albino)
          (b) recessive epistasis

4.12. (a) dominant and recessive interaction (b) F_1: all wild type; F_2: 13 wild type : 3 star (c) 69%

4.13. (a) duplicate dominant genes with only the double recessive genotype producing non-feathered shanks (b) $\frac{8}{15}$

4.14. (a) P: $A_1A_1a_2a_2 \times a_1a_1A_2A_2$; F_1: $A_1a_1A_2a_2$
          (b) $\frac{9}{16}$ colored : $\frac{7}{16}$ colorless (c) $\frac{1}{7}A_1A_1a_2a_2 : \frac{2}{7}A_1a_1a_2a_2 : \frac{1}{7}a_1a_1A_2A_2 : \frac{2}{7}a_1a_1A_2a_2 : \frac{1}{7}a_1a_1a_2a_2$

4.15. (a) $9:3:4$ (b) recessive epistasis (c) 32 white : 24 yellow : 72 red

4.16. (a) 15 triangular : 1 ovoid (b) duplicate dominant interaction

4.17. (a) 13 colorless : 3 colored (b) $\frac{3}{13}$

4.18. (a) F_1: all black; F_2: $\frac{9}{16}$ black : $\frac{3}{16}$ brown : $\frac{4}{16}$ albino (b) $\frac{1}{4}BBcc : \frac{1}{2}Bbcc : \frac{1}{4}bbcc$

4.19. (a) duplicate recessive interaction (b) 9 high cyanide : 7 low cyanide (c) $A\text{-}Bb \times AABb$ (d) $\frac{2}{9}$

4.20. (a) $\frac{3}{8}$ red : $\frac{3}{8}$ cream : $\frac{1}{4}$ white; $\frac{1}{8}AACc : \frac{1}{8}AAcc : \frac{1}{4}AaCc : \frac{1}{4}Aacc : \frac{1}{8}aaCc : \frac{1}{8}aacc$
          (b) $Aacc \times AaCc$ (or) $Aacc \times AaCC$
          (c) 9 red : 3 cream : 4 white
          (d) $AaCc \times aaCc$ (or) $AaCc \times aacc$

4.21. (a) $IIrr \times iiRR$ (b) F_1: all white; F_2: $\frac{12}{16}$ white : $\frac{3}{16}$ red : $\frac{1}{16}$ yellow (c) 16 yellow : 48 red : 192 white

4.22. (a) F_1: all purple; F_2: $\frac{9}{16}$ purple : $\frac{3}{16}$ red : $\frac{4}{16}$ white
          (b) $\frac{4}{9}AACCprprRR : \frac{4}{9}AACCprprRr : \frac{1}{9}AACCprprrr$; 8 red : 1 white

4.23. (a) F_1: all white; F_2: 13 white : 3 colored (c) $IiCc \times Iicc$
          (b) dominant and recessive interaction (d) $IiCc \times iiCc$

4.24. (a) $\frac{9}{16}$ purple centered : $\frac{7}{16}$ yellow centered
          (b) $\frac{1}{4}$ purple centered : $\frac{3}{4}$ yellow centered (c) all purple centered

4.25. (a) no (b) dominant epistasis where $Y\text{-}R\text{-}$ or $yyR\text{-}$ produce purple, $Y\text{-}rr$ = yellow, and $yyrr$ = white
          (c) $\frac{3}{4}$ purple : $\frac{3}{16}$ yellow : $\frac{1}{16}$ white (d) one (e) The appearance of seed traits requires one less generation of rearing than that for tissues found in the sporophyte.

4.26. (a) 9 disc : 6 sphere : 1 elongated
          (b) duplicate genes with cumulative effect (c) $\frac{2}{3}$ sphere : $\frac{2}{9}$ disc : $\frac{1}{9}$ elongate

4.27. (a) $A^yACc \times A^yAcc$ (where A^y allele is lethal when homozygous)
          (b) 2 yellow : 1 agouti : 1 albino (c) none

4.28. (a) solid symbol (b) diagonal lines (c) open symbol (d) recessive epistasis (e) duplicate genes with cumulative effect

4.29.   (*a*) duplicate recessive interaction (*b*) *A-B-* (wild type), *aa- -* or *- -bb* or *aabb* (platinum); *AaB-* (I1, 2), *A-Bb* (I3, 4), *A-B-* (I5, 6, II3), *aaBB* (II1), *AAbb* (II2), *AaBb* (III1 thru 8), either *aa* or *bb* or both (II4, 5, III9 thru 16) (*c*) 9 wild type : 7 platinum

4.30.   The following set of genotypes is only one of several possible solutions: *aaB-* (III1, 2, 3, 4, 5, 6), *A-* or *bb* or both (II1), *a- - -* (I1, 2), *aaBb* (I3, 4, II2, 3), *aabb* (II4, III7, 8).

4.31.   The following set of genotypes is only one of several possible solutions: *AaB-* (I1, 2), *A-Bb* (I3, 4), *A-B-* (II1, 4, 5), *aaB-* (II2), *Aabb* (II3), *AaBb* (III1, 2, 3), *aa* or *bb* or both (III4, 5).

4.32.   (*a*) 3 (*b*) P: $AABBCC \times aabbcc$; F_1: $AaBbCc$

4.33.   27 solid black : 9 spotted black : 9 solid brown : 3 spotted brown : 16 albino

4.34.   (*a*) 27 colored : 37 colorless (*b*) $\frac{1}{37}$ (*c*) $\frac{1}{27}AACCRR$: $\frac{2}{27}AACCRr$: $\frac{2}{27}AACcRR$: $\frac{4}{27}AACcRr$: $\frac{2}{27}AaCCRR$: $\frac{4}{27}AaCCRr$: $\frac{4}{27}AaCcRR$: $\frac{8}{27}AaCcRr$

4.35.   (*a*) 25% (*b*) F_1: all white; F_2: 52 white : 9 red : 3 yellow

4.36.   (*a*) 9 colored : 55 colorless (*b*) $\frac{48}{55}$ (*c*) $\frac{16}{81}$

4.37.   (*a*) The gene for thalassemia is dominant to its normal allele, causing mild anemia when heterozygous, but is lethal when homozygous (*b*) 75% (*c*) 56.25%

4.38.   (*a*) 3 loci involved; one possesses a dominant inhibitor of color (*I-*) and the other two possess different recessive inhibitors of color (*cc* and *oo*). Only the genotype *iiC-O-* produces colored birds; all other genotypes produce white feathers. (*b*) White Leghorn (*CCOOII*), White Wyandotte (*ccOOii*), White Silkie (*CCooii*) (*c*) 55 white : 9 colored (*d*) $\frac{20}{55}$

4.39.   (*a*) Three pairs of factors contribute to seed color: *R* = color, *r* = colorless; *Pr* = purple, *pr* = red; *Y* = yellow, *y* = white. The R-locus exhibits recessive epistasis over the Pr-locus (hence the 9 : 3 : 4 ratio), i.e. the dominant gene *R* is necessary for any color to be produced by the Pr-alleles. The R-locus exhibits dominant epistasis over the Y-locus (hence the 12 : 3 : 1 ratio), i.e. segregation of alleles at the Y-locus can only be expressed in colorless (*rr*) seeds. First cross: $RrPrprYy \times RrPrprYy = 9:3:3:1$. Second cross: $RrprprYy \times RrprprYy = 12:3:1$. Third cross: $RrPrpryy \times RrPrpryy = 9:3:4$. (*b*) First cross: 1 purple : 1 red : 1 yellow : 1 white; Second cross: 2 red : 1 yellow : 1 white. Third cross: 2 white : 1 red : 1 purple. (*c*) $\frac{9}{16}$ purple : $\frac{3}{16}$ red : $\frac{1}{8}$ yellow : $\frac{1}{8}$ white

4.40.   (*a*) F_1: all colored; F_2: $\frac{81}{256}$ colored : $\frac{175}{256}$ non-colored (*b*) 19.75% (*c*) 4% (*d*) 2 (*e*) 3 (*f*) 93.75%

Chapter 5

The Genetics of Sex

THE IMPORTANCE OF SEX

We are probably too accustomed to thinking of sex in terms of the males and females of our own or domestic species. Plants also have sexes; at least we know that there are male and female portions of a flower. All organisms, however, do not possess only two sexes. Some of the lowest forms of plant and animal life may have several sexes. For example, in one variety of the ciliated protozoan *Paramecium bursaria* there are eight sexes or "mating types" all morphologically identical. Each mating type is physiologically incapable of conjugating with its own type, but may exchange genetic material with any of the seven other types within the same variety. In most higher organisms, the number of sexes has been reduced to just two. These sexes may reside in different individuals or within the same individual. An animal possessing both male and female reproductive organs is usually referred to as a *hermaphrodite*. In plants where *staminate* (male) and *pistillate* (female) flowers occur on the same plant, the term of preference is *monoecious*. Moreover, most of our flowering plants have both male and female parts within the same flower (perfect flower). Relatively few angiosperms are *dioecious*, i.e., having the male and female elements in different individuals. Among the common cultivated crops known to be dioecious are asparagus, date palm, hemp, hops, and spinach.

Whether or not there are two or more sexes, or whether or not these sexes reside in the same or different individuals is relatively unimportant. The importance of sex itself is that it is a mechanism which provides for the great amount of genetic variability characterizing most natural populations. The evolutionary process of natural selection depends upon this genetic variability to supply the raw material from which the better adapted types usually survive to reproduce their kind. Many subsidiary mechanisms have evolved to insure cross fertilization in most species as a means for generating new genetic combinations in each generation.

SEX DETERMINING MECHANISMS

Most mechanisms for the determination of sex are under genetic control and may be classified into one of the following categories.

1. Sex Chromosome Mechanisms.

(a) Heterogametic Males. In man, and apparently in all other mammals, the presence of the Y chromosome may determine a tendency to maleness. Normal males are chromosomally XY and females are XX. This produces a 1:1 sex ratio in each generation. Since the male produces two kinds of gametes as far as the sex chromosomes are concerned, he is said to be the *heterogametic* sex. The female, producing only one kind of gamete, is the *homogametic* sex. This mode of sex determination is commonly referred to as the XY method.

Example 5.1. XY Method of Sex Determination.

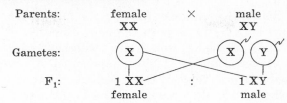

In some insects, especially those of the orders Hemiptera (true bugs) and Orthoptera (grasshoppers and roaches), males are also heterogametic, but produce either X-bearing sperm or gametes without a sex chromosome. In males of these species, the X chromosome has no homologous pairing partner because there is no Y chromosome present. Thus males exhibit an odd number in their chromosome complement. The one-X and two-X condition determines maleness and femaleness respectively. If the single X chromosome of the male is always included in one of the two types of gametes formed, then a 1:1 sex ratio will be produced in the progeny. This mode of sex determination is commonly referred to as the XO method where the O symbolizes the lack of a chromosome analogous to the Y of the XY system.

Example 5.2. XO Method of Sex Determination.

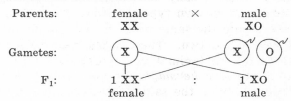

(b) *Heterogametic Females.* This method of sex determination is found in a comparatively large group of animals including the butterflies, moths, caddis flies, silkworms, and in some birds and fishes. The one-X and two-X condition in these species determines femaleness and maleness respectively. The females of some species have a chromosome similar to that of the Y in man. In these cases, the chromosomes are sometimes labeled Z and W instead of X and Y respectively in order to call attention to the fact that the female (ZW) is the heterogametic sex and the male (ZZ) is the homogametic sex. The females of other species, for example the domestic chicken, have no homologue to the single sex chromosome as in the case of the XO mechanism discussed previously. To point out this difference, the symbols ZZ and ZO may be used to designate males and females respectively. A 1:1 sex ratio is expected in either case.

Example 5.3. ZO Method of Sex Determination.

Example 5.4. ZW Method of Sex Determination.

2. Genic Balance.

The presence of the Y-chromosome in *Drosophila,* though it is essential for male fertility, apparently has nothing to do with the determination of sex. Instead, the factors for maleness residing in all of the autosomes are "weighed" against the factors for femaleness residing on the X chromosome(s). If each haploid set of autosomes carries factors with a male-determining value equal to one, then each X-chromosome carries factors with a female-determining value of $1\frac{1}{2}$. Let A represent a haploid set of autosomes. In a normal male (AAXY), the male : female determinants are in the ratio $2 : 1\frac{1}{2}$ and therefore the balance is in favor of maleness. A normal female (AAXX) has a male : female ratio of $2 : 3$ and therefore the balance is in favor of femaleness. Several abnormal combinations of chromosomes have confirmed this hypothesis. For example, an individual with three sets of autosomes and two X chromosomes has a ratio of $3 : 3$ which makes its genetic sex neutral, and indeed phenotypically it appears as a sterile intersex.

3. Haplodiploidy.

Male bees are known to develop parthenogenetically from unfertilized eggs (arrhenotoky) and are therefore haploid. Females (both workers and queens) originate from fertilized (diploid) eggs. Sex chromosomes are not involved in this mechanism of sex determination which is characteristic of the insect order Hymenoptera including the ants, bees, wasps, etc. The quantity and quality of food available to the diploid larva determines whether that female will become a sterile worker or a fertile queen. Thus environment here determines sterility or fertility but does not alter the genetically determined sex. The sex ratio of the offspring is under the control of the queen. Most of the eggs laid in the hive will be fertilized and develop into worker females. Those eggs which the queen chooses not to fertilize (from her store of sperm in the seminal receptacle) will develop into fertile haploid males. Queen bees usually mate only once during their lifetime.

4. Single Gene Effects.

(a) Complementary Sex Factors. At least two members of the insect order Hymenoptera are known to produce males by homozygosity at a single gene locus as well as by haploidy. This has been confirmed in the tiny parasitic wasp *Bracon hebetor* (often called *Habrobracon juglandis*), and more recently in bees also. At least nine sex alleles are known at this locus in *Bracon* and may be represented by $s^a, s^b, s^c, \ldots, s^i$. All females must be heterozygotes such as $s^a s^b, s^a s^c, s^d s^f$, etc. If an individual is homozygous for any of these alleles such as $s^a s^a, s^c s^c$, etc., it develops into a diploid male (usually sterile). Haploid males, of course, would carry only one of the alleles at this locus, e.g. s^a, s^c, s^g, etc.

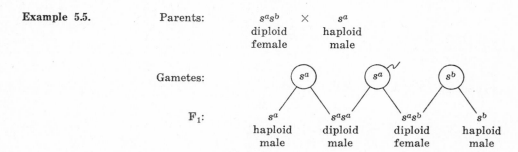

Among the diploid progeny we expect 1 $s^a s^a$ male : 1 $s^a s^b$ female. Among the haploid progeny we expect 1 s^a male : 1 s^b male.

(*b*) *The "Transformer" Gene of Drosophila.* A recessive gene (*tra*) on chromosome 3 of *Drosophila*, when homozygous, transforms a diploid female into a sterile male. The X/X, *tra/tra* individuals resemble normal males in external and internal morphology with the exception that the testes are much reduced in size. The gene is without effect in normal males. The presence of this gene can considerably alter the sex ratio (see Problem 5.1). The significance of these kinds of genes resides in the fact that a mechanism of sex determination based on numerous genes throughout the genome can apparently be nullified by a single gene substitution.

(*c*) *"Mating Type" in Microorganisms.* In microorganisms such as the alga *Chlamydomas* and the fungi *Neurospora* and yeast, sex is under control of a single gene. Haploid individuals possessing the same allele of this "mating type" locus usually cannot fuse with each other to form a zygote, but haploid cells of opposite (complementary) allelic constitution at this locus may fuse.

SEX-LINKED INHERITANCE

Any gene located on the X chromosome (mammals, *Drosophila*, and others) or on the analogous Z chromosome (in birds and other species with the ZO or ZW mechanism of sex determination) is said to be *sex-linked*. The first sex-linked gene found in *Drosophila* was the recessive white eye mutation. Reciprocal crosses involving autosomal traits yield comparable results. This is not true with sex-linked traits as shown below. When white eyed females are crossed with wild type (red eyed) males, all the male offspring have white eyes like their mother and all the female offspring have red eyes like their father.

Example 5.6.   Parents: X^w/X^w ♀   × X^+/Y ♂
                                   white female   wild type male

            Gametes: X^w X^+ Y

                 F_1: X^w/X^+ X^w/Y
                           red females   white males

This criss-cross method of inheritance is characteristic of sex-linked genes. This peculiar type of inheritance is due to the fact that the Y chromosome carries no alleles homologous to those at the white locus on the X chromosome. In fact, in most organisms with the Y-type chromosome, the Y is virtually devoid of known genes. Thus males carry only one allele for sex-linked traits. This one-allelic condition is termed *hemizygous* in contrast to the homozygous or heterozygous possibilities in the female. If the F_1 of Example 5.6 mate among themselves to produce an F_2, a 1 red : 1 white phenotypic ratio is expected in both the males and females.

Example 5.7. F_1: X^+/X^w × X^w/Y
                                red female   white male

		X^+	X^w
F_2:	X^w	X^+/X^w red female	X^w/X^w white female
	Y	X^+/Y red male	X^w/Y white male

The reciprocal cross, where the sex-linked mutation appears in the male parent, results in the disappearance of the trait in the F_1 and its reappearance only in the males of the F_2. This type of skip-generation inheritance also characterizes sex-linked genes.

Example 5.8.

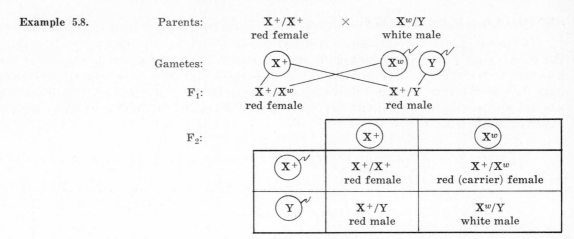

Thus a 3 red : 1 white phenotypic ratio is expected in the total F_2 disregarding sex, but only the males show the mutant trait. The phenotypic ratio among the F_2 males is 1 red : 1 white. All F_2 females are phenotypically wild type.

Whenever working with problems involving sex-linkage in this book, be sure to list the ratios for males and females separately unless specifically directed by the problem to do otherwise.

In normal diploid organisms with sex determining mechanisms like that of man or *Drosophila,* a trait governed by a sex-linked recessive gene usually manifests itself in the following manner: (1) it is usually found more frequently in the male than in the female of the species, (2) it fails to appear in females unless it also appeared in the paternal parent, (3) it seldom appears in both father and son, then only if the maternal parent is heterozygous. On the other hand, a trait governed by a sex-linked dominant gene usually manifests itself by: (1) being found more frequently in the female than in the male of the species, (2) being found in all female offspring of a male which shows the trait, (3) failing to be transmitted to any son from a mother which did not exhibit the trait herself.

VARIATIONS OF SEX-LINKAGE

The sex chromosomes (X and Y) often are of unequal size, shape and/or staining qualities. The fact that they pair during meiosis is indication that they contain at least some homologous segments. Genes on the homologous segments are said to be *incompletely sex-linked* or *partially sex-linked* and may recombine by crossing over just as do the gene loci on homologous autosomes. Special techniques are required to demonstrate the presence of such genes on the X chromosome and few examples are known. Genes on the non-homologous segment of the X chromosome are said to be *completely sex-linked* and exhibit the peculiar mode of inheritance described in the preceding sections. In man, a few genes are known to reside in the non-homologous portion of the Y-chromosome. In such cases, the trait would be expressed only in males and would always be transmitted from father to son. Such completely Y-linked genes are called *holandric genes* (Fig. 5-1).

Fig. 5-1. Diagram of X and Y chromosomes showing homologous and non-homologous regions

SEX-INFLUENCED TRAITS

The genes governing sex-influenced traits may reside on any of the autosomes or on the homologous portions of the sex chromosomes. The expression of dominance or recessiveness by the alleles of sex-influenced loci is reversed in males and females due, in large part, to the difference in the internal environment provided by the sex hormones. Thus examples of sex-influenced traits are most readily found in the higher animals with well-developed endocrine systems.

Example 5.9. The gene for pattern baldness in man exhibits dominance in men, but acts recessively in women.

Genotypes	Phenotypes	
	Men	Women
$b'b'$	bald	bald
$b'b$	bald	non-bald
bb	non-bald	non-bald

SEX-LIMITED TRAITS

Some genes may only come to expression in one of the sexes either because of differences in the internal hormonal environment or because of anatomical dissimilarities. For example, we know that bulls have many genes for milk production which they may transmit to their daughters, but they or their sons are unable to express this trait. The production of milk is therefore limited to variable expression in only the female sex. When the penetrance of a gene in one sex is zero, the trait will be *sex-limited*.

Example 5.10. Chickens have a recessive gene for cock-feathering which is penetrant only in the male environment.

Genotype	Phenotypes	
	Males	Females
HH	hen-feathering	hen-feathering
Hh	hen-feathering	hen-feathering
hh	cock-feathering	hen-feathering

SEX REVERSAL

Female chickens (ZO) that have laid eggs have been known to undergo not only a reversal of the secondary sexual characteristics such as development of cock-feathering, spurs, and crowing, but also the development of testes and even the production of sperm cells (primary sexual characteristics). This may occur when, for example, disease destroys the ovarian tissue, and in the absence of the female sex hormones the rudimentary testicular tissue present in the center of the ovary is allowed to proliferate. In solving problems involving sex reversals, it must be remembered that the functional male derived through sex-reversal will still remain genetically female (ZO).

SEXUAL PHENOMENA IN PLANTS

Most flowering plants are monoecious and therefore do not have sex chromosomes. Indeed, the ability of mitotically produced cells with exactly the same genetic endowment to produce tissues with different sexual functions in a perfect flower speaks clearly for the bipotentiality of such plant cells. Well-known examples of dioecism usually are under the genetic control of a single gene locus. However, at least one well-documented case of chromosomal sexuality is known in plants, *viz*, in the genus *Melandrium* (a member of the pink family). Here the Y-chromosome determines a tendency to maleness just as it does in man. Pistillate plants are XX and staminate plants are XY.

The ability of gametes produced by the same individual to unite and produce viable and fertile offspring is common among many families of flowering plants. Self-fertilization is also known to occur in a few of the lower animal groups. The perfect flowers of some monoecious plants fail to open (*cleistogamy*) until after the pollen has matured and accomplished self-fertilization. Self-fertilization is obligatory in barley, beans, oats, peas, soybeans, tobacco, tomato, wheat and many other crops. In some species, self-fertilization as well as cross-fertilization may occur to varying degrees. For example, cotton and sorghum commonly experience more than 10% cross-fertilization. Still other monoecious species have developed genetic mechanisms which prevent self-fertilization or the development of zygotes produced by the union of identical gametes, making cross-fertilization obligatory. Self-incompatibility in monoecious species can become as efficient in enforcing cross-fertilization as would be exhibited under a dioecious mechanism of sex determination.

Solved Problems

SEX DETERMINING MECHANISMS

5.1. An autosomal recessive gene (*tra*), when homozygous, transforms a *Drosophila* female (X/X) into a phenotypic male. All such "transformed" males are sterile. The gene is without effect in males (X/Y). A cross is made between a female heterozygous at the *tra*-locus and a male homozygous recessive at the same locus. What is the expected sex ratio in the F_1 and F_2?

Solution:

We will use a slash mark (/) to separate alleles or homologous chromosomes, and a comma (,) to separate one gene locus from another.

Parents: X/X, +/*tra*   ×   X/Y, *tra*/*tra*
            normal female   normal male

Gametes: (X +) (X *tra*)   (X *tra*) (Y *tra*)

F_1:

	X +	X *tra*
X *tra*	X/X, +/*tra* normal females	X/X, *tra*/*tra* "transformed" males
Y *tra*	X/Y, +/*tra* normal males	X/Y, *tra*/*tra* normal males

The F_1 phenotypic proportions thus appear as $\frac{3}{4}$ males : $\frac{1}{4}$ females.

F$_2$:   The "transformed" F$_1$ males are sterile and hence do not contribute gametes to the F$_2$. Two kinds of matings must be considered. First mating $= \frac{1}{2}$ of all possible matings:

$$\text{X/X, } +/tra \quad \times \quad \text{X/Y, } +/tra$$
$$\text{females} \qquad\qquad \text{males}$$

Offspring:

	X +	X *tra*
X +	X/X, $+/+$ female	X/X, $+/tra$ female
X *tra*	X/X, $+/tra$ female	X/X, tra/tra "transformed" male
Y +	X/Y, $+/+$ male	X/Y, $+/tra$ male
Y *tra*	X/Y, $+/tra$ male	X/Y, tra/tra male

Thus F$_2$ offspring from this mating type appear in the proportions $\frac{3}{8}$ female : $\frac{5}{8}$ male. But this type of mating constitutes only half of all possible matings. Therefore the contribution to the total F$_2$ from this mating is $\frac{1}{2} \cdot \frac{3}{8} = \frac{3}{16}$ female : $\frac{1}{2} \cdot \frac{5}{8} = \frac{5}{16}$ male. Second mating $= \frac{1}{2}$ of all possible matings:

$$\text{X/X, } +/tra \quad \times \quad \text{X/Y, } tra/tra$$
$$\text{females} \qquad\qquad \text{males}$$

This is the same as the original parental mating and hence we expect $\frac{3}{4}$ males : $\frac{1}{4}$ females. Correcting these proportions for the frequency of this mating, we have $\frac{1}{2} \cdot \frac{3}{4} = \frac{3}{8}$ males : $\frac{1}{2} \cdot \frac{1}{4} = \frac{1}{8}$ females. Summary of the F$_2$ from both matings: males $= \frac{5}{16} + \frac{3}{8} = \frac{11}{16}$; females $= \frac{3}{16} + \frac{1}{8} = \frac{5}{16}$.

SEX-LINKED INHERITANCE

5.2.   There is a dominant sex-linked gene B which places white bars on an adult black chicken as in the Barred Plymouth Rock breed. Newly hatched chicks, which will become barred later in life, exhibit a white spot on the top of the head. (*a*) Diagram the cross through the F$_2$ between a homozygous barred male and a non-barred female. (*b*) Diagram the reciprocal cross through the F$_2$ between a homozygous non-barred male and a barred female. (*c*) Will both of the above crosses be useful in sexing F$_1$ chicks at hatching?

Solution:

(*a*)   Parents: Z^B/Z^B $\times$ Z^b/O
                        barred male   non-barred female

("O" represents the lack of a homologue to the Z or sex-chromosome.)

Gametes: B b O

F$_1$: B/b ———— B/O
              barred male   barred female

F$_2$:

	B	O
B	B/B barred male	B/O barred female
b	B/b barred male	b/O non-barred female

(b)   Parents:

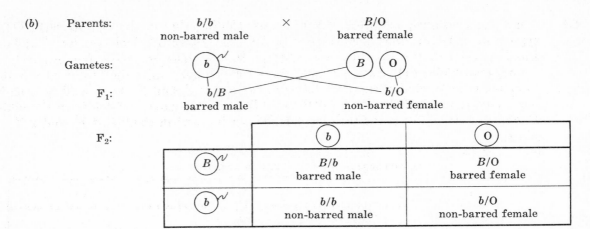

(c)   No. Only the cross shown in (b) would be diagnostic in sexing F_1 chicks at birth through the use of this genetic marker. Only male chicks will have a light spot on their heads.

5.3.   A recessive sex-linked gene (h) prolongs the blood-clotting time, resulting in what is commonly called "bleeder's disease" (hemophilia). From the information in the pedigree, answer the following questions. (a) If II2 marries a normal man, what is the chance of her first child being a hemophilic boy? (b) Suppose her first child is actually hemophilic. What is the probability that her second child will be a hemophilic boy? (c) If II3 marries a hemophilic man, what is the probability that her first child will be normal? (d) If the mother of I1 was phenotypically normal, what phenotype was her father? (e) If the mother of I1 was hemophilic, what phenotype was her father?

Solution:

(a)   Since II4 is a hemophilic male (hY), the hemophilic allele is on an **X** chromosome which he received from his mother (I1). But I1 is phenotypically normal and therefore must be heterozygous or a carrier of hemophilia of genotype Hh. I2 and II1 are both normal males (HY). Therefore the chance of II2 being a carrier female (Hh) is $\frac{1}{2}$. When a carrier woman marries a normal man (HY), 25% of their children are expected to be hemophilic boys (hY). The combined probability that she is a carrier and will produce a hemophilic boy is $\frac{1}{2} \cdot \frac{1}{4} = \frac{1}{8}$.

(b)   Because her first child was hemophilic, she *must* be a carrier. One-quarter of the children from carrier mothers (Hh) × normal fathers (HY) are expected to be hemophilic boys (hY).

(c)   II3 (like II2) has a 50% chance of being a carrier of hemophilia (Hh). If she marries a hemophilic man (hY), $\frac{1}{2}$ of their children (both boys and girls) are expected to be hemophilic. The combined chance of II3 being a carrier and producing a hemophilic child is $\frac{1}{2} \cdot \frac{1}{2} = \frac{1}{4}$. Therefore the probability that her first child is normal is the complementary fraction, $\frac{3}{4}$.

(d)   It is impossible to deduce the phenotype of the father of I1 from the information given because the father could be either normal or hemophilic and still produce a daughter (I1) which is heterozygous normal (Hh), depending upon the genotype of the normal mother:

(1)   HH   ×   hY   =   Hh(I1)
       normal mother   hemophilic father   carrier daughter

(2)   Hh   ×   HY   =   Hh(I1)
       carrier mother   normal father   carrier daughter

(e)   In order for a hemophilic mother (hh) to produce a normal daughter (Hh), her father must possess the dominant normal allele (HY) and therefore would have normal blood clotting time.

5.4. A mutant sex-linked condition called "notch" (N) is lethal in *Drosophila* when hemizygous in males or when homozygous in females. Heterozygous females (Nn) have small notches in the tips of their wings. Homozygous recessive females (nn) or hemizygous males (nY) have normal wings (wild type). (*a*) Other than within sex, calculate the expected phenotypic ratios in the viable F_1 and F_2 when wild type males are mated to notched females. (*b*) What is the ratio of males : females in the viable F_1 and F_2? (*c*) What is the ratio of notched : wild type in the viable F_1 and F_2?

Solution:

(*a*)   Parents: nY $\times$ Nn
                      wild type males   notched females

F_1:

	N	n
n	Nn notched females	nn wild type females
Y	NY lethal	nY wild type males

The ratio of F_1 viable phenotypes is 1 wild type female : 1 notched female : 1 wild type male.

F_2:   There are two kinds of matings to be considered: (1) $Nn \times n$Y, (2) $nn \times n$Y. The first mating gives results identical to those of the F_1. The second mating produces equal numbers of wild type males and females. The two kinds of matings are expected to occur with equal frequency and therefore the contribution which each phenotype makes to the total F_2 must be halved.

1st Mating

$\frac{1}{4}$ notched females $\times \frac{1}{2}$ = $\frac{1}{8}$
$\frac{1}{4}$ wild females $\times \frac{1}{2}$ = $\frac{1}{8}$
$\frac{1}{4}$ wild males $\times \frac{1}{2}$ = $\frac{1}{8}$
$\frac{1}{4}$ lethal males $\times \frac{1}{2}$ = $\frac{1}{8}$

2nd Mating

$\frac{1}{2}$ wild females $\times \frac{1}{2}$ = $\frac{1}{4}$ = $\frac{2}{8}$
$\frac{1}{2}$ wild males $\times \frac{1}{2}$ = $\frac{1}{4}$ = $\frac{2}{8}$

The ratio of viable F_2 phenotypes thus becomes 3 wild type females : 3 wild type males : 1 notched female.

(*b*) By inspection of the data in part (*a*), it is clear that the sex ratio in the viable F_1 is 2 females : 1 male, and in the F_2 it is 4 females : 3 males.

(*c*) Similarly, the ratio for wing phenotypes in the viable F_1 is 2 wild : 1 notched, and in the F_2 it is 6 wild : 1 notched.

5.5. A recessive sex-linked gene in *Drosophila* (v) produces vermilion eye color when homozygous in females or when hemizygous in males. An autosomal recessive on chromosome 2 (bw) produces brown eye color. Individuals which are homozygous recessive at both the brown and the vermilion loci have white eyes. (*a*) Determine the phenotypic expectations among the F_1 and F_2 when homozygous wild type females are crossed to males which are white eyed due to the interaction of the brown and vermilion loci. (*b*) Another recessive gene called "scarlet" (st) on chromosome 3 also produces white eye when homozygous in combination with homozygous recessive brown (st/st, bw/bw). Providing at least one bw^+ allele is present, homozygous scarlet, homozygous or hemizygous vermilion, or both produce a nearly identical eye color which we shall call "orange-red". What phenotypic ratio is expected among the F_1 and F_2 progeny from testcrossing wild type females homozygous at all three loci?

Solution:

(*a*)   P: bw^+/bw^+, v^+/v^+ $\times$ bw/bw, v/Y
                      wild type females   white eyed males

          F_1:   1/2 bw^+/bw, v^+/v =   wild type females
                      1/2 bw^+/bw, v^+/Y   =   wild type males

F$_2$:

	$bw^+\ v^+$	$bw\ v^+$	$bw^+\ Y$	$bw\ Y$
$bw^+\ v^+$	$bw^+/bw^+,\ v^+/v^+$ wild type	$bw^+/bw,\ v^+/v^+$ wild type	$bw^+/bw^+,\ v^+/Y$ wild type	$bw^+/bw,\ v^+/Y$ wild type
$bw^+\ v$	$bw^+/bw^+,\ v^+/v$ wild type	$bw^+/bw,\ v^+/v$ wild type	$bw^+/bw^+,\ v/Y$ vermilion	$bw^+/bw,\ v/Y$ vermilion
$bw\ v^+$	$bw^+/bw,\ v^+/v^+$ wild type	$bw/bw,\ v^+/v^+$ brown	$bw^+/bw,\ v^+/Y$ wild type	$bw/bw,\ v^+/Y$ brown
$bw\ v$	$bw^+/bw,\ v^+/v$ wild type	$bw/bw,\ v^+/v$ brown	$bw^+/bw,\ v/Y$ vermilion	$bw/bw,\ v/Y$ white

F$_2$ summary:

Females	Males
3/4 wild type	3/8 wild type 1/8 brown
1/4 brown	3/8 vermilion 1/8 white

(b)   P: $bw^+/bw^+,\ st^+/st^+,\ v^+/v^+$ $\times$ $bw/bw,\ st/st,\ v/Y$
                        wild type females   white eyed males

F$_1$:   1/2 $bw^+/bw,\ st^+/st,\ v^+/v$ = wild type females
        1/2 $bw^+/bw,\ st^+/st,\ v^+/Y$ = wild type males

F$_2$:   **Females:**

Females:

$\frac{3}{4}bw^+/-$	$\frac{3}{4}st^+/-$ —— $v^+/-$	= wild type	9/16
	$\frac{1}{4}st/st$ —— $v^+/-$	= orange-red	3/16
$\frac{1}{4}bw/bw$	$\frac{3}{4}st^+/-$ —— $v^+/-$	= brown	3/16
	$\frac{1}{4}st/st$ —— $v^+/-$	= white	1/16

Males:

$\frac{3}{4}bw^+/-$	$\frac{3}{4}st^+/-$	$\frac{1}{2}v^+/Y$ = wild type	9/32
		$\frac{1}{2}v/Y$ = orange-red	9/32
	$\frac{1}{4}st/st$	$\frac{1}{2}v^+/Y$ = orange-red	3/32
		$\frac{1}{2}v/Y$ = orange-red	3/32
$\frac{1}{4}bw/bw$	$\frac{3}{4}st^+/-$	$\frac{1}{2}v^+/Y$ = brown	3/32
		$\frac{1}{2}v/Y$ = white	3/32
	$\frac{1}{4}st/st$	$\frac{1}{2}v^+/Y$ = white	1/32
		$\frac{1}{2}v/Y$ = white	1/32

F$_2$ summary: **Females:** 9/16 wild type, 3/16 orange-red, 3/16 brown, 1/16 white
                         Males: 9/32 wild type, 15/32 orange-red, 3/32 brown, 5/32 white

VARIATIONS OF SEX LINKAGE

5.6.   The recessive incompletely sex-linked gene called "bobbed" bb causes the bristles of *Drosophila* to be shorter and of smaller diameter than the normal bristles produced by its dominant wild type allele bb^+. Determine the phenotypic expectations of the F$_1$ and F$_2$ when bobbed females are crossed with each of the two possible heterozygous males.

Solution:

Recall that an incompletely sex-linked gene has an allele on the homologous portion of the Y-chromosome in a male. The wild type allele in heterozygous males may be on either the X or the Y, thus making possible two types of crosses.

First Cross:

Parents: $X^{bb}X^{bb}$ $\times$ $X^{bb+}Y^{bb}$

                  bobbed females   wild type males

F_1: $X^{bb}X^{bb+}$ and $X^{bb}Y^{bb}$

                  all females wild type   all males bobbed

F_2:

	X^{bb}	X^{bb+}
X^{bb}	$X^{bb}X^{bb}$ bobbed female	$X^{bb}X^{bb+}$ wild type female
Y^{bb}	$X^{bb}Y^{bb}$ bobbed male	$X^{bb+}Y^{bb}$ wild type male

Thus $\frac{1}{2}$ of the F_2 females are bobbed and $\frac{1}{2}$ are wild type; $\frac{1}{2}$ of the F_2 males are bobbed and $\frac{1}{2}$ are wild type.

Second Cross:

Parents: $X^{bb}X^{bb}$ $\times$ $X^{bb}Y^{bb+}$

                  bobbed female   wild type male

F_1: $X^{bb}X^{bb}$ and $X^{bb}Y^{bb+}$

                  all females bobbed   all males wild type

F_2:

	X^{bb}	Y^{bb+}
X^{bb}	$X^{bb}X^{bb}$ bobbed females	$X^{bb}Y^{bb+}$ wild type males

Thus all F_2 females are bobbed and all males are wild type.

SEX INFLUENCED TRAITS

5.7. Let us consider two sex-influenced traits simultaneously, pattern baldness and short index finger, both of which are dominant in men and recessive in women. A heterozygous bald man with long index finger marries a heterozygous long-fingered, bald woman. Determine the phenotypic expectations for their children.

Solution:

   Let us first select appropriate symbols and define the phenotypic expression of the three genotypes in each sex.

Genotypes	Males	Females	Genotype	Males	Females
B^1B^1	bald	bald	F^1F^1	short-finger	short-finger
B^1B^2	bald	non-bald	F^1F^2	short-finger	long-finger
B^2B^2	non-bald	non-bald	F^2F^2	long-finger	long-finger

P: B^1B^2, F^2F^2 $\times$ B^1B^1, F^1F^2

            bald, long-fingered man   bald, long-fingered woman

F_1:

$\frac{1}{2}B^1B^1$ $\Big\langle$

$\frac{1}{2}F^1F^2$ $= \frac{1}{4}B^1B^1F^1F^2$ bald, short (men) / bald, long   (women)

$\frac{1}{2}F^2F^2$ $= \frac{1}{4}B^1B^1F^2F^2$ bald, long (men) / bald, long   (women)

$\frac{1}{2}B^1B^2$ $\Big\langle$

$\frac{1}{2}F^1F^2$ $= \frac{1}{4}B^1B^2F^1F^2$ bald, short (men) / non-bald, long (women)

$\frac{1}{2}F^2F^2$ $= \frac{1}{4}B^1B^2F^2F^2$ bald, long (men) / non-bald, long (women)

F_1 summary: **Men:**   1/2 bald, short-fingered : 1/2 bald, long-fingered
Women: 1/2 bald, long-fingered : 1/2 non-bald, long-fingered

SEX-LIMITED TRAITS

5.8.   Cock-feathering in chickens is a trait limited to expression only in males and determined by the autosomal recessive genotype hh. The dominant allele (H) produces hen-feathered males. All females are hen-feathered regardless of genotype. A cock-feathered male is mated to three females, each of which produces a dozen chicks. Among the 36 progeny are 15 hen-feathered males, 18 hen-feathered females and 3 cock-feathered males. What are the most probable genotypes of the three parental females?

Solution:

In order for both hen-feathered (H-) and cock-feathered (hh) males to be produced, at least one of the females had to be heterozygous (Hh) or recessive (hh). The following female genotype possibilities must be explored:

(a) $2\,HH, 1\,Hh$ (c) $1\,HH, 1\,Hh, 1\,hh$ (e) $2\,Hh, 1\,hh$ (g) $2\,HH, 1\,hh$

(b) $1\,HH, 2\,Hh$ (d) $3\,Hh$ (f) $1\,Hh, 2\,hh$ (h) $2\,hh, 1\,HH$

Obviously, the more hh or Hh hen genotypes, proportionately more cock-feathered males are expected in the progeny. The ratio of 15 hen-feathered males : 3 cock-feathered males is much greater than the 1 : 1 ratio expected when all three females are heterozygous (Hh).

P: hh × Hh
cock-feathered male   hen-feathered females

F_1: $\frac{1}{2}Hh$ hen-feathered males, $\frac{1}{2}hh$ cock-feathered males

Possibility (d) is therefore excluded. Possibilities (e) and (f), which both contain one or more hh genotypes in addition to one or more Hh genotypes, must also be eliminated because these matings would produce even more cock-feathered males than possibility (d). In possibility (g), the $2\,HH : 1\,hh$ hens are expected to produce an equivalent ratio of 2 hen-feathered (Hh) : 1 cock-feathered (hh) males. This 2 : 1 ratio should be expressed in the 18 male offspring as 12 hen-feathered : 6 cock-feathered. These numbers compare fairly well with the observed 15 : 3, but possibility (h) would be even less favorable because even more cock-feathered males would be produced. Let us see if one of the remaining three possibilities will give us expected values closer to our observations.

Possibility (c): $\frac{1}{3}HH$ $\Big\}$
P: hh × $\frac{1}{3}Hh$ $\Big\rangle$ hen-feathered females
cock-feathered male $\frac{1}{3}hh$ $\Big\}$

F_1: $\frac{1}{3}(hh \times HH)$ $=$ $\frac{1}{3}Hh$ hen-feathered males

$\frac{1}{3}(hh \times Hh)$ $=$ $\begin{cases} \frac{1}{3} \cdot \frac{1}{2} = \frac{1}{6}Hh \text{ hen-feathered males} \\ \frac{1}{3} \cdot \frac{1}{2} = \frac{1}{6}hh \text{ cock-feathered males} \end{cases}$

$\frac{1}{3}(hh \times hh)$ $=$ $\frac{1}{3}hh$ cock-feathered males

Summary: Hen-feathered males $= \frac{1}{3} + \frac{1}{6} = \frac{1}{2}$, Cock-feathered males $= \frac{1}{6} + \frac{1}{3} = \frac{1}{2}$

Again this disagrees with the observations and must be excluded.

Possibility (b):

P: hh × $\frac{1}{3}HH$ $\Big\}$
cock-feathered male $\frac{2}{3}Hh$ $\Big\rangle$ hen-feathered females

F_1: $\frac{1}{3}(hh \times HH) = \frac{1}{3}Hh$ hen-feathered males

$\frac{2}{3}(hh \times Hh) = \begin{cases} \frac{2}{3} \cdot \frac{1}{2} = \frac{2}{6}Hh \text{ hen-feathered males} \\ \frac{2}{3} \cdot \frac{1}{2} = \frac{2}{6}hh \text{ cock-feathered males} \end{cases}$

Summary: Hen-feathered males $= \frac{1}{3} + \frac{2}{6} = \frac{2}{3}$,   Cock-feathered males $= \frac{2}{6}$ or $\frac{1}{3}$

These expectations are no closer to the observations than those of possibility (g).

Possibility (a):

P: hh $\times$ $\frac{2}{3}HH$ $\left.\begin{array}{l} \\ \\ \end{array}\right\}$ hen-feathered females
        cock-feathered male $\frac{1}{3}Hh$

F_1: $\frac{2}{3}(hh \times HH) = \frac{2}{3}Hh$ hen-feathered males

$\frac{1}{3}(hh \times Hh) = \begin{cases} \frac{1}{3} \cdot \frac{1}{2} = \frac{1}{6}Hh \text{ hen-feathered males} \\ \frac{1}{3} \cdot \frac{1}{2} = \frac{1}{6}hh \text{ cock-feathered males} \end{cases}$

Summary: Hen-feathered males $= \frac{2}{3} + \frac{1}{6} = \frac{5}{6}$,   Cock-feathered males $= \frac{1}{6}$

Set the observation of 3 cock-feathered males equal to the $\frac{1}{6}$, then 5 times 3 or 15 hen-feathered males should represent the $\frac{5}{6}$. These expectations agree perfectly with the observations and therefore it is most probable that two of the females were HH and one was Hh.

SEX REVERSAL

5.9.   Suppose that a hen's ovaries are destroyed by disease, allowing its rudimentary testes to develop. Further suppose that this hen was carrying the dominant sex-linked gene B for barred feathers, and upon sex reversal was then crossed to a non-barred female. What phenotypic proportions are expected in the F_1 and F_2?

Solution:

Remember that sex determination in chickens is by the ZO method and that sex reversal does not change this chromosomal constitution. Furthermore at least one sex-chromosome (Z) is essential for life.

P: BO $\times$ bO
            barred female   normal non-barred female
            sex reversed to a
            functional male

F_1:

	B	O
b	Bb barred male	bO non-barred female
O	BO barred female	OO lethal

The proportions are thus $\frac{1}{3}$ males (all barred) : $\frac{2}{3}$ females (half barred and half non-barred).

F_2:   Two equally frequent kinds of matings are possible among the F_1 birds. First mating $= \frac{1}{2}$ of all matings.

Bb $\times$ bO
barred male   non-barred female

Progeny Expectations		Correction for Frequency of Mating		Proportion of Total F_2
$\frac{1}{4}Bb$	$\cdot$	$\frac{1}{2}$	$=$	$\frac{1}{8}Bb$ barred males
$\frac{1}{4}bb$	$\cdot$	$\frac{1}{2}$	$=$	$\frac{1}{8}bb$ non-barred males
$\frac{1}{4}BO$	$\cdot$	$\frac{1}{2}$	$=$	$\frac{1}{8}BO$ barred females
$\frac{1}{4}bO$	$\cdot$	$\frac{1}{2}$	$=$	$\frac{1}{8}bO$ non-barred females

Second mating $= \frac{1}{2}$ of all matings.

$$Bb \quad \times \quad BO$$
barred male   barred female

Progeny Expectations	Correction for Frequency of Mating		Proportion of Total F_2
$\frac{1}{4}BB$	$\cdot$	$\frac{1}{2}$ $=$	$\frac{1}{8}BB$ $\Big\}$ $\frac{1}{4}$ barred males
$\frac{1}{4}Bb$	$\cdot$	$\frac{1}{2}$ $=$	$\frac{1}{8}Bb$
$\frac{1}{4}BO$	$\cdot$	$\frac{1}{2}$ $=$	$\frac{1}{8}BO$ barred females
$\frac{1}{4}bO$	$\cdot$	$\frac{1}{2}$ $=$	$\frac{1}{8}bO$ non-barred females

Summary of the F_2:   Barred males $= \frac{1}{8} + \frac{1}{4} = \frac{3}{8}$ Barred females $= \frac{1}{8} + \frac{1}{8} = \frac{1}{4}$

Non-barred males $= \frac{1}{8}$ Non-barred females $= \frac{1}{8} + \frac{1}{8} = \frac{1}{4}$

SEXUAL PHENOMENA IN PLANTS

5.10. A recessive gene in monoecious corn called "tassel-seed" (*ts*), when homozygous, produces only seeds where the staminate inflorescence (tassel) normally appears. No pollen is produced. Thus individuals of genotype *ts/ts* are functionally reduced to a single sex, that of the female. On another chromosome, the recessive gene called "silkless" (*sk*), when homozygous produces ears with no pistils (silks). Without silks, none of these ears can produce seed and individuals of genotype *sk/sk* are reduced to performing only male functions (production of pollen in the tassel). The recessive gene for tassel-seed is epistatic to the silkless locus. (*a*) What sex-ratio is expected in the F_1 and F_2 from the cross *ts/ts, sk$^+$/sk$^+$* (female) × *ts$^+$/ts$^+$, sk/sk* (male)? (*b*) How could the genes for tassel-seed and silkless be used to establish male and female plants (dioecious) that would continue, generation after generation, to produce progeny in the ratio of 1 male : 1 female?

Solution:

(*a*)   P: *ts/ts, sk$^+$/sk$^+$*   ×   *ts$^+$/ts$^+$, sk/sk*
          female   male

F_1:   *ts$^+$/ts, sk$^+$/sk*
                  monoecious
          (both male and female flowers)

F_2: $\frac{9}{16}$ *ts$^+$/-, sk$^+$/-* $=$ $\frac{9}{16}$ monoecious
          $\frac{3}{16}$ *ts$^+$/-, sk/sk* $=$ $\frac{3}{16}$ male
          $\frac{3}{16}$ *ts/ts, sk$^+$/-* $\Big\}$ $=$ $\frac{4}{16}$ female
          $\frac{1}{16}$ *ts/ts, sk/sk*

(*b*)   P: *ts/ts, sk/sk*   ×   *ts$^+$/ts, sk/sk*
          female   male

F_1: $\frac{1}{2}$ *ts$^+$/ts, sk/sk*   males
          $\frac{1}{2}$ *ts/ts, sk/sk*   females

Subsequent generations would continue to exhibit a 1 : 1 sex ratio for these dioecious plants.

5.11. Pollen tubes containing the same self-incompatibility allele as that found in the diploid tissue of the style grow so slowly that fertilization cannot occur before the flower withers. Pollen produced by a plant of genotype S^1S^3 would be of two types, S^1 and S^3. If this pollen were to land on the stigma of the same plant (S^1S^3), none of the pollen tubes would grow. If these pollen grains (S^1 and S^3) were to alight on a

		Male Parent			
		A	B	C	D
Female Parent	A	—	$\frac{1}{4}$C, $\frac{1}{4}$D $\frac{1}{4}$E, $\frac{1}{4}$F	$\frac{1}{2}$C $\frac{1}{2}$D	$\frac{1}{2}$C $\frac{1}{2}$D
	B	$\frac{1}{4}$C, $\frac{1}{4}$D $\frac{1}{4}$E, $\frac{1}{4}$F	—	$\frac{1}{2}$C $\frac{1}{2}$E	$\frac{1}{2}$D $\frac{1}{2}$F
	C	$\frac{1}{2}$A $\frac{1}{2}$D	$\frac{1}{2}$B $\frac{1}{2}$E	—	$\frac{1}{2}$D $\frac{1}{2}$A
	D	$\frac{1}{2}$A $\frac{1}{2}$C	$\frac{1}{2}$B $\frac{1}{2}$F	$\frac{1}{2}$A $\frac{1}{2}$C	—

stigma of genotype S^1S^2, then only the tubes containing the S^3 allele would be compatible with the alleles in the tissue of the style. If these pollen grains were to alight on a stigma of genotype S^2S^4, all of the pollen tubes would be functional. Four plant varieties (A, B, C and D) are crossed, with the results listed in the table above. Notice that two additional varieties (E and F) appear in the progeny. Determine the genotypes for all six varieties in terms of four self-sterility alleles (S^1, S^2, S^3 and S^4).

Solution:

None of the genotypes are expected to be homozygous for the self-incompatibility alleles because pollen containing the same allele present in the maternal tissue is not functional and therefore homozygosity is prevented. Thus six genotypes are possible with four self-incompatibility alleles: S^1S^2, S^1S^3, S^1S^4, S^2S^3, S^2S^4, S^3S^4. Crosses between genotypes with both alleles in common produce no progeny (e.g. A × A, B × B, etc.). Crosses between genotypes with only one allele in common produce offspring in the ratio of 1:1 (e.g. $S^1S^2 ♀ × S^1S^3 ♂ = \frac{1}{2}S^1S^3 : \frac{1}{2}S^2S^3$). Crosses between genotypes with none of their self-incompatibility alleles in common produce progeny in the ratio 1:1:1:1 (e.g. $S^1S^2 × S^3S^4 = \frac{1}{4}S^1S^3 : \frac{1}{4}S^1S^4 : \frac{1}{4}S^2S^3 : \frac{1}{4}S^2S^4$). Turning now to the table of results, we find the cross B ♀ × A ♂ produces offspring in the ratio 1:1:1:1 and therefore neither B nor A contains any alleles in common. If we assume that variety B has the genotype S^1S^4, then variety A must have the genotype S^2S^3 (the student's solution to this problem may differ from the one presented here in the alleles arbitrarily assigned as a starting point). The cross C ♀ × A ♂ produces offspring in the ratio 1:1, indicating one pair of alleles in common. Since we have already designated variety A to be of genotype S^2S^3, let us arbitrarily assign the genotype S^1S^2 to variety C. The cross D ♀ × A ♂ also indicates that one allele is held in common by these two varieties. Let us assign the genotype S^1S^3 to variety D. The genotype for variety E may now be determined from the cross C ♀ × B ♂.

P: S^1S^2(C) ♀   × S^1S^4(B) ♂

F₁: $\frac{1}{2}S^1S^4$ = variety B, $\frac{1}{2}S^2S^4$ = variety E

Likewise, the genotype for variety F may now be determined from the cross D ♀ × B ♂.

P: S^1S^3(D) ♀   × S^1S^4(B) ♂

F₁: $\frac{1}{2}S^1S^4$ = variety B, $\frac{1}{2}S^3S^4$ = variety F

Summary of genotypes for all six varieties:

A = S^2S^3 B = S^1S^4 C = S^1S^2 D = S^1S^3 E = S^2S^4 F = S^3S^4

The student should satisfy himself that the other results shown in the table are compatible with the genotypic assumptions shown above.

Supplementary Problems

SEX DETERMINATION AND SEX-LINKED INHERITANCE

Heterogametic Males (XY and XO methods)

5.12. A sex-linked recessive gene c produces red-green color blindness in man. A normal woman whose father was color blind marries a color blind man. (a) What genotypes are possible for the mother of the color blind man? (b) What are the chances that the first child from this marriage will be a color blind boy? (c) Of all the girls produced by these parents, what percentage is expected to be color blind? (d) Of all the children (sex unspecified) from these parents, what proportion is expected to be normal?

5.13. The gene for yellow body color y in *Drosophila* is recessive and sex-linked. Its dominant allele y^+ produces wild type body color. What phenotypic ratios are expected from the crosses (a) yellow male × yellow female, (b) yellow female × wild type male, (c) wild type female (homozygous) × yellow male, (d) wild type (carrier) female × wild type male, (e) wild type (carrier) female × yellow male?

5.14. A narrow reduced eye called "bar" is a dominant sex-linked condition (B) in *Drosophila*, and the full wild type eye is produced by its recessive allele B^+. A homozygous wild type female is mated to a bar-eyed male. Determine the F_1 and F_2 genotypic and phenotypic expectations.

5.15. Sex determination in the grasshopper is by the XO method. The somatic cells of a grasshopper are analyzed and found to contain 23 chromosomes. (a) What sex is this individual? (b) Determine the frequency with which different types of gametes (number of autosomes and sex chromosomes) can be formed in this individual. (c) What is the diploid number of the opposite sex?

5.16. Male house cats may be black or yellow. Females may be black, tortoise-shell pattern, or yellow. (a) If these colors are governed by a sex-linked locus, how can these results be explained? (b) Using appropriate symbols, determine the phenotypes expected in the offspring from the cross yellow female × black male. (c) Do the same for the reciprocal cross of part (b). (d) A certain kind of mating produces females, half of which are tortoise-shell and half are black; half the males are yellow and half are black. What colors are the parental males and females in such crosses? (e) Another kind of mating produces offspring, $\frac{1}{4}$ of which are yellow males, $\frac{1}{4}$ yellow females, $\frac{1}{4}$ black males and $\frac{1}{4}$ tortoise-shell females. What colors are the parental males and females in such crosses?

5.17. In the plant genus *Melandrium*, sex determination is similar to that in man. A sex-linked gene (l) is known to be lethal when homozygous in females. When present in the hemizygous condition in males (lY), it produces blotchy patches of yellow-green color. The homozygous or heterozygous condition of the wild type allele (LL or Ll) in females, or the hemizygous condition in males (LY) produces normal dark green color. From a cross between heterozygous females and yellow-green males, predict the phenotypic ratio expected in the progeny.

5.18. The recessive gene for white eye color in *Drosophila* (w) is sex-linked. Another recessive sex-linked gene governing eye color is vermilion (v), which when homozygous in females or hemizygous in males together with the autosomal gene for brown eye (bw/bw), also produces white eye. White genotypes (wY, ww) are epistatic to the other loci under consideration. (a) What phenotypic results are expected among progeny from mating a white-eyed male of genotype (bw/bw, vw^+/Y) with a white-eyed female of genotype (bw^+/bw, vw/v^+w)? *Hint.* See Problem 5.5. (b) What phenotypic proportions are expected in the progeny from the mating of a vermilion female heterozygous at the brown locus but not carrying the white allele with a male which is white due to the w allele but heterozygous at the brown locus and hemizygous for the vermilion allele? (c) Determine the expected phenotypic ratio in the F_1 and F_2 from the reciprocal cross of Problem 5.5(a).

Heterogametic Females (ZW and ZO methods)

5.19. A recessive sex-linked gene (k) influences a slower growth rate of the primary feathers of chickens than its dominant allele (k^+) for fast feathering. This trait can be used for sexing chicks within a few days after hatching. (a) If fast feathering females are crossed to slow feathering males, what phenotypic ratio is expected among the F_1 and F_2? (b) What are the expected F_1 and F_2 phenotypic ratios from crossing fast feathering males (k^+/k^+) to slow feathering females? (c) What are the expected F_1 and F_2 phenotypic ratios from crossing fast feathering males (k^+/k) to slow feathering females?

5.20. Silver-colored plumage in poultry is due to a dominant sex-linked gene (S) and gold-colored plumage to its recessive allele (s). List the phenotypic and genotypic expectations of the progeny from the matings (a) $s/O\,♀ \times S/S\,♂$, (b) $s/O\,♀ \times S/s\,♂$, (c) $S/O\,♀ \times S/s\,♂$, (d) $S/O\,♀ \times s/s\,♂$.

5.21. In the Rosy Gier variety of carrier pigeon, a cross was made between gray-headed females and creamy-headed males. The F_1 ratio was 1 gray-headed female : 1 gray-headed male : 1 creamy-headed male. (*a*) How may these results be explained? (*b*) Diagram this cross using appropriate symbols.

5.22. Chickens have an autosomal dominant gene (*C*) that produces a short-legged phenotype called "creeper" in heterozygotes. Normal legs are produced by the recessive genotype (*cc*). The homozygous dominant genotype (*CC*) is lethal. A dominant sex-linked gene (*B*) produces barred plumage, the recessive allele (*b*) produces non-barred plumage. (*a*) Determine the phenotypic expectations among progeny (of both sexes) from the cross of a barred creeper female and a non-barred creeper male. (*b*) Determine the phenotypic ratios within each sex for part (*a*). (*c*) Two chickens were mated and produced progeny in the following proportions: $\frac{1}{12}$ non-barred males, $\frac{1}{6}$ non-barred creeper females, $\frac{1}{12}$ barred males, $\frac{1}{12}$ non-barred females, $\frac{1}{6}$ non-barred creeper males, $\frac{1}{6}$ barred creeper males, $\frac{1}{12}$ barred females and $\frac{1}{6}$ barred creeper females. What are the genotypes and phenotypes of the parents?

5.23. A dominant autosomal inhibitor (*I*-) as well as a recessive autosomal inhibitor (*cc*) prevents any color from being produced in chickens. The genotypes *I-C-*, *I-cc* and *iicc* all produce white chickens; only the genotype *iiC-* produces colored birds. A recessive sex-linked gene *k* produces slow growth of the primary wing feathers. Its dominant allele k^+ produces fast feathering. A white (*IICC*) slow feathering male is mated to a white (*iicc*) fast feathering female. What are the F_1 and F_2 phenotypic expectations?

5.24. The presence of feathers on the shanks of the Black Langshan breed of chickens is due to the dominant alleles at either or both of two autosomal loci. Non-feathered shanks are the result of the double recessive genotype. A dominant sex-linked gene (*B*) places white bars on a black bird. Its recessive allele (*b*) produces non-barred (black) birds. Trihybrid barred males with feathered shanks are mated to dihybrid non-barred females with feathered shanks. Determine the F_1 phenotypic expectations.

Genic Balance

5.25. In *Drosophila*, the ratio between the number of X chromosomes and the number of sets of autosomes (A) is called the "sex index". Diploid females have a sex-index (ratio X/A) = 2/2 = 1.0. Diploid males have a sex index of $\frac{1}{2} = 0.5$. Sex index values between 0.5 and 1.0 give rise to intersexes. Values over 1.0 or under 0.5 produce weak and inviable flies called superfemales (meta-females) and supermales (meta-males) respectively. Calculate the sex index and the sex phenotype in the following individuals: (*a*) AAX, (*b*) AAXXY, (*c*) AAAXX, (*d*) AAXX, (*e*) AAXXX, (*f*) AAAXXX, (*g*) AAY.

Haplodiploidy

5.26. If the diploid number of the honey bee is 16, (*a*) how many chromosomes will be found in the somatic cells of the drone (male), (*b*) how many bivalents will be seen during the process of gametogenesis in the male, (*c*) how many bivalents will be seen during the process of gametogenesis in the female?

5.27. Seven eye colors are known in the honey bee, each produced by a recessive gene at a different locus: brick (*bk*), chartreuse (*ch*), ivory (*i*), cream (*cr*), snow (*s*), pearl (*pe*) and garnet (*g*). Suppose that a wild type queen heterozygous at the brick locus (bk^+/bk) was to be artificially inseminated with a mixture of sperm from seven haploid drones each exhibiting a different one of the seven mutant eye colors. Further assume that the semen contribution of each male contains equal concentrations of sperm, that each sperm has an equal opportunity to enter fertilization, and that each zygote thus formed has an equal opportunity to survive. (*a*) What percentage of the drone offspring is expected to be brick-eyed? (*b*) What percentage of worker offspring is expected to be brick-eyed?

Single Gene Effects

5.28. In the single-celled haploid plant *Chlamydomonas*, there are two mating types, (+) and (−). There is no morphological distinction between the (+) sex and the (−) sex in either the spore stage or the gamete stage (isogametes). The fusion of (+) and (−) gametes produces a 2n zygote which immediately undergoes meiosis producing four haploid spores, two of which are (+) and two are (−). (*a*) Could a pair of genes for sex account for the 1 : 1 sex ratio? (*b*) Does the foregoing information preclude some other form of sex-determination? Explain.

5.29. Sex determination in the wasp *Bracon* is either by sex-alleles or haplodiploidy. A recessive gene called "veinless" (*v*) is known to assort independently of the sex alleles; the dominant allele v^+ results in wild type. For each of the eight crosses listed below, determine the relative frequencies of progeny phenotypes within each of 3 categories: (1) haploid males, (2) diploid males, (3) females. (*a*) $v/v, s^a/s^b \times v^+, s^a$, (*b*) $v/v, s^a/s^b \times v^+, s^c$, (*c*) $v/v, s^a/s^b \times v, s^b$, (*d*) $v/v, s^a/s^b \times v, s^c$, (*e*) $v/v^+, s^a/s^b \times v, s^a$, (*f*) $v/v^+, s^a/s^b \times v, s^c$, (*g*) $v^+/v^+, s^a/s^b \times v, s^a$, (*h*) $v^+/v^+, s^a/s^b \times v, s^c$.

VARIATIONS OF SEX-LINKAGE

5.30. An Englishman by the name of Edward Lambert was born in 1717. His skin was like thick bark which had to be shed periodically. The hairs on his body were quill-like and he subsequently has been referred to as the "porcupine man". He had six sons, all of which exhibited the same trait. The trait appeared to be transmitted from father to son through four generations. None of the daughters ever exhibited the trait. In fact, it has never been known to appear in females. (*a*) Could this be an autosomal sex-limited trait? (*b*) How is this trait probably inherited?

5.31. Could a recessive mutant gene in humans be located on the X chromosome if a woman exhibiting the recessive trait and a normal man had a normal son? Explain.

5.32. A holandric gene is known in man which causes long hair to grow on the external ears. When men with hairy ears marry normal women, (*a*) what percentage of their sons would be expected to have hairy ears, (*b*) what proportion of the daughters is expected to show the trait, (*c*) what ratio of hairy eared : normal children is expected?

SEX-INFLUENCED TRAITS

5.33. A certain type of white forelock in man appears to follow the sex-influenced mode of inheritance, being dominant in men and recessive in women. Using the allelic symbols w and w', indicate all possible genotypes and the phenotypes thereby produced in men and women.

5.34. The sex-influenced gene governing the presence of horns in sheep exhibits dominance in males but acts recessively in females. When the Dorset breed (both sexes horned) with genotype hh is crossed to the Suffolk breed (both sexes polled or hornless) with the genotype $h'h'$, what phenotypic ratios are expected in the F_1 and F_2?

5.35. The fourth (ring) finger of man may be longer or shorter than the second (index) finger. The short index finger is thought to be produced by a gene which is dominant in men and recessive in women. What kinds of children and with what frequency would the following marriages be likely to produce: (*a*) heterozygous short-fingered man × short-fingered women, (*b*) heterozygous long-fingered woman × homozygous short-fingered man, (*c*) heterozygous short-fingered man × heterozygous long-fingered woman, (*d*) long-fingered man × short-fingered woman?

5.36. In the Ayrshire breed of dairy cattle, mahogany-and-white color is dependent upon a gene C^M which is dominant in males and recessive in females. Its allele for red-and-white (C^R) acts as a dominant in females but recessive in males. (*a*) If a red-and-white male is crossed to a mahogany-and-white female, what phenotypic and genotypic proportions are expected in the F_1 and F_2? (*b*) If a mahogany-and-white cow has a red-and-white calf, what sex is the calf? (*c*) What genotype is *not* possible for the sire of the calf in part (*b*)?

5.37. Long eared goats mated to short eared goats produce an ear of intermediate length in the F_1 and an F_2 consisting of $\frac{1}{4}$ long, $\frac{1}{2}$ intermediate, and $\frac{1}{4}$ short in both males and females. Non-bearded male goats mated to bearded female goats produce bearded male progeny and non-bearded female progeny. The F_2 males have $\frac{3}{4}$ bearded and $\frac{1}{4}$ non-bearded, while the F_2 females have $\frac{3}{4}$ non-bearded and $\frac{1}{4}$ bearded. A bearded male with ears of intermediate length whose father and mother were both non-bearded is mated with a non-bearded, intermediate-eared half-sib (sib = sibling = a brother or sister; half-sibs are half-brothers or half-sisters) by the same father but out of a bearded mother. List the phenotypic expectations among the progeny.

5.38. A sex-linked recessive gene in man produces color blind men when hemizygous and color blind women when homozygous. A sex-influenced gene for pattern baldness is dominant in men and recessive in women. A heterozygous bald, color blind man marries a non-bald woman with normal vision whose father was non-bald and color blind and whose mother was bald with normal vision. List the phenotypic expectations for their children.

SEX-LIMITED TRAITS

5.39. A dominant sex-limited gene is known to affect premature baldness in men but is without effect in women. (*a*) What proportion of the male offspring from parents, both of which are heterozygous, is expected to be bald prematurely? (*b*) What proportion of all their children is expected to be prematurely bald?

5.40. The down of baby junglefowl chicks of genotype S- is darkly striped, whereas the recessive genotype *ss* produces in both sexes an unstriped yellowish-white down. In the adult plumage, however, the character behaves as a sex-limited trait. Males, regardless of genotype, develop normal junglefowl plumage. Females of genotype S- bear normal junglefowl plumage but the recessive *ss* is a creamy-buff color. A male bird unstriped at birth is mated to three females, each of which lays 16 eggs. Among the 48 progeny there are 32 unstriped chicks and 16 striped. At maturity there are 16 with creamy-buff and 32 with normal junglefowl plumage. What are the most probable genotypes of the three parental females?

5.41. In the clover butterfly, all males are yellow, but females may be yellow if they are of the homozygous recessive genotype *yy* or white if they possess the dominant allele (Y-). What phenotypic proportions, exclusive of sex, are expected in the F_1 from the cross $Yy \times Yy$?

5.42. The barred plumage pattern in chickens is governed by a dominant sex-linked gene B. The gene for cock-feathering *h* is recessive in males, its dominant allele H producing hen-feathering. Normal females are hen-feathered regardless of genotype (sex-limited trait). Non-barred females heterozygous at the hen-feathered locus are crossed to a barred, hen-feathered male whose father was cock-feathered and non-barred. What phenotypic proportions are expected among the progeny?

PEDIGREES

5.43. Could the trait represented by the solid symbols in the pedigree on the right be explained on the basis of (*a*) a dominant sex-linked gene, (*b*) a recessive sex-linked gene, (*c*) a holandric gene, (*d*) a sex-limited autosomal dominant, (*e*) a sex-limited autosomal recessive, (*f*) a sex-influenced autosomal gene dominant in males, (*g*) a sex-influenced autosomal gene recessive in males?

5.44.

Legend:
○ = wild type female
□ = wild type male
● = mutant female
■ = mutant male

Could the assumption of a sex-linked recessive mutant gene be supported by the above pedigree? Explain?

5.45.

Legend:
□ = normal male
○ = normal female
■ = mutant male
● = mutant female

(*a*) Could the above pedigree be used as support for a holandric gene?

(*b*) Does the above pedigree contradict the assumption of a sex-linked recessive gene for the mutant trait?

(*c*) If a mating between III2 and III3 produced a mutant female offspring, which of the above two hypotheses would apply? List the genotype of each individual in the pedigree, using appropriate symbols.

5.46. Could the trait represented by the solid symbols in the pedigree shown below be produced by (*a*) an autosomal dominant, (*b*) an autosomal recessive, (*c*) a sex-linked dominant, (*d*) a sex-linked recessive, (*e*) a sex-limited gene, (*f*) a holandric gene, (*g*) a sex-influenced gene?

SEX REVERSALS

5.47. Suppose that a female undergoes sex reversal to become a functional male and is then mated to a normal female. Determine the expected F_1 sex ratios from such matings in species with (a) ZW method of sex determination, (b) XY method of sex determination.

5.48. The hemp plant is dioecious, probably resulting from an XY mechanism of sex determination. Early plantings (May-June) yield the normal $1:1$ sex ratio. Late plantings in November, however, produce all female plants. If this difference is due to the length of daylight, it should be possible to rear both XY females and XY males under controlled conditions in the greenhouse. What sex ratio would be expected among seedlings grown early in the year from crosses between XY males and XY females?

5.49. Suppose that a hen carrying the recessive sex-linked allele k for slow feathering underwent a sex reversal and sired chicks from hens carrying the dominant allele k^+ for fast feathering. What genotypic and phenotypic proportions are expected in the F_1 and F_2?

SEXUAL PHENOMENA IN PLANTS

5.50. A completely pistillate inflorescence (female flower) is produced in the castor bean by the recessive genotype nn. Plants of genotype NN and Nn have mixed pistillate and staminate flowers in the inflorescence. Determine the types of flowers produced in the progeny from the following crosses: (a) $NN♀ \times Nn♂$, (b) $Nn♀ \times Nn♂$, (c) $nn♀ \times Nn♂$.

5.51. Asparagus is a dioecious plant in which maleness (staminate plants) is governed by a dominant gene P and femaleness (pistillate plants) by its recessive allele p. Sometimes pistillate flowers are found to have small non-functional anthers, and then again some staminate flowers may be found to possess immature pistils. Very rarely a staminate plant may be found to produce seed, most likely by self-fertilization. (a) What sex ratio is expected among the F_1 from an exceptional staminate-seed plant of genotype Pp when selfed? (b) When the staminate F_1 plants from part (a) are crossed to normal pistillate plants (pp), what sex ratio is expected in the progeny? (c) What type of mating gives a $1:1$ sex ratio?

5.52. Sex determination in the dioecious plant *Melandrium album* (*Lychnis dioica*) is by the XY method. A sex-linked gene governs leaf size, the dominant allele B producing broad leaves and the recessive allele b producing narrow leaves. Pollen grains bearing the recessive allele are inviable. What phenotypic results are expected from the following crosses?

	Seed Parent		Pollen Parent
(a)	homozygous broad-leaf	$\times$	narrow-leaf
(b)	heterozygous broad-leaf	$\times$	narrow-leaf
(c)	heterozygous broad-leaf	$\times$	broad leaf

5.53. Partial dioecy can be attained in a monoecious plant by the action of a single gene locus which prevents the production of viable gametes in one of the two types of gametangia (organ bearing gametes). The male-sterile condition is ordinarily recessive in most plant species where it has been studied. (a) Suppose that we artificially cross a pollen parent (Ss) onto a male-sterile (egg) parent of genotype ss. Determine the phenotypic ratio in the F_1 and F_2 (assuming complete randomness of mating, including selfing, among the F_1 types). (b) Determine the F_1 and F_2 expectancies in part (a) when the parental cross is $ss \times SS$. (c) If a locus (A), assorting independently of the male sterility locus (S), is jointly considered in the cross $ssAA \times Ssaa$, determine the F_1 and F_2 expectancies for the genotypes $S\text{-}A\text{-}$, $S\text{-}aa$, $ssA\text{-}$ and $ssaa$. (d) Do likewise for part (c) where the parental cross is $ssAA \times SSaa$.

5.54. Two or more genes may cooperate to restrict selfing. An example is known in monoecious sorghum where the action of two complementary genes produces an essentially male plant by making the female structures sterile. Plants heterozygous at both loci ($Fs_1/fs_1, Fs_2/fs_2$) result in female sterile plants with no effect on their production of pollen. Whenever three dominant genes are present ($Fs_1/Fs_1, Fs_2/fs_2$ or $Fs_1/fs_1, Fs_2/Fs_2$), dwarf plants are produced which fail to develop a head. Although not yet observed, a genotype with all four dominant alleles would presumably also be dwarf and headless. All other genotypes produce normal plants. If these loci assort independently of one another, determine the F_1 phenotypic expectancies from the crosses (a) $Fs_1/fs_1, Fs_2/fs_2 \times Fs_1/fs_1, fs_2/fs_2$, (b) $Fs_1/fs_1, Fs_2/fs_2 \times Fs_1/Fs_1, fs_2/fs_2$.

5.55. In some cases of self-incompatibility, pollen tube growth is so slow that the style withers and dies before fertilization can occur. Sometimes, if pollination is artificially accomplished in the bud stage, the pollen tube can reach the ovary before the style withers. In this case it is possible to produce a genotype homozygous at the self sterility locus. (a) What would be the expected results from natural pollination of such a homozygote (S^1S^1) by a heterozygote containing one allele in common (S^1S^3)? (b) What would be the result of the reciprocal cross of part (a)? (c) What would be the result of natural pollination of S^1S^1 by S^2S^3? (d) Would the reciprocal cross of part (c) make any difference in the progeny expectations?

5.56. Two heteromorphic types of flowers are produced in many species of the plant genus *Primula*. One type called "pin" has short anthers and a long style. The other type called "thrum" has highly placed anthers and a short style. Thrum is produced by a dominant gene (S) and pin by the recessive allele (s). The only pollinations that are compatible are those between styles and anthers of the same height, i.e. between thrum style and pin anther or between thrum anther and pin style. (a) What genotype do all thrum plants possess? (b) If both the pin and thrum are heterozygous for an independently segregating allelic pair (Aa), what genotypic ratio is expected in the next generation?

5.57. The self-incompatibility mechanism of many plants probably involves a series of multiple alleles similar to that found in *Nicotiana*. In this species, pollen tubes grow very slowly or not at all down the style that contains the same allele at the self-incompatibility locus (S). List the genotypic ratio of progeny sporophytes expected from the following crosses:

	Seed Parent		Pollen Parent
(a)	S_1S_2	$\times$	S_1S_2
(b)	S_1S_2	$\times$	S_1S_3
(c)	S_1S_2	$\times$	S_3S_4
(d)	How much of the pollen is compatible in each of the above three crosses?		

5.58. A cross is made between two plants of the self-sterile genotype $S^1S^2 \times S^3S^4$. If all the F_1 progeny are pollinated only by plants of genotype S^2S^3, what genotypic proportions are expected in the F_2?

Answers to Supplementary Problems

5.12. (a) Cc or cc (b) $\frac{1}{4}$ (c) 50% (d) $\frac{1}{2}$

5.13. (a) all offspring yellow (b) all females wild type, all males yellow (c) all offspring wild type (d) all females wild type : $\frac{1}{2}$ wild type males : $\frac{1}{2}$ yellow males (e) females and males : $\frac{1}{2}$ wild type : $\frac{1}{2}$ yellow

5.14. F_1: B^+/B bar eyed females, B^+/Y wild type males; F_2 females: $\frac{1}{2}B^+/B^+$ wild type : $\frac{1}{2}B^+/B$ bar eye; F_2 males: $\frac{1}{2}B^+/Y$ wild type : $\frac{1}{2}B/Y$ bar eye

5.15. (a) male (b) $\frac{1}{2}(11A + 1X) : \frac{1}{2}(11A)$ (c) 24

5.16.   (*a*) a pair of codominant sex-linked alleles.

	Females	Males
black	$C^B C^B$	$C^B Y$
tortoise-shell	$C^B C^Y$	—
yellow	$C^Y C^Y$	$C^Y Y$

(*b*) all males yellow, all females tortoise-shell   (*c*) all males black, all females tortoise-shell (*d*) tortoise-shell female $\times$ black male   (*e*) tortoise-shell female $\times$ yellow male

5.17. $\frac{1}{3}$ dark green females : $\frac{1}{3}$ males with yellow-green patches : $\frac{1}{3}$ males dark green

5.18.   (*a*) males all white eyed; females: $\frac{1}{4}$ vermilion : $\frac{1}{4}$ wild type : $\frac{1}{4}$ white : $\frac{1}{4}$ brown   (*b*) males and females: $\frac{3}{4}$ vermilion : $\frac{1}{4}$ white   (*c*) males and females: $\frac{3}{8}$ wild type : $\frac{3}{8}$ vermilion : $\frac{1}{8}$ brown : $\frac{1}{8}$ white

5.19.   (*a*) F$_1$: fast males, slow females; F$_2$: males and females: $\frac{1}{2}$ fast : $\frac{1}{2}$ slow   (*b*) F$_1$: all fast; F$_2$ males fast; F$_2$ females: $\frac{1}{2}$ fast : $\frac{1}{2}$ slow   (*c*) F$_1$ both males and females: $\frac{1}{2}$ fast : $\frac{1}{2}$ slow; F$_2$ males: $\frac{5}{8}$ fast : $\frac{3}{8}$ slow; F$_2$ females: $\frac{1}{4}$ fast : $\frac{3}{4}$ slow

5.20.   (*a*) silver females (*S/O*), silver males (*S/s*)   (*b*) males: $\frac{1}{2}$ silver (*S/s*) : $\frac{1}{2}$ gold (*s/s*); females: $\frac{1}{2}$ silver (*S/O*) : $\frac{1}{2}$ gold (*s/O*)   (*c*) males: all silver ($\frac{1}{2}$*S/S* : $\frac{1}{2}$*S/s*); females: $\frac{1}{2}$ silver (*S/O*) : $\frac{1}{2}$ gold (*s/O*) (*d*) all males silver (*S/s*), all females gold (*s/O*)

5.21.   (*a*) Sex-linked gene with one allele lethal when hemizygous in females or homozygous in males.

	Male	Female
gray	HH	HW
cream	HH^1	—
lethal	H^1H^1	H^1W

(*b*)   P: $HW \times HH^1$; F$_1$: $\frac{1}{3}$ HH gray male : $\frac{1}{3}$ HH^1 cream male : $\frac{1}{3}$ HW gray female

5.22.   (*a*) $\frac{1}{6}$ non-bar, normal leg females : $\frac{1}{6}$ bar, normal leg male : $\frac{1}{3}$ non-bar, creeper female : $\frac{1}{3}$ bar, creeper male
(*b*) males: $\frac{2}{3}$ bar, creeper : $\frac{1}{3}$ bar, normal leg; females: $\frac{2}{3}$ non-bar, creeper : $\frac{1}{3}$ non-bar, normal leg
(*c*) bar, creeper male (*CcBb*) $\times$ non-bar, creeper female (*CcbO*)

5.23.   F$_1$: males: white, fast; females: white, slow; F$_2$ males and females: $\frac{13}{32}$ white, fast : $\frac{13}{32}$ white, slow : $\frac{3}{32}$ colored, fast : $\frac{3}{32}$ colored, slow

5.24.   Males and females: $\frac{15}{32}$ bar, feathered : $\frac{15}{32}$ non-bar, feathered : $\frac{1}{32}$ bar, non-feathered : $\frac{1}{32}$ non-bar, non-feathered

5.25.   (*a*) 0.5 male   (*c*) 0.67 intersex   (*e*) 1.5 superfemale
(*b*) 1.0 female   (*d*) 1.0 female   (*f*) 1.0 female (triploid)   (*g*) lethal

5.26.   (*a*) 8   (*b*) none; meiosis cannot occur in haploid males   (*c*) 8

5.27.   (*a*) 50%   (*b*) 7.14%

5.28.   (*a*) Yes   (*b*) No.   A sex chromosome mechanism could be operative without a morphological difference in the chromosomes, gametes, or spores.

5.29.

	Haploid Males		Diploid Males		Females	
	Wild type	Veinless	Wild type	Veinless	Wild type	Veinless
(*a*)	0	all	all	0	all	0
(*b*)	0	all	0	0	all	0
(*c*)	0	all	0	all	0	all
(*d*)	0	all	0	0	0	all
(*e*)	$\frac{1}{2}$	$\frac{1}{2}$	$\frac{1}{2}$	$\frac{1}{2}$	$\frac{1}{2}$	$\frac{1}{2}$
(*f*)	$\frac{1}{2}$	$\frac{1}{2}$	0	0	$\frac{1}{2}$	$\frac{1}{2}$
(*g*)	all	0	all	0	all	0
(*h*)	all	0	0	0	all	0

5.30.   (a) No. It is highly unlikely that a mutant autosomal sex-limited gene would be transmitted to all his sons through four generations without showing segregation. (b) holandric gene (Y-linked)

5.31.   Yes, if it was incompletely sex-linked and the father carried the dominant normal gene on the homologous portion of his Y chromosome.

5.32.   (a) 100%   (b) none   (c) 1 hairy : 1 normal

5.33.

Genotypes	Men	Women		Genotypes
w dominant in men:				w' dominant in men:
ww	forelock	forelock		$w'w'$
ww'	forelock	normal	(or)	$w'w$
$w'w'$	normal	normal		ww

5.34. F_1: all males horned, all females polled; F_2 males: $\frac{3}{4}$ horned : $\frac{1}{4}$ polled; F_2 females: $\frac{3}{4}$ polled : $\frac{1}{4}$ horned

5.35.   (a) all males short; females: $\frac{1}{2}$ short : $\frac{1}{2}$ long   (b) same as (a)   (c) males: $\frac{3}{4}$ short : $\frac{1}{4}$ long; females: $\frac{1}{4}$ short : $\frac{3}{4}$ long   (d) all males short, all females long

5.36.   (a) F_1: $C^M C^R$ mahogany males, $C^M C^R$ red females; F_2 males and females: $\frac{1}{4}C^M C^M$: $\frac{1}{2}C^M C^R$: $\frac{1}{4}C^R C^R$; F_2 males: $\frac{3}{4}$ mahogany : $\frac{1}{4}$ red; F_2 females: $\frac{1}{4}$ mahogany : $\frac{3}{4}$ red (b) female (c) $C^M C^M$

5.37.

Phenotype	Males	Females
bearded, long eared	3/16	1/16
bearded, intermediate eared	3/8	1/8
bearded, short eared	3/16	1/16
non-bearded, long eared	1/16	3/16
non-bearded, intermediate eared	1/8	3/8
non-bearded, short eared	1/16	3/16

5.38.

Phenotype	Daughters	Sons
bald, normal vision	1/8	3/8
bald, color blind	1/8	3/8
non-bald, normal vision	3/8	1/8
non-bald, color blind	3/8	1/8

5.39.   (a) $\frac{3}{4}$ (b) $\frac{3}{8}$

5.40. $2ss : 1SS$ or $2Ss : 1ss$

5.41. $\frac{5}{8}$ yellow : $\frac{3}{8}$ white

5.42.   Males: $\frac{3}{8}$ barred, hen-feathered : $\frac{1}{8}$ barred, cock-feathered : $\frac{3}{8}$ non-barred, hen-feathered : $\frac{1}{8}$ non-barred, cock-feathered; females: $\frac{1}{2}$ barred, hen-feathered : $\frac{1}{2}$ non-barred, hen-feathered

5.43.   (a) no   (b) yes   (c) no   (d) yes   (e) yes   (f) yes   (g) no

5.44.   No. Under the assumption, III1 must be of heterozygous genotype and therefore should be phenotypically normal; III2 must carry the recessive mutant in hemizygous condition and therefore should be phenotypically mutant.

5.45.   (a) yes   (b) no   (c) sex-linked recessive gene; Aa (I1, II1, 3, III2), aY (I2, II2, 4, III1, 3)

5.46.   (a) through (f) no   (g) yes (if black is dominant in males and recessive in females)

5.47.   (a) 2 females : 1 male   (b) all females

5.48.   2 males : 1 female

5.49. F_1: $\frac{1}{3}k^+/k$ fast males : $\frac{1}{3}k^+/O$ fast females : $\frac{1}{3}k/O$ slow females; F_2: $(\frac{1}{8}k^+/k^+ + \frac{1}{4}k^+/k) = \frac{3}{8}$ **fast** males : $\frac{1}{8}k/k$ slow males : $\frac{1}{4}k^+/O$ fast females : $\frac{1}{4}k/O$ slow females

5.50.   (a) all mixed   (b) $\frac{3}{4}$ mixed : $\frac{1}{4}$ pistillate   (c) $\frac{1}{2}$ mixed : $\frac{1}{2}$ pistillate

5.51.   (a) $\frac{3}{4}$ staminate : $\frac{1}{4}$ pistillate   (b) $\frac{2}{3}$ staminate : $\frac{1}{3}$ pistillate   (c) $Pp \times pp$

5.52.   (a) only broad-leaved males   (b) $\frac{1}{2}$ broad-leaved males : $\frac{1}{2}$ narrow-leaved males   (c) all **females** broad-leaved; $\frac{1}{2}$ males broad-leaved : $\frac{1}{2}$ males narrow-leaved

5.53.   (a) F_1: $\frac{1}{2}$ male sterile : $\frac{1}{2}$ male fertile (normal = monoecious); F_2: $\frac{3}{8}$ male sterile : $\frac{5}{8}$ **normal** (b) F_1: all normal; F_2: $\frac{1}{4}$ male sterile : $\frac{3}{4}$ normal   (c) F_1: $\frac{1}{2}SsAa$ normal : $\frac{1}{2}ssAa$ male sterile; F_2: $\frac{15}{32}S\text{-}A\text{-}$: $\frac{9}{32}ssA\text{-}$: $\frac{5}{32}S\text{-}aa$: $\frac{3}{32}ssaa$ (d) F_1: $SsAa$ normal; F_2: $\frac{9}{16}S\text{-}A\text{-}$: $\frac{3}{16}S\text{-}aa$: $\frac{3}{16}ssA\text{-}$: $\frac{1}{16}ssaa$

5.54.   (a) $\frac{1}{8}$ dwarf : $\frac{1}{4}$ female sterile : $\frac{5}{8}$ normal (monoecious)   (b) $\frac{1}{2}$ normal : $\frac{1}{4}$ female sterile : $\frac{1}{4}$ dwarf

5.55.   (a) all S^1S^3 (b) no progeny   (c) $\frac{1}{2}S^1S^2$: $\frac{1}{2}S^1S^3$ (d) no

5.56.   (a) Ss (b) $\frac{1}{8}AASs$: $\frac{1}{4}AaSs$: $\frac{1}{8}aaSs$: $\frac{1}{8}AAss$: $\frac{1}{4}Aass$: $\frac{1}{8}aass$

5.57.   (a) none   (b) $\frac{1}{2}S_1S_3$: $\frac{1}{2}S_2S_3$ (c) $\frac{1}{4}S_1S_3$: $\frac{1}{4}S_1S_4$: $\frac{1}{4}S_2S_3$: $\frac{1}{4}S_2S_4$ (d) a = none, $b = \frac{1}{2}$, c = all

5.58. $\frac{1}{4}S_1S_2$: $\frac{1}{3}S_2S_3$: $\frac{1}{12}S_1S_3$: $\frac{1}{12}S_2S_4$: $\frac{1}{4}S_3S_4$

Chapter 6

Linkage and Chromosome Mapping

RECOMBINATION AMONG LINKED GENES

1. Linkage.

When two or more genes reside in the same chromosome, they are said to be *linked*. They may be linked together on one of the autosomes or connected together on the sex chromosome (Chapter 5). Genes on different chromosomes are distributed into gametes independently of one another (Mendel's Law of Independent Assortment). Genes on the same chromosome, however, tend to stay together during the formation of gametes. Thus the results of testcrossing dihybrid individuals will yield different results, depending upon whether the genes are linked or on different chromosomes.

Example 6.1. Genes on different chromosomes assort independently, giving a $1:1:1:1$ testcross ratio.

Parents: $AaBb$ $\times$ $aabb$

Gametes: (AB) (Ab) (aB) (ab) (ab)

F_1: $\frac{1}{4} AaBb : \frac{1}{4} Aabb : \frac{1}{4} aaBb : \frac{1}{4} aabb$

Example 6.2. Linked genes do not assort independently, but tend to stay together in the same combinations as they were in the parents. Genes to the left of the slash line (/) are on one chromosome and those to the right are on the homologous chromosome.

Parents: AB/ab $\times$ ab/ab

Gametes: (AB) (ab) (ab)

F_1: $\frac{1}{2} AB/ab : \frac{1}{2} ab/ab$

Large deviations from a $1:1:1:1$ ratio in the testcross progeny of a dihybrid could be used as evidence for linkage. Linked genes do not always stay together, however, because homologous non-sister chromatids may exchange segments of varying length with one another during meiotic prophase. Recall from Chapter 1 that homologous chromosomes pair with one another in a process called "synapsis" and that the points of genetic exchange, called "chiasmata", produce recombinant gametes through crossing over.

2. Crossing Over.

During meiosis each chromosome replicates, forming two identical sister chromatids; homologous chromosomes pair (synapse) and crossing over occurs between non-sister chromatids. This latter process involves the breakage and reunion of only two of the four strands at any given point on the chromosomes. In the diagram below, a crossover occurs in the region between the A and B loci.

Synapsis and crossing over   End of meiosis I   End of meiosis II

Notice that two of the meiotic products (*AB* and *ab*) have the genes linked in the same way as they were in the parental chromosomes. These products are produced from chromatids that were not involved in crossing over and are referred to as *non-crossover* or *parental* types. The other two meiotic products (*Ab* and *aB*) produced by crossing over have recombined the original linkage relationships of the parent into two new forms called *recombinant* or *crossover* types.

The alleles of double heterozygotes (dihybrids) at two linked loci may appear in either of two positions relative to one another. If the two dominant (or wild type) alleles are on one chromosome and the two recessives (or mutants) on the other (*AB/ab*), the linkage relationship is called *coupling phase*. When the dominant allele of one locus and the recessive allele of the other occupy the same chromosome (*Ab/aB*), the relationship is termed *repulsion phase*. Parental and recombinant gametes will be of different types, depending upon how these genes are linked in the parent.

Example 6.3. Coupling Parent: *AB/ab*

Gametes:

Parental: (*AB*) (*ab*)

Recombinant: (*Ab*) (*aB*)

Example 6.4. Repulsion Parent: *Ab/aB*

Gametes:

Non-crossover: (*Ab*) (*aB*)

Crossover: (*AB*) (*ab*)

3. Chiasma Frequency.

A pair of synapsed chromosomes (bivalent) consists of four chromatids called a *tetrad*. Every tetrad usually experiences at least one chiasma somewhere along its length. Generally speaking, the longer the chromosome the greater the number of chiasmata. Each type of chromosome within a species has a characteristic (or average) number of chiasmata. The frequency with which a chiasma occurs between any two genetic loci also has a characteristic or average probability. The further apart two genes are located on a chromosome, the greater the opportunity for a chiasma to occur between them. The closer two genes are linked, the smaller the chance for a chiasma occurring between them. These chiasmata probabilities are useful in predicting the proportions of parental and recombinant gametes expected to be formed from a given genotype. The percentage of crossover (recombinant) gametes formed by a given genotype is a direct reflection of the frequency with which a chiasma forms between the genes in question. Only when a crossover forms *between* the gene loci under consideration will recombination be detected.

Example 6.5.   Crossing over outside the A-B region fails to recombine these markers.

When a chiasma forms between two gene loci, only half of the meiotic products will be of crossover type.   Therefore chiasma frequency is twice the frequency of crossover products.

$$\text{Chiasma \%} = 2(\text{crossover \%}) \quad \text{or} \quad \text{Crossover \%} = \tfrac{1}{2}(\text{chiasma \%})$$

Example 6.6.   If a chiasma forms between the loci of genes A and B in 30% of the tetrads of an individual of genotype AB/ab, then 15% of the gametes will be recombinant (Ab or aB) and 85% will be parental (AB or ab).

Example 6.7.   Suppose progeny from the testcross $Ab/aB \times ab/ab$ were found in the proportions 40% Ab/ab, 40% aB/ab, 10% AB/ab and 10% ab/ab.   The genotypes AB/ab and ab/ab were produced from crossover gametes.   Thus 20% of all gametes formed by the dihybrid parent were crossover types.   This means that a chiasma occurs between these two loci in 40% of all tetrads.

4. Multiple Crossovers.

When two strand double crossovers occur between two genetic markers, the products, as detected through the progeny phenotypes, are only parental types.

In order to detect these double crossovers, a third gene locus (C) between the outside markers must be used.

If there is a certain probability that a crossover will form between the *A* and *C* loci and another independent probability of a crossover forming between the *C* and *B* loci, then the probability of a double crossover is the product of the two independent probabilities.

> **Example 6.8.**   If a crossover between the *A* and *C* loci occurs in 20% of the tetrads and between *C* and *B* loci in 10% of the tetrads in an individual of genotype *ACB/acb*, then 2% (0.2 × 0.1) of the gametes are expected to be of double crossover types *AcB* and *aCb*.

Odd numbers of two strand crossovers (1, 3, 5, etc.) between two gene loci produce detectable recombinations between the outer markers, but even numbers of two strand crossovers (2, 4, 6, etc.) do not.

5. Limits of Recombination.

If two gene loci are so far apart in the chromosome that the probability of a chiasma forming between them is 100%, then 50% of the gametes will be parental type (non-crossover) and 50% recombinant (crossover) type. When such dihybrid individuals are testcrossed, they are expected to produce progeny in a 1 : 1 : 1 : 1 ratio as would be expected for genes on different chromosomes. Recombination between two linked genes cannot exceed 50% even when multiple crossovers occur between them.

GENETIC MAPPING

1. Map Distance.

The places where genes reside in the chromosome (loci) are positioned in linear order analogous to beads on a string. There are two major aspects to genetic mapping: (i) the determination of the linear order with which the genetic units are arranged with respect to one another (gene order) and (ii) the determination of the relative distances between the genetic units (gene distance). The unit of distance which has the greatest utility in predicting the outcome of certain types of matings is an expression of the probability that crossing over will occur between the two genes under consideration. One unit of map distance (centimorgan) is therefore equivalent to 1% crossing over.

> **Example 6.9.**   If the genotype *Ab/aB* produces 8% each of the crossover gametes *AB* and *ab*, then the distance between *A* and *B* is estimated to be 16 map units.

> **Example 6.10.**   If the map distance between the loci *B* and *C* is 12 units, then 12% of the gametes of genotype *BC/bc* should be crossover types; i.e. 6% *Bc* and 6% *bC*.

Each chiasma produces 50% crossover products. Fifty percent crossing over is equivalent to 50 map units. If the average (mean) number of chiasmata is known for a chromosome pair, the total length of the map for that linkage group may be predicted:

$$\text{Total length} \quad = \quad \text{mean number of chiasmata} \times 50$$

2. Two-Point Testcross.

The easiest way to detect crossover gametes in a dihybrid is through the testcross progeny. Suppose we testcross dihybrid individuals in coupling phase (*AC/ac*) and find in the progeny phenotypes 37% dominant at both loci, 37% recessive at both loci, 13% dominant at the first locus and recessive at the second, and 13% dominant at the second locus and recessive at the first. Obviously the last two groups (genotypically *Ac/ac* and *aC/ac*) were produced by crossover gametes from the dihybrid parent. Thus 26% of all gametes (13 + 13) were of crossover types and the distance between the loci *A* and *C* is estimated to be 26 map units.

3. Three-Point Testcross.

Double crossovers usually do not occur between genes less than 5 map units apart. For genes further apart, it is advisable to use a third marker between the other two in order to detect any double crossovers. Suppose that we testcross trihybrid individuals of genotype *ABC/abc* and find in the progeny the following:

36% *ABC/abc*	9% *Abc/abc*	4% *ABc/abc*	1% *AbC/abc*
36% *abc/abc*	9% *aBC/abc*	4% *abC/abc*	1% *aBc/abc*

72% Parental type : 18% Single crossovers : 8% Single crossovers : 2% Double crossovers
between A and B   between B and C
(region I)   (region II)

To find the distance *A-B* we must count all crossovers (both singles and doubles) that occurred in region I = 18% + 2% = 20% or 20 map units between the loci *A* and *B*. To find the distance *B-C* we must again count all crossovers (both singles and doubles) that occurred in region II = 8% + 2% = 10% or 10 map units between the loci *B* and *C*. The *A-C* distance is therefore 30 map units when double crossovers are detected in a three point linkage experiment and 26 map units when double crossovers are undetected in the two-point linkage experiment above.

Without the middle marker (*B*), double crossovers would appear as parental types and hence we *underestimate* the true map distance (crossover percentage). In this case the 2% double crossovers would appear with the 72% parental types, making a total of 74% parental types and 26% recombinant types. Therefore for any three linked genes whose distances are known, the amount of *detectable* crossovers (recombinants) between the two outer markers *A* and *C* when the middle marker *B* is missing is: (*A-B* crossover percentage) plus (*B-C* crossover percentage) minus (2 × double crossover percentage).

Example 6.11. Given distances *A-B* = 20, *B-C* = 10, *A-C* = 30 map units, the percentage of detectable crossovers from the dihybrid testcross *AC/ac* × *ac/ac* = 0.20 + 0.10 − 2(0.20)(0.10) = 0.30 − 2(0.02) = 0.30 − 0.04 = 0.26 or 26% (13% *Ac/ac* and 13% *aC/ac*).

4. Gene Order.

The additivity of map distances allows us to place genes in their proper linear order. Three linked genes may be in any one of three different orders, depending upon which gene is in the middle. We will ignore left and right end alternatives for the present. If double crossovers do not occur, map distances may be treated as completely additive units. When we are given the distances *A-B* = 12, *B-C* = 7, *A-C* = 5, we should be able to determine the correct order.

Case 1. Let us assume that *A* is in the middle.

| B | 12 | A | | A | 5 | C |

| B | 7 | C |

The distances *B-C* are not equitable. Therefore *A* cannot be in the middle.

Case 2. Let us assume that *B* is in the middle.

| A | 12 | B | | B | 7 | C |

| A | 5 | C |

The distances *A-C* are not equitable. Therefore *B* cannot be in the middle.

Case 3.   Let us assume that C is in the middle.

A	5	C	C	7	B

A	12	B

The distances A-B are equitable. Therefore C must be in the middle. Most students should be able to perceive the proper relationships intuitively.

(a) Linkage Relationships From A Two-Point Testcross.

Parental combinations will tend to stay together in the majority of the progeny and the crossover types will always be the least frequent classes. From this information, the mode of linkage (coupling or repulsion) may be determined for the dihybrid parent.

Example 6.12.   P: Dihybrid Parent $\times$ Testcross Parent
                        Aa, Bb ab/ab
              (linkage relationships unknown)

      F_1:   42% $AaBb$ ⎫   Parental types   8% $Aabb$ ⎫   Recombinant types
                42% $aabb$ ⎭   8% $aaBb$ ⎭

The testcross parent contributes ab to each progeny. The remaining genes come from the dihybrid parent. Thus A and B must have been on one chromosome of the dihybrid parent and a and b on the other, i.e. in coupling phase (AB/ab), because these were the combinations that appeared with greatest frequency in the progeny.

Example 6.13.   P: Dihybrid Parent $\times$ Testcross Parent
                        Aa, Bb ab/ab
              (linkage relationships unknown)

      F_1:   42% $Aabb$ ⎫   Parental types   8% $AaBb$ ⎫   Recombinant types
                42% $aaBb$ ⎭   8% $aabb$ ⎭

By reasoning similar to that in Example 6.12, A and b must have been on one chromosome of the dihybrid parent and a and B on the other, i.e. in repulsion phase (Ab/aB).

(b) Linkage Relationships From A Three-Point Testcross.

In a testcross involving three linked genes, the parental types are expected to be most frequent and the double crossovers to be the least frequent. The gene order is determined by manipulating the parental combinations into the proper order for the production of double crossover types.

Example 6.14.   P: Trihybrid Parent $\times$ Testcross Parent
                        Aa, Bb, Cc abc/abc
              (linkage relationships unknown)

      F_1:   36% $Aabbcc$ 9% $aabbCc$ 4% $AabbCc$ 1% $AaBbCc$

             36% $aaBbCc$ 9% $AaBbcc$ 4% $aaBbcc$ 1% $aabbcc$

             72%   18%   8%   2%

The 72% group is composed of parental types because non-crossover gametes are always produced in the highest frequency. Obviously the only contribution the testcross parent makes to all the progeny is abc. Thus the trihybrid parent must have had A, b and c on one chromosome and a, B and C on the other. But which locus is in the middle? Again, three cases can be considered.

     Case 1.   Can we produce the least frequent double crossover types (2% of the F_1) if the B locus is in the middle?

$$\begin{array}{ccc} A & b & c \\ \diagdown\diagup & \diagdown\diagup & \\ a & B & C \end{array} \quad \times \quad abc/abc \quad = \quad ABc/abc \text{ and } abC/abc$$

These are not double crossover types and therefore the B locus is not in the **middle**.

Case 2. Can we produce the double crossover types if the C locus is in the middle? Remember to keep A, b and c on one chromosome and a, B and C on the other when switching different loci to the middle position.

$$\begin{array}{ccc} A & c & b \\ \diagdown\diagup & \diagdown\diagup & \\ a & C & B \end{array} \quad \times \quad acb/acb \quad = \quad ACb/acb \text{ and } acB/acb$$

These are not double crossover types and therefore the C locus is not in the middle.

Case 3. Can we produce the double crossover types if the A locus is in the middle?

$$\begin{array}{ccc} b & A & c \\ \diagdown\diagup & \diagdown\diagup & \\ B & a & C \end{array} \quad \times \quad bac/bac \quad = \quad bac/bac \text{ and } BAC/bac$$

These are the double crossover types and we conclude that the A locus is in the middle.

Now that we know the gene order and the parental linkage relationships, we can deduce the single crossovers. Let us designate the distance B-A as region I, and the A-C distance as region II. Single crossovers in region I:

$$\begin{array}{ccc} b & A & c \\ \diagdown\diagup & & \\ B & a & C \end{array} \quad \times \quad bac/bac \quad = \quad baC/bac \text{ and } BAc/bac$$

Single crossovers in region II:

$$\begin{array}{ccc} b & A & c \\ & \diagdown\diagup & \\ B & a & C \end{array} \quad \times \quad bac/bac \quad = \quad bAC/bac \text{ and } Bac/bac$$

5. Recombination Percentage vs. Map Distance.

In a two-point linkage experiment, the greater the unmarked distance (i.e. without segregating loci) between two genes, the greater the chance of double crossovers (and other even numbers of crossovers) occurring without detection. Therefore the most reliable estimates of the amount of crossing over will be gained from closely linked genes. Double crossovers do not occur within a distance of 10 to 12 map units in *Drosophila*. The minimum double crossover distance will vary between different species. Within this minimum distance, recombination percentage is equivalent to map distance. Outside this minimum distance, the relationship between recombination percentage and map distance becomes nonlinear as illustrated in Fig. 6-1. The true map distance will thus be underestimated by the recombination fraction, and at large distances they virtually become independent of each other.

Fig. 6-1. Relationship between map distance and recombination percentage.

6. Genetic vs. Physical Maps.

The frequency of crossing over usually varies in different segments of the chromosome, but is a highly predictable event between any two gene loci. Therefore the actual physical distances between linked genes bears no direct relationship to the map distances calculated on the basis of crossover percentages. The linear order, however, is identical in both cases.

7. Combining Map Segments.

Segments of map determined from three-point linkage experiments may be combined whenever two of the three genes are held in common.

Example 6.15. Consider three map segments.

$$(1)\quad a \overset{8}{\rule{2cm}{0.4pt}} b \overset{10}{\rule{2.5cm}{0.4pt}} c$$

$$(2)\quad c \overset{10}{\rule{2.5cm}{0.4pt}} b \overset{22}{\rule{5cm}{0.4pt}} d$$

$$(3)\quad c \overset{30}{\rule{7cm}{0.4pt}} e \overset{2}{\rule{0.5cm}{0.4pt}} d$$

Superimpose each of these segments by aligning the genes shared in common.

$$(1)\qquad\qquad\qquad a \overset{8}{\rule{2cm}{0.4pt}} b \overset{10}{\rule{2.5cm}{0.4pt}} c$$

$$(2)\quad d \overset{22}{\rule{5cm}{0.4pt}} b \overset{10}{\rule{2.5cm}{0.4pt}} c$$

$$(3)\quad d \overset{2}{\rule{0.5cm}{0.4pt}} e \overset{30}{\rule{7cm}{0.4pt}} c$$

Then combine the three segments into one map.

The a to d distance $= (d \text{ to } b) - (a \text{ to } b) = 22 - 8 = 14$.
The a to e distance $= (a \text{ to } d) - (d \text{ to } e) = 14 - 2 = 12$.

$$d \overset{2}{\rule{0.5cm}{0.4pt}} e \overset{12}{\rule{3cm}{0.4pt}} a \overset{8}{\rule{2cm}{0.4pt}} b \overset{10}{\rule{2.5cm}{0.4pt}} c$$

Additional segments of map added in this manner can produce a total linkage map over 100 map units long. However, as explained previously, the maximum recombination between any two linked genes is 50%. That is, genes very far apart on the same chromosome may behave as though they were on different chromosomes (assorting independently).

All other factors being equal, the greater the number of individuals in an experiment, the more accurate the linkage estimates should be. Therefore in averaging the distances from two or more replicate experiments, the linkage estimates may be *weighted* according to the sample size. For each experiment, multiply the sample size by the linkage estimate. Add the products and divide by the total number of individuals from all experiments.

Example 6.16. Let $n =$ number of individuals, $d =$ map distance.

Experiment	n	d	nd
1	239	12.3	2,940
2	652	11.1	7,237
3	966	12.9	12,461
	1857		22,638

$22{,}638/1857 = 12.2$ map units (weighted average)

8. Interference and Coincidence.

In most of the higher organisms, the formation of one chiasma actually reduces the probability of another chiasma forming in an immediately adjacent region of the chromosome. This reduction in chiasma formation may be thought of as being due to a physical inability of the chromatids to bend back upon themselves within certain minimum distances. The net result of this *interference* is the observation of fewer double crossover types than would be expected according to map distances. The strength of interference varies in different segments of the chromosome and is usually expressed in terms of a *coefficient of coincidence,* or the ratio between the observed and the expected double crossovers.

$$\text{Coefficient of Coincidence } = \frac{\% \text{ observed double crossovers}}{\% \text{ expected double crossovers}}$$

Coincidence is the complement of interference.

$$\text{Coincidence + Interference } = \text{ 1.0}$$

When interference is complete (1.0), no double crossovers will be observed and coincidence becomes zero. When we observe all the double crossovers expected, coincidence is unity and interference becomes zero. When interference is 30% operative, coincidence becomes 70%, etc.

> **Example 6.17.** Given the map distances $A\text{-}B = 10$ and $B\text{-}C = 20$, then $0.1 \times 0.2 = 0.02$ or 2% double crossovers are expected if there is no interference. Suppose we observe 1.6% double crossovers in a testcross experiment.
>
> $$\text{Coincidence } = \text{ 1.6/2.0 } = \text{ 0.8}$$
>
> This simply means that we observed only 80% of the double crossovers that were expected on the basis of combining independent probabilities (map distances).
>
> $$\text{Interference } = \text{ 1.0} - \text{0.8 } = \text{ 0.2}$$
>
> Thus 20% of the expected double crossovers did not form due to interference.

The percentage of double crossovers that will probably be observed can be predicted by multiplying the expected double crossovers by the coefficient of coincidence.

> **Example 6.18.** Given a segment of map, $a \quad \overset{10}{\underline{\qquad}} \quad b \quad \overset{20}{\underline{\qquad\qquad}} \quad c$, with 40% interference, we expect $0.1 \times 0.2 = 0.02$ or 2% double crossovers on the basis of combining independent probabilities. However, we will only observe 60% of those expected because of the interference. Therefore we should observe $0.02 \times 0.6 = 0.012$ or 1.2% double crossover types.

LINKAGE ESTIMATES FROM F_2 DATA

1. Sex-Linked Traits.

In organisms where the male is XY or XO, the male receives only the Y chromosome from the paternal parent (or no chromosome homologous with the X in the case of XO sex determination). The Y contains, on its differential segment, no alleles homologous to those on the X chromosome received from the maternal parent. Thus for completely sex-linked traits the parental and recombinant gametes formed by the female can be observed directly in the F_2 males, regardless of the genotype of the F_1 males.

> **Example 6.19.** Consider in *Drosophila* the recessive sex-linked bristle mutant scute (*sc*), and on the same chromosome the gene for vermilion eye color (*v*).
>
> P: $\frac{+\ +}{+\ +}$ ♀♀   × $\frac{sc\ v}{\longrightarrow}$ ♂♂   ($\longrightarrow$ = Y chromosome)
>
>   wild type females   scute, vermilion males

F_1: $\dfrac{+\ +}{sc\ v}$ ♀♀   and $\dfrac{+\ +}{\longrightarrow}$ ♂♂

        wild type females   wild type males

F_2:

♀ \ ♂	+ +	Y
Parental Gametes	+ +	+ +/+ + wild type	+ +/Y wild type
	sc v	+ +/sc v wild type	sc v/Y scute, vermilion
Crossover Gametes	+ v	+ +/+ v wild type	+ v/Y vermilion
	sc +	+ +/sc + wild type	sc +/Y scute
		Females	Males

Example 6.20. Let us consider the same two sex-linked genes as in Example 6.19, using scute parental males and vermilion parental females.

P: $\dfrac{+\ v}{+\ v}$ ♀♀   × $\dfrac{sc\ +}{\longrightarrow}$ ♂♂

        vermilion females   scute males

F_1: $\dfrac{+\ v}{sc\ +}$ ♀♀   × $\dfrac{+\ v}{\longrightarrow}$ ♂♂

        wild type females   vermilion males

F_2:

♀ \ ♂	+ v	Y
Parental Gametes	+ v	+ v/+ v vermilion	+ v/Y vermilion
	sc +	+ v/sc + wild type	sc +/Y scute
Crossover Gametes	+ +	+ v/+ + wild type	+ +/Y wild type
	sc v	+ v/sc v vermilion	sc v/Y scute, vermilion
		Females	Males

If the original parental females are double recessive (testcross parent), then both male and female progeny of the F_2 can be used to estimate the percentage of crossing over.

Example 6.21.   P: $\dfrac{sc\ v}{sc\ v}$ ♀♀   × $\dfrac{+\ +}{\longrightarrow}$ ♂♂

                scute, vermilion females   wild type males

        F_1: $\dfrac{sc\ v}{+\ +}$ ♀♀   × $\dfrac{sc\ v}{\longrightarrow}$ ♂♂

                wild type females   scute, vermilion males

F$_2$:

♀ \ ♂	sc v	Y
Parental Gametes sc v	sc v/sc v scute, vermilion	sc v/Y scute, vermilion
++	+ +/sc v wild type	+ +/Y wild type
Crossover Gametes sc +	sc +/sc v scute	sc +/Y scute
+ v	+ v/sc v vermilion	+ v/Y vermilion
	Females	Males

In organisms where the female is the heterogametic sex (ZW or ZO methods of sex determination), the F$_2$ females can be used for detection of crossing over between sex-linked genes. If the male is used as a testcross parent, both males and females of the F$_2$ can be used to estimate the strength of the linkage.

2. Autosomal Traits.

A poor alternative to the testcross method for determining linkage and estimating distances is by allowing dihybrid F$_1$ progeny to produce an F$_2$ either by random mating among the F$_1$ or, in the case of plants, by selfing the F$_1$. Such an F$_2$ which obviously does not conform to the 9 : 3 : 3 : 1 ratio expected for genes assorting independently may be considered evidence for linkage. Two methods for estimating the degree of linkage from F$_2$ data are presented below.

(a) Square Root Method.

The frequency of double recessive phenotypes in the F$_2$ may be used as an estimator of the frequency of non-crossover gametes when the F$_1$ is in coupling phase, and as an estimator of the frequency of crossover gametes when the F$_1$ is in repulsion phase.

Example 6.22. F$_1$ in coupling phase. *AB/ab*

F$_2$: The frequency of *ab* gametes = $\frac{1}{2}$ of the frequency of all non-crossover gametes. If the crossover percentage is 20%, we would expect 80% non-crossover gametes (40% *AB* and 40% *ab*). The probability of two *ab* gametes uniting to form the double recessive *ab/ab* = $(0.4)^2$ = 0.16 or 16%. Now, if we do not know the crossover percentage, but the F$_2$ data tells us that 16% are double recessive, then the percentage of non-crossover gametes = $2\sqrt{\text{freq. of double recessives}}$ = $2\sqrt{0.16}$ = 2(0.4) = 0.8 or 80%. If 80% are non-crossovers, the other 20% must be crossover types. Therefore the map distance between *A* and *B* is estimated at 20 units.

Example 6.23. F$_1$ in repulsion phase. *Ab/aB*

F$_2$: The reasoning is similar to that in Example 6.22. With 20% crossing over we expect 10% of the gametes to be *ab*. The probability of two of these gametes uniting to form the double recessive *(ab/ab)* = $(0.1)^2$ = 0.01 or 1%. Now, if we do not know the crossover percentage, but the F$_2$ data tells us that 1% are double recessives, then the percentage of crossover gametes = $2\sqrt{\text{freq. of double recessives}}$ = $2\sqrt{0.01}$ = 2(0.1) = 0.2 or 20%.

(b) Product-Ratio Method.

An estimate of the frequency of recombination from double heterozygous (dihybrid) F$_1$ parents can be ascertained from F$_2$ phenotypes *R-S-*, *R-ss*, *rrS-* and *rrss* appearing in the frequencies *a*, *b*, *c* and *d* respectively. The ratio of crossover to parental types, called the *product ratio*, is a function of recombination.

$$\text{For coupling data:} \quad \text{x} = bc/ad$$

$$\text{For repulsion data:} \quad \text{x} = ad/bc$$

The recombination fraction represented by the value of x may be read directly from a product ratio table (Table 6.1). The product-ratio method utilizes all of the F_2 data available and not just the double recessive class as in the square root method. The product-ratio method should therefore yield more accurate estimates of recombination than the square root method.

Table 6.1.   Recombination Fraction Estimated by the Product Ratio Method

Recombination Fraction	Ratio of Products		Recombination Fraction	Ratio of Products	
	ad/bc (Repulsion)	bc/ad (Coupling)		ad/bc (Repulsion)	bc/ad (Coupling)
.00	.000000	.000000	.26	.1608	.1467
.01	.000200	.000136	.27	.1758	.1616
.02	.000801	.000552	.28	.1919	.1777
.03	.001804	.001262	.29	.2089	.1948
.04	.003213	.002283	.30	.2271	.2132
.05	.005031	.003629			
.06	.007265	.005318	.31	.2465	.2328
.07	.009921	.007366	.32	.2672	.2538
.08	.01301	.009793	.33	.2892	.2763
.09	.01653	.01262	.34	.3127	.3003
.10	.02051	.01586	.35	.3377	.3259
.11	.02495	.01954	.36	.3643	.3532
.12	.02986	.02369	.37	.3927	.3823
.13	.03527	.02832	.38	.4230	.4135
.14	.04118	.03347	.39	.4553	.4467
.15	.04763	.03915	.40	.4898	.4821
.16	.05462	.04540	.41	.5266	.5199
.17	.06218	.05225	.42	.5660	.5603
.18	.07033	.05973	.43	.6081	.6034
.19	.07911	.06787	.44	.6531	.6494
.20	.08854	.07671	.45	.7013	.6985
.21	.09865	.08628	.46	.7529	.7510
.22	.1095	.09663	.47	.8082	.8071
.23	.1211	.1078	.48	.8676	.8671
.24	.1334	.1198	.49	.9314	.9313
.25	.1467	.1328	.50	1.0000	1.0000

Source: F. R. Immer and M. T. Henderson, "Linkage studies in barley," *Genetics*, **28**: 419-440, 1943.

Example 6.24.   Coupling Data.

P:	$RS/RS \quad \times \quad rs/rs$	
F_1:	RS/rs (coupling phase)	
F_2:	Phenotypes	Numbers
(a)	$R-S-$	1221
(b)	$R-ss$	219
(c)	$rrS-$	246
(d)	$rrss$	243

$$\text{x (for coupling data)} = \frac{bc}{ad} = \frac{(219)(246)}{(1221)(243)} = \frac{53,874}{296,703} = 0.1816$$

Locating the value of x in the body of the coupling column (Table 6.1), we find that 0.1816 lies between the values 0.1777 and 0.1948 which corresponds to recombination fractions of 0.28 and 0.29 respectively. Therefore, without interpolation, recombination is approximately 28%.

Example 6.25. Repulsion Data.

P: Ve/Ve $\times$ vE/vE

F$_1$: Ve/vE (repulsion phase)

	Phenotypes	Numbers
(a)	$V\text{-}E\text{-}$	36
(b)	$V\text{-}ee$	12
(c)	$vvE\text{-}$	16
(d)	$vvee$	2

$$x \text{ (for repulsion data)} = \frac{ad}{bc} = \frac{(36)(2)}{(12)(16)} = \frac{72}{192} = 0.3750$$

Locating the value of x in the body of the repulsion column, we find that 0.3750 lies between the values 0.3643 and 0.3927 which corresponds to recombination fractions of 0.36 and 0.37 respectively. Therefore recombination is approximately 36%.

USE OF GENETIC MAPS

1. Predicting Results of a Dihybrid Cross.

If the map distance between any two linked genes is known, the expectations from any type of mating may be predicted by use of the gametic checkerboard.

Example 6.26. Given genes A and B 10 map units apart and parents $AB/AB \male\male \times ab/ab \female\female$, the F$_1$ will all be heterozygous in coupling phase (AB/ab). Ten percent of the F$_1$ gametes are expected to be of crossover types (5% Ab and 5% aB). Ninety percent of the F$_1$ gametes are expected to be parental types (45% AB and 45% ab). The F$_2$ can be derived by use of the gametic checkerboard, combining independent probabilities by multiplication.

		Parental Types		Crossover Types	
		0.45 AB	0.45 ab	0.05 Ab	0.05 aB
Parental Types	0.45 AB	.2025 AB/AB	.2025 AB/ab	.0225 AB/Ab	.0225 AB/aB
	0.45 ab	.2025 ab/AB	.2025 ab/ab	.0225 ab/Ab	.0225 ab/aB
Crossover Types	0.05 Ab	.0225 Ab/AB	.0225 Ab/ab	.0025 Ab/Ab	.0025 Ab/aB
	0.05 aB	.0225 aB/AB	.0225 aB/ab	.0025 aB/Ab	.0025 aB/aB

Summary of Phenotypes: 0.7025 or $70\frac{1}{4}$% $A\text{-}B\text{-}$

0.0475 or $4\frac{3}{4}$% $A\text{-}bb$

0.0475 or $4\frac{3}{4}$% $aaB\text{-}$

0.2025 or $20\frac{1}{4}$% $aabb$

2. Predicting Results of a Trihybrid Testcross.

Map distances or crossover percentages may be treated as any other probability estimates. Given a particular kind of mating, the map distances involved, and either the coincidence or interference for this region of the chromosome, we should be able to predict the results in the offspring generation.

Example 6.27.   Parents: $AbC/aBc \times abc/abc$

                     Map: a 10 b 20 c

         Interference: 40%

Step 1. For gametes produced by the trihybrid parent determine the parental types, single crossovers in each of the two regions, and the double crossover types.

F_1:		Step 1		Steps 2 thru 5
Parental Types	AbC	35.6%		71.2%
	aBc	35.6%		
Singles in Region I	ABc	4.4%		8.8%
	abC	4.4%		
Singles in Region II	Abc	9.4%		18.8%
	aBC	9.4%		
Double Crossovers	ABC	0.6%		1.2%
	abc	0.6%		
		100.0%		

Step 2. The frequency of double crossovers expected to be observed is calculated by multiplying the two decimal equivalents of the map distances by the coefficient of coincidence.

$$0.1 \times 0.2 \times 0.6 = 0.012 \text{ or } 1.2\%$$

This percentage is expected to be equally divided (0.6% each) between the two double crossover types.

Step 3. Calculate the single crossovers in region II (between b and c) and correct it for the double crossovers which also occurred in this region:

$$20\% - 1.2\% = 18.8\%$$

equally divided into two classes = 9.4% each.

Step 4. The single crossovers in region I (between a and b) are calculated in the same manner as step 3:

$$10\% - 1.2\% = 8.8\%$$

divided equally among the two classes = 4.4% each.

Step 5. Total all the single crossovers and all the double crossovers and subtract from 100% to obtain the percentage of parental types:

$$100 - (8.8 + 18.8 + 1.2) = 71.2\%$$

to be equally divided among the two parental classes = 35.6% each.

For convenience, we need not write out the entire genotype or phenotype of the progeny because, for example, when the gamete AbC from the dihybrid parent unites with the gamete produced by the testcross parent (abc), obviously the genotype is AbC/abc. Phenotypically it will exhibit the dominant trait at the A locus, the recessive trait at the B locus and the dominant trait at the C locus. All this could be predicted directly from the gamete AbC.

An alternative method for predicting F_1 progeny types is by combining the probabilities of crossovers and/or non-crossovers in appropriate combinations. This method can be used only when there is no interference.

Example 6.28.   Parents: $ABC/abc \times abc/abc$

         Coincidence: 1.0

Map:

$$\begin{array}{c}\overset{\text{I}}{10}\qquad\qquad\overset{\text{II}}{20}\end{array}$$

$$a\text{———}b\text{————————}c$$

No. of progeny: 2000

Step 1.   Determine the parental, single crossover and double crossover progeny types expected.

F_1:		Step 1	Steps 2 thru 5
Parental Types	ABC		720
	abc		720
Singles in Region I	Abc		80
	aBC		80
Singles in Region II	ABc		180
	abC		180
Double Crossovers	AbC		20
	aBc		20
			2000

Step 2.   The number of double crossovers expected to appear in the progeny is $0.1 \times 0.2 \times 2000 = 40$, equally divided between the two double crossover types (20 each).

Step 3.   The probability of a single crossover occurring in region I is 10%. Hence there is a 90% chance that a crossover will not occur in that region. The combined probability that a crossover will not occur in region I and will occur in region II is $(0.9)(0.2) = 0.18$ and the number of region II single crossover progeny expected is $0.18(2000) = 360$, equally divided between the two classes (180 each).

Step 4.   Likewise the probability of a crossover occurring in region I and not in region II is $0.1(0.8) = 0.08$ and the number of region I single crossover progeny expected is $0.08(2000) = 160$, equally divided among the two classes (80 each).

Step 5.   The probability that a crossover will not occur in region I and region II is $0.9(0.8) = 0.72$ and the number of parental type progeny expected is $0.72(2000) = 1440$, equally divided among the two parental types (720 each).

CROSSOVER SUPPRESSION

Many extrinsic and intrinsic factors are known to contribute to the crossover rate. Among these are the effects of sex, age, temperature, proximity to the centromere or heterochromatic regions (darkly staining regions presumed to carry little genetic information), chromosomal aberrations such as inversions, and many more. Two specific cases of crossover suppression are presented in this section: (1) complete absence of crossing over in male *Drosophila* and (2) the maintenance of balanced lethal systems as permanent trans heterozygotes through the prevention of crossing over.

1. Absence of Crossing Over in Male Drosophila.

One of the unusual characteristics of *Drosophila* is the apparent absence of crossing over in males. This fact is shown clearly by the non-equivalent results of reciprocal crosses.

Example 6.29.   Testcross of heterozygous females.

Consider two genes on the third chromosome of *Drosophila*, hairy (h) and scarlet (st), approximately 20 map units apart.

P: $h +/+ st \,♀♀$ $\times$ $h\,st/h\,st \,♂♂$
              wild type females   hairy, scarlet males

F₁:

	♂ / ♀	(h st)
80% Parental Types	40% (h +)	h +/h st = 40% hairy
	40% (+ st)	+ st/h st = 40% scarlet
20% Recombinant Types	10% (h st)	h st/h st = 10% hairy and scarlet
	10% (+ +)	+ +/h st = 10% wild type

Example 6.30.   Testcross of heterozygous males (reciprocal cross of Example 6.29).

P: h st/h st ♀♀   ×   h +/+ st ♂♂
        hairy, scarlet females   wild type males

F₁:

	♂ / ♀	h st
Only Parental Types	(h +)	h +/h st = 50% hairy
	(+ st)	+ st/h st = 50% scarlet

When dihybrid males are crossed to dihybrid females (both in repulsion phase) the progeny will always appear in the ratio 2 : 1 : 1 regardless of the degree of linkage between the genes.   The double recessive class never appears.

Example 6.31. P: h +/+ st ♀♀   ×   h +/+ st ♂♂
                    wild type females   wild type males

F₁:

		50% (h +)	50% (+ st)
80% Parental Types	40% (h +)	h +/h + 20% hairy	h +/+ st 20% wild type
	40% (+ st)	+ st/h + 20% wild type	+ st/+ st 20% scarlet
20% Recombinant Types	10% (h st)	h st/h + 5% hairy	h st/+ st 5% scarlet
	10% (+ +)	+ +/h + 5% wild type	+ +/+ st 5% wild type

Summary: 50% wild type ⎤
          25% hairy   ⎬ 2 : 1 : 1
          25% scarlet   ⎦

Drosophila is not unique in this respect.   For example, crossing over is completely suppressed in female silkworms.   Other examples of complete and partial suppression of crossing over are common in genetic literature.

2. Balanced Lethal Systems.

A gene which is lethal when homozygous and linked to another lethal with the same mode of action can be maintained in permanent dihybrid condition in repulsion phase when associated with a genetic condition which prevents crossing over (see "inversions" in Chapter 8).   Balanced lethals breed true and their behavior simulates that of a homozygous genotype.   These systems are commonly used to maintain laboratory cultures of lethal, semilethal, or sterile mutants.

Example 6.32.   Two dominant genetic conditions, curly wings (Cy) and plum eye color (Pm), are linked on chromosome 2 of *Drosophila* and associated with a chromosomal inversion which prevents crossing over. Cy or Pm are lethal when homozygous.   Half the progeny from repulsion heterozygotes die, and the viable half are repulsion heterozygotes just like the parents.

P: $Cy\,Pm^+/Cy^+\,Pm$ ♀♀   × $Cy\,Pm^+/Cy^+\,Pm$ ♂♂
            curly, plum females   curly, plum males

F$_1$:

	$Cy\,Pm^+$	$Cy^+\,Pm$
$Cy\,Pm^+$	$Cy\,Pm^+/Cy\,Pm^+$ dies	$Cy\,Pm^+/Cy^+\,Pm$ curly, plum
$Cy^+\,Pm$	$Cy^+\,Pm/Cy\,Pm^+$ curly, plum	$Cy^+\,Pm/Cy^+\,Pm$ dies

Balanced lethals may be used to determine on which chromosome an unknown genetic unit resides (see Problem 6.12).   Sex-linked genes make themselves known through the non-equivalence of progeny from reciprocal matings (Chapter 5).   Without the aid of a balanced lethal system, the assignment of an autosomal gene to a particular linkage group may be made through observation of the peculiar genetic ratios obtained from abnormal individuals possessing an extra chromosome (trisomic) bearing the gene under study (Chapter 8).

TETRAD ANALYSIS IN ASCOMYCETES

Recall from Chapter 1 the life cycles of bread mold and yeast, two common ascomycetes (sac fungi).   All four of the products of a single meiotic event are housed in the ascus. In the case of yeast the ascospores representing the four chromatids of meiosis are in no special order, but in the bread mold *Neurospora* the ascospores are linearly ordered in the ascus in the same sequence as the chromatids were on the meiotic metaphase plate.   The recovery and investigation of all of the products from a single meiotic event is called *tetrad analysis*.

Each ascus of *Neurospora*, when analyzed for a segregating pair of alleles, reveals one of two linear ratios: (1) 4 : 4 ratio, attributed to *first division segregation* and (2) 2 : 2 : 2 : 2 ratio resulting from *second division segregation*.

1. First Division Segregation.

A cross between a culture with a wild type (c^+) spreading form of mycelial growth and one with a restricted form of growth called colonial (c) is diagrammed in Fig. 6-2(a) below.   If the ascospores are removed one by one from the ascus in linear order and each is grown as a separate culture, a linear ratio of 4 colonial : 4 wild type indicates that a first division segregation has occurred.   That is, during first meiotic anaphase both of the c^+ chromatids moved to one pole and both of the c chromatids moved to the other pole.   The 4 : 4 ratio indicates that *no crossing over* has occurred between the gene and its centromere. The further the gene locus is from the centromere, the greater is the opportunity for crossing over to occur in this region.   Therefore if the meiotic products of a number of asci are analyzed and most of them are found to exhibit a 4 : 4 pattern, then the locus of c must be close to the centromere.

colonial (*c*)   wild type (*c*⁺)

Fig. 6-2.   Neurospora spore patterns

2. Second Division Segregation.

Let us now investigate the results of a crossover between the centromere and the *c* locus (Fig. 6-2(*b*)).   Note that crossing over in meiotic prophase results in a *c*⁺ chromatid and a *c* chromatid being attached to the same centromere.   Hence *c*⁺ and *c* fail to separate from each other during first anaphase.   During second anaphase, sister chromatids move to opposite poles, thus affecting segregation of *c*⁺ from *c*.   The 2 : 2 : 2 : 2 linear pattern is indicative of a second division segregation ascus produced by *crossing over* between the gene and its centromere.

RECOMBINATION MAPPING WITH TETRADS

1. Ordered Tetrads.

The frequency of crossing over between the centromere and the gene in question is a reflection of its map distance from the centromere.   Thus the percentage of asci showing second division segregation is a measure of linkage intensity. It must be remembered, however, that one crossover event gives one second division ascus, but that only half of the *ascospores* in that ascus are recombinant type. Therefore to convert second division asci frequency to crossover frequency, we divide the former by two.

2. Unordered Tetrads.

The meiotic products of most ascomycetes are usually not in a linear order as in the ascus of *Neurospora*. Let us analyze unordered tetrads involving two linked genes from the cross $++ \times ab$. The fusion nucleus is diploid ($++/ab$) and immediately undergoes meiosis. If a crossover does not occur between these two loci or if a two-strand double crossover occurs between them, the resulting meiotic products will be of two kinds, equally frequent, resembling the parental combinations. Such a tetrad is referred to as a *parental ditype* (PD).

A four-strand double crossover between the two genes results in two kinds of products, neither of which are parental combinations. This tetrad is called a *nonparental ditype* (NPD), and is the rarest of the tetrad double crossovers.

A *tetratype* (TT) is produced by either a single crossover or a three-strand double crossover (of two types) between the two genes.

$\frac{1}{4}++, \frac{1}{4}+b, \frac{1}{4}a+, \frac{1}{4}ab$

Whenever the number of parental ditypes and non-parental ditypes are statistically non-equivalent, this may be considered evidence for linkage between the two genes. To estimate the amount of recombination between the two markers, we use the formula:

$$\text{Recombination Frequency} = \frac{\text{NPD} + \frac{1}{2}\text{TT}}{\text{total number of tetrads}}$$

The derivation of the above formula becomes clear when we analyze these diagrams and see that all of the products from a NPD tetrad are recombinant, but only half of the products from a TT tetrad are recombinant. Recombination frequency is not always equivalent to crossover frequency (map distance). If a third genetic marker was present midway between the loci of a and b, the three-strand double crossovers could be distinguished from the single crossovers and crossover frequency could thus be determined. Recombination frequency analysis of two widely spaced genes thereby can establish only minimum map distances between the two genes.

Solved Problems

RECOMBINATION AMONG LINKED GENES

6.1. In the adjacent human pedigree where the male parent does not appear, it is assumed that he is phenotypically normal. Both hemophilia (h) and color blindness (c) are sex-linked recessives. Insofar as possible, determine the genotypes for each individual in the pedigree.

Solution:

Let us begin with males first because, being hemizygous for sex-linked genes, the linkage relationships on their single X chromosome is obvious from their phenotype. Thus I1, I2 and III3 are all hemophilic with normal color vision and therefore must be hC/Y. Non-hemophilic, color blind males II1 and II3 must be Hc/Y. Normal males II2, II6 and III1 must possess both dominant alleles HC/Y. III2 is both hemophilic and color blind and therefore must possess both recessives hc/Y. Now let us determine the female genotypes. I3 is normal but produces sons, half of which are color blind and half normal. The X chromosome contributed by I3 to her color blind sons II1 and II3 must have been Hc; the X chromosome she contributed to her normal sons II2 and II6 must have been HC. Therefore the genotype for I3 is Hc/HC.

Legend:
□ ○   Non-hemophilic, normal vision
▨   Color blind male
▧   Hemophilic male
▦   Hemophilic and color blind male

Normal females II4, II5 and II7 each receive hC from their father (I2), but could have received either Hc or HC on the X chromosome they received from their mother (I3). II4 has a normal son (III1) to which she gives HC; therefore II4 is probably hC/HC, although it is possible for II4 to be hC/Hc and produce a HC gamete by crossing over. II5, however, could not be hC/HC and produce a son with both hemophilia and color blindness (III2); therefore II5 must be hC/Hc, in order to give the crossover gamete hc to her son.

GENETIC MAPPING

6.2. Two dominant mutants in the first linkage group of the guinea pig govern the traits pollex (Px), which is the ativistic return of thumb and little toe, and rough fur (R). When dihybrid pollex, rough pigs (with identical linkage relationships) were crossed to normal pigs, their progeny fell into four phenotypes: 79 rough, 103 normal, 95 rough, pollex and 75 pollex. (*a*) Determine the genotypes of the parents. (*b*) Calculate the amount of recombination between Px and R.

Solution:

(a) The parental gametes always appear with greatest frequency, in this case 103 normal and 95 rough, pollex. This means that the two normal genes were on one chromosome of the dihybrid parent and the two dominant mutations on the other (i.e., coupling linkage).

P: $Px\,R/px\,r$ $\times$ $px\,r/px\,r$
     pollex, rough   normal

(b) The 79 rough and 75 pollex types are recombinants, constituting 154 out of 352 individuals = 0.4375 or approximately 43.8% recombination.

6.3. A kidney-bean shaped eye is produced by a recessive gene k on the third chromosome of *Drosophila*. Orange eye color, called "cardinal" is produced by the recessive gene cd on the same chromosome. Between these two loci is a third locus with a recessive allele e producing ebony body color. Homozygous kidney, cardinal females are mated to homozygous ebony males. The trihybrid F_1 females are then testcrossed to produce the F_2. Among 4000 F_2 progeny are the following:

1761 kidney, cardinal	97 kidney
1773 ebony	89 ebony, cardinal
128 kidney, ebony	6 kidney, ebony, cardinal
138 cardinal	8 wild type

(a) Determine the linkage relationships in the parents and F_1 trihybrids.

(b) Estimate the map distances.

Solution:

(a) The parents are homozygous lines:

    $k\,e^{*}\,cd/k\,e^{+}\,cd\,♀♀$ $\times$ $k^{+}\,e\,cd^{+}/k^{+}\,e\,cd^{+}\,♂♂$
     kidney, cardinal   ebony

The F_1 is then trihybrid:

    $k\,e^{+}\,cd/k^{+}\,e\,cd^{+}$
     wild type

The linkage relationships in the trihybrid F_1 can also be determined directly from the F_2. By far the most frequent F_2 phenotypes are kidney, cardinal (1761) and ebony (1773), indicating that kidney and cardinal were on one chromosome in the F_1 and ebony on the other.

(b) Crossing over between the loci k and e produces the kidney, ebony (128) and cardinal (138) offspring. Double crossovers are the triple mutants (6) and wild type (8). Altogether there are $128 + 138 + 6 + 8 = 280$ crossovers between k and e:

$$280/4000 \;=\; 0.07 \text{ or } 7\% \text{ crossing over } = \; 7 \text{ map units}$$

Crossovers between e and cd produced the single crossover types kidney (97) and ebony, cardinal (89). Double crossovers again must be counted in this region.

$$97 + 89 + 6 + 8 \;=\; 200 \text{ crossovers between } e \text{ and } cd$$
$$200/4000 \;=\; 0.05 \text{ or } 5\% \text{ crossing over } = \; 5 \text{ map units}$$

6.4. The map distances for six genes in the second linkage group of the silkworm *Bombyx mori* are shown in the table on the right. Construct a genetic map which includes all of these genes.

	Gr	Rc	S	Y	P	oa
Gr	—	25	1	19	7	20
Rc	25	—	26	6	32	5
S	1	26	—	20	6	21
Y	19	6	20	—	26	1
P	7	32	6	26	—	27
oa	20	5	21	1	27	—

Solution:

Step 1. It makes little difference where one begins to solve this kind of problem, so we shall begin at the top. The Gr-Rc distance is 25 map units, and the Gr-S distance is 1 unit. Therefore the relationship of these three genes may be either

(a) $\underline{S^1Gr \qquad\qquad\qquad 25 \qquad\qquad\qquad Rc}$

or

(b) $\underline{Gr^1S \qquad\qquad\qquad 24 \qquad\qquad\qquad Rc}$

The table, however, tells us that the distance S-Rc is 26 units. Therefore alternative (a) must be correct, i.e., Gr is between S and Rc.

Step 2. The Gr-Y distance is 19 units. Again two alternatives are possible:

(c) $\underline{S^1Gr \qquad\qquad 19 \qquad\qquad Y \quad 6 \quad Rc}$

or

(d) $\underline{Y \qquad\qquad 18 \qquad\qquad S^1Gr \qquad 25 \qquad Rc}$

In the table we find that the distance Y-$Rc = 6$. Hence possibility (c) must be correct, i.e., Y lies between the loci of Gr and Rc.

Step 3. The distance Gr-P is 7 map units. Two alternatives for these loci are

(e) $\underline{S^1Gr \quad 7 \quad P \qquad 12 \qquad Y \quad 6 \quad Rc}$

or

(f) $\underline{P \quad 6 \quad S^1Gr \qquad 19 \qquad Y \quad 6 \quad Rc}$

The distance P-S is read from the table, and thus alternative (f) must be correct.

Step 4. There are 20 units between Gr and oa. These two genes may be in one of two possible relationships:

(g) $\underline{P \quad 6 \quad S^1Gr \qquad 19 \qquad\qquad Y^1oa \quad 5 \quad Rc}$

or

(h) $\underline{oa \quad 13 \quad P \quad 6 \quad S^1Gr \qquad 19 \qquad\qquad Y \quad 6 \quad Rc}$

The table indicates that Y and oa are 1 map unit apart. Therefore (g) is the completed map.

6.5. Three recessive genes in linkage group V of the tomato are a producing absence of anthocyanin pigment, hl producing hairless plants, and j producing jointless fruit stems (pedicels). Among 3000 progeny from a trihybrid testcross, the following phenotypes were observed:

259 hairless	268 anthocyaninless, jointless, hairless
40 jointless, hairless	941 anthocyaninless, hairless
931 jointless	32 anthocyaninless
260 normal	269 anthocyaninless, jointless

(a) How were the genes originally linked in the trihybrid parent? (b) Estimate the distance between the genes.

Solution:

(a) The most frequent phenotypes observed among the offspring are the jointless (931) and anthocyaninless, hairless (941). Hence j was on one chromosome of the trihybrid parent, a and hl on the other. The double crossover (DCO) types are the least frequent phenotypes: jointless, hairless (40) and anthocyaninless (32).

Case 1. If jointless is in the middle, we could not obtain the double crossover types as given:

P: $\dfrac{A\,j\,Hl}{a\,J\,hl}$

F$_1$: DCO $\begin{cases} A\,J\,Hl = \text{normal} \\ a\,j\,hl = \text{triple mutant} \end{cases}$

Case 2. If h was in the middle, the double crossover types could be formed. Therefore the parental genotype is as shown below:

P: $\dfrac{J\,hl\,a}{j\,Hl\,A}$

F$_1$: DCO $\begin{cases} J\,Hl\,a = \text{anthocyaninless} \\ j\,hl\,A = \text{jointless, hairless} \end{cases}$

(b) Now that the genotype of the trihybrid parent is known, we can predict the single crossover types.

P: $\dfrac{J \; hl \; a}{j \; Hl \; A}$

F_1:   Single crossovers (SCO) between j and hl (region I) yield:

$$\text{SCO(I)} \begin{cases} J \, Hl \, A & = \text{ normal } (260) \\ j \, hl \, a & = \text{ jointless, hairless, anthocyaninless } (268) \end{cases}$$

Therefore the percentage of *all* crossovers (singles and doubles) that occurred between j and hl is $260 + 268 + 32 + 40 = 600/3000 = 0.2 = 20\%$ or 20 map units.

Similarly the single crossovers between hl and a (region II) may be obtained.

P: $\dfrac{J \; hl \; a}{j \; Hl \; A}$

F_1: $\text{SCO(II)} \begin{cases} J \, hl \, A & = \text{ hairless } (259) \\ j \, Hl \, a & = \text{ jointless, anthocyaninless } (269) \end{cases}$

$259 + 269 + 32 + 40 = 600/3000 = 0.2 = 20\%$ or 20 map units

Note the similarity of numbers between the SCO(II) jointless, anthocyaninless (269) and the SCO(I) triple mutant (268). Attempts to obtain map distances by matching pairs with similar numbers could, as this case proves, lead to erroneous estimates. The single crossover types in each region must first be determined in order to avoid such errors.

6.6. The recessive mutation called "lemon" (le) produces a pale yellow body color in the parasitic wasp *Bracon hebetor*. This locus exhibits 12% recombination with a recessive eye mutation called "canteloupe" (c). Canteloupe shows 14% recombination with a recessive mutation called "long" (l), causing antennal and leg segments to elongate. Canteloupe is the locus in the middle. A homozygous lemon female is crossed with a hemizygous long male (males are haploid). The F_1 females are then testcrossed to produce the F_2. (a) Diagram the crosses and the expected F_1 and F_2 female genotypes and phenotypes. (b) Calculate the amount of wild types expected among the F_2 females.

Solution:

(a)   P: $le \, l^+/le \, l^+$ ♀   × $le^+ \, l$ ♂
                     lemon   long

F_1: $le \, l^+/le^+ \, l$ ♀♀   × $le \, l$ ♂♂
                     wild type   lemon, long

F_2:

	♀ ＼ ♂	$le \, l$
Parental Types	$le \, l^+$	$le \, l^+/le \, l$ lemon
	$le^+ \, l$	$le^+ \, l/le \, l$ long
Recombinant Types	$le \, l$	$le \, l/le \, l$ lemon, long
	$le^+ \, l^+$	$le^+ \, l^+/le \, l$ wild type

(b) Since the canteloupe locus is not segregating in this cross, double crossovers will appear as parental types. The percentage of recombination expected to be observed is $0.12 + 0.14 - 2(0.12)(0.14) = 0.2264 = 22.64\%$. Half of the recombinants are expected to be wild type: $22.64\%/2 = 11.32\%$ wild type.

6.7.   Several three-point testcrosses were made in maize utilizing the genes booster (*B*, a dominant plant color intensifier), liguleless leaf (*lg₁*), virescent seedling (*v₄*, yellowish-green), silkless (*sk*, abortive pistils), glossy seedling (*gl₂*), and tassel seed (*ts₁*, pistillate terminal inflorescence).   Using the information from the following testcrosses, map this region of the chromosome.

Testcross #1. Trihybrid parent is heterozygous for booster, liguleless, tassel seed.

Testcross Progeny

71 booster, liguleless, tassel seed   17 tassel seed
111 wild type   24 booster, liguleless
48 liguleless   6 booster
35 booster, tassel seed   3 liguleless, tassel seed

Testcross #2. Trihybrid parent is heterozygous for booster, liguleless, tassel seed.

Testcross Progeny

57 tassel seed   21 liguleless, tassel seed
57 booster, liguleless   21 booster, liguleless, tassel seed
20 wild type   8 booster, tassel seed
31 booster   7 liguleless

Testcross #3. Trihybrid parent is heterozygous for booster, liguleless, silkless.

Testcross Progeny

52 silkless   56 booster, liguleless
8 booster, silkless   13 liguleless
2 booster, liguleless, silkless   131 liguleless, silkless
148 booster

Testcross #4. Trihybrid parent is heterozygous for booster, liguleless, silkless.

Testcross Progeny

6 booster   3 liguleless, silkless
137 booster, silkless   30 silkless
291 booster, liguleless, silkless   34 booster, liguleless
142 liguleless   339 wild type

Testcross #5. Trihybrid parent is heterozygous for liguleless, virescent, glossy.

Testcross Progeny

431 wild type   128 virescent, glossy
399 liguleless, virescent, glossy   153 liguleless
256 virescent   44 glossy
310 liguleless, glossy   51 virescent, liguleless

Testcross #6. Trihybrid parent is heterozygous for booster, liguleless, virescent.

Testcross Progeny

60 wild type   18 virescent
37 liguleless, booster, virescent 23 liguleless, booster
32 virescent, booster   11 booster
34 liguleless   12 virescent, liguleless

Testcross #7. Trihybrid parent is heterozygous for virescent, liguleless, booster.

Testcross Progeny

25 booster   8 booster, virescent
11 booster, liguleless   2 liguleless, booster, virescent

Solution:

Following the procedures established in this chapter, we determine from each of the testcrosses the gene order (which gene is in the middle) and the percent crossing over in each region. Note that the results of testcrosses #1 and #2 may be combined, recognizing that the linkage relationships are different in the trihybrid parents. Likewise, the results of #3 and #4 may be combined, as well as #6 with #7. The analysis of these seven testcrosses are summarized below in tabular form.

Testcross No.	Trihybrid Parent	Parental Type Progeny	Recombinant Progeny			Total
			Region I	Region II	DCO	
1	$\dfrac{+\ +\ +}{lg_1\ B\ ts_1}$	111 71	35 48	17 24	6 3	315
2	$\dfrac{+\ +\ ts_1}{lg_1\ B\ +}$	57 57	31 21	20 21	8 7	222
		296	135	82	24	537
			25.1%	15.3%	4.5%	
3	$\dfrac{+\ B\ +}{lg_1\ +\ sk}$	148 131	52 56	8 13	0 2	410
4	$\dfrac{+\ +\ +}{lg_1\ B\ sk}$	339 291	137 142	30 34	6 3	982
		909	387	85	11	1392
			27.8%	6.1%	0.8%	
5	$\dfrac{+\ +\ +}{lg_1\ gl_2\ v_4}$	431 399	128 153	256 310	44 51	
		830	281	566	95	1772
			15.9%	31.9%	5.4%	
6	$\dfrac{+\ +\ +}{lg_1\ B\ v_4}$	60 37	32 34	18 23	11 12	227
7	$\dfrac{+\ B\ +}{lg_1\ +\ v_4}$	25 0	0 11	8 0	0 2	46
		122	77	49	25	273
			28.2%	17.9%	9.2%	

To find the map distances between lg_1 and B in the first two testcrosses, we add the double crossovers (4.5%) to the region I single crossovers (25.1%) = 29.6% or 29.6 map units. Likewise, to find the map distance between B and ts_1, we add 4.5% to the region II single crossovers (15.3%) = 19.8% or 19.8 map units. Thus this segment of map becomes

$$lg_1 \underset{}{\overset{29.6}{\rule{6cm}{0.4pt}}} B \underset{}{\overset{19.8}{\rule{4cm}{0.4pt}}} ts_1$$

Three other map segments are similarly derived from testcross data:

#3 and #4 $lg_1 \overset{28.6}{\rule{5cm}{0.4pt}} B \overset{6.9}{\rule{1.5cm}{0.4pt}} sk$

#5 $lg_1 \overset{21.3}{\rule{3cm}{0.4pt}} gl_2 \overset{37.3}{\rule{7cm}{0.4pt}} v_4$

#6 and #7 $lg_1 \overset{37.4}{\rule{6cm}{0.4pt}} B \overset{27.1}{\rule{4cm}{0.4pt}} v_4$

Now let us combine all four maps into one:

The weighted average distance lg_1-B is determined next:

Expt.	No. in Expt. x	Distance y	xy
1, 2	537	29.6	15,895.2
3, 4	1392	28.6	39,811.2
6, 7	273	37.4	10,210.2
	2202		65,916.6

$$65{,}916.6/2202 \; = \; 29.9 \text{ map units (weighted average)}$$

The sk-ts_1 distance $= (B\text{-}ts_1) - (B\text{-}sk) = 19.8 - 6.9 = 12.9$ map units.

The gl_2-B distance has two estimators:

(1) $(lg_1\text{-}B) - (lg_1\text{-}gl_2) = 29.9 - 21.3 = 8.6$

(2) $(gl_2\text{-}v_4) - (B\text{-}v_4) = 37.3 - 27.1 = 10.2$

All other factors being equal, the second estimate is likely to be less accurate because of the greater distances involved. There is no easy way to accurately average these two values. We will arbitrarily use the estimate of 8.6 map units until more definitive experimental results are obtained.

Likewise, the ts_1-v_4 distance has two estimators:

(1) $(B\text{-}v_4) - (B\text{-}ts_1) = 27.1 - 19.8 = 7.3$

(2) $(gl_2\text{-}v_4) - [(gl_2\text{-}B) + (B\text{-}ts_1)] = 37.3 - (8.6 + 19.8) = 8.9$

Again, the second estimate is likely to be less accurate because of the distances involved, and we will use 7.3 map units as our estimate of the ts_1-v_4 distance. The unified map now appears as follows:

| lg_1 | 21.3 | gl_2 | 8.6 | B | 6.9 | sk | 12.9 | ts_1 | 7.3 | v_4 |

Additional experimental data may considerably modify certain portions of this genetic map. It should always be remembered that these maps are only estimates, and as such are continually subject to refinements.

LINKAGE ESTIMATES FROM F_2 DATA

6.8. Two dominant sex-linked traits are known in the mouse (*Mus musculus*): bent (*Bn*), appearing as a short crooked tail, and tabby (*Ta*) with dark transverse stripes. Homozygous bent, tabby females are mated to normal (wild type) males. All of the F_1 offspring are mated together to produce an F_2. Inadvertently, the male-female data from the F_2 was not recorded. Among 200 F_2 offspring were found 141 bent, tabby, 47 wild type, 7 tabby and 5 bent.

(a) Estimate the amount of recombination between bent and tabby assuming that the male : female ratio is 1 : 1.

(b) Estimate the amount of recombination when the male : female ratio is variable and unreliable in this colony.

Solution:

(a) P: $Bn\,Ta/Bn\,Ta$ ♀♀ × $bn\,ta$/Y ♂♂
     bent, tabby females   normal males

   F_1: $Bn\,Ta/bn\,ta$ ♀♀ × $Bn\,Ta$/Y ♂♂
     bent, tabby females   bent, tabby males

F₂:

♀ \ ♂	Bn Ta	Y
Parental Types Bn Ta	Bn Ta/Bn Ta bent, tabby	Bn Ta/Y bent, tabby
bn ta	bn ta/Bn Ta bent, tabby	bn ta/Y wild type (47)
Recombinant Types Bn ta	Bn ta/Bn Ta bent, tabby	Bn ta/Y bent (5)
bn Ta	bn Ta/Bn Ta bent, tabby	bn Ta/Y tabby (7)

Females   Males

If we assume that the male : female ratio is 1 : 1, then out of 200 offspring, half of them or (100) should have been males. The difference $100 - (47 + 5 + 7) = 41$ estimates the probable number of bent, tabby males. The estimate of recombination from the male data $= (5 + 7)/100 = 0.12$ or 12%.

(b) If the male : female ratio is unreliable, then we might better use the 47 wild type males as an estimator of the number of bent, tabby males. The estimated total number of males $= 47 + 47 + 5 + 7 = 106$. The amount of recombination $= (5 + 7)/106 = 0.113$ or 11.3%.

6.9. White eyes (w/w females; w/Y males) in *Drosophila* can be produced by the action of a sex-linked recessive gene. White eyes can also be produced through the interaction of two other genes; the recessive sex-linked gene v for vermilion eye color, and the autosomal recessive gene bw for brown eye color (see Problem 5.5). Consider the parental cross: $bw/bw, w^+v^+/w\,v$ ♀♀ (brown-eyed females) $\times$ $bw/bw, w\,v/Y$ ♂♂ (white-eyed males), where the F₁ progeny consists of 70 brown-eyed and 130 white-eyed individuals. Estimate the distance between the sex-linked genes w and v.

Solution:

F₁:

♀ \ ♂	bw/, w v/	bw/, Y/
Parental Types bw/, w⁺v⁺/	bw/bw, w⁺v⁺/w v brown	bw/bw, w⁺v⁺/Y brown
bw/, w v/	bw/bw, w v/w v white	bw/bw, w v/Y white
Recombinant Types bw/, w⁺v/	bw/bw, w⁺v/w v white	bw/bw, w⁺v/Y white
bw/, w v⁺/	bw/bw, w v⁺/w v white	bw/bw, w v⁺/Y white

Only the genotypes of the brown offspring are known for certain. The 70 brown offspring constitute only one-half of the offspring produced by non-crossover maternal gametes. Therefore we *estimate* that 70 of the white individuals were also produced by non-crossover maternal gametes. Thus 140 out of 200 F₁ flies are estimated to be parental type offspring = 70%. The other 30% must be crossover types. The best estimate of linkage between the white and vermilion loci would be 30 map units.

6.10. Elongate tomato fruit is produced by plants homozygous for a recessive gene o, round fruit shape is produced by the dominant allele at this locus (O). A compound inflorescence is the result of another recessive gene s, simple inflorescence is produced by the dominant allele at this locus (S). A Yellow Pear variety (with elongate fruit and simple inflorescence) is crossed to a Grape Cluster variety (with round fruit and compound inflorescence). The F_1 plants are randomly crossed to produce the F_2. Among 259 F_2 are found 126 round, simple: 63 round, compound: 66 long, simple: 4 long, compound. Estimate the amount of recombination by the "square root method."

Solution:

P: oS/oS × Os/Os
         Yellow Pear Variety   Grape Cluster Variety
            (long, simple)   (round, compound)

F_1: oS/Os
            (round, simple)

F_2:

		Parental Gametes		Crossover Gametes	
		oS	Os	os	OS
Parental Gametes	oS	oS/oS long, simple	oS/Os round, simple	oS/os long, simple	oS/OS round, simple
	Os	Os/oS round, simple	Os/Os round, compound	Os/os round, compound	Os/OS round, simple
Crossover Gametes	os	os/oS long, simple	os/Os round, compound	os/os long, compound	os/OS round, simple
	OS	OS/oS round, simple	OS/Os round, simple	OS/os round, simple	OS/OS round, simple

Notice that the double recessive phenotype (long, compound) occupies only one of the 16 frames in the gametic checkerboard. This genotype is produced by the union of two identical double recessive gametes (os). If we let x = the frequency of formation of os gametes, then x^2 = frequency of occurrence of the os/os genotype (long, compound phenotype) = $4/259$ = 0.0154. Thus, $x = \sqrt{0.0154} = 0.124$. But x estimates only half of the crossover gametes. Therefore $2x$ estimates all of the crossover gametes = $2(0.124) = 0.248$ or 24.8% recombination.

USE OF GENETIC MAPS

6.11. The genes for two nervous disorders, waltzer (v) and jittery (ji) are 18 map units apart on chromosome 10 in mice. A phenotypically normal F_1 group of mice carrying these two genes in coupling phase is being maintained by a commercial firm. An order arrives for two dozen young mice each of waltzer, jittery, and waltzer plus jittery. Assuming that the average litter size is seven offspring, and including a 10% safety factor to insure the recovery of the needed number of offspring, calculate the minimum number of females that need to be bred.

Solution:

F_1: $v\,ji/++$

F_2:   If 18% are crossover types, then 82% should be parental types.

		.41 *v ji*	.41 + +	.09 *v* +	.09 + *ji*
82% **Parental** **Type**	.41 *v ji*	.1681 *v ji/v ji* waltzer and jittery	.1681 *v ji/+ +* wild type	.0369 *v ji/v +* waltzer	.0369 *v ji/+ ji* jittery
	.41 + +	.1681 *+ +/v ji* wild type	.1681 *+ +/+ +* wild type	.0369 *+ +/v +* wild type	.0369 *+ +/+ ji* wild type
18% **Crossover** **Types**	.09 *v* +	.0369 *v +/v ji* waltzer	.0369 *v +/+ +* wild type	.0081 *v +/v +* waltzer	.0081 *v +/+ ji* wild type
	.09 + *ji*	.0369 *+ ji/v ji* jittery	.0369 *+ ji/+ +* wild type	.0081 *+ ji/v +* wild type	.0081 *+ ji/+ ji* jittery

Summary: wild type   = .6681 or 66.81%

waltzer and jittery = .1681 or 16.81%

waltzer   = .0819 or 8.19%

jittery   = .0819 or 8.19%

Waltzer or jittery phenotypes are least frequent and hence are the limiting factors. If 8.19% of all the progeny are expected to be waltzers, how many offspring need to be raised to produce 24 waltzers? $.0819x = 24$, $x = 24/.0819 = 293.04$ or approximately 293 progeny. Adding the 10% safety factor, $293 + 29.3 = 322.3$ or approximately 322 progeny.

If each female has 7 per litter, how many females need to be bred? $322/7 = 46$ females.

CROSSOVER SUPPRESSION

6.12. Suppose you are given a strain of *Drosophila* exhibiting an unknown abnormal genetic trait (mutation). We mate the mutant females to males from a balanced lethal strain ($Cy\,Pm^+/Cy^+\,Pm,\,D\,Sb^+/D^+\,Sb$) where curly wings ($Cy$) and plum eye ($Pm$) are on chromosome 2 and dichaete wing (D) and stubble bristles (Sb) are on chromosome 3. Homozygosity for either curly, plum, dichaete or stubble is lethal. The trait does not appear in the F_1. The F_1 males with curly wings and stubby bristles are then backcrossed to the original mutant females. In the progeny the mutation appears in equal association with curly and stubble. *Drosophila melanogaster* has a haploid number of 4 including an X, 2, 3 and 4 chromosome. (a) Determine whether the mutation is a dominant or a recessive. (b) To which linkage group (on which chromosome) does the mutation belong?

Solution:

(a) If the mutation was a dominant (let us designate it M), then each member of the strain (pure line) would be of genotype MM. Since the trait does not appear in our balanced lethal stock, they must be homozygous recessive (M^+M^+). Crosses between these two lines would be expected to produce only heterozygous genotypes (M^+M) and would be phenotypically of the mutant type. But since the mutant type did not appear in the F_1, the mutation must be a recessive (now properly redesignated m). The dominant wild type allele may now be designated m^+.

(b) Let us assume that this is a sex-linked recessive mutation. The F_1 males receive their single X chromosome from the mutant female (mm). Therefore all males of the F_1 should exhibit the mutant trait because males would be hemizygous for all sex-linked genes (mY). Since the mutant type did not appear in the F_1, our recessive mutation could not be sex-linked.

Let us assume that our recessive mutation is on the second chromosome. The curly, stubble F_1 males carry the recessive in the heterozygous condition ($Cy\,m^+/Cy^+\,m,\,Sb/Sb^+$). Notice that we omit the designation of loci with which we are not concerned. When these carrier males are then backcrossed to the original mutant females ($Cy^+\,m/Cy^+\,m,\,Sb^+/Sb^+$), the F_2 expectations are as follows:

$Cy\ m^+/Cy^+\ m,\ Sb/Sb^+$ curly, stubble $Cy^+\ m/Cy^+\ m,\ Sb/Sb^+$ *mutant*, stubble

$Cy\ m^+/Cy^+\ m,\ Sb^+/Sb^+$ curly $Cy^+\ m/Cy^+\ m,\ Sb^+/Sb^+$ *mutant*

Note that the mutant cannot appear with curly. Therefore our recessive mutation is not on chromosome 2.

Let us then assume that our mutant gene is on the third chromosome. When F_1 carrier males (Cy/Cy^+, $Sb\ m^+/Sb^+\ m$) are backcrossed to the original mutant females (Cy^+/Cy^+, $Sb^+\ m/Sb^+\ m$), the F_2 expectations are as follows:

$Cy/Cy^+,\ Sb\ m^+/Sb^+\ m$ curly, stubble $Cy^+/Cy^+,\ Sb\ m^+/Sb^+\ m$ stubble

$Cy/Cy^+,\ Sb^+\ m/Sb^+\ m$ curly, *mutant* $Cy^+/Cy^+,\ Sb^+\ m/Sb^+\ m$ *mutant*

Note that the mutant cannot appear with stubble. Hence our recessive mutation is not on chromosome 3.

If the mutant is not sex-linked, not on 2 nor on 3, then obviously it must be on the fourth chromosome. Let us prove this. When F_1 carrier males (Cy/Cy^+, Sb/Sb^+, m^+/m) are backcrossed to the original mutant females (Cy^+/Cy^+, Sb^+/Sb^+, m/m), the F_2 expectations are as follows:

Note that our recessive mutant occurs in equal association with curly and stubble which satisfies the conditions of the problem. We conclude that this mutation is on the fourth chromosome.

RECOMBINATION MAPPING WITH TETRADS

6.13. A strain of *Neurospora* requiring methionine (m) was crossed to a wild type (m^+) strain with the results shown below. How far is this gene from its centromere?

No. of Asci	Spores			
	1 + 2	3 + 4	5 + 6	7 + 8
6	+	m	+	m
5	m	+	+	m
6	m	+	m	+
7	+	m	m	+
40	m	m	+	+
36	+	+	m	m

Solution:

Non-crossover asci are those which appear with greatest frequency = 40 + 36 = 76 out of 100 total asci. The other 24/100 of these asci are crossover types. While 24% of the asci are crossover types, only half of the spores in these asci are recombinant. Therefore the distance from the gene to the centromere is 12 map units. The origin of each of the crossover type asci is as follows:

($+m+m$ or $m++m$)   ($m++m$)   ($m+m+$ or $+m+m$)   ($+mm+$)

6.14. Two linked genes are involved in a *Neurospora* cross: $(a +) \times (+ b)$, where a is closest to the centromere. Diagram the simplest explanation to account for the following spore patterns: (a) $(a\,b)(+\,b)(a\,+)(+\,+)$, (b) $(+\,b)(a\,+)(+\,b)(a\,+)$, (c) $(a\,+)(+\,b)(a\,b)(+\,+)$.

Solution:

(a) Two kinds of double crossover events can account for this spore pattern.

(1)   This four strand double crossover can be symbolized as $(2, 3)(1, 4)$ which indicates that the first crossover involves strands 2 and 3 and the second crossover involves strands 1 and 4.

(2)   This two strand double crossover can be symbolized $(1, 4)(1, 4)$. Note that the readings of the two spore patterns are reversed left to right, but otherwise are in the same linear order. Both of these patterns are possible for either kind of crossover depending upon the first meiotic metaphase orientation of the chromosomes.

(b) A single crossover $(2, 3)$ gives the right to left pattern; a single crossover $(1, 4)$ gives the left to right pattern.

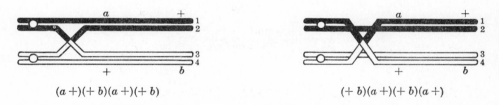

(c) A three strand double crossover $(2, 3)(2, 4)$ gives the right to left spore pattern; a three strand double $(1, 4)(2, 4)$ reverses the pattern.

6.15. Two strains of *Neurospora*, one mutant for gene a, the other mutant for gene b, are crossed. Results are shown below. Determine the linkage relationships between these two genes.

	Percent of Asci	Spores			
		$1 + 2$	$3 + 4$	$5 + 6$	$7 + 8$
(1)	79	$a +$	$a +$	$+ b$	$+ b$
(2)	14	$a +$	$+ +$	ab	$+ b$
(3)	6	$a +$	ab	$+ +$	$+ b$
(4)	1	$a +$	$+ b$	$a +$	$+ b$

Solution:

Pattern (1) represents the non-crossover types showing first division segregation (4 : 4) for both a and b. Pattern (2) shows second division segregation (2 : 2 : 2 : 2) for a, but first division segregation for b. Genes which show high frequency of second division segregation are usually further from the centromere than genes with low frequency of second division segregation. Judging by the relatively high frequency of pattern (2) these are probably single crossovers and we suspect that a is more distal from its centromere than b.

Pattern (3), indicating first division segregation for a and second division segregation for b, cannot be generated by a single crossover if a and b are linked as shown above, but requires a double crossover.

$$\Rightarrow \quad (+\,a)(b\,a)(+\,+)(b\,+)$$

Furthermore, pattern (4) could be produced from the linkage relationships as assumed above by a single crossover in region I.

$$\Rightarrow \quad (+\,a)(b\,+)(+\,a)(b\,+)$$

Double crossovers are expected to be much less frequent than single crossovers. Under the above assumptions, double crossover pattern (3) is more frequent than one of the single crossover patterns (4). This does not make sense, and thus our assumption must be wrong. The locus of a must be further from the centromere than b, but it need not be on the same side of the centromere with b. Let us place a on the other side of the centromere.

Now a single crossover in region I produces pattern (2), a single crossover in region II produces pattern (3), and a two strand double crossover (I, II) produces pattern (4). The percentage of asci are numerically acceptable under this assumption.

The distance a-centromere $= \frac{1}{2}(\text{SCO I} + \text{DCO}) = \frac{1}{2}(14 + 1) = 7.5$ map units.

The distance centromere-b $= \frac{1}{2}(\text{SCO II} + \text{DCO}) = \frac{1}{2}(6 + 1) = 3.5$ map units.

6.16. The cross $(abc) \times (+++)$ is made in an ascomycete with unordered tetrads. From the analysis of 100 asci, determine the linkage relationships between these three loci as completely as the data allow.

(1) 40 $(abc)(abc)(+++)(+++)$　　　(3) 10 $(a+c)(++c)(ab+)(+b+)$

(2) 42 $(ab+)(ab+)(++c)(++c)$　　　(4) 8 $(a++)(+++)(abc)(+bc)$

Solution:

Pattern (1) is parental ditype (PD) for *ab*, *ac* and *bc*. Pattern (2) is PD for *ab*, nonparental ditype (NPD) for *ac* and *bc*. Pattern (3) is tetratype (TT) for *ab* and *ac*, NPD for *bc*. Pattern (4) is TT for *ab* and *ac*, PD for *bc*. For each pair of markers the relative frequencies of each type of tetrad is as follows:

	PD	NPD	TT
ab	$\dfrac{40}{\underline{42}}$ $82/100 = 0.82$	0	$\dfrac{10}{\underline{8}}$ $18/100 = 0.18$
ac	$40/100 = 0.40$	$42/100 = 0.42$	$\dfrac{10}{\underline{8}}$ $18/100 = 0.18$
bc	$\dfrac{40}{\underline{8}}$ $48/100 = 0.48$	$\dfrac{42}{\underline{10}}$ $52/100 = 0.52$	0

For the *ab* pair, PD's are not equivalent with NPD's. Thus *a* and *b* must be linked. For pairs *ac* and *bc*, PD's are roughly equivalent with NPD's. Thus *c* must be assorting independently on another chromosome. The recombination frequency between *a* and *b* $= \dfrac{\text{NPD} + \frac{1}{2}\text{TT}}{\text{total number of tetrads}} = \dfrac{0 + \frac{1}{2}(18)}{100} = 9\%$ or 9 map units. Single crossovers between either *b* and its centromere or *c* and its centromere or both would produce TT's for *bc*. Since none occurred we can assume that the locus of *b* and *c* are both very near their respective centromeres.

Supplementary Problems

RECOMBINATION AMONG LINKED GENES

6.17. There is 21% crossing over between the locus of *p* and that of *c* in the rat. Suppose that 150 primary oocytes could be scored for chiasmata within this region of the chromosome. How many of these oocytes would be expected to have a chiasma between these two genes?

6.18. The longest chromosome in the sweet pea has a minimum uncorrected map length (based on known genetic markers) of 118 units. Cytological observations of the longest chromosome in meiotic cells revealed an average chiasmata frequency of 2.96 per tetrad. Calculate the maximum number of crossover units remaining in this chromosome for the mapping of new genes outside the range already known.

GENETIC MAPPING

6.19. The distances between 8 loci in the second chromosome of *Drosophila* are presented in the following table. Construct a genetic map to include these eight loci. The table is symmetrical above and below the diagonal.

	d	*dp*	*net*	*J*	*ed*	*ft*	*cl*	*ho*
d	—	18	31	10	20	19	14.5	27
dp		—	13	28	2	1	3.5	9
net			—	41	11	12	16.5	4
J				—	30	29	24.5	37
ed					—	1	5.5	7
ft						—	4.5	8
cl							—	12.5
ho								—

6.20. The recessive gene sh produces shrunken endosperm in corn kernels and its dominant allele sh^+ produces full, plump kernels. The recessive gene c produces colorless endosperm and its dominant allele c^+ produces colored endosperm. Two homozygous plants are crossed, producing an F_1 all phenotypically plump and colored. The F_1 plants are testcrossed and produce 149 shrunken, colored : 4,035 shrunken, colorless : 152 plump, colorless : 4,032 plump, colored. (a) What were the phenotypes and genotypes of the original parents? (b) How are the genes linked in the F_1? (c) Estimate the map distance between sh and c.

6.21. The presence of one of the Rh antigens on the surface of the red blood cells (Rh-positive) in man is produced by a dominant gene R, Rh-negative cells are produced by the recessive genotype rr. Oval shaped erythrocytes (elliptocytosis or ovalocytosis) are caused by a dominant gene E, its recessive allele e producing normal red blood cells. Both of these genes are linked approximately 20 map units apart on one of the autosomes. A man with elliptocytosis, whose mother had normally shaped erythrocytes and a homozygous Rh-positive genotype and whose father was Rh-negative and heterozygous for elliptocytosis, marries a normal Rh-negative woman. (a) What is the probability of their first child being Rh-negative and elliptocytotic? (b) If their first child is Rh-positive, what is the chance that it will also be elliptocytotic?

6.22. The Rh genotypes, as discussed in Problem 6.21, are given for each individual in the pedigree shown below. Solid symbols represent elliptocytotic individuals. (a) List the E locus genotypes for each individual in the pedigree. (b) List the *gametic contribution* (for both loci) of the elliptocytotic individuals (of genotype Rr) beside each of their offspring in which it can be detected. (c) How often in part (b) did R segregate with E and r with e? On the basis of random assortment, in how many of the offspring of part (b) would we expect to find R segregating with e or r with E? (e) If these genes assort independently, calculate the probability of R segregating with E and r with e in all 10 cases. (f) Is the solution to part (c) suggestive of linkage between these two loci? (g) Calculate part (e) if the siblings III1 and II2 were identical twins (developed from a single egg). (h) How are these genes probably linked in I1?

6.23. A hereditary disease called "retinitis pigmentosa" in man causes excessive pigmentation of the retina with consequent partial or complete blindness. It is caused by a dominant incompletely sex-linked gene R. Afflicted individuals appear as solid symbols in the pedigree.

(a) Determine the genotypes, insofar as possible, for each individual in the pedigree, designating the chromosome (**X** or **Y**) in which the mutant gene probably resides in the afflicted individuals. Label each individual produced by a crossover gamete "CO". (b) Only in the gametes of afflicted males does the opportunity exist for the mutant gene to crossover from the **X** to the **Y** chromosome. Beginning with afflicted males, wherein the location of the mutant gene is known for certain, determine the number of opportunities (progeny) for the detection of such crossovers. (c) How many crossovers were actually observed? (d) What percentage crossing over does this represent?

6.24. Two recessive genes in *Drosophila* (*b* and *vg*) produce black body and vestigial wings respectively. When wild type flies are testcrossed, the F_1 are all dihybrid in coupling phase. Testcrossing the F_1 produced 1930 wild type : 1888 black and vestigial : 412 black : 370 vestigial. (a) Calculate the distance between *b* and *vg*. (b) Another recessive gene *cn* lies between the loci of *b* and *vg*, producing cinnabar eye color. When wild type flies are testcrossed, the F_1 are all trihybrid. Testcrossing the F_1 produced 664 wild type : 652 black, cinnabar, vestigial : 72 black, cinnabar : 68 vestigial : 70 black : 61 cinnabar, vestigial : 4 black, vestigial : 8 cinnabar. Calculate the map distances. (c) Do the *b-vg* distances calculated in parts (a) and (b) coincide? Explain. (d) What is the coefficient of coincidence?

6.25. In corn, a dominant gene *C* produces colored aleurone; its recessive allele *c* produces colorless. Another dominant gene *Sh* produces full, plump kernels; its recessive allele *sh* produces shrunken kernels due to collapsing of the endosperm. A third dominant gene *Wx* produces normal starchy endosperm and its recessive allele *wx* produces waxy starch. A homozygous plant from a seed with colorless, plump and waxy endosperm is crossed to a homozygous plant from a seed with colored, shrunken and starchy endosperm. The F_1 is testcrossed to a colorless, shrunken, waxy strain. The progeny seed exhibits the following phenotypes: 113 colorless, shrunken, starchy : 4 colored, plump, starchy : 2,708 colorless, plump, waxy : 626 colorless, plump, starchy : 2 colorless, shrunken, waxy : 116 colored, plump, waxy : 2,538 colored, shrunken, starchy : 601 colored, shrunken, waxy. (a) Construct a genetic map for this region of the chromosome. Round all calculations to the nearest tenth of a percent. (b) Calculate the interference in this region.

6.26. A gene called "forked" (*f*) produces shortened, bent or split bristles and hairs in *Drosophila*. Another gene called "outstretched" (*od*) results in wings being carried at right angles to the body. A third gene called "garnet" (*g*) produces pinkish eye color in young flies. Wild type females heterozygous at all three loci were crossed to wild type males. The F_1 data appears below.

F_1: Females: all wild type

     Males:

        57 garnet, outstretched
      419 garnet, forked
       60 forked
        1 outstretched, forked
        2 garnet
      439 outstretched
       13 wild type
        9 outstretched, garnet, forked
      1000

(a) Which gene is in the middle? (b) What was the linkage relationship between alleles at the forked and outstretched loci in the maternal parent? (c) What was the linkage relationship between alleles at the forked and garnet loci in the maternal parent? (d) On what chromosome do these three genes reside? (e) Calculate the map distances. (f) How much interference is operative?

6.27. Maize plants homozygous for the recessive gene "variable sterile" (*va*) exhibit irregular distribution of chromosomes during meiosis. Yellowish-green seedlings are the result of another recessive gene called "virescent" (*v*). A third recessive called "glossy" (*gl*) produces shiny leaves. All three of these genes are linked. Two homozygous plants were crossed and produced an all normal F_1. When the F_1 was testcrossed, progeny phenotypes appeared as follows:

60 virescent	4 variable sterile, virescent
48 virescent, glossy	40 variable sterile
7 glossy	62 variable sterile, glossy
270 variable sterile, virescent, glossy	235 wild type

(a) What were the genotypes and phenotypes of the original parents? (b) Diagram the linkage relationships in the F_1. (c) Determine the gene order. (d) Calculate the amount of recombination observed. (e) How much interference is operative?

6.28.   Five sex-linked recessive genes of *Drosophila* (*ec*, *sc*, *v*, *cv* and *ct*) produce traits called echinus, scute, vermilion, crossveinless and cut respectively. Echinus is a mutant producing rough eyes with large facets. Scute manifests itself by the absence or reduction in the number of bristles on certain parts of the body. Vermilion is a bright orange-red eye color. Crossveinless prevents the development of supporting structures in the wings. Cut produces scalloped and pointed wings with manifold (pleiotropic) effects in other parts of the body. At the beginning of our experiments we do not know the gene order. From the results of the following three experiments, construct a genetic map for this region of the X chromosome. Whenever possible use weighted averages.

       Experiment 1. Echinus females crossed to scute, crossveinless males produced all wild type females and all echinus males in the F_1. When the F_1 females were testcrossed, the results (including both male and female progeny) were as follows:

810 echinus	89 scute
828 scute, crossveinless	62 echinus, scute
88 crossveinless	103 echinus, crossveinless

       Experiment 2. Crossveinless females crossed to echinus, cut males produced all wild type females and all crossveinless males in the F_1. When the F_1 females were testcrossed, the results (including both male and female progeny) were as follows:

2207 crossveinless	223 crossveinless, cut
2125 echinus, cut	217 echinus
273 echinus, crossveinless	5 wild type
265 cut	3 echinus, crossveinless, cut

       Experiment 3. Cut females crossed to vermilion, crossveinless males produced all wild type females and cut males in the F_1. When the F_1 females were testcrossed, the results (including both male and female progeny) were as follows:

766 vermilion, crossveinless	73 vermilion
759 cut	85 crossveinless, cut
140 vermilion, cut	2 wild type
158 crossveinless	2 vermilion, crossveinless, cut

LINKAGE ESTIMATES FROM F_2 DATA

6.29.   Two recessive sex-linked genes are known in chickens (ZO method of sex determination), rapid feathering (*sl*) and gold plumage (*s*). The dominant alleles produce slow feathering (*Sl*) and silver plumage (*S*) respectively. Females of the Silver Penciled Rock breed, with slow feathering and silver plumage, are crossed to males of the Brown Leghorn breed, with rapid feathering and gold plumage. The F_2 progeny data appear below:

	Slow, silver	Rapid, silver	Slow, gold	Rapid, gold
Males	94	40	7	127
Females	117	28	7	156

(a) Determine the F_1 genotypes and phenotypes. (b) In what linkage phase are the F_1 males? (c) Calculate the amount of recombination expected to occur between these two loci in males.

6.30.   Assume the genotype *AB/AB* is testcrossed and produces an F_2 consisting of 37 *A-B-*, 11 *A-bb*, 12 *aaB-* and 4 *aabb*. Estimate the percentage recombination between *A* and *B* by the square-root method.

6.31.   Two recessive genes in the third linkage group of corn produce crinkly leaves and dwarf plants respectively. A pure crinkly plant is pollinated by a pure dwarf plant. The F_2 progeny consist of 104 normal : 43 dwarf : 51 crinkly : 2 dwarf, crinkly. Using the square-root method, estimate the amount of recombination between these two loci.

6.32.   Colored kernel is dominant to colorless in corn; full kernel is dominant to shrunken. A pure colored, full variety is crossed to a colorless, shrunken variety. In the F_2 there was 73% colored, full : 2% colored, shrunken : 2% colorless, full : 23% colorless, shrunken. Estimate, by square-root method, the crossover percentage between these two genes.

6.33. Several sex-linked genes in chickens are known, among which are the S locus governing plumage color, the K locus controlling the rate of feather development, and the Id locus which determines whether or not melanin pigment can develop in the dermis. F_2 data is shown below, where X and Y represent dominant phenotypes and x and y represent recessive phenotypes.

	Coupling				Repulsion			
	XY	Xy	xY	xy	XY	Xy	xY	xy
S and Id	157	171	145	177	83	108	91	75
K and S	603	94	159	648	12	24	26	9

Using the product ratio method, estimate the amount of recombination between S and Id and between K and S using a weighted average of the estimates derived from coupling and repulsion data.

6.34. The results of selfing dihybrid sweet peas have been reported by several investigators. Let us consider five loci on the "D chromosome":

D_1, d_1 = tendril vs. acacia leaves
D_2, d_2 = bright vs. dull flower color
D_3, d_3 = presence vs. absence of flake modifier
D_4, d_4 = hairy vs. glabrous (smooth)
D_5, d_5 = full vs. picotee flower pattern

Ten experiments were carried through the F_2 generation with the following results (let X and Y represent dominant phenotypes and x and y represent recessive phenotypes):

		Coupling Series				Repulsion Series			
		XY	Xy	xY	xy	XY	Xy	xY	xy
(1)	D_1D_2	634	192	163	101	2263	809	882	124
(2)	D_1D_3	286	11	19	79	—	—	—	—
(3)	D_1D_4	3217	790	784	544	692	278	300	58
(4)	D_1D_5	—	—	—	—	3112	1126	1114	277
(5)	D_2D_3	992	273	265	124	296	97	88	20
(6)	D_2D_4	1580	482	421	148	1844	592	603	171
(7)	D_2D_5	1438	443	424	162	1337	465	415	128
(8)	D_3D_4	200	52	44	35	—	—	—	—
(9)	D_3D_5	373	112	103	42	—	—	—	—
(10)	D_4D_5	1076	298	283	188	2537	1003	993	131

(a) Using the product ratio method (Table 6.1) determine the crossover values for each experiment accurate to two decimal places. (b) Where the estimates are available in both coupling and repulsion, take a weighted average of the two and express all 10 crossover values to two decimal places on the same map. (c) The distance calculated from experiments (D_1D_2) plus (D_1D_3) is not the same as the distance from the experiment involving (D_2D_3). Why? (d) What is the total map distance represented by the map in part (b)? (e) To what average chiasma frequency does the answer to part (d) correspond?

6.35. The duplicate recessive genes (r_1 and r_2) produce a short, velvetlike fur called "rex". Two rex rabbits of different homozygous genotypes were mated and produced an F_1 which was then test-crossed to produce 64 rex and 6 normal testcross progeny. (a) Assuming independent assortment, how many normal and rex phenotypes would be expected among 70 progeny? (b) Do the data indicate linkage? (c) What is the genotype and the phenotype of the F_1? (d) What is the genotype and phenotype of the testcross individuals? (e) Calculate the map distance.

6.36. A dominant gene C is necessary for any pigment to be developed in rabbits. Its recessive allele c produces albino. Black pigment is produced by another dominant gene B and brown pigment by its recessive allele b. The C-locus exhibits recessive epistasis over the B-locus. Homozygous brown rabbits mated to albinos of genotype $ccBB$ produce an F_1 which is then testcrossed to produce the F_2. Among the F_2 progeny were found 17 black, 33 brown and 50 albino. (a) Assuming independent assortment, what F_2 ratio is expected? (b) Do the F_2 results approximate the expectations in part (a)? (c) What are the genotypes and phenotypes of the F_1? (d) What are the genotypes and phenotypes of the testcross individuals? (e) Estimate the map distance between these two genes.

USE OF GENETIC MAPS

6.37.   Two loci are known to be in linkage group IV of the rat. Kinky hairs in the coat and vibrissae (long nose "whiskers") are produced in response to the recessive genotype kk and a short, stubby tail is produced by the recessive genotype st/st. The dominant alleles at these loci produce normal hairs and tails, respectively. Given 30 map units between the loci of k and st, determine the expected F_1 phenotypic proportions from heterozygous parents which are (a) both in coupling phase, (b) both in repulsion phase, (c) one in coupling and the other in repulsion phase.

6.38.   In mice, the genes frizzy (fr) and albino (c) are linked on chromosome 1 at a distance of 20 map units. Dihybrid wild type females in repulsion phase are mated to dihybrid wild type males in coupling phase. Predict the offspring phenotypic expectations.

6.39.   Deep yellow hemolymph (blood) in silkworm larvae is the result of a dominant gene Y at locus 25.6 (i.e., 25.6 crossover units from the end of the chromosome). Another dominant mutation Rc, 6.2 map units from the Y locus, produces a yellowish-brown cocoon (rusty). Between these two loci is a recessive mutant oa governing mottled translucency in the larval skin, mapping at locus 26.7. Rc and oa are separated by 5.1 crossover units. An individual which is homozygous for yellow blood, mottled translucent larval skin and wild type cocoon color is crossed to an individual of genotype $Y^+ oa^+ Rc/Y^+ oa^+ Rc$ which spins a rusty cocoon. The F_1 males are then testcrossed to produce 3000 F_2 progeny. Coincidence is assumed to be 10%. (a) Predict the numbers within each phenotypic class that will appear in the F_2 (to the nearest whole numbers). (b) On the basis of probabilities, how many more F_2 progeny would need to be produced in order to recover one each of the DCO phenotypes?

6.40.   The eyes of certain mutant *Drosophila* have a rough texture due to abnormal facet structure. Three of the mutants which produce approximately the same phenotype (mimics) are sex-linked recessives: roughest (rst), rugose (rg) and roughex (rux). The loci of these genes in terms of their distances from the end of the X chromosome are 2, 11, and 15 map units respectively. (a) From testcrossing wild type females of genotype $\dfrac{rst\ +\ rux}{+\ \ rg\ \ +}$, predict the number of wild type and rough-eyed flies expected among 20,000 progeny. Assume no interference. (b) Approximately how many rough-eyed progeny flies are expected for every wild type individual? (c) If the females of part (a) were of genotype $\dfrac{rst\ rg\ rux}{+\ \ +\ \ +}$, what would be the approximate ratio of wild type : rough-eyed progeny?

6.41.   In Asiatic cotton, a pair of factors (R and r) controls the presence or absence respectively of anthocyanin pigmentation. Another gene, about ten map units away from the R-locus, controls chlorophyll production. The homozygous recessive genotype at this locus (yy) produces a yellow (chlorophyll deficient) plant which dies early in the seedling stage. The heterozygote Yy is phenotypically green and indistinguishable from the dominant homozygote YY. Obviously, testcrosses are not possible for the Y-locus. When dihybrids are crossed together, calculate the expected phenotypic proportions among the seedlings and among the mature F_1 when parents are (a) both in coupling phase, (b) both in repulsion phase, (c) one in coupling and one in repulsion position. (d) Which method (in parts (a), (b) or (c)) is expected to produce the greatest mortality?

6.42.   The "agouti" hair pattern, commonly found in many wild animals, is characterized by a small band of light pigment near the tip of the hair. In the rabbit, the agouti locus has a dominant allele A which puts the narrow band of light pigment on the hair (agouti pattern). Its recessive allele a results in non-agouti (black coat). Approximately 28 map units from the agouti locus is a gene which regulates the size of the agouti band; wide-banded agouti being produced by the recessive allele w and normal (narrow) agouti band by the dominant allele W. Midway between these two loci is a third locus controlling body size. The dominant allele at this locus (Dw) produces normal growth, but the recessive allele dw produces a dwarf which dies shortly after birth. Assume the genotype of a group of trihybrid females has the A and Dw loci in coupling, and the A and W loci in repulsion. These females are mated to a group of wide-banded agouti males of genotype $A\,dw\,w/a\,Dw\,w$. (a) Predict the phenotypic percentages (to the nearest decimal) expected in the F_1 at birth. (b) How much genetic death loss is anticipated? (c) Predict the phenotypic percentages expected in the F_1 when mature.

CROSSOVER SUPPRESSION

6.43. A black bodied *Drosophila* is produced by a recessive gene *b* and vestigial wings by another recessive gene *vg* on the same chromosome. These two loci are approximately 20 map units apart. Predict the progeny phenotypic expectations from (*a*) the mating of repulsion phase females × coupling phase males, (*b*) the reciprocal cross of part (*a*), (*c*) the mating where both parents are in repulsion phase.

6.44. Poorly developed mucous glands in the female silkworm *Bombyx mori* causes eggs to be easily separated from the papers on which they are laid. This is a dominant genetic condition; its wild type recessive allele Ng^+ produces normally "glued" eggs. Another dominant gene *C*, 14 map units from *Ng*, produces a golden-yellow color on the outside of the cocoon and nearly white inside. Its recessive wild type allele C^+ produces normally pigmented or wild type cocoon color. A pure "glueless" strain is crossed to a pure golden strain. The F_1 females are then mated to their brothers to produce the F_2. Predict the number of individuals of different phenotypes expected to be observed in a total of 500 F_2 offspring. *Hint.* Crossing over does not occur in female silkworms.

6.45. Two autosomal recessive genes, "dumpy" (*dp*, a reduction in wing size) and "net" (*net*, extra veins in the wing) are linked on chromosome 2 of *Drosophila*. Homozygous wild type females are crossed to net, dumpy males. Among 800 F_2 offspring were found: 574 wild type : 174 net, dumpy : 25 dumpy : 27 net. Estimate the map distance.

6.46. Suppose that an abnormal genetic trait (mutation) appeared suddenly in a female of a pure culture of *Drosophila melanogaster*. We mate the mutant female to a male from a balanced lethal strain (*Cy/Pm, D/Sb*, where curly (*Cy*) and plum (*Pm*) are on chromosome 2 and dichaete (*D*) and stubble (*Sb*) are on chromosome 3). About half of the F_1 progeny (both males and females) exhibit the mutant phenotype. The F_1 mutant males with curly wings and stubble bristles are then mated to unrelated virgin wild type females. In the F_2 the mutant trait never appears with stubble. Recall that this species of *Drosophila* has chromosomes **X**, 2, 3 and 4. Could the mutation be (*a*) an autosomal recessive, (*b*) a sex-linked recessive, (*c*) an autosomal dominant, (*d*) a sex-linked dominant? (*e*) In which chromosome does the mutant gene reside? (*f*) Suppose the mutant trait in the F_2 appeared in equal association with curly and stubble. In which chromosome would the mutant gene reside? (*g*) Suppose the mutant trait in the F_2 appeared only in females. In which chromosome would the mutant gene reside? (*h*) Suppose the mutant trait in the F_2 never appeared with curly. In which chromosome would the mutant gene reside?

RECOMBINATION MAPPING WITH TETRADS

6.47. Given the adjoining meiotic metaphase orientation in *Neurospora*, determine the simplest explanation to account for the following spore patterns. *Hint.* See Problem 6.14.

(*a*) $(+b)(a+)(a+)(+b)$	(*e*) $(ab)(++)(a+)(+b)$	(*i*) $(ab)(a+)(++)(+b)$
(*b*) $(a+)(+b)(+b)(a+)$	(*f*) $(a+)(++)(ab)(+b)$	(*j*) $(a+)(ab)(++)(+b)$
(*c*) $(++)(a+)(ab)(+b)$	(*g*) $(ab)(+b)(++)(a+)$	(*k*) $(a+)(ab)(+b)(++)$
(*d*) $(++)(ab)(a+)(+b)$	(*h*) $(a+)(+b)(++)(ab)$	(*l*) $(ab)(a+)(+b)(++)$

6.48. A certain strain of *Neurospora* cannot grow unless adenine is in the culture medium. Adenineless is a recessive mutation (*ad*). Another strain produces yellow conidia (*ylo*). Below are shown the results from crossing these two strains. Calculate the map distance between these two genes.

No. of Asci	Meiotic Products
106	$(ad+)(ad+)(+ylo)(+ylo)$
14	$(ad+)(ad\ ylo)(++)(+ylo)$

6.49. A strain of *Neurospora*, unable to synthesize the vitamin thiamine (*t*), is crossed to a strain unable to synthesize the amino acid arginine (*a*).

No. of Asci	Ascospores			
	Pair 1	Pair 2	Pair 3	Pair 4
37	$++$	$++$	at	at
33	$+t$	$+t$	$a+$	$a+$
34	at	at	$++$	$++$
36	$a+$	$a+$	$+t$	$+t$

What information can be gleaned from these results for use in mapping these two loci?

6.50. Two strains of *Neurospora*, one mutant for gene x and the other for gene y, were crossed with results as shown below. Determine the gene order and calculate the map distance of each gene from its centromere.

No. of Asci	Meiotic Products
52	$(+\,y)(+\,y)(x\,+)(x\,+)$
2	$(+\,+)(xy)(+\,y)(x\,+)$
17	$(x\,+)(+\,y)(x\,+)(+\,y)$
1	$(xy)(x\,+)(+\,+)(+\,y)$
6	$(+\,y)(xy)(+\,+)(x\,+)$
1	$(+\,y)(x\,+)(+\,+)(xy)$
15	$(x\,+)(+\,y)(+\,y)(x\,+)$
1	$(+\,+)(+\,y)(xy)(x\,+)$
5	$(xy)(+\,y)(+\,+)(x\,+)$

6.51. A riboflavineless strain (r) of *Neurospora* is crossed with a tryptophaneless strain (t) to give

No. of Asci	Meiotic Products	No. of Asci	Meiotic Products
129	$(r+)(r+)(+t)(+t)$	13	$(rt)(r+)(+t)(++)$
1	$(+t)(r+)(r+)(+t)$	17	$(r+)(rt)(++)(+t)$
2	$(r+)(+t)(r+)(+t)$	17	$(r+)(rt)(+t)(++)$
1	$(r+)(+t)(+t)(r+)$	2	$(r+)(++)(rt)(+t)$
15	$(rt)(r+)(++)(+t)$	1	$(rt)(++)(r+)(+t)$

Construct a map which includes these two genes.

6.52. Two of the three genes $(s, t$ or $u)$ are linked, the third assorts independently and is very tightly linked to its centromere. Analyze the unordered tetrads produced by the cross $(stu) \times (+\,+\,+)$. *Hint.* See Problem 6.16.

No. of Tetrads	Tetrads
59	$(stu)(stu)(+\,+\,+)(+\,+\,+)$
53	$(s+u)(s+u)(+\,t+)(+\,t+)$
26	$(st+)(+\,t+)(s+u)(+\,+u)$
30	$(s+\,+)(+\,+\,+)(stu)(+\,tu)$
32	$(stu)(+\,t+)(s+u)(+\,+\,+)$

Answers to Supplementary Problems

6.17. 63

6.18. 30 units

6.19. $\underset{4}{net} \quad \underset{7}{ho} \quad \underset{1}{ed} \quad \underset{1}{ft} \quad \underset{3.5}{dp} \quad \underset{14.5}{cl} \qquad \underset{10}{d} \qquad J$

6.20. (a) $sh\,c/sh\,c$ (shrunken, colorless) $\times$ $sh^+\,c^+/sh^+\,c^+$ (plump, colored)   (c) 3.6 map units
(b) $sh^+\,c^+/sh\,c$ (coupling phase)

6.21. (a) $\frac{2}{5}$ (b) $\frac{1}{5}$

6.22. (a) all open symbols = ee, all solid symbols = Ee (b) re (II1, II2, III6), RE (II5, 9, III2-5, 7)
(c) all 10 cases   (d) 5 each   (e) 1/1024   (f) yes   (g) 1/512   (h) RE/re (coupling phase)

6.23. (a) all open symbols rr; all afflicted individuals Rr; location of mutant gene is on **X** chromosome in II1, III2, 3, 5, 8, IV2, 4, 9, 10, 17, 18, 19, 21, V3, 5, 12, 16, 17, 18, 19, 20; location of mutant gene is on Y chromosome in IV7, V6, 7, 10, 13, 14, 15; crossover individuals are IV6, 7, 11, 13, 14, V5, 11, 12; location of mutant gene in I1 is unknown.   (b) 27 opportunities; they are IV1, 2, 4, 6, 7, 9-14, 21, V5-15, 19-22   (c) 8   (d) 29.63%

6.24. (a) 17 map units (b) $b\text{-}cn = 8.9$ map units; $cn\text{-}vg = 9.5$ map units (c) No. In part (a), two-point testcross cannot detect double crossovers which then appear as parental types, thus underestimating the true map distance. (d) 0.89

6.25. (a) $c \quad \overset{3.5}{\underline{\hspace{1.2cm}}} \quad sh \quad \overset{18.4}{\underline{\hspace{3.5cm}}} \quad wx$ (b) 86.1%

6.26. (a) f (b) repulsion phase (c) coupling phase (d) **X** chromosome (sex-linked) (e) $g\text{-}f = 12.0$, $f\text{-}od = 2.5$ (f) none

6.27. (a) $va^+\,gl^+\,v^+/va^+\,gl^+\,v^+$ (wild type) $\times$ $va\,gl\,v/va\,gl\,v$ (variable sterile, glossy, virescent) (b) $va^+\,gl^+\,v^+/va\,gl\,v$ (c) gl is in the middle (d) $va\text{-}gl = 13.6\%$, $gl\text{-}v = 18.3\%$ (e) 39%

6.28.

Experiment 1: $sc \quad \overset{7.6}{\underline{\hspace{1.5cm}}} \quad ec \quad \overset{9.7}{\underline{\hspace{1.5cm}}} \quad cv$

Experiment 2: $ec \quad \overset{10.3}{\underline{\hspace{1.5cm}}} \quad cv \quad \overset{8.4}{\underline{\hspace{1.2cm}}} \quad ct$

Experiment 3: $cv \quad \overset{8.2}{\underline{\hspace{1.2cm}}} \quad ct \quad \overset{15.2}{\underline{\hspace{2cm}}} \quad v$

Combined Map: $sc \quad \overset{7.6}{\underline{\hspace{1.5cm}}} \quad ec \quad \overset{10.1}{\underline{\hspace{2cm}}} \quad cv \quad \overset{8.3}{\underline{\hspace{1.5cm}}} \quad ct \quad \overset{15.2}{\underline{\hspace{2.5cm}}} \quad v$

6.29. (a) $Sl\,S/sl\,s$ (slow, silver males) $\times$ $sl\,s/\text{O}$ (rapid, gold females) (b) coupling phase (c) 14.2%

6.30. 50%

6.31. 20%

6.32. 4%

6.33.

Genes	Coupling	Repulsion	Weighted Average
S and Id	0.48	0.44	0.47
K and S	0.15	0.27	0.16

6.34. (a)

Genes	D_1D_2	D_1D_3	D_1D_4	D_1D_5	D_2D_3	D_2D_4	D_2D_5	D_3D_4	D_3D_5	D_4D_5
Coupling	0.40	0.08	0.36	—	0.42	0.48	0.47	0.35	0.46	0.38
Repulsion	0.37	—	0.40	0.45	0.45	0.48	0.48	—	—	0.35

(b)

(c) (1) Undetected double crossovers underestimate the true distance in the D_2D_3 experiment. (2) Sampling error in different experiments yields slightly different estimates of the true values. (d) 117 map units (e) 2.34 chiasmata per tetrad

6.35. (a) 52.5 rex : 17.5 normal (b) Yes (c) R_1r_2/r_1R_2, normal (d) r_1r_2/r_1r_2, rex (e) 17.14 map units

6.36. (a) 2 albino : 1 black : 1 brown (b) No (c) Cb/cB, black (d) cb/cb, albino (e) 34 map units

6.37.

Phenotype	(a)	(b)	(c)
normal	.6225	.5225	.5525
kinky hair	.1275	.2275	.1975
stub tail	.1275	.2275	.1975
kinky hair, stub tail	.1225	.0225	.0525

6.38. 54% wild type : 21% frizzy : 21% albino : 4% frizzy, albino

6.39. (a) 1408 yellow, mottled : 1408 rusty : 16 yellow, rusty : 16 mottled : 76 yellow, mottled, rusty : 76 wild type. Note: rounding errors may allow one whole individual difference in each of these phenotypic classes. (b) 32,651

6.40. (a) 19,964 rough-eyed : 36 wild type (b) approximately 1 : 555 (c) approximately 1 : 1.289

6.41. (a)(b)(c)

	Seedlings			Adult		
	(a)	(b)	(c)	(a)	(b)	(c)
normal chlorophyll, anthocyanin present	.7025	.5025	.5225	.9367	.6700	.6967
normal chlorophyll, anthocyanin absent	.0475	.2475	.2275	.0633	.3300	.3033
yellow, anthocyanin present	.0475	.2475	.2275			
yellow, anthocyanin absent	.2025	.0025	.0225			

(d) All three crosses = 25% mortality.

6.42. (a) 40.9% wide agouti : 22.0% black : 18.9% narrow agouti, dwarf : 12.1% narrow agouti : 3.1% wide agouti, dwarf : 3.0% black, dwarf (b) 25% (c) 54.5% wide agouti : 29.3% black : 16.1% narrow agouti

6.43. (a) 55% wild type : 20% black : 20% vestigial : 5% black, vestigial
(b), (c) 50% wild type : 25% black : 25% vestigial

6.44. 250 glueless, golden : 125 glueless : 125 golden

6.45. 13 map units

6.46. A dominant trait may appear suddenly in a population by mutation of a recessive wild type gene to a dominant allelic form. Such a mutant individual would be heterozygous. (a) No (b) No (c) Yes (d) No (e) Chromosome 3 (f) Chromosome 4 (g) X chromosome (sex-linked) (h) Chromosome 2

6.47. (a) (1, 3) (b) (2, 4) (c) (1, 3)(1, 3) or (1, 3)(2, 4) (d) (1, 3)(2, 3) or (1, 3)(1, 4) (e) (2, 3)(1, 3) or (1, 4)(1, 3) (f) (2, 3)(2, 3) or (1, 4)(2, 3) (g) (2, 4)(1, 3) or (2, 4)(2, 4) (h) (2, 4)(2, 3) or (2, 4)(1, 4) (i) (1, 3) (j) (2, 3) (k) (2, 4) (l) (1, 4)

6.48. 5.83 map units

6.49. Gene a is segregating independently of t, and both loci are closely linked to their respective centromeres.

6.50. Centromere to y = 18.5 map units; centromere to x = 26.5 map units

6.51.

6.52. Genes u and s are linked on the same side of the centromere with u closest to the centromere. Centromere to u = 16 units, u to s = 14 units. Gene t is on another chromosome and very closely linked to its centromere.

Chapter 7

The Binomial and Chi-Square Distributions

THE BINOMIAL EXPANSION

In $(p + q)^n$, the p and q represent the probabilities of alternative independent events, and the power n to which the binomial is raised represents the number of trials. The sum of the factors in the binomial must add to unity; thus

$$p + q = 1$$

Recall from Chapter 2 that when two independent events are occurring with the probabilities p and q, then the probability of their joint occurrence is pq. That is, the combined probability is the product of the independent events. When alternative possibilities exist for the satisfaction of the conditions of the problem, the probabilities are combined by addition.

Example 7.1. In two tosses of a coin, with $p = $ heads $= \frac{1}{2}$ and $q = $ tails $= \frac{1}{2}$, there are four possibilities.

First Toss		Second Toss		Probability
heads (p)	(and)	heads (p)	=	p^2
heads (p)	(and)	tails (q)	=	pq
tails (q)	(and)	heads (p)	=	pq
tails (q)	(and)	tails (q)	=	q^2
				1.0

which may be expressed as follows:

$$\underset{\text{(two heads)}}{p^2} \quad + \quad \underset{\text{(one head : one tail)}}{2pq} \quad + \quad \underset{\text{(two tails)}}{q^2} \quad = \quad 1.0$$

Example 7.2. Expanding the binomial $(p + q)^2$ produces the same expression as in the previous example. Thus $(p + q)^2 = p^2 + 2pq + q^2$.

Example 7.3. When a coin is tossed three times, the probabilities for any combination of heads and/or tails can be found from $(p + q)^3 = p^3 + 3p^2q + 3pq^2 + q^3$.

Let $p = $ probability of heads $= \frac{1}{2}$ and $q = $ probability of tails $= \frac{1}{2}$.

No. of Heads	No. of Tails	Term	Probability
3	0	p^3	$(\frac{1}{2})^3 = \frac{1}{8}$
2	1	$3p^2q$	$3(\frac{1}{2})^2(\frac{1}{2}) = \frac{3}{8}$
1	2	$3pq^2$	$3(\frac{1}{2})(\frac{1}{2})^2 = \frac{3}{8}$
0	3	q^3	$(\frac{1}{2})^3 = \frac{1}{8}$

The expansion of $(p + q)^3$ is found by multiplying $(p^2 + 2pq + q^2)$ by $(p + q)$. This process can be extended for higher powers, but obviously becomes increasingly laborious. A short method for expanding $(p + q)$ to any power (n) may be performed by following these rules. (1) The coefficient of the first term is one. The power of the first factor (p) is n, and that of (q) is zero (note: any factor to the zero power is unity).   (2) Thereafter in each term, multiply the coefficient by the power of p and divide by the number of that term in the expansion.   The result is the coefficient of the *next* term.   (3) Also thereafter, the power of p will decrease by one and the power of q will increase by one in each term of the expansion. (4) The fully expanded binomial will have $(n+1)$ terms.   The coefficients are symmetrical about the middle term(s) of the expansion.

Summary:

Term	Coefficient	Powers	
		p	q
1	1	n	0
2	$n(1)/1$	$n-1$	1
3	$n(n-1)/1 \cdot 2$	$n-2$	2
4	$n(n-1)(n-2)/1 \cdot 2 \cdot 3$	$n-3$	3
.	.	.	.
.	.	.	.
.	.	.	.
$n+1$	1	0	n

1. Single Terms of the Expansion.

The coefficients of the binomial expansion represent the number of ways in which the conditions of each term may be satisfied. The number of combinations (C) of n different things taken k at a time is expressed by

$$_nC_k = \frac{n!}{(n-k)!\,k!} \tag{7.1}$$

where $n!$ (called "factorial n") $= n(n-1)(n-2)\dots 1$.   ($0! = 1$ by definition.)

Example 7.4.   If $n=4$, then $n! = 4(4-1)(4-2)(4-3) = 4 \cdot 3 \cdot 2 \cdot 1 = 24$.

Example 7.5.   The number of ways to obtain two heads in three tosses of a coin is

$$_3C_2 = \frac{3!}{(3-2)!\,2!} = \frac{3 \times 2 \times 1}{(1) \times 2 \times 1} = 3$$

These three combinations are HHT, HTH, THH.

Formula (7.1) can be used for calculating the coefficients in a binomial expansion,

$$(p+q)^n = \sum_{k=0}^{n} {_nC_k}\, p^{n-k} q^k = \sum_{k=0}^{n} \frac{n!}{(n-k)!\,k!} p^{n-k} q^k \tag{7.2}$$

where $\sum_{k=0}^{n}$ means to sum what follows as k increases by one unit in each term of the expansion from zero to n.   This method is obviously much more laborious than the short method presented previously.   However, it does have utility in the calculation of one or a few specific terms of a large binomial expansion.   To represent this formula in another way, we can let p = probability of the occurrence of one event (e.g. a success) and q = probability of the occurrence of the alternative event (e.g. a failure); then the probability that in n trials a success will occur s times and a failure will occur f times is given by

$$\left(\frac{n!}{s!\,f!}\right)(p^s)(q^f) \tag{7.3}$$

2. The Multinomial Distribution.

The binomial distribution may be generalized to accommodate any number of variables. If events $e_1, e_2, \dots, e_k$ can occur with probabilities $p_1, p_2, \dots, p_k$ respectively, then the probability that $e_1, e_2, \dots, e_k$ will occur $k_1, k_2, \dots, k_n$ times respectively is

$$\frac{N!}{k_1!\,k_2!\,\dots\,k_n!} p_1^{k_1} p_2^{k_2} \dots p_n^{k_n} \tag{7.4}$$

where $k_1 + k_2 + \cdots + k_n = N$.

TESTING GENETIC RATIOS

1. Sampling Theory.

If we toss a coin, we expect that half of the time it will land heads up and half of the time tails up. This hypothesized probability is based upon an infinite number of coin tossings wherein the effects of chance deviations from 0.5 in favor of either heads or tails cancel one another. All actual experiments, however, involve finite numbers of observations and therefore some deviation from the expected numbers (sampling error) is to be anticipated. Let us assume that there is no difference between the observed results of a coin-tossing experiment and the expected results that cannot be accounted for by chance alone (*null hypothesis*). How great a deviation from the expected 50-50 ratio in a given experiment should be allowed before the null hypothesis is rejected? Conventionally, the null hypothesis in most biological experiments is rejected when the deviation is so large that it could be accounted for by chance less than 5% of the time. Such results are said to be *significant*. When the null hypothesis is rejected at the 5% level, we take one chance in twenty of discarding a valid hypothesis. It must be remembered that statistics can never render absolute proof of the hypothesis, but merely sets limits to our uncertainty. If we wish to be even more certain that the rejection of the hypothesis is warranted we could use the 1% level, often called *highly significant,* in which case the experimenter would be taking only one chance in a hundred of rejecting a valid hypothesis.

2. Sample Size.

If our coin tossing experiment is based on small numbers, we might anticipate relatively large deviations from the expected values to occur quite often by chance alone. However, as the sample size increases the deviation should become proportionately less, so that in a sample of infinite size the plus and minus chance deviations cancel each other completely to produce the 50-50 ratio.

3. Degrees of Freedom.

Assume a coin is tossed 100 times. We may arbitrarily assign any number of heads from 0 to 100 as appearing in this hypothetical experiment. However, once the number of heads is established, the remainder is tails and must add to 100. In other words, we have $n - 1$ *degrees of freedom* (df) in assigning numbers at random to the n classes within an experiment.

> **Example 7.6.** In an experiment involving three phenotypes ($n = 3$), we can fill two of the classes at random, but the number in the third class must constitute the remainder of the total number of individuals observed. Therefore we have $3 - 1 = 2$ degrees of freedom.

> **Example 7.7.** A $9 : 3 : 3 : 1$ dihybrid ratio has four phenotypes ($n = 4$). There are $4 - 1 = 3$ degrees of freedom.

The number of degrees of freedom in these kinds of problems is the number of variables (n) under consideration minus one. For most genetic problems, the degrees of freedom will be one less than the number of phenotypic classes. Obviously the more variables involved in an experiment the greater the total deviation may be by chance.

4. Chi-Square Test.

In order to evaluate a genetic hypothesis, we need a test which can convert deviations from expected values into the probability of such inequalities occurring by chance. Furthermore, this test must also take into consideration the size of the sample and the number of variables (degrees of freedom). The chi-square test (pronounced ki-; symbolized χ^2) includes all of these factors.

$$\chi^2 = \sum_{i=1}^{n} \frac{(o_i - e_i)^2}{e_i} = \frac{(o_1 - e_1)^2}{e_1} + \frac{(o_2 - e_2)^2}{e_2} + \cdots + \frac{(o_n - e_n)^2}{e_n} \qquad (7.5)$$

where $\sum_{i=1}^{n}$ means to sum what follows it as the i classes increase from 1 to n, o represents the number of observations within a class, e represents the number expected in the class according to the hypothesis under test and n is the number of classes. The value of chi-square may then be converted into the probability that the deviation is due to chance by entering Table 7.1 at the appropriate number of degrees of freedom.

Table 7.1.   Chi-Square Distribution

Degrees of Freedom	Probability										
	0.95	0.90	0.80	0.70	0.50	0.30	0.20	0.10	0.05	0.01	0.001
1	0.004	0.02	0.06	0.15	0.46	1.07	1.64	2.71	3.84	6.64	10.83
2	0.10	0.21	0.45	0.71	1.39	2.41	3.22	4.60	5.99	9.21	13.82
3	0.35	0.58	1.01	1.42	2.37	3.66	4.64	6.25	7.82	11.34	16.27
4	0.71	1.06	1.65	2.20	3.36	4.88	5.99	7.78	9.49	13.28	18.47
5	1.14	1.61	2.34	3.00	4.35	6.06	7.29	9.24	11.07	15.09	20.52
6	1.63	2.20	3.07	3.83	5.35	7.23	8.56	10.64	12.59	16.81	22.46
7	2.17	2.83	3.82	4.67	6.35	8.38	9.80	12.02	14.07	18.48	24.32
8	2.73	3.49	4.59	5.53	7.34	9.52	11.03	13.36	15.51	20.09	26.12
9	3.32	4.17	5.38	6.39	8.34	10.66	12.24	14.68	16.92	21.67	27.88
10	3.94	4.86	6.18	7.27	9.34	11.78	13.44	15.99	18.31	23.21	29.59
	Nonsignificant								Significant		

Source: R. A. Fisher and F. Yates, *Statistical Tables for Biological, Agricultural and Medical Research* (6th edition), Table IV, Oliver & Boyd, Ltd., Edinburgh, by permission of the authors and publishers.

An alternative method for computing chi-square in problems involving *only two phenotypes* will give the same result as the conventional method and often makes computation easier,

$$\chi^2 = \frac{(a - rb)^2}{r(a + b)} \qquad (7.6)$$

where a and b are the numbers in the two phenotypic classes and r is the expected ratio of a to b.

(a) *Chi-Square Limitations.*

The chi-square test as used for analyzing the results of genetic experiments has two important limitations. (1) It must be used only on the numerical data itself, never on percentages or ratios derived from the data. (2) It cannot properly be used for experiments wherein the expected frequency within any phenotypic class is less than 5.

(b) *Correction For Small Samples.*

The formula from which the chi-square table is derived is based upon a continuous distribution, namely that of the "normal" curve (see Chapter 11). Such a distribution might be expected when we plot the heights of a group of people. The most frequent class would be the average height and successively fewer people would be in the taller or shorter phenotypes. All sizes are possible from the shortest to the tallest, i.e. heights form a *continuous distribution*. However, the kind of genetic problems in the previous chapters of this book involve separate or *discrete phenotypic classes* such as blue eyes vs. brown eyes. A correction should therefore be applied in the calculation of chi-square to correct for this lack of continuity. The "Yates' Correction for Continuity" is applied as follows:

$$\chi^2 \text{ (corrected)} = \sum_{i=1}^{n} \frac{[|o_i - e_i| - 0.5]^2}{e_i} = \frac{[|o_1 - e_1| - 0.5]^2}{e_1} + \frac{[|o_2 - e_2| - 0.5]^2}{e_2}$$
$$+ \cdots + \frac{[|o_n - e_n| - 0.5]^2}{e_n} \qquad (7.7)$$

This correction usually makes little difference in the chi-square of most problems, but may become an important factor near the critical values. Yates' correction should be routinely applied whenever only one degree of freedom exists, or in small samples where each expected frequency is between 5 and 10. If the corrected and uncorrected methods each lead to the same conclusion, there is no difficulty. However, if these methods do not lead to the same conclusion, then either more data needs to be collected or a more sophisticated statistical test should be employed. Most genetic texts make no mention of this correction. Therefore problems in this book requiring the application of Yates' correction will be limited to those in the section entitled "Correction for Small Samples" in both the Solved and Supplementary Problems.

Solved Problems

THE BINOMIAL EXPANSION

7.1. Expand the binomial $(p + q)^5$.

Solution:

1st term:	$1p^5q^0$;	coefficient of 2nd term $= (5 \cdot 1)/1$
2nd term:	$5p^4q^1$;	coefficient of 3rd term $= (4 \cdot 5)/2$
3rd term:	$10p^3q^2$;	coefficient of 4th term $= (3 \cdot 10)/3$
4th term:	$10p^2q^3$;	coefficient of 5th term $= (2 \cdot 10)/4$
5th term:	$5p^1q^4$;	coefficient of 6th term $= (1 \cdot 5)/5$
6th term:	$1p^0q^5$	

Summary: $(p + q)^5 = p^5 + 5p^4q + 10p^3q^2 + 10p^2q^3 + 5pq^4 + q^5$

7.2. Expand $(p + q)^2$ by formula (7.2).

Solution:

$$(p + q)^n = \sum_{k=0}^{n} \frac{n!}{(n-k)!\,k!} p^{n-k} q^k$$

$$(p + q)^2 = \frac{2!}{(2-0)!\,0!} p^{2-0} q^0 + \frac{2!}{(2-1)!\,1!} p^{2-1} q^1 + \frac{2!}{(2-2)!\,2!} p^{2-2} q^2$$

$$= p^2 + 2pq + q^2$$

Note that $0! = 1$, and $x^0 = 1$ where x is any number.

7.3. Find the middle term of the expansion $(p + q)^{10}$ by application of formula (7.2).

Solution:

The middle term of the expansion $(p + q)^{10}$ is the 6th term since there are $(n + 1)$ terms in the expansion. The power of q starts at zero in the first term and increases by one in each successive term so that the sixth term would have q^5, and so $k = 5$. Then the 6th term is

$$\frac{n!}{(n-k)!\,k!} p^{n-k} q^k = \frac{10 \cdot 9 \cdot 8 \cdot 7 \cdot 6 \cdot 5!}{(10-5)!\,5!} p^{10-5} q^5 = \frac{10 \cdot 9 \cdot 8 \cdot 7 \cdot 6}{5 \cdot 4 \cdot 3 \cdot 2 \cdot 1} p^5 q^5 = 252 p^5 q^5$$

7.4. A multiple allelic series is known with seven alleles.   How many kinds of matings are possible?

Solution:

$$\begin{array}{l}\text{No. of genotypes} \\ \text{possible}\end{array} = \begin{array}{l}\text{No. of different allelic} \\ \text{combinations (heterozygotes)}\end{array} + \begin{array}{l}\text{No. of genotypes with two} \\ \text{of the same alleles (homozygotes)}\end{array}$$

$$= \frac{n!}{(n-k)!\,k!} + n = \frac{7!}{5!\,2!} + 7 = \frac{7 \cdot 6 \cdot 5!}{2 \cdot 5!} + 7$$

$$= 21 + 7 = 28 \text{ genotypes}$$

$$\begin{array}{l}\text{No. of different} \\ \text{matings}\end{array} = \begin{array}{l}\text{No. of matings between} \\ \text{unlike genotypes}\end{array} + \begin{array}{l}\text{No. of matings between} \\ \text{identical genotypes}\end{array}$$

$$= \frac{28!}{26!\,2!} + 28 = \frac{28 \cdot 27 \cdot 26!}{2 \cdot 26!} + 28 = 406$$

7.5. Determine the probability of obtaining 6 heads and 3 tails in 9 tosses of a coin by applying formula (*7.3*).

Solution:

In tossing a coin, we may consider heads to be a success (s) and tails a failure (f). The probability of obtaining 6 successes and 3 failures in 9 trials is

$$\frac{n!}{s!\,f!}\,p^s q^f = \frac{9!}{6!\,3!}\,p^6 q^3 = \frac{9 \cdot 8 \cdot 7 \cdot 6!}{1 \cdot 2 \cdot 3 \cdot 6!}\,p^6 q^3 = 84 p^6 q^3$$

If the probability of obtaining a head (p) is equal to the probability of obtaining a tail (q) $= \frac{1}{2}$, then $84 p^6 q^3 = 84(\frac{1}{2})^9 = 84/512 = 21/128$.

7.6. The M-N blood types of humans are under the genetic control of a pair of codominant alleles as explained in Example 2.9, page 24. In families of size six where both parents are blood type MN, what is the chance of finding 3 children of type M, 2 of type MN, and 1 N?

Solution:

P: $L^M L^N \ \times \ L^M L^N$

F_1: $\frac{1}{4} L^M L^M = \text{type M}$

$\frac{1}{2} L^M L^N = \text{type MN}$

$\frac{1}{4} L^N L^N = \text{type N}$

Let $p_1 =$ probability of child being type M $= \frac{1}{4}$
$p_2 =$ probability of child being type MN $= \frac{1}{2}$
$p_3 =$ probability of child being type N $= \frac{1}{4}$

Let $k_1 =$ number of children of type M required $= 3$
$k_2 =$ number of children of type MN required $= 2$
$k_3 =$ number of children of type N required $= 1$

$$N = \sum k_i = 6$$

$$(p_1 + p_2 + p_3)^N = \frac{N!}{k_1!\,k_2!\,k_3!}\,p_1^{k_1} p_2^{k_2} p_3^{k_3} \qquad \text{Formula (7.4)}$$

$$(p_1 + p_2 + p_3)^6 = \frac{6!}{3!\,2!\,1!}(\tfrac{1}{4})^3(\tfrac{1}{2})^2(\tfrac{1}{4}) = \frac{6 \cdot 5 \cdot 4 \cdot 3!}{2 \cdot 3!}(\tfrac{1}{4})^4(\tfrac{1}{2})^2 = \frac{15}{256}$$

CHI-SQUARE TEST

7.7. (*a*) A coin is tossed 10 times and lands heads up 6 times and tails up 4 times. Are these results consistent with the expected 50-50 ratio? (*b*) If the coin is tossed 100 times with the same relative magnitude of deviation from the expected ratio, is the hypothesis still acceptable? (*c*) What conclusion can be drawn from the results of parts (*a*) and (*b*)?

Solution:

(a)

Phenotypic Classes	Observed (o)	Expected (e)	Deviations (o − e)	(o − e)²	(o − e)²/e
Heads	6	$\frac{1}{2}(10) = 5$	1	1	1/5 = 0.2
Tails	4	$\frac{1}{2}(10) = 5$	−1	1	1/5 = 0.2
	10	10	0		$\chi^2 = 0.4$

Two mathematical check points are always present in the chi-square calculations. (1) The total of the expected column must equal the total observations. (2) The sum of the deviations should equal zero. The squaring of negative deviations converts all values to a positive scale. The number of degrees of freedom is the number of phenotypes minus one $(2 - 1 = 1)$. We enter Table 7.1 on the first line (df = 1) and find the computed value of 0.4 lying in the body of the table between the values 0.15 and 0.46 corresponding to the probabilities 0.7 and 0.5 shown at the top of the respective columns. This implies that the magnitude of the deviation in our experimental results could be anticipated by chance alone in more than 50% but less than 70% of an infinite number of experiments of comparable size. This range of values is far above the critical probability value of 0.05 or 5%. Therefore we accept the null hypothesis and conclude that our coin is conforming to the expected probabilities of heads = $\frac{1}{2}$ and tails = $\frac{1}{2}$.

(b) In (a), heads appeared in 60% and tails in 40% of the tosses. The same relative magnitude of deviations will now be considered in a sample of size 100. In problems such as this, where expected values are equivalent in all the phenotypic classes, chi-square may be calculated more rapidly by adding the squared deviations and making a single division by the expected number.

Phenotypes	o	e	(o − e)	(o − e)²
Heads	60	$\frac{1}{2}(100) = 50$	10	100
Tails	40	$\frac{1}{2}(100) = 50$	−10	100
	100	100	0	$\chi^2 = 200/50 = 4.0$

With df = 1, this χ^2 value lies between 6.64 and 3.84 corresponding to the probabilities 0.01 and 0.05 respectively. This means that a deviation as large as or larger than the one observed in this experiment is to be anticipated by chance alone in less than 5% of an infinite number of trials of similar size. This is in the "critical region" and we are therefore obliged to reject the null hypothesis and conclude that our coin is not conforming to the expected 50-50 ratio. Either of two explanations may be involved: (1) this is not a normal well-balanced coin or (2) our experiment is among the one in twenty (5%) expected to have a large deviation produced by chance alone.

(c) The results of parts (a) and (b) demonstrate the fact that larger samples provide a more critical test of a hypothesis than small samples. Proportionately larger deviations have a greater probability of occurring by chance in small samples than in large samples.

7.8. In the garden pea, yellow cotyledon color is dominant to green, and inflated pod shape is dominant to the constricted form. When both of these traits were considered jointly in self-fertilized dihybrids, the progeny appeared in the following numbers: 193 green, inflated: 184 yellow, constricted: 556 yellow, inflated: 61 green, constricted. Test the data for independent assortment.

Solution:

P: $Gg\,Cc$ × $Gg\,Cc$
         yellow, inflated   yellow inflated

F_1:   (expectations) $\frac{9}{16}$ $G\text{-}\ C\text{-}$ yellow, inflated
                          $\frac{3}{16}$ $G\text{-}\ cc$ yellow, constricted
                          $\frac{3}{16}$ $gg\ C\text{-}$ green, inflated
                          $\frac{1}{16}$ $gg\ cc$ green, constricted

Phenotypes	Observed	Expected	Deviation d	d^2	d^2/e
yellow, inflated	556	$\frac{9}{16}(994) = 559.1$	-3.1	9.61	0.017
yellow, constricted	184	$\frac{3}{16}(994) = 186.4$	-2.4	5.76	0.031
green, inflated	193	$\frac{3}{16}(994) = 186.4$	6.6	43.56	0.234
green, constricted	61	$\frac{1}{16}(994) = 62.1$	-1.1	1.21	0.019
	994	994.0	0		$\chi^2 = 0.301$

$$df = 4 - 1 = 3, \quad P > 0.95$$

This is not a significant chi-square value, and thus we accept the null-hypothesis, i.e. the magnitude of the deviation $(o - e)$ is to be expected by chance alone in greater than 95% of an infinite number of experiments of comparable size. This is far above the critical value of 5% necessary for acceptance of the hypothesis. We may therefore accept the data as being in conformity with a $9:3:3:1$ ratio, indicating that the gene for cotyledon color assorts independently of the gene for pod form.

7.9. Pure red fleshed tomatoes crossed with yellow fleshed tomatoes produced an all red F_1. Among 400 F_2 plants, 90 were yellow. It is hypothesized that a single pair of alleles is involved such that $Y- = $ red and $yy = $ yellow. Test this hypothesis by use of formula (7.6).

Solution:

P: $\quad\quad\quad YY$ (red) $\times$ yy (yellow)

F_1: $\quad\quad\quad\quad\quad Yy$ (red)

F_2: $\quad$ (expectations) $\frac{3}{4} Y-$ (red)

$\quad\quad\quad\quad\quad\quad\quad\quad \frac{1}{4} yy$ (yellow)

Let $a = $ number of yellow fleshed fruits $= 90$, $b = $ number of red fleshed fruits $= 400 - 90 = 310$, $r = $ expected ratio of a to $b = \frac{1}{3}$. Then

$$\chi^2 = \frac{(a - rb)^2}{r(a+b)} = \frac{[90 - \frac{1}{3}(310)]^2}{\frac{1}{3}(90+310)} = 1.33$$

$$df = 1, \quad P = 0.2\text{-}0.3$$

This is not a significant value and hence we may accept the hypothesis.

Some work can be saved in this method by always letting the larger number $= a$. Let $a = $ number of red fleshed fruits $= 310$, $b = $ number of yellow fleshed fruits $= 90$, $r = $ expected ratio of a to $b = 3$. Then

$$\chi^2 = \frac{[310 - 3(90)]^2}{3(400)} = \frac{(40)^2}{1200} = 1.33$$

7.10. A total of 160 families with four children were surveyed with the following results:

Girls	4	3	2	1	0
Boys	0	1	2	3	4
Families	7	50	55	32	16

Is the family distribution consistent with the hypothesis of equal numbers of boys and girls?

Solution:

Let $a = $ probability of a girl $= \frac{1}{2}$, $b = $ probability of a boy $= \frac{1}{2}$.

$$(a+b)^4 \quad = \quad a^4 \quad + \quad 4a^3b \quad + \quad 6a^2b^2 \quad + \quad 4ab^3 \quad + \quad b^4$$

4 girls	3 girls	2 girls	1 girl	0 girls
0 boys	1 boy	2 boys	3 boys	4 boys

$$= \quad (\tfrac{1}{2})^4 \quad + \quad 4(\tfrac{1}{2})^3(\tfrac{1}{2}) \quad + \quad 6(\tfrac{1}{2})^2(\tfrac{1}{2})^2 \quad + \quad 4(\tfrac{1}{2})(\tfrac{1}{2})^3 \quad + \quad (\tfrac{1}{2})^4$$

$$= \quad 1/16 \quad + \quad 4/16 \quad + \quad 6/16 \quad + \quad 4/16 \quad + \quad 1/16$$

Expected number with 4 girls and 0 boys $= \tfrac{1}{16}(160) = 10$

3 girls and 1 boy $= \tfrac{4}{16}(160) = 40$

2 girls and 2 boys $= \tfrac{6}{16}(160) = 60$

1 girl and 3 boys $= \tfrac{4}{16}(160) = 40$

0 girls and 4 boys $= \tfrac{1}{16}(160) = 10$.   Then

$$\chi^2 = \frac{(7-10)^2}{10} + \frac{(50-40)^2}{40} + \frac{(55-60)^2}{60} + \frac{(32-40)^2}{40} + \frac{(16-10)^2}{10} = 9.02$$

$$df = 5-1 = 4, \quad P = 0.05\text{-}0.10$$

This value is close to, but less than, the critical value 9.49. We may therefore accept the hypothesis, but the test would be more definitive if it could be run on a larger sample. It is a well-known fact that a greater mortality occurs in males than in females and therefore an attempt should be made to ascertain family composition on the basis of sex of *all* children *at birth* including prematures, aborted fetuses, etc.

Correction for Small Samples.

7.11. In Problem 7.7(*b*), it was shown that observations of 60:40 produced a significant chi-square at the 5% level when uncorrected for continuity. Apply Yates' correction for continuity and retest the data.

Solution:

o	e	$[|o-e|-0.5]$	$[|o-e|-0.5]^2$
60	50	$10-0.5 = 9.5$	90.25
40	50	$10-0.5 = 9.5$	90.25
			$\chi^2 = 180.50/50 = 3.61$

Notice that the correction 0.5 is always applied to the *absolute value* $|o-e|$ of the deviation of expected from observed numbers. This is not a significant chi-square value. Because the data is discrete (jumping from unit to unit) there is a tendency to underestimate the probability, causing too many rejections of the null hypothesis. Yates' correction removes this bias and produces a more accurate test near the critical values (column headed by a probability of 0.05 in Table 7.1).

Supplementary Problems

THE BINOMIAL EXPANSION

7.12. Black hair in the guinea pig is dominant to white hair. In families of five offspring where both parents are heterozygous black, with what frequency would we expect to find (*a*) 3 whites and 2 blacks, (*b*) 2 whites and 3 blacks, (*c*) 1 white and 4 blacks, (*d*) all whites?

7.13. In families of size three, what is the probability of finding the oldest child to be a girl and the youngest a boy?

7.14. In families of five children, what is the probability of finding (a) 3 or more boys, (b) 3 or more boys or 3 or more girls?

7.15. A dozen strains of corn are available for a cross-pollination experiment. How many different ways can these strains be paired?

7.16. Five coat colors in mice are agouti, cinnamon, black, chocolate and albino. (a) List all of the possible crosses between different phenotypes. (b) Verify the number of different crosses by applying formula (7.1), page 140.

7.17. In mice litters of size 8, determine (a) the most frequently expected number of males and females, (b) the term of the binomial part (a) represents, (c) the percentage of all litters of size 8 expected to have 4 males and 4 females.

7.18. There are at least 12 alleles at the sex-linked "white" locus in *Drosophila*. Find the number of possible (a) genotypes, (b) types of matings.

7.19. White plumage in chickens can result from the action of a recessive genotype *cc* or from the action of an independently assorting dominant gene *I*. The White Plymouth Rock breed has genotype *ccii* and the White Leghorn breed has genotype *CCII*. The hybrid bird produced by crossing these two breeds is also white. How frequently in clutches (a nest of eggs; a brood of chicks) of 10 chicks produced by hybrid birds would you expect to find 5 colored and 5 white chicks?

7.20. A case of dominant interaction among coat colors has been discovered in the dog: *B-* results in black, *bb* in brown; *I-* inhibits color development, *ii* allows color to be produced. White dogs of genotype *BBII* testcrossed to brown dogs produce all white puppies in the F_1. In the F_2, determine the fraction of all litters of size 6 which is expected to contain 3 white, 1 black and 2 brown puppies.

7.21. A pair of alleles in the rat, *C* and *c*, act on coat color in such a way that the genotypes *CC* and *Cc* allow pigment to be produced, but the genotype *cc* prevents any pigment from being produced (albinos). Black rats possess the dominant gene *R* of an independently assorting locus. Cream rats are produced by the recessive genotype *rr*. When black rats of genotype *RRCC* are testcrossed to albino rats, the F_1 is all black. Determine the percentage of F_2 litters of size seven which is expected to have 4 black, 2 cream and 1 albino.

7.22. Two independently assorting loci, each with codominant allelic pairs, are involved in the shape and color characteristics of radishes. The shape may be long or round, due to different homozygous genotypes, or oval due to the heterozygous genotype. The color may be red or white due to different homozygous genotypes, or purple due to the heterozygous genotype. A long white variety is crossed to a round red variety. The F_1 is all oval purple. A dozen seeds are saved from each self-pollinated F_1 plant and grown out the next season in sibling groups. Assuming 100% germination, determine the proportion of plants in each group of a dozen progeny expected to exhibit 5 oval, purple: 3 oval, white: 2 round, purple: 1 long, purple: 1 round, red.

TESTING GENETIC RATIOS

7.23. Determine the number of degrees of freedom when testing the ratios (a) 3:1, (b) 9:3:3:1, (c) 1:2:1, (d) 9:3:4. Find the number of degrees of freedom in applying a chi-square test to the results from (e) testcrossing a dihybrid, (f) testcrossing a trihybrid, (g) trihybrid × trihybrid cross, (h) mating repulsion dihybrid *Drosophila* males and females.

7.24. Two phenotypes appear in an experiment in the numbers 4:16. (a) How well does this sample fit a 3:1 ratio? Would a sample with the same proportional deviation fit a 3:1 ratio if it were (b) 10 times larger than (a), (c) 20 times larger than (a)?

7.25. The flowers of four o'clock plants may be red, pink, or white. Reds crossed to whites produced only pink offspring. When pink flowered plants were crossed they produced 113 red, 129 white and 242 pink. It is hypothesized that these colors are produced by a single gene locus with codominant alleles. Is this hypothesis acceptable on the basis of a chi-square test?

7.26. A heterozygous genetic condition called "creeper" in chickens produces shortened and deformed legs and wings, giving the bird a squatty appearance. Matings between creepers produced 775 creeper : 388 normal progeny. (a) Is the hypothesis of a 3:1 ratio acceptable? (b) Does a 2:1 ratio fit the data better? (c) What phenotype is probably produced by the gene for creeper when in homozygous condition?

7.27. Genetically pure white dogs, when testcrossed to brown dogs, produce an all white F_1. Data on 190 F_2 progeny: 136 white, 41 black, 13 brown. These coat colors are postulated to be under the genetic control of two loci exhibiting dominant epistasis ($12:3:1$ ratio expected). (a) Test this hypothesis by chi-square. (b) When the F_1 was backcrossed to the brown parental type, the following numbers of phenotypes appeared among 70 progeny: 39 white, 19 black, 12 brown. Are these results consistent with the hypothesis?

7.28. Pure black rats, when testcrossed to albinos, produce only black F_1 offspring. The F_2 in one experiment was found to consist of 43 black, 14 cream and 22 albino. The genetic control of these coat colors is postulated to involve two gene loci with recessive epistasis ($9:3:4$ ratio expected). Is the genetic hypothesis consistent with the data?

7.29. Colored aleurone in corn is hypothesized to be produced by the interaction of two dominant alleles in the genotype A-C-; all other genotypes at these two loci produce colorless aleurone. A second hypothesis proposes that a third locus is also involved in this interaction such that only the genotypes A-C-R- produce colored aleurone; all other genotypes at these three loci produce colorless aleurone. A pure colored strain is crossed to a pure colorless strain. The F_1 exhibits only kernels with colored aleurone. The F_2 exhibits 3300 colored : 2460 colorless. (a) Analyze the data by chi-square under each of the hypotheses. (b) Which of the two hypotheses is supported by the data?

7.30. The results of phenotypic analysis of 96 F_2 progeny in two replicate experiments is shown below.

Experiment	Phenotype-1	Phenotype-2
1	70	26
2	76	20

Calculate chi-square for each experiment assuming a   (a) $3:1$ ratio,   (b) $13:3$ ratio.   (c) Which hypothesis is most consistent with the data?

7.31. A total of 320 families of six children each were surveyed with the results shown below. Does this distribution indicate that boys and girls are occurring with equal frequency?

No. of girls	6	5	4	3	2	1	0
No. of boys	0	1	2	3	4	5	6
No. of families	6	33	71	99	69	37	5

7.32. Yellowish-green corn seedlings are produced by a gene called "virescent-4" (v_4). A dark brown color of the outer seed coat called "chocolate pericarp" is governed by a dominant gene Ch. A virescent-4 strain is crossed to a strain homozygous for chocolate pericarp. The F_1 is then testcrossed. The resulting progeny are scored for phenotype with the following results: 216 green seedling, light pericarp: 287 green seedling, chocolate pericarp: 293 virescent seedling, light pericarp: 204 virescent seedling, chocolate pericarp. (a) Are these results compatible with the hypothesis of independent assortment? (b) Perform a genetic analysis of the data in the light of the results of part (a).

7.33. Purple anthocyanin pigment in tomato stems is governed by a dominant gene A, and its recessive allele a produces green stem. Hairy stem is governed by a dominant gene Hl, and hairless stem by its recessive allele hl. A dihybrid purple, hairy plant is testcrossed and produces 73 purple, hairy : 12 purple, hairless : 75 green, hairless : 9 green, hairy. (a) Is the F_1 purple : green ratio compatible with the expectation for alleles (i.e. a $1:1$ ratio)? (b) Is the F_1 hairy : hairless ratio compatible with the expectation for alleles (i.e. a $1:1$ ratio)? (c) Test the F_1 data for independent assortment (i.e. a $1:1:1:1$ ratio). What conclusion do you reach?

7.34. In guinea pigs, it is hypothesized that a dominant allele L governs short hair and its recessive allele l governs long hair. Codominant alleles at an independently assorting locus are assumed to govern hair color, such that $C^y C^y =$ yellow, $C^y C^w =$ cream and $C^w C^w =$ white. From the cross $Ll\,C^y C^w \times Ll\,C^y C^w$, the following progeny were obtained: 50 short cream : 21 short yellow : 23 short white : 21 long cream : 7 long yellow : 6 long white. Are the data consistent with the genetic hypothesis?

Correction for Small Samples

7.35. A dominant gene in corn (*Kn*) results in the proliferation of vascular tissues in a trait called "knotted leaf". A heterozygous knotted leaf plant is testcrossed to a normal plant producing 153 knotted leaf and 178 normal progeny. Apply Yates' correction in the calculation of chi-square testing a 1 : 1 ratio. Are these results consistent with the hypothesis?

7.36. Observations of 30 : 3 in a genetic experiment are postulated to be in conformity with a 3 : 1 ratio. Is a 3 : 1 ratio acceptable at the 5% level on the basis of (*a*) an uncorrected chi-square test, (*b*) a corrected chi-square test?

Answers to Supplementary Problems

7.12. (*a*) 90/1024   (*b*) 270/1024   (*c*) 405/1024   (*d*) 1/1024   **7.14.** (*a*) $\frac{1}{2}$ (*b*) 1.0

7.13. $\frac{1}{4}$ **7.15.** 66

7.16. (*a*) (1) agouti × cinnamon   (2) agouti × black   (3) agouti × chocolate   (4) agouti × albino   (5) cinnamon × black   (6) cinnamon × chocolate   (7) cinnamon × albino   (8) black × chocolate   (9) black × albino   (10) chocolate × albino

7.17. (*a*) 4 males : 4 females   (*b*) 5th   (*c*) 27.34%

7.18. (*a*) Males = 12; females = 78   (*b*) 936

7.19. $252(13/16)^5(3/16)^5 \cong 2.1\%$ by 4 place logarithms   **7.21.** 9.25%

7.20. 1215/65,536   **7.22.** $332,640/4,294,967,296 \cong 7.745 \times 10^{-5}$

7.23. (*a*) 1 (*b*) 3 (*c*) 2 (*d*) 2 (*e*) 3 (*f*) 7 (*g*) 7 (*h*) 2 (2 : 1 : 1 ratio expected; see "crossover suppression" in Chapter 6)

7.24. (*a*) $\chi^2 = 0.27$; P = 0.5-0.7; acceptable   (*b*) $\chi^2 = 2.67$; P = 0.1-0.2; acceptable   (*c*) $\chi^2 = 5.33$; P = 0.01-0.05; not acceptable

7.25. Yes. $\chi^2 = 1.06$; P = 0.5-0.7; acceptable

7.26. (*a*) $\chi^2 = 43.37$; P < 0.001; not acceptable   (*b*) $\chi^2 = 0.000421$; P > 0.95; a 2 : 1 ratio fits the data almost perfectly   (*c*) lethal

7.27. (*a*) $\chi^2 = 1.22$; P = 0.5-0.7; acceptable   (*b*) Yes; expected 2 : 1 : 1 ratio; $\chi^2 = 2.32$; P = 0.3-0.5

7.28. Yes; $\chi^2 = 0.35$; P = 0.8-0.9

7.29. (*a*) 2 genes = 9 : 7 ratio expected; $\chi^2 = 2.54$; P = 0.1-0.2
　　　3 genes = 37 : 27 ratio expected; $\chi^2 = 12.02$; P < 0.001
(*b*) 2 gene hypothesis

7.30. (*a*) *Experiment 1*: $\chi^2 = 0.22$; P = 0.5-0.7.   *Experiment 2*: $\chi^2 = 0.88$; P = 0.3-0.5.
(*b*) *Experiment 1*: $\chi^2 = 4.38$; P = 0.05-0.01.   *Experiment 2*: $\chi^2 = 0.27$; P = 0.5-0.7.
(*c*) 3 : 1 ratio

7.31. Yes. $\chi^2 = 2.83$; P = 0.8-0.9; the distribution is consistent with the assumption that boys and girls occur with equal frequency.

7.32. (*a*) No. $\chi^2 = 25.96$; P < 0.001   (*b*) v_4 is linked to *Ch*, exhibiting approximately 42% recombination

7.33. (*a*) Yes. $\chi^2 = 0.006$; P = 0.90-0.95   (*b*) Yes. $\chi^2 = 0.077$; P = 0.7-0.8   (*c*) $\chi^2 = 95.6$; P < 0.001; the observations do not conform to a 1 : 1 : 1 : 1 ratio, therefore genes *a* and *hl* are probably linked.

7.34. Yes; $\chi^2 = 2.69$; P = 0.7-0.8

7.35. Yes; $\chi^2 = 1.74$; P = 0.1-0.2

7.36. (*a*) No. $\chi^2 = 4.45$; P < 0.05   (*b*) Yes. $\chi^2 = 3.64$; P > 0.05

Chapter 8

Cytogenetics

THE UNION OF CYTOLOGY WITH GENETICS

Perhaps one reason Mendel's discoveries were not appreciated by the scientific community of his day (1865) was that the mechanics of mitosis and meiosis had not yet been discovered. During the years 1870-1900 rapid advances were made in the study of cells (*cytology*). At the turn of the century, when Mendel's laws were rediscovered, the cytological basis was available to render the statistical laws of genetics intelligible in terms of physical units. *Cytogenetics* is the hybrid science which attempts to correlate cellular events, especially those of the chromosomes, with genetic phenomena.

VARIATION IN CHROMOSOME NUMBERS

Each species has a characteristic number of chromosomes. Most higher organisms are diploid, with two sets of homologous chromosomes: one set donated by the father, the other set by the mother. Variation in the number of sets of chromosomes (*ploidy*) is commonly encountered in nature. It is estimated that one-third of the angiosperms (flowering plants) have more than two sets of chromosomes (polyploid). The term *euploidy* is applied to organisms with chromosome numbers that are multiples of some basic number (n).

1. **Euploidy.**

(*a*) *Monoploid.* One set of chromosomes (n) is characteristically found in the nuclei of some lower organisms such as fungi. Monoploids in higher organisms are usually smaller and less vigorous than the normal diploids. Few, monoploid animals survive. A notable exception exists in male bees and wasps. Monoploid plants are known but are usually sterile.

(*b*) *Triploid.* Three sets of chromosomes ($3n$) can originate by the union of a monoploid gamete (n) with a diploid gamete ($2n$). The extra set of chromosomes of the triploid is distributed in various combinations to the germ cells, resulting in genetically unbalanced gametes. Because of the sterility which characterizes triploids, they are not commonly found in natural populations.

(*c*) *Tetraploid.* Four sets of chromosomes ($4n$) can arise in body cells by the somatic doubling of the chromosome number. Doubling is accomplished either spontaneously or it can be induced in high frequency by exposure to chemicals such as the alkaloid *colchicine*. Tetraploids are also produced by the union of unreduced diploid ($2n$) gametes.

(i) *Autotetraploid.* The prefix "auto" indicates that the ploidy involves only homologous chromosome sets. Somatic doubling of a diploid produces four sets of homologous chromosomes (autotetraploid). Union of unreduced diploid gametes from the same species would accomplish the same result. Meiotic chromosome pairing usually produces quadrivalents (four synapsing chromosomes) which can produce genetically balanced gametes if *disjunction* is by two's, i.e. two chromosomes of the quadrivalent going to one pole and the other two to the opposite pole. If

151

disjunction is not stabilized in this fashion for all quadrivalents, the gametes will be genetically unbalanced. Sterility will be expressed in proportion to the production of unbalanced gametes.

(ii) *Allotetraploid.* The prefix "allo" indicates that non-homologous sets of chromosomes are involved. The union of unreduced ($2n$) gametes from different diploid species could produce, in one step, an allotetraploid which appears and behaves like a new species. Alternatively, two diploid plant species may hybridize to produce a sterile diploid F_1. The sterility results from the failure of each set of chromosomes to provide sufficient genetic homology to affect pairing. The sterile diploid can become fertile if it undergoes doubling of the chromosome number. The allotetraploid thus produced has two matched sets of chromosomes which can pair just as effectively as in the diploid. Double diploids of this kind, found only in plants, are called *amphidiploids*.

Example 8.1.   Let the two sets of chromosomes of one diploid species be *AA* and the other *BB*.

$$P: \qquad AA \ \times \ BB$$

$$F_1: \qquad AB \quad \text{(sterile hybrid)}$$
$$\text{(chromosome doubling)}$$

$$\text{Amphidiploid:} \qquad AABB \text{ (fertile)}$$

(d) *Polyploid.*   This term can be applied to any organism with more than $2n$ chromosomes. Ploidy levels higher than tetraploid are not commonly encountered in natural populations, but some of our most important crops are polyploid. For example, common bread wheat is hexaploid ($6n$), some strawberries are octaploid ($8n$), etc. Some triploids as well as tetraploids exhibit a more robust phenotype than their diploid counterparts, often having larger leaves, flowers and fruits (*gigantism*). Many commercial fruits and ornamentals are polyploids. Sometimes a specialized tissue within a diploid organism will be polyploid. For example, some liver cells of humans are polyploid. A common polyploid with which the reader should already be familiar is the triploid endosperm tissue of corn and other grains. Polyploids offer an opportunity for studying *dosage effects,* i.e. how two or more alleles of one locus behave in the presence of a single dose of an alternative allele. Dominance refers to the masking effect which one allele has over another allele. When one allele in the pollen is able to mask the effect of a double dose of another allele in the resulting endosperm, the former is said to exhibit *xenia* over the latter.

Example 8.2.   In corn, starchy endosperm is governed by a gene *S* which shows xenia with respect to its allele for sugary endosperm (*s*). Four genotypes are possible for these triploid cells: starchy $= SSS, SSs, Sss$; sugary $= sss$.

The term *haploid,* strictly applied, refers to the *gametic* chromosome number. For diploids ($2n$) the haploid number is n; for an allotetraploid ($4n$) the haploid (reduced) number is $2n$; for an allohexaploid ($6n$) the haploid number is $3n$; etc. Lower organisms such as bacteria and viruses are called haploids because they have a single set of genetic elements. However, since they do not form gametes comparable to those of higher organisms, the term monoploid would seem to be more appropriate.

2. Aneuploidy.

Variations in chromosome number may occur which do not involve whole sets of chromosomes, but only parts of a set. The term *aneuploidy* is given to variations of this nature, and the suffix "-somic" is a part of their nomenclature.

(a) **Monosomic.** Diploid organisms which are missing one chromosome of a single pair are monosomics with the genomic formula $2n-1$. The single chromosome without a pairing partner may go to either pole during meiosis, but more frequently will lag at anaphase and fails to be included in either nucleus. Monosomics can thus form two kinds of gametes, (n) and $(n-1)$. In plants, the $n-1$ gametes seldom function. In animals, loss of one whole chromosome often results in genetic unbalance which is manifested by high mortality or reduced fertility.

(b) **Trisomic.** Diploids which have one extra chromosome are represented by the chromosomal formula $2n+1$. One of the pairs of chromosomes has an extra member, so that a trivalent structure may be formed during meiotic prophase. If two chromosomes of the trivalent go to one pole and the third goes to the opposite pole, then gametes will be $(n+1)$ and (n) respectively. Trisomy can produce different phenotypes, depending upon which chromosome of the complement is present in triplicate. In man, the presence of one small extra chromosome (autosome 21) has a very deleterious effect resulting in Down's syndrome, formerly called mongolism.

(c) **Tetrasomic.** When one chromosome of an otherwise diploid organism is present in quadruplicate, this is expressed as $2n+2$. A quadrivalent may form for this particular chromosome during meiosis which then has the same problem as that discussed for autotetraploids.

(d) **Double trisomic.** If two different chromosomes are each represented in triplicate, the double trisomic can be symbolized as $2n+1+1$.

(e) **Nullosomic.** An organism which has lost a chromosome pair is a nullosomic. The result is usually lethal to diploids $(2n-2)$. Some polyploids, however, can lose two homologues of a set and still survive. For example, several nullosomics of hexaploid wheat $(6n-2)$ exhibit reduced vigor and fertility but can survive to maturity because of the genetic redundancy in polyploids.

VARIATION IN CHROMOSOME SIZE

In general, chromosomes of most organisms are too small and too numerous to be considered as good subjects for cytological investigation. *Drosophila* was considered to be a favorable organism for genetic studies because it produces large numbers of progeny within the confines of a small bottle in a short interval of time. Many distinctive phenotypes can be recognized in laboratory strains. It was soon discovered that crossing over does not occur in male fruit flies, thereby making it especially useful for genetic analyses. Later, its unusual sex mechanism was found to be a balance between male determiners on the autosomes and female determiners on the sex chromosomes. Although it had been known for over 30 years that some species of dipterans had extra large chromosomes in certain organs of the body, their utility in cytogenetic studies of *Drosophila* was not recognized until about 1934. There are only four pairs of chromosomes in the diploid complement of *D. melanogaster,* but their size in reproductive cells and most body cells is quite small. Unusually large chromosomes, 100 times as large as those in other parts of the body, are found in the larval salivary gland cells. These giant chromosomes (Fig. 8-1 below) are thought to be composed of many (100-1000) chromatin strands (*chromonemata*) fused together (*polytene*). The chromosome pairs are in a continual prophase condition with close somatic pairing between homologues throughout their length. Distinctive crossbanding is presumed to be groups of *chromomeres* (highly coiled areas) of the chromonema replicates. The crossbanding pattern of each chromosome is a constant characteristic within a species. Abnormal genetic behavior can sometimes be correlated with aberrations which are easily observed in the giant chromosome.

Courtesy of B. P. Kaufmann

Fig. 8-1. Salivary gland chromosomes of *Drosophila melanogaster*.

VARIATION IN THE ARRANGEMENT OF CHROMOSOME SEGMENTS

1. Translocations.

Chromosomes occasionally undergo spontaneous rupture, or can be induced to rupture in high frequency by ionizing radiations. The broken ends of such chromosomes behave as though they were "sticky" and may rejoin into non-homologous combinations (*translocations*). A reciprocal translocation involves the exchange of segments between two non-homologous chromosomes. During meiosis, an individual which is heterozygous for a reciprocal translocation must form a cross-shaped configuration in order to affect pairing of all homologous segments.

Example 8.3. Assume that a reciprocal translocation occurs between chromosomes 1-2 and 3-4.

The only way that functional gametes can be formed from a translocation heterozygote is by the alternate disjunction of chromosomes.

Example 8.4. At the end of the meiotic prophase begun in Example 8.3, a ring of four chromosomes is formed. If the adjacent chromosomes move to the poles as indicated in the diagram below, all of the gametes will contain some extra segments (duplications) and some pieces will be missing (deficiencies).

Example 8.5.   By forming a "figure-8", alternate disjunction produces functional gametes.

Translocation heterozygotes have several distinctive manifestations. (1) Semi-sterility is usually characteristic of translocation heterozygotes because of adjacent disjunctions as shown in Example 8.4. (2) Some genes which formerly assorted independently, will exhibit linkage relationships after translocation has occurred; a single reciprocal translocation will reduce the number of linkage groups by one. (3) The phenotypic expression of a gene may be modified when it is translocated to a new position in the genome. *Position effects* are particularly evident when genes in euchromatin (lightly staining areas usually containing genetic elements) are shifted near heterochromatic regions (darker staining areas presumably devoid of active genes).

(a) ***Translocation Complexes.*** In the evening primrose of the genus *Oenothera,* an unusual series of reciprocal translocations has occurred involving all 7 of its chromosome pairs. If we label each chromosome end with a different number, the normal set of 7 chromosomes would be 1-2, 3-4, 5-6, 7-8, 9-10, 11-12 and 13-14; a translocation set would be 2-3, 4-5, 6-7, 8-9, 10-11, 12-13 and 14-1. A multiple translocation heterozygote like this would form a ring of 14 chromosomes during meiosis. Different lethals in each of the two haploid sets of 7 chromosomes enforces structural heterozygosity. Since only alternate segregation from the ring can form viable gametes, each group of 7 chromosomes behaves as though it were a single large linkage group with recombination confined to the pairing ends of each chromosome. Each set of 7 chromosomes which is inherited as a single unit is called a "Renner complex".

Example 8.6.   In *O. lamarckiana,* one of the Renner complexes is called *gaudens* and the other is called *velans*. This species is largely self-pollinated. The lethals become effective in the zygotic stage so that only the *gaudens-velans* (G-V) zygotes are viable. *Gaudens-gaudens* (G-G) or *velans-velans* (V-V) zygotes are lethal.

Example 8.7.   The two complexes in *O. muricata* are called *rigens* (R) and *curvans* (C).   Gametic lethals in each complex act differentially in the gametophytes.   Pollen with the *rigens* complex are inactive; eggs with the *curvans* complex are inhibited.   Only the *curvans* pollen and the *rigens* eggs are functional to give the *rigens-curvans* complex in the zygote.

2. Inversions.

Assume that the normal order of segments within a chromosome is (1-2-3-4-5-6) and that breaks occur in regions 2-3 and 5-6, and that the broken piece is reinserted in reverse order.   The inverted chromosome now has segments (1-2-5-4-3-6).   One way in which inversions might arise is shown in Fig. 8-2.   An inversion heterozygote has one chromosome in the inverted order and its homologue in the normal order.   During meiosis the synaptic configuration attempts to maximize the pairing between homologous regions in the two chromosomes.   This is usually accomplished by a loop in one of the chromosomes.   Crossing over within the inverted segment gives rise to crossover gametes which are inviable because of duplications and deficiencies.   Chromatids which are not involved in crossing over will be viable.   Thus as we have seen with translocations, inversions produce semisterility and altered linkage relationships.   Inversions are sometimes called "crossover suppressors".   Actually they do not prevent crossovers from occurring but they do prevent the crossover products from functioning.   Genes within the inverted segment are thus held together and transmitted as one large linked group.   Balanced lethal systems (Chapter 6) involve either a translocation or an inversion to prevent the recovery of crossover products and thus maintain heterozygosity generation after generation.   In some organisms, these "inversions" have a selective advantage under certain environmental conditions and become more prevalent in the population than the standard chromosome order.   Two types of inversion heterozygotes will be considered in which crossing over occurs within the inverted segment.

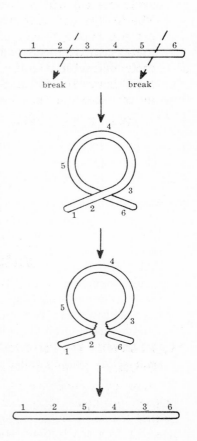

Fig. 8-2.   Origin of an inversion

*(a) **Pericentric inversion.***   The centromere lies within the inverted region.   First meiotic anaphase figures appear normal, but the two chromatids of each chromosome usually have arms of unequal length depending upon where the crossover occurred.   Half of the products contain duplications and deficiencies and do not function.   The other half of the gametes are functional: one-quarter have the normal chromosome order, one-quarter have the inverted arrangement.

Example 8.8.   Assume an inversion heterozygote as shown below with crossing over in region 3-4.

Synapsis and Crossing Over   First Anaphase

(b) *Paracentric inversion.*   The centromere lies outside the inverted segment. Crossing over within the inverted segment produces a *dicentric* chromosome (possessing two centromeres) which forms a bridge from one pole to the other during first anaphase. The bridge will rupture somewhere along its length and the resulting fragments will contain duplications and/or deficiencies.   Also, an *acentric* fragment (without a centromere) will be formed; and since it usually fails to move to either pole, it will not be included in the meiotic products.   Again, half of the products are non-functional, one-quarter are functional with a normal chromosome, and one-quarter are functional with an inverted chromosome.

Example 8.9.   Assume an inversion heterozygote as shown below with crossing over in region 4-5.

Synapsis and Crossing Over   First Anaphase

VARIATION IN THE NUMBER OF CHROMOSOMAL SEGMENTS

1. Deletions (Deficiencies).

Loss of a chromosomal segment may be so small that it includes only a single gene or part of a gene.   In this case the phenotypic effects may resemble those of a mutant allele at that locus.   For example, the "notch" phenotype of *Drosophila* discussed in Problem 5.4, page 81, is a sex-linked deletion which acts like a dominant mutation; a deletion at another sex-linked locus behaves as a recessive mutation, producing yellow body color when homozygous.   Deletions never back mutate to the normal condition, because a lost piece of chromosome cannot be replaced.   In this way, as well as others to be explained in subsequent chapters, a deletion can be distinguished from a gene mutation.   A loss of any considerable portion of a chromosome is usually lethal to a diploid organism because of genetic unbalance. When an organism heterozygous for a pair of alleles, *A* and *a*, loses a small portion of the chromosome bearing the dominant allele, the recessive allele on the other chromosome will become expressed phenotypically.   This is called *pseudodominance*, but it is a misnomer because the condition is hemizygous rather than dizygous at this locus.

Example 8.10. A deficiency in the segment of chromosome bearing the dominant gene *A* allows the recessive allele *a* to become phenotypically expressed.

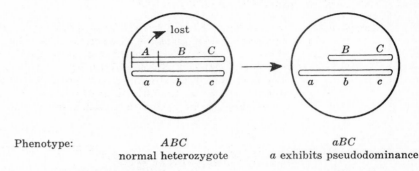

Phenotype: *ABC*   *aBC*
           normal heterozygote   *a* exhibits pseudodominance

A deletion heterozygote may be detected cytologically during meiotic prophase when the forces of pairing cause the normal chromosome segment to bulge away from the region in which the deletion occurs (Fig. 8-3).

Overlapping deletions have been extensively used to locate the physical position of genes in the chromosome (cytological mapping).

Deletion involving *CDE*

Fig. 8-3. Synapsis in a deletion heterozygote

Example 8.11. A laboratory stock of *Drosophila* females is heterozygous in coupling phase for two linked genes at the tip of the X chromosome, *ac* (achaete) and *sc* (scute). A deletion in one chromosome shows pseudodominance for both achaete and scute. In other individuals, another deletion displays pseudodominance only for achaete. Obviously, these two deletions overlap. In the giant chromosomes of *Drosophila*, the absence of these segments of chromosome is easily seen. The actual location of the scute gene resides in the band or bands which differentiate the two overlapping deletions.

X chromosome with *ac*⁺, *sc*⁺ / X chromosome with *ac*, *sc*

Close pairing of two X chromosomes in a heterozygous female *ac sc/ac*⁺ *sc*⁺

Locus of achaete ——————— Locus of scute

Pseudodominant for achaete and scute

Pseudodominant for achaete

2. Duplications (Additions).

Extra segments in a chromosome may arise in a variety of ways. Generally speaking, their presence is not as deleterious to the organism as a deficiency. It is assumed that some duplications are useful in the evolution of new genetic material. Because the old genes can continue to provide for the present requirements of the organism, the superfluous genes may be free to mutate to new forms without a loss in immediate adaptability. Genetic redundancy, of which this is one type, may protect the organism from the effects of a deleterious recessive gene or from an otherwise lethal deletion. During meiotic pairing the chromosome bearing the duplicated segment forms a loop to maximize the juxtaposition of homologous regions. In some cases, extra genetic material is known to cause a distinct phenotypic effect. Relocation of chromosomal material without altering its quantity may result in an altered phenotype (position effect).

Example 8.12.   A reduced eye size in *Drosophila*, called "bar eye", is known to be associated with a duplicated region on the X chromosome. Genetically the duplication behaves as a dominant factor. Wild type flies arise in homozygous bar-eye cultures with a frequency of about 1 in 1600. With approximately the same frequency, a very small eye called "double-bar" is also produced. These unusual phenotypes apparently arise in a pure bar culture by improper synapsis and unequal crossing over as shown below, where the region (*a-b-c-d*) is a duplication.

VARIATION IN CHROMOSOME MORPHOLOGY

It has already been shown that a translocation can change the structure of the chromosome both genetically and morphologically. The length of the chromosome may be longer or shorter, depending upon the size of the translocated piece. An inversion does not normally change the length of the chromosome, but if the inversion includes the centromere (pericentric) the position of the centromere may be changed considerably. Deletions or duplications, if viable, may sometimes be detected cytologically by a change in the size of the chromosome (or banding pattern in the case of the giant chromosomes of *Drosophila*), or by the presence of "bulges" in the pairing figure. Chromosomes with unequal arm lengths may be changed to *isochromosomes* having arms of equal length and genetically homologous with each other, by an abnormal transverse division of the centromere. The telocentric X chromosome of *Drosophila* may be changed to an "attached-X" form by a misdivision of the centromere (Fig. 8-4).

Fig. 8-4.   Origin of an attached-X chromosome.

The shape of a chromosome may change at each division once it has been broken. Following reduplication of a broken chromosome, the "sticky" ends of the sister chromatids fuse. When the chromatids move to opposite poles, a bridge is formed. The bridge will break somewhere along its length and the cycle repeats at the next division. This sequence of events is called a *breakage-fusion-bridge cycle*. Mosaic tissue can be produced by a breakage-fusion-bridge cycle appearing as irregular patches of an unexpected phenotype on a background of normal tissue (*variegation*). The size of the unusual trait generally bears an inverse relationship to the period of development at which the original break occurred. That is, the earlier a break occurs, the larger will be the size of the abnormal tissue. Chromosomes are not always rod shaped. Occasionally ring chromosomes are encountered in higher organisms. Crossing over between ring chromosomes can lead to bizarre anaphase figures.

Example 8.13.   A single exchange in a ring homozygote produces a double bridge at first anaphase.

Solved Problems

VARIATION IN CHROMOSOME NUMBERS

8.1.   An autotetraploid of genotype $AAaa$ forms only diploid gametes by random assortment from the quadrivalents.   The locus of A is very close to the centromere so that crossing over in that area is negligible.   (*a*) Determine the expected frequencies of zygotes produced by selfing.   (*b*) What reduction in the frequency of the recessive phenotype is anticipated by this autotetraploid in comparison with a selfed diploid of genotype Aa?

Solution:

(*a*)   For genes which are tightly linked to their centromeres, the distribution of alleles into gametes follows the same pattern as chromosomal assortment.   Let us first use a checkerboard to determine the kinds and frequencies of different combinations of alleles by two's expected in the gametes of the autotetraploid.   Note that the diagonal represents the nonexistent possibility of a given chromosome (or allele) with itself in a gamete. The table is symmetrical above and below the diagonal.

	A	A	a	a
A	—	AA	Aa	Aa
A		—	Aa	Aa
a			—	aa
a				—

Ratio of possible gametes: $1\,AA : 4\,Aa : 1\,aa = 1/6\,AA : 2/3\,Aa : 1/6\,aa$.   Using these gametic expectations, let us now construct a zygotic checkerboard for the prediction of progeny genotypes.

	$1/6\,AA$	$2/3\,Aa$	$1/6\,aa$
$1/6\,AA$	$1/36\,AAAA$	$2/18\,AAAa$	$1/36\,AAaa$
$2/3\,Aa$	$2/18\,AAAa$	$4/9\,AAaa$	$2/18\,Aaaa$
$1/6\,aa$	$1/36\,AAaa$	$2/18\,Aaaa$	$1/36\,aaaa$

Ratio of offspring genotypes: $1/36\,AAAA$ (quadruplex) : $8/36\,AAAa$ (triplex)   : $18/36\,AAaa$ (duplex) : $8/36\,Aaaa$ (simplex)   : $1/36\,aaaa$ (nulliplex).

(*b*)   If one dose of the dominant allele is sufficient to phenotypically mask one or more doses of the recessive allele, then the phenotypic ratio is expected to be $35\,A : 1a$.   One-quarter of the offspring of a selfed diploid heterozygote (Aa) is expected to be of the recessive phenotype.   The reduction in the frequency of the recessive trait is from 1/4 to 1/36, or 9 fold.   When homozygous genotypes produce a less desirable phenotype than heterozygotes, polyploidy can act as a buffer to reduce the incidence of homozygotes.

8.2. Assume an autopolyploid of genotype $AAaa$ with the locus of A 50 map units or more from the centromere so that a crossover always occurs in this area. In this case, the *chromatids* will assort independently. Assuming random assortment of chromatids to the gametes by two's, determine (*a*) the expected genotypic ratio of the progeny which results from selfing this autopolyploid, (*b*) the increase in the incidence of heterozygous genotypes compared with selfed diploids of genotype Aa.

Solution:

(*a*) Random assortment of 8 chromatids of the autotetraploid during meiotic prophase requires a gametic checkerboard with 64 squares.

	A	A	A	A	a	a	a	a
A	$-$	AA	AA	AA	Aa	Aa	Aa	Aa
A		$-$	AA	AA	Aa	Aa	Aa	Aa
A			$-$	AA	Aa	Aa	Aa	Aa
A				$-$	Aa	Aa	Aa	Aa
a					$-$	aa	aa	aa
a						$-$	aa	aa
a							$-$	aa
a								$-$

Summary of gametic types: $6\,AA : 16\,Aa : 6\,aa$ or $3 : 8 : 3$. Using these gametic expectations, we can now construct a zygotic checkerboard to generate the expected progeny.

	$3\,AA$	$8\,Aa$	$3\,aa$
$3\,AA$	$9\,AAAA$	$24\,AAAa$	$9\,AAaa$
$8\,Aa$	$24\,AAAa$	$64\,AAaa$	$24\,Aaaa$
$3\,aa$	$9\,AAaa$	$24\,Aaaa$	$9\,aaaa$

Summary of progeny genotypes: $9\,AAAA$ (quadruplex) : $48\,AAAa$ (triplex) : $82\,AAaa$ (duplex) : $48\,Aaaa$ (simplex) : $9\,aaaa$ (nulliplex).

(*b*) Selfing a diploid of genotype Aa produces 50% heterozygous progeny. Selfing the autotetraploid produces $178/196 = 91\%$ heterozygous progeny. The increase from 50% to 91% is $41/50 = 82\%$.

8.3. Pericarp is the outermost layer of the corn kernel and is maternal in origin. A dominant gene (B) produces brown pericarp, and its recessive allele (b) produces colorless pericarp. Tissue adjacent to the pericarp is aleurone (triploid). Purple pigment is deposited in the aleurone when the dominant gene C is present; its recessive allele c results in colorless aleurone. Aleurone is actually a single specialized layer of cells of the endosperm. The color of endosperm itself is modified by a pair of alleles. Yellow is governed by the dominant allele Y and white by the recessive allele y. Both C and Y show xenia to their respective alleles. A plant which is $bbCcYy$ is pollinated by a plant of genotype $BbCcYy$. (*a*) What phenotypic ratio is expected among the progeny kernels? (*b*) If the F$_1$ is pollinated by plants of genotype $bbccyy$, in what color ratio will the resulting F$_2$ kernels be expected to appear?

Solution:

(a) If pericarp is colorless, then the color of the aleurone shows through. If aleurone is also color-less, then the color of the endosperm becomes visible. Since the maternal parent is bb, the pericarp on all F_1 seeds will be colorless. Any seeds with C will have purple aleurone. Only if the aleurone is colorless (ccc) can the color of the endosperm be seen.

Parents: $bbCcYy\,♀ \quad × \quad BbCcYy\,♂$

F_1: $\frac{3}{4}\,C\text{-}\text{-} \qquad = \qquad \frac{3}{4}$ purple

$$\frac{1}{4}\,ccc \left\langle \begin{array}{lll} \frac{3}{4}\,Y\text{-}\text{-} & = & \frac{3}{16}\ \text{yellow} \\[4pt] \frac{1}{4}\,yyy & = & \frac{1}{16}\ \text{white (colorless)} \end{array} \right.$$

(b) Half of the F_1 embryos is expected to be Bb and will thus lay down a brown pericarp around their seeds (F_2); the other half is expected to be bb and will envelop its seeds with a colorless pericarp. Thus half of the seeds on the F_1 plants will be brown. Of the remaining half which has colorless pericarp, we need show only as much of the genotype as is necessary to establish the phenotype.

bb	F_1		Diploid Fusion Nucleus		Sperm Nucleus		Triploid Tissue
$\frac{1}{2}\times$	$\frac{1}{4}\,CC$	$=$	$\frac{1}{8}\,CC$	$+$	c	$=$	$\frac{1}{8}\,CCc$ purple
$\frac{1}{2}\times$	$\frac{1}{2}\,Cc$	$=\ \frac{1}{4}$	$\begin{cases}\frac{1}{8}\,CC \\ \frac{1}{8}\,cc\begin{cases}\frac{1}{16}\,YY \\ \frac{1}{16}\,yy\end{cases}\end{cases}$	$\begin{matrix}+\\+\\+\end{matrix}$	$\begin{matrix}c\\cy\\cy\end{matrix}$	$\begin{matrix}=\\=\\=\end{matrix}$	$\begin{matrix}\frac{1}{8}\,CCc\text{ purple}\\\frac{1}{16}\,cccYYy\text{ yellow}\\\frac{1}{16}\,cccyyy\text{ white}\end{matrix}$
$\frac{1}{2}\times$	$\frac{1}{4}\,cc$	$=\ \frac{1}{8}$	$\begin{cases}\frac{1}{16}\,ccYY \\ \frac{1}{16}\,ccyy\end{cases}$	$\begin{matrix}+\\+\end{matrix}$	$\begin{matrix}cy\\cy\end{matrix}$	$\begin{matrix}=\\=\end{matrix}$	$\begin{matrix}\frac{1}{16}\,cccYYy\text{ yellow}\\\frac{1}{16}\,cccyyy\text{ white}\end{matrix}$

Summary of F_2 seed colors: $\frac{1}{2}$ brown : $\frac{1}{4}$ purple : $\frac{1}{8}$ yellow : $\frac{1}{8}$ white.

8.4.   Eyeless is a recessive gene (ey) on the tiny fourth chromosome of *Drosophila*. A male trisomic for chromosome 4 with the genotype $+\,+\,ey$ is crossed to a disomic eyeless female of genotype $ey\,ey$. Determine the genotypic and phenotypic ratios expected among the progeny by random assortment of the chromosomes to the gametes.

Solution:

Three types of segregation are possible in the formation of gametes in the triploid.

(1) $+\ (+)\ ey$ (2) $+\ (+)\ ey$ (3) $(+)\ +\ ey$

$\quad$ ($+\ (+)$)   (ey)   ($+$)   ($(+)\ ey$)   ($(+)$)   ($+\ ey$)

Summary of sperm genotypes: $1\,++\ :\ 2\,+\,ey\ :\ 2\,+\ :\ 1\,ey$.

The union of these sperms with eggs of genotype ey results in the following progeny:

$$\left.\begin{array}{l} 1\ +\,+\,ey \\ 2\ +\,ey\,ey \\ 2\ +\,ey \end{array}\right\} \ =\ 5\ \text{wild type}$$

$$1\ ey\,ey \qquad\qquad = \ 1\ \text{eyeless}$$

VARIATION IN THE ARRANGEMENT OF CHROMOSOME SEGMENTS

8.5.   In 1931 Stern found two different translocations in *Drosophila* from which he developed females possessing heteromorphic X chromosomes. One X chromosome had a piece of the Y chromosome attached to it; the other X was shorter and had a piece of chromosome IV attached to it. Two sex-linked genes were used as markers for detecting crossovers, the recessive trait carnation eye color (*car*) and the dominant trait bar eye (*B*). Dihybrid bar females with heteromorphic chromosomes (both mutant alleles on the X portion of the X-IV chromosome) were crossed to hemizygous carnation males with normal chromosomes. The results of this experiment provided cytological proof that genetic crossing over involves an actual physical exchange between homologous chromosome segments. Diagram the expected cytogenetic results of this cross showing all genotypes and phenotypes.

Solution:

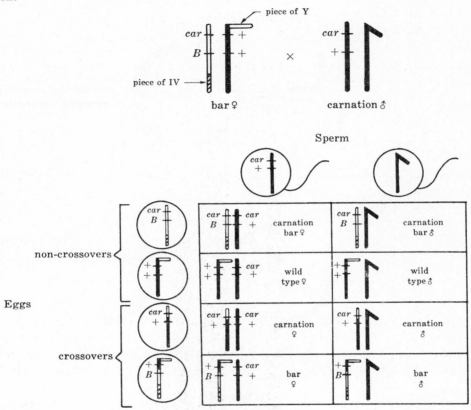

The existence of a morphologically normal **X** chromosome in recombinant male progeny with carnation eyes provides cytological proof that genetic crossing over is correlated with **physical** exchange between homologous chromosomes in the parents. Similarly, all other phenotypes correlate with the cytological picture.

8.6. Consider an organism with four pairs of chromosomes in standard order, the ends of which we shall label 1-2, 3-4, 5-6, 7-8. Strain A crossed to the standard strain gives a ring of four plus two bivalents during meiotic prophase. Strain B crossed to the standard strain also gives a ring of four plus two bivalents. In each of the four situations which follow, explain how a cross of strain A × strain B could produce (*a*) four bivalents, (*b*) ring of four plus two bivalents, (*c*) two rings of four, (*d*) ring of six plus one bivalent.

Solution:

A ring of four indicates a reciprocal translocation involving two nonhomologous chromosomes. As a starting point, let us assume that strain A has experienced a single reciprocal translocation so that the order is 1-3, 2-4, 5-6, 7-8. Strain B also shows a ring of four with the standard, but we do not know whether the translocation involves the same chromosome as strain A or different chromosomes. The results of crossing A × B will indicate which of the B chromosomes have undergone translocations.

(*a*) Formation of only bivalents indicates that complete homology exists between the chromosomes in strains A and B. Therefore strain B has the same translocation as that in strain A.

(*b*) A ring of four indicates that the same chromosomes which were interchanged in strain A are also involved in strain B, but with different end arrangements.

     A: 1-3, 2-4, 5-6, 7-8
     B: 1-4, 2-3, 5-6, 7-8

(*c*) Two rings of four chromosomes each indicate that B differs from A by two translocations.

     A: 1-3, 2-4, 5-6, 7-8
     B: 1-4, 2-3, 5-7, 6-8

(*d*) A ring of six indicates that B differs from A by three translocations.

     A: 1-3, 2-4, 5-6, 7-8
     B: 1-2, 3-5, 4-6, 7-8

8.7. The centromere of chromosome V in corn is about 7 map units from the end. The gene for light yellow (virescent) seedling (*v*) is 10 map units from this end, and a gene which shortens internode length called brevis (*bv*) is 12 map units from this end. The break point of a translocation (*T*) is 20 map units from this end. A translocation heterozygote involving chromosomes V and VIII of genotype $+\ bv\ t/v + T$ is pollinated by a normal (non-translocated, *t*) plant of genotype $v\ bv\ t/v\ bv\ t$. If gametes are formed exclusively by alternate segregation from the ring of chromosomes formed by the translocation heterozygote, predict the ratio of progeny genotypes and phenotypes from this cross (considering multiple crossovers to be negligible).

Solution:
First let us diagram the effect which crossing over will have between the centromere and the point of translocation. We will label the ends of chromosome V with 1-2, and of chromosome VIII with 3-4. A cross-shaped pairing figure is formed during meiosis.

Gametes

Functional   Non-functional

Alternate segregation produces half functional and half non-functional (duplication-deficiency) gametes. Note that the non-functional gametes derive only from the crossover chromatids. Thus recovery of chromatids which experience a crossover between the centromere and the point of translocation is prevented. The combination of genes in this region of the chromosome is prevented from being broken up by crossing over and are thus transmitted as a unit. This situation is analogous to the block of genes within an inversion which are similarly held together as a genetic unit. Non-crossover chromatids will form two types of functional gametes with equal frequency: $+ bv\, t$ and $v + T$. Expected zygotes are: $\frac{1}{2} + bv\, t/v\, bv\, t$ = brevis, homozygous for the normal chromosome order and $\frac{1}{2} v + T/v\, bv\, t$ = virescent, heterozygous for the translocation.

8.8. Shrunken endosperm of corn is governed by a recessive gene sh and waxy endosperm by another recessive wx. Both of these loci are linked on chromosome 9. A plant which is heterozygous for a translocation involving chromosomes 8 and 9 and which developed from a plump, starchy kernel is pollinated by a plant from a shrunken, waxy kernel with normal chromosomes. The progeny is

> 171 shrunken, starchy, normal ear
>
> 205 plump, waxy, semi-sterile ear
>
> 82 plump, starchy, normal ear
>
> 49 shrunken, waxy, semi-sterile ear
>
> 17 shrunken, starchy, semi-sterile ear
>
> 40 plump, waxy, normal ear
>
> 6 plump, starchy, semi-sterile ear
>
> 3 shrunken, waxy, normal ear.

(a) How far is each locus from the point of translocation?   (b) Diagram and label the pairing figure in the plump, starchy parent.

Solution:

(a) The point of translocation may be considered as a gene locus because it produces a phenotypic effect, namely semisterility. The conventional symbol for translocation is T, and t is used for the normal chromosome without a translocation. Gene order in the parents must be

$$\frac{+\ wx\ T}{sh\ +\ t} \quad \times \quad \frac{sh\ wx\ t}{sh\ wx\ t}$$

in order for double crossovers to produce the least frequent phenotypes

$$+ + T\ =\ \text{plump, starchy, semi-sterile ear}$$
$$sh\ wx\ t\ =\ \text{shrunken, waxy, normal ear}$$

The map distances are calculated in the usual way for a three point testcross.

> Distance $sh\text{-}wx\ =\ (82+49+6+3)/573\ =\ $ **24.4 map units.**
>
> Distance $wx\text{-}T\ =\ (17+40+6+3)/573\ =\ $ **11.5 map units.**
>
> Distance $sh\text{-}T\ =\ 24.4+11.5\ =\ $ **35.9 map units.**

(b)

8.9. An inversion heterozygote possesses one chromosome in the normal order
$\overset{a\ b\ c\ d\ e\ f\ g\ h}{\bullet\rule{2cm}{0.4pt}}$ and one in the inverted order $\overset{a\ b\ f\ e\ d\ c\ g\ h}{\bullet\rule{2cm}{0.4pt}}$. A four strand
double crossover occurs in the areas *f-e* and *d-c*. Diagram and label the first ana-
phase figures.

Solution:

A somewhat easier way to diagram the synapsing chromosomes when crossing over is only
within the inversion is shown below. This is obviously not representative of the actual pairing
figure. Let the crossover in the *c-d* region involve strands 2 and 3, and the crossover in the *e-f*
region involve strands 1 and 4.

Synapsis

First Anaphase

(double bridge)

plus

$\left(\begin{array}{c}\text{two acentric}\\ \text{fragments}\end{array}\right)$

8.10. Eight regions of a dipteran chromosome are easily recognized cytologically and
labeled *a* through *h*. Four different races within this species have the chromosomal
orders as listed:

(1) *ahbdcfeg*,   (2) *aedcfbhg*,   (3) *ahbdgefc*,   (4) *aefcdbhg*

Assuming that each race evolved by a single inversion from another race, show how
the four races could have originated.

Solution:

An inversion in (1) involving *cfeg* produces the order for (3).

(1) *a h b d c̲f̲e̲g̲*   ⟶   (3) *a h b d g e f c*

No single inversion in (3) can produce any of the other chromosomal orders. However, a different
inversion in (1) can produce the order for (4).

(1) *a h̲b̲d̲c̲f̲eg*   ⟶   (4) *a e f c d b h g*

Race 4 in turn can give rise to (2) by a single inversion.

(4) *a e̲f̲c̲d̲b h g*   ⟶   (2) *a e d c f b h g*

If (1) was the original ancestor, the evolutionary pattern would be $2 \leftarrow 4 \leftarrow 1 \rightarrow 3$. If (2) was the original ancestor, the evolutionary pattern would be $2 \rightarrow 4 \rightarrow 1 \rightarrow 3$. If (3) was the original ancestor, the evolutionary pattern would be $3 \rightarrow 1 \rightarrow 4 \rightarrow 2$. If (4) was the original ancestor, the evolutionary pattern would be $2 \leftarrow 4 \rightarrow 1 \rightarrow 3$. Since we do not know which of the four was the original ancestor, we can briefly indicate all of these possibilities by using double-headed arrows: $2 \leftrightarrow 4 \leftrightarrow 1 \leftrightarrow 3$.

VARIATION IN CHROMOSOME MORPHOLOGY

8.11. Yellow body color in *Drosophila* is produced by a recessive gene y at the end of the X chromosome. A yellow male is mated to an attached-X female ($\hat{XX}$) heterozygous for the y allele. Progeny are of two types, yellow females and wild type females. What insight does this experiment offer concerning the stage (2 strand or 4 strand) at which crossing over occurs?

Solution:

Let us assume that crossing over occurs in the two strand stage, i.e. before the chromosome replicates into two chromatids.

The yellow male produces gametes with either a y-bearing X chromosome or one with the Y chromosome which is devoid of genetic markers. Trisomic X ($\hat{XXX}$) flies seldom survive (super-females). Those with $\hat{XXY}$ will be viable heterozygous wild type attached-X females. Crossing over fails to produce yellow progeny when it occurs in the two strand stage.

Let us assume that crossing over occurs after replication of the chromosome, i.e. in the four strand stage:

Yellow ♀

Wild type ♀

The appearance of yellow females in the progeny is proof that crossing over occurs in the four strand stage.

8.12. Data from *Drosophila* studies indicate that non-crossover (NCO) rings are recovered in equal frequencies with NCO rods from ring-rod heterozygotes. What light does this information shed on the occurrence of sister strand crossing over?

Solution:

Let us diagram the results of a sister strand crossover in a rod and in a ring chromosome.

(*a*) Rod Chromosome

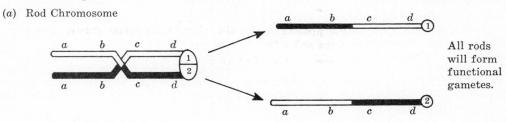

All rods will form functional gametes.

(*b*) Ring Chromosome

The double bridge at anaphase will rupture and produce nonfunctional gametes with duplications or deficiencies. These would fail to be recovered in viable offspring. The fact that both rings and rods are recovered with equal frequency argues against the occurrence of sister-strand crossing over.

Supplementary Problems

VARIATION IN CHROMOSOME NUMBER

8.13. Abyssinian oat (*Avena abyssinica*) appears to be a tetraploid with 28 chromosomes. The common cultivated oat (*Avena sativa*) appears to be a hexaploid in this same series. How many chromosomes does the common oat possess?

8.14. If two alleles, *A* and *a*, exist at a locus, five genotypic combinations can be formed in an autotetraploid: quadruplex (*AAAA*), triplex (*AAAa*), duplex (*AAaa*), simplex (*Aaaa*), nulliplex (*aaaa*). Assume *A* exhibits xenia over *a*. For each of these five genotypes determine the expected phenotypic ratio (*A* : *a*) when (*a*) the locus is tightly linked to its centromere (chromosomal assortment) and the genotype is selfed, (*b*) the locus is assorting chromosomally and the genotype is testcrossed, (*c*) the locus is far from its centromere so that chromatids assort independently and the genotype is selfed, (*d*) the locus assorts by chromatids and the genotype is testcrossed.

8.15. The loci of genes *A* and *B* are on different chromosomes. A dihybrid autotetraploid plant of genotype *AAaaBBbb* is self pollinated. Assume that only diploid gametes are formed and that the loci of *A* and *B* are very close to their respective centromeres (chromosomal segregation). Find the phenotypic expectations of the progeny.

8.16. The European raspberry (*Rubus idaeus*) has 14 chromosomes. The dewberry (*Rubus caesius*) is a tetraploid with 28 chromosomes. Hybrids between these two species are sterile F_1 individuals. Some unreduced gametes of the F_1 are functional in backcrosses. Determine the chromosome number and level of ploidy for each of the following: (*a*) F_1, (*b*) F_1 backcrossed to *R. idaeus*, (*c*) F_1 backcrossed to *R. caesius*, (*d*) chromosome doubling of F_1 (*R. maximus*).

8.17. There are 13 pairs of chromosomes in Asiatic cotton (*Gossypium arboreum*) and also 13 pairs in an American species *G. thurberi*. Interspecific crosses between *arboreum* and *thurberi* are sterile because of highly irregular chromosome pairing during meiosis. The American cultivated cotton (*Gossypium hirsutum*) has 26 pairs of chromosomes. Crosses of *arboreum* × *hirsutum* or *thurberi* × *hirsutum* produce triploids with 13 bivalents (pairs of chromosomes) and 13 univalents (single unpaired chromosomes). How can this cytological information be used to interpret the evolution of *hirsutum*?

8.18. The flinty endosperm character in maize is produced whenever two or all three of the alleles in this triploid tissue are *F*. In the presence of its alternative allele *F'* in double or triple dose, a floury endosperm is produced. White endosperm color is produced by a triple dose of a recessive allele *y*, its dominant allele *Y* exhibiting xenia and producing yellow endosperm. The loci of F and Y assort independently. (*a*) In crosses between parents of genotype *FF'Yy*, what phenotypic ratio is expected in the progeny seed? (*b*) Pollen from a plant of genotype *FF'Yy* is crossed onto a plant of genotype *FFyy*. Compare the phenotypic ratios produced by this cross with its reciprocal cross.

8.19. The diploid number of an organism is $2n = 10$. (a) How many different trisomics could be formed? (b) How many different double trisomics could be formed?

8.20. The diploid number of an organism is 12. How many chromosomes would be expected in (a) a monosomic, (b) a trisomic, (c) a tetrasomic, (d) a double trisomic, (e) a nullisomic, (f) a monoploid, (g) a triploid, (h) an autotetraploid?

8.21. Sugary endosperm of corn is regulated by a recessive gene s on chromosome IV and starchy endosperm by its dominant allele S. Assuming $n+1$ pollen grains are nonfunctional, predict the genotypic and phenotypic ratios of endosperm expected in the progeny from the cross of (a) diploid ss pollinated by trisomic-IV of genotype SSs, (b) diploid Ss pollinated by trisomic-IV of genotype SSs.

8.22. A dominant gene w^+ produces yellow flowers in a certain plant species and its recessive allele w produces white flowers. Plants trisomic for the chromosome bearing the color locus will produce n and $n+1$ functional female gametes, but viable pollen has only the n number. Find the phenotypic ratio expected from each of the following crosses:

	Seed Parent		Pollen Parent
(a)	$+ + w$	$\times$	$+ + w$
(b)	$+ w\, w$	$\times$	$+ + w$
(c)	$+ + w$	$\times$	$+ w$
(d)	$+ w\, w$	$\times$	$+ w$

8.23. Shrunken endosperm is the product of a recessive gene sh on chromosome III of corn; its dominant allele Sh produces full, plump kernels. Another recessive gene pr on chromosome V gives red color to the aleurone, and its dominant allele Pr gives purple. A diploid plant of genotype $Sh/sh, Pr/pr$ was pollinated by a plant trisomic for chromosome III of genotype $Sh/Sh/sh, Pr/pr$. If $n+1$ pollen grains are non-functional, determine the phenotypic ratio expected in the progeny endosperms.

8.24. Normal women possess two sex chromosomes (**XX**) and normal men have a single X chromosome plus a Y chromosome which carries male determiners. Rarely a woman is found with marked abnormalities of primary and secondary sexual characteristics, having only one X chromosome (**XO**). The phenotypic expressions of this monosomic-X state is called Turner's syndrome. Likewise, men are occasionally discovered with an **XXY** constitution exhibiting corresponding abnormalities called Kleinfelter's syndrome. Color blindness is a sex-linked recessive trait. (a) A man and his wife both had normal vision, but one of their children was a color blind Turner girl. Diagram this cross, including the gametes which produced this child. (b) In another family the mother is color blind and the father has normal vision. Their child is a Kleinfelter with normal vision. What gametes produced this child? (c) Suppose the same parents in part (b) produced a color blind Kleinfelter. What gametes produced this child? (d) The normal diploid number for man is 46. Mongoloids are trisomic for chromosome 21. At least one case of mongoloid-Kleinfelter has been recorded. How many chromosomes would this individual be expected to possess?

VARIATION IN ARRANGEMENT OF CHROMOSOME SEGMENTS

8.25. Colorless aleurone of corn kernels is a trait governed by a recessive gene c and is in the same linkage group (IX) with another recessive gene wx governing waxy endosperm. In 1931 Creighton and McClintock found a plant with one normal IX chromosome, but its homologue had a knob on one end and a translocated piece from another chromosome on the other end. A dihybrid colored, starchy plant with the heteromorphic IX chromosome shown below was testcrossed to a colorless, waxy plant with normal chromosomes. The results of this experiment provided cytological proof that genetic crossing over involves an actual physical exchange between homologous chromosome segments. Diagram the results of this cross, showing all genotypes and phenotypes.

colorless, waxy   colored, starchy

8.26. Nipple shaped tips on tomato fruit is the phenotypic expression of a recessive gene *nt* on chromosome V. A heterozygous plant (*Nt/nt*) which is also heterozygous for a reciprocal translocation involving chromosomes V and VIII is testcrossed to a plant with normal chromosomes. The progeny were: 48 normal fruit, fertile : 19 nipple fruit, fertile : 11 normal fruit, semisterile : 37 nipple fruit, semisterile. What is the genetic position of the locus of gene *Nt* with respect to the point of translocation?

8.27. Given a pericentric inversion heterozygote with one chromosome in normal order (1 2 3 4 . 5 6 7 8) and the other in the inverted order (1 5 . 4 3 2 6 7 8), diagram the first anaphase figure when a 4-strand double crossover occurs involving the regions between 4 and the centromere (.) and between the centromere and 5.

8.28. A four-strand double crossover occurs in an inversion heterozygote. The normal chromosome order is (. 1 2 3 4 5 6 7 8); the inverted chromosome order is (. 1 2 7 6 5 4 3 8). One crossover is between 1 and 2 and the other is between 5 and 6. Diagram and label the first anaphase figures.

8.29. Diagram and label the first anaphase figure produced by an inversion heterozygote whose normal chromosome is (. *a b c d e f g h*) and with the inverted order (. *a b f e d c g h*). Assume that a two-strand double crossover occurs in the regions c-d and e-f.

8.30. A chromosome with segments in the normal order is (. *a b c d e f g h*). An inversion heterozygote has the abnormal order (. *a b f e d c g h*). A three-strand double crossover occurs involving the regions between *a* and *b* and between *d* and *e*. Diagram and label the first and second anaphase figures.

8.31. Given the pairing figure for an inversion heterozygote with 3 crossovers as indicated on the right, diagram the first anaphase.

8.32. Four races of a species are characterized by variation in the segmental order (*a* through *h*) of a certain chromosome.

Race 1: *a b c d e f g h*   Race 3: *g f e a c d b h*
Race 2: *g f e b d c a h*   Race 4: *a c b d e f g h*

A fifth race, with still a different chromosomal order, is postulated to have existed in the past but is now extinct. Explain the evolutionary origin of these races in terms of single inversion differences. *Hint.* See Problem 8.10.

8.33. A species of the fruit fly is differentiated into five races on the basis of differences in the banding patterns of one of its giant chromosomes. Eight regions of the chromosome are designated *a* through *h*. If each of these races is separated by a single overlapping inversion, devise a scheme to account for the evolution of the five races: (1) *a d g h f c b e*, (2) *f h g d a c b e*, (3) *f h c a d g b e*, (4) *f h g b c a d e*, (5) *f a d g h c b e*.

VARIATION IN THE NUMBER OF CHROMOSOME SEGMENTS

8.34. In higher animals, even very small deficiencies, when homozygous, are usually lethal. A recessive gene *w* in mice results in an abnormal gait called "waltzing". A waltzing male was crossed to several homozygous normal females. Among several hundred offspring one was found to be a waltzer female. Presumably, a deficiency in the chromosome carrying the *w*⁺ allele caused the waltzing trait to appear as pseudodominant. The pseudodominant waltzer female was then crossed to a homozygous normal male and produced only normal offspring. (*a*) List two possible genotypes for the normal progeny from the above cross. (*b*) Suppose that two males, one of each genotype produced in part (*a*), were backcrossed to their pseudodominant mother and each produced 12 zygotes. Assuming that homozygosity for the deletion is lethal, calculate the expected combined number of waltzer and normal progeny.

VARIATION IN CHROMOSOME MORPHOLOGY

8.35. Vermilion eye color in *Drosophila* is a sex-linked recessive condition; bar eye is a sex-linked dominant condition. An attached-X female with vermilion eyes, also having a Y chromosome ($\overset{\wedge}{XX}Y$) is mated to a bar eyed male. (*a*) Predict the phenotypic ratio which is expected in the F_1 flies. (*b*) How much death loss is anticipated in the F_1 generation? (*c*) What phenotypic ratio is expected in the F_2?

8.36. Two recessive sex-linked traits in *Drosophila* are garnet eye (*g*) and forked bristle (*f*). The attached-X chromosomes of females heterozygous for these genes are diagrammed on the right.

A crossover between two chromatids attached to the same centromere is called a reciprocal exchange; a crossover between two chromatids attached to different centromeres is a non-reciprocal exchange. Approximately 7% of the daughters from these attached-X females were + +/*f g*, 7% were *f* +/+ +, 7% were *f g*/+ *g* and the remainder were *f* +/+ *g*. (*a*) Which of the single exchanges (A, B, C, or D in the diagram) could produce the daughters (1) + +/*f g* and *f* +/+ *g*, (2) *f* +/+ + and *f g*/+ *g*? (*b*) Are chromatids attached to the same centromere more likely to be involved in an exchange than chromatids attached to different centromeres? (*c*) Does the fact that neither homozygous wild type nor garnet-forked progeny were found shed any light on the number of chromatids which undergo exchange at any one locus?

8.37. Given the ring homozygote of Fig. 8-5, diagram the first anaphase figure when crossovers occur at positions (*a*) A and B, (*b*) A and C, (*c*) A and D.

Fig. 8-5

Fig. 8-6

8.38. Given the ring-rod heterozygote of Fig. 8-6, diagram the first anaphase figure when crossovers occur at positions (*a*) A and B, (*b*) A and C, (*c*) A and D.

Answers to Supplementary Problems

8.13. 42

8.14.

Genotype	(*a*)	(*b*)	(*c*)	(*d*)
quadruplex	all *A*	all *A*	all *A*	all *A*
triplex	all *A*	all *A*	783 *A* : 1 *a*	27 *A* : 1 *a*
duplex	35 *A* : 1 *a*	5 *A* : 1 *a*	20.8 *A* : 1 *a*	3.7 *A* : 1 *a*
simplex	3 *A* : 1 *a*	1 *A* : 1 *a*	2.48 *A* : 1 *a*	0.87 *A* : 1 *a*
nulliplex	all *a*	all *a*	all *a*	all *a*

8.15. 1225 *AB* : 35 *Ab* : 35 *aB* : 1 *ab*

8.16. (*a*) 21, triploid (*b*) 28, tetraploid (*c*) 35, pentaploid (*d*) 42, hexaploid

8.17. Half of the chromosomes of *hirsutum* have homology with *arboreum*, and the other half with *thurberi*. Doubling the chromosome number of the sterile hybrid (*thurberi* × *arboreum*) could produce an amphidiploid with the cytological characteristics of *hirsutum*.

8.18. (a) $\frac{3}{8}$ flinty, yellow : $\frac{1}{8}$ flinty, white : $\frac{3}{8}$ floury, yellow : $\frac{1}{8}$ floury, white

(b)

	Original Cross	Reciprocal Cross
flinty, white	$\frac{1}{2}$	$\frac{1}{4}$
flinty, yellow	$\frac{1}{2}$	$\frac{1}{4}$
floury, white		$\frac{1}{4}$
floury, yellow		$\frac{1}{4}$

8.19. (a) 5 (b) 10

8.20. (a) 11 (b) 13 (c) 14 (d) 14 (e) 10 (f) 6 (g) 18 (h) 24

8.21. (a) 2 *Sss* (starchy) : 1 *sss* (sugary) (b) $\frac{1}{3}$ *SSS* : $\frac{1}{6}$ *SSs* : $\frac{1}{3}$ *Sss* : $\frac{1}{6}$ *sss* : $\frac{5}{6}$ starchy : $\frac{1}{6}$ sugary

8.22. (a) 17 yellow : 1 white (b) 5 yellow : 1 white (c) 11 yellow : 1 white (d) 3 yellow : 1 white

8.23. $\frac{15}{24}$ plump, purple : $\frac{5}{24}$ plump, red : $\frac{3}{24}$ shrunken, purple : $\frac{1}{24}$ shrunken, red

8.24. (a) P: $X^C X^c \times X^C Y$; gametes: X^c O ; F_1: $X^c O$ (b) X^c $X^C Y$ (c) $X^c X^c$ Y (d) 48

8.25.

	Non-crossovers			Crossovers	
	colorless, starchy	colored, waxy		colorless, waxy	colored, starchy

8.26. 26.1 map units from the point of translocation.

8.27.

8.28.

8.29.

8.30. First anaphase: a diad, a loop chromatid and an acentric fragment; second anaphase: the diad splits into two monads, the loop forms a bridge and the acentric fragment becomes lost.

8.31. Two loop chromatids and two acentric fragments.

8.32.   If the order of the extinct race (5) was *g f e d b c a h* or *a c d b e f g h*, then: 1 ↔ 4 ↔ 5 ↔ 2 ↔ 3.

8.33.

8.34.   (*a*) +/*w* and +/(−) (heterozygous deficiency)   (*b*) 9 waltzers : 12 normals

8.35.   (*a*) All daughters have vermilion eyes (X͡XY); all sons have bar eyes (XY).   (*b*) 50% death loss; nullo-X is lethal (YY); superfemales (X͡XX) usually die.   (*c*) Same as part (*a*).

8.36.   (*a*) (1) D or C (2) B or A   (*b*) No.   Reciprocal vs. non-reciprocal exchanges are occurring in a 1 : 1 ratio, indicating that chromatids attached to the same centromere are involved in an exchange with the same frequency as chromatids attached to different centromeres. Daughters with genotype *f* +/+ *g* resulting from single crossovers of type C cannot be distinguished from non-exchange chromatids. (*c*) Two exchanges in the garnet-forked region involving all four strands, as well as one non-reciprocal exchange between *f* and the centromere, are required to give homozygous wild type and garnet-forked daughters. Their absence is support for the assumption that only two of the four chromatids undergo exchange at any one locus.

8.37.   (*a*)   **8.38.**   (*a*)

(*b*)   (*b*)

(*c*)   (*c*)

Chapter 9

The Chemical Basis of Heredity

NUCLEIC ACIDS

The chromosomes of higher organisms are composed of nucleoprotein, i.e. a conjugate of nucleic acids (organic acids found predominantly in the nucleus of the cell) and proteins such as histones and/or protamines. Only the nucleic acids carry genetic information. The function of the protein components of chromosomes has not been established. Some experiments with histones suggest that they may be agents of gene repression.

The nucleic acid which serves as the carrier of genetic information in all organisms other than some viruses is *deoxyribonucleic acid* (DNA). The double helical structure of this extremely long molecule is shown in Fig. 9-1. The backbone of the helix is composed of two chains with alternating sugar-phosphate units. The sugar is a pentose (5-carbon) called *deoxyribose,* differing from its close relative called *ribose* by one oxygen atom in the 2' position (Fig. 9-2 below). The phosphate group (PO_4) links adjacent sugars through a 3'-5' phosphodiester linkage; in one chain the linkages are polarized 3'-5', in the other chain they are in the reverse order 5'-3'. The steps in the spiral staircase (i.e. the units connecting one strand of DNA to its polarized complement) consist of paired organic bases of four species (symbolized A, G, T, C) classified into two groups, the *purines* and the *pyrimidines.* Purines only pair with pyrimidines and vice versa, thus producing a symmetrical double helix. Furthermore, the base pairs are linked in such a manner that the number of bonds between them is always maximized. For this reason, adenine (A) pairs only with thymine (T) and guanine (G) only with cytosine (C) (Fig. 9-3 below). A base plus its sugar and a phosphate group is called a *nucleotide.* The DNA molecule is thus a long *polymer* (i.e. a macromolecule composed of a number of similar or identical subunits, *monomers,* covalently bonded) of thousands of nucleotide pairs, even in such simple organisms as viruses.

Another class of nucleic acids, called *ribonucleic acid* (RNA), is slightly different from DNA in the following respects.

(1) RNA is considered to be single stranded; DNA is double stranded.

(2) RNA contains ribose sugar; DNA contains deoxyribose sugar.

Fig. 9-1. Diagram of Watson-Crick model of **DNA**

174

Fig. 9-2.   Structure of nucleic acids

Fig. 9-3.   Base pairing in DNA, diagrammatic

(3) RNA contains the pyrimidine uracil (U) instead of thymine (U pairs with A).

Uracil

(4) RNA molecules are generally much shorter than DNA molecules.

RNA functions primarily in protein synthesis, acting in one capacity as a messenger (mRNA) carrying information from the instructions coded into the DNA to the ribosomal sites of protein synthesis in the cell. Ribosomes contain a special form of RNA called ribosomal RNA (rRNA), which constitutes the bulk of cellular RNA. A third kind of RNA, called transfer RNA (tRNA), attaches to amino acids and during protein synthesis brings them each into proper positioning with other amino acids using the mRNA-ribosome complex as a template. In some of the plant viruses, such as tobacco mosaic virus (TMV), DNA is absent and RNA functions as genetic material.

DNA REPLICATION

The hydrogen bonds linking base pairs together are relatively weak bonds. At the time of replication the two strands of the DNA separate along this line of weakness in zipperlike fashion. Each single strand then becomes a template for the formation of another complementary strand by attracting free nucleotides to their complementary sites and the linking of adjacent nucleotides under the direction of the enzyme DNA-polymerase (Fig. 9-4).

GENETIC CODE

Biochemical reactions are mediated by enzymes. All enzymes are proteins. Proteins are polymers of subunits (monomers) called amino acids, often spoken of as "residues". Each amino acid has an amino group (NH_2) at one end and a carboxyl group (COOH) at the other end. Twenty different kinds of amino acids occur naturally in proteins. Each enzyme consists of a certain number of amino acid residues in a precisely ordered sequence. The blueprint for making proteins is coded in the nucleotide sequence of DNA. The number of nucleotides which code for an amino acid is termed a *codon*. There are 20 common amino acids but only 4 different nucleotides. Obviously a singlet code (i.e. one nucleotide coding for one amino acid) could code for only 4 amino acids. A doublet code (i.e. two nucleotides coding for one amino acid) allows for only 16 combinations. Mathematically, therefore, a triplet code (i.e. three nucleotides coding for one amino acid) is the smallest coding unit (codon) that can accommodate the 20 amino acids.

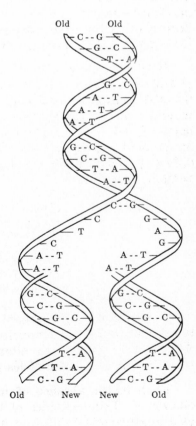

Fig. 9-4. Replication of DNA

The first experimental evidence supporting the triplet code concept was provided by the study of single base pair additions in the single linkage group of a bacterial virus (phage T4). If the transcription of a functional genetic unit (*cistron*) of DNA into mRNA is always read from a fixed position, then the first six codons in one chain of a DNA cistron might be as follows:

$$\begin{array}{cccccc}
1 & 2 & 3 & 4 & 5 & 6 \\
\text{TCA} & \text{GGC} & \text{TAA} & \text{AGT} & \text{CGG} & \text{TCG}
\end{array}$$

The addition of a single base (e.g. G) at the end of the second codon would shift all other codons one nucleotide out of register and prevent the correct reading of all codons to the right of the base addition.

$$\begin{array}{ccccccc}
1 & 2 & 3 & 4 & 5 & 6 & \\
\text{TCA} & \text{GGC} & \boxed{\text{G}}\text{TA} & \text{AAG} & \text{TCG} & \text{GTC} & \text{G}
\end{array}$$

By successively adding bases in a nearby region, it should be possible to place the reading of the codons back into register. It was found that one or two base additions failed to produce a functionally normal protein. But three base additions apparently can place the reading of the codons back into register for all codons to the right of the third base addition.

$$\begin{array}{ccccccc}
1 & 2 & 3 & 4 & 5 & 6 & 7 \\
\text{TCA} & \boxed{\text{A}}\text{GG} & \text{C}\boxed{\text{G}}\text{T} & \text{A}\boxed{\text{C}}\text{A} & \text{AGT} & \text{CGG} & \text{TCG}
\end{array}$$

$$\underbrace{\phantom{\text{TCA AGG CGT ACA}}}_{\substack{\text{Missense Codons} \\ \text{(out of register)}}} \qquad \underbrace{\phantom{\text{AGT CGG TCG}}}_{\substack{\text{Codons in} \\ \text{correct register}}}$$

The same has also been found to be true for single nucleotide deletions. Three deletions or multiples thereof can correct the reading frame in the synthesis of an active protein. Several other lines of evidence indicate that the codon is a sequence of three nucleotides and the genetic code is generally referred to as a "triplet code".

High concentrations of ribonucleotides in the presence of the enzyme polynucleotide phosphorylase can generate synthetic mRNA molecules *in vitro* by forming an internucleotide 3'-5' phosphodiester bond. In this way a number of uracil molecules can become linked together to form a synthetic poly-U with mRNA activity. The addition of poly-U to bacterial cell extracts results in the limited synthesis of polypeptides containing only the amino acid phenylalanine. Thus 3 uracils probably code for phenylalanine. Mixtures of different ribonucleotides can also form synthetic mRNA molecules with the nucleotides in random order.

Example 9.1. Poly-AU made from a mixture of adenine and uracil in concentrations of 2 : 1 respectively is expected to form **AAA** triplets most frequently, AAU (or AUA or UAA) triplets would be next in frequency, AUU (or UAU or UUA) triplets next, and UUU triplets would be least frequent. The frequencies with which various amino acids are incorporated into polypeptides under direction of the synthetic poly-AU can then be correlated with the expected frequencies of various triplets, allowing tentative assignment of specific triplets to specific amino acids.

A combination of organic chemical and enzymatic techniques can be used to prepare synthetic polyribonucleotides with known repeating sequences as, for example, AUAUAUAU... which alternately codes for the amino acids isoleucine and tyrosine, CUCUCUCU... which codes for leucine and serine alternately, etc.

Even in the absence of mRNA and protein synthesis, a trinucleotide will bind to a ribosome. Trinucleotides of known sequence can then be used to specifically bind one out of a mixture of 20 different amino acids to ribosomes *in vitro*. For example, UUG binds only leucine-loaded tRNA to ribosomes, UGU binds only cysteine-loaded tRNA, etc.

The genetic code is *degenerate* because more than one codon exists for most amino acids. The code is basically the same for all organisms. Apparently only three of the 64 possible three letter codons fail to code for any amino acid. Such codons are termed *nonsense* triplets. The mRNA codons for the twenty amino acids are listed in Table 9.1.

Table 9.1. mRNA Codons

		Second Letter				
		U	C	A	G	
First Letter	U	UUU UUC } Phe UUA UUG } Leu	UCU UCC UCA UCG } Ser	UAU UAC } Tyr UAA UAG } Nonsense	UGU UGC } Cys UGA Nonsense UGG Try	U C A G
	C	CUU CUC CUA CUG } Leu	CCU CCC CCA CCG } Pro	CAU CAC } His CAA CAG } Gln	CGU CGC CGA CGG } Arg	U C A G
	A	AUU AUC } Ileu AUA AUG Met	ACU ACC ACA ACG } Thr	AAU AAC } Asn AAA AAG } Lys	AGU AGC } Ser AGA AGG } Arg	U C A G
	G	GUU GUC GUA GUG } Val	GCU GCC GCA GCG } Ala	GAU GAC } Asp GAA GAG } Glu	GGU GGC GGA GGG } Gly	U C A G
						Third Letter

The abbreviated names of amino acids are as follows: ala = alainine, arg = arginine, asn = asparagine, asp = aspartic acid, cys = cysteine, gln = glutamine, glu = glutamic acid, gly = glycine, his = histidine, ileu = isoleucine, leu = leucine, lys = lysine, met = methionine, phe = phenylalanine, pro = proline, ser = serine, thr = threonine, try = tryptophan, tyr = tyrosine, val = valine.

PROTEIN SYNTHESIS

The coded information in DNA is *transcribed* into the coded sequence of the mRNA presumably by using one strand of DNA as a template. The mechanism for selection of the appropriate strand is unknown at the present time. The mRNA moves from the nucleus to the cytoplasm. There the message is unidirectionally read beginning at the 5'-hydroxyl end by one or more ribosomes (*polysomes*). The 5' end of mRNA corresponds to the N-terminal amino acid in the completed protein. The ribosome serves as a binding site where mRNA and tRNA interact (Fig. 9-5 below). Messenger RNA is very unstable in bacterial systems and must be continually replaced by newly synthesized molecules.

If each of the 20 amino acids is recognized by its own species of tRNA, then at least 20 species of tRNA would exist in the cytoplasm. The attachment of an amino acid to its tRNA molecule is mediated by a specific enzyme in a process called *activation* or *loading*. Somewhere on the tRNA is a sequence of three nucleotides (the *anticodon*) which is complementary to the mRNA codon. The affinity of the complementary triplets brings each amino acid into its proper relationship with other amino acids in the growing polypeptide chain. Two other enzyme fractions link the amino group and carboxyl group of adjacent

Fig. 9-5. Diagram of protein synthesis

amino acids together by a *peptide bond*. The tRNA molecule is released both from its amino acid and from the mRNA. The tRNA is then free to activate another free amino acid of the same species. When the ribosome reaches the end of the messenger, *translation* of the nucleotide code into an amino acid sequence is completed. At this stage the polypeptide (protein) possesses its primary and probably its secondary structures. The linear sequence of amino acids forms the primary structure; at least some portion of many proteins have a secondary structure in the form of an alpha-helix. The protein chain may then fold back upon itself, forming internal bonds (including strong disulfide bonds) which stabilize its tertiary structure into a precisely and often intricately folded pattern. Two or more tertiary structures may unite into a functional quarternary structure. For example, hemoglobin consists of four polypeptide chains, two identical α-chains and two identical β-chains. A protein does not become an active enzyme until it has assumed its tertiary or quarternary pattern (Fig. 9-6 below). Any subsequent disturbance of its final configuration may inactivate the enzyme. For example, heating destroys enzymatic activity because bonds, which hold the protein in its higher structural forms, are ruptured. The shape of an active enzyme molecule is believed to fit its *substrate* (the substance which is catalyzed by the enzyme) in a way that is analogous to a lock and key situation (Fig. 9-7).   An altered enzyme, either genetically or physically, may not fit the substrate and therefore would be incapable of catalyzing its conversion into the normal product.

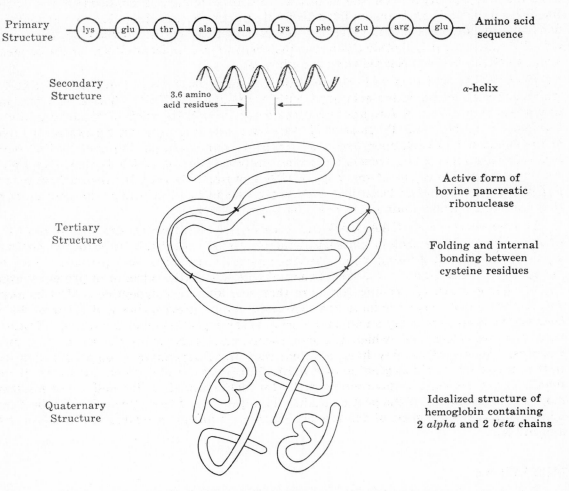

Fig. 9-6.   Stages in the development of a functional protein

Fig. 9-7.   Diagram of enzymatic action

Bacterial ribosomes consist of two major subunits, a larger 50S subunit and a smaller 30S subunit (S = Svedberg units, a sedimentation coefficient for molecules in an ultra-centrifuge).   More than 30 different proteins are found associated with rRNA in ribosomes. The specific function which these constituents perform has yet to be elucidated.   Three sites are presumed to exist on functional ribosomes: (1) a *decoding site* which binds the loaded tRNA thru base pairing with mRNA, (2) a *condensing site* which joins the amino acid to the growing polypeptide chain, (3) an *exit site* at which the tRNA becomes detached from the polypeptide, mRNA and ribosome. During protein synthesis, mRNA is bound to the 30S subunit. Each transfer RNA molecule enters the decoding site, moves to the condensing site, transfers its amino acid to the carboxyl end of the polypeptide, moves to the exit site where the polypeptide chain is transferred to the adjacent tRNA on the condensing site, and tRNA is then released from the ribosome.

Each tRNA consists of 75 to 80 nucleotides in a specific order. The 3' end of all tRNA's which is bound to the amino acid apparently terminates in $CCA^{3'}$. The 5' end terminates in a guanine residue. A few unusual bases occur in tRNA's, such as pseudouradilic acid, inosinic acid and others. Portions of tRNA's have a helical structure formed by the folding of the single strand back upon itself and complementary base pairing over limited regions. Several three-dimensional models have been proposed, one of which is shown in Fig. 9-5. An unpaired region in one of the loops of tRNA presumably contains the anticodon triplet. Perhaps one of the other loops in tRNA is the *recognition site* where the specific enzyme that loads the specific amino acid onto the 3' end attaches.

The nonsense codons UAA, UAG and UGA do not code for any amino acid and thereby presumably terminate protein synthesis. Bacterial proteins often have N-formyl-methionine at the N-terminal (beginning) end. Presumably the codon AUG (and perhaps GUG), when appearing at the beginning of a messenger molecule, acts as the initiator of protein synthesis. In polycistronic mRNA (coding for more than one kind of polypeptide), AUG coding for formylmethionine may terminate the synthesis of one polypeptide and initiate the next because the N-formyl group on an amino acid prevents peptide bond formation. There may be a "trimming enzyme" which removes formylmethionine from the ends of completed proteins. Some codons may have different meanings, depending upon where they occur in the message: if at the beginning of mRNA, AUG may initiate protein synthesis; if in the middle of the message, it may code normally for methionine; if at the end of the message, it may act as terminator of the peptide chain. The specificity of genetic coding can be changed by altering any component of the readout machinery including enzymes, ribosomes, tRNA and mRNA.

MUTATIONS

Non-enzymatic or structural proteins constitute the bulk of organic matter in living systems. Most proteins are complex, high molecular weight molecules. The exact sequence of amino acids in proteins is known for only a few, including hemoglobin, insulin, bovine pancreatic ribonuclease, tobacco mosaic virus protein, lysozyme and tryptophan synthetase. The normal human hemoglobin (Hb A) has about 140 amino acid residues in each of its α and β chains. The sequence in the β^A chain has been determined to be

val - his - leu - thr - pro - glu - glu - lys - etc.
 1   2   3   4   5   6   7   8

An abnormal hemoglobin (Hb S) is produced by individuals with a mutant allele, resulting in a deformity of the red blood cell called "sickling". In a heterozygous condition this allele produces a mild anemia; in a homozygous condition the severity of the anemia may be lethal. The difference between Hb A and Hb S is that the latter has valine substituted for glutamic acid in the sixth position of the β^S chain. Another potentially lethal abnormal hemoglobin (Hb C) is known in which the glutamic acid of the sixth position is replaced by lysine. One of the codons for glutamic acid is GAA. If a mutation occurred which changed the first A to a U, then the codon GUA (a *missense* triplet) would be translated as valine. The substitution of A for G would produce the missense codon AAA which codes for lysine.

Thus a change in a single nucleotide in the hemoglobin gene can produce a substitution of one amino acid in a chain of about 140 residues with profound phenotypic consequences!

Fortunately most genes are relatively stable and mutation is a rare event. The great majority of genes have mutation rates of 1×10^{-5} to 1×10^{-6}, i.e. one gamete in 100,000 to one gamete in a million would contain a mutation at a given locus. However in a higher organism containing 10,000 genes, one gamete in 10 to one gamete in 100 would be expected to contain at least one mutation. The rate at which a given gene mutates under specified environmental conditions is as much a characteristic of the gene as is its phenotypic expression. The mutation rate of each gene is probably dependent to some extent upon the residual genotype. The only effect which some genes exhibit is to increase the mutation rate of another locus. These kinds of genes are called "mutator genes".

> **Example 9.2.** A dominant gene called "dotted" (*Dt*) on chromosome 9 in corn causes a recessive gene *a* governing colorless aleurone, on chromosome 3, to mutate quite frequently to its allele *A* for colored aleurone. Plants which are *aaDt-* often have kernels with dots of color in the aleurone produced by mutation of *a* to *A*. The size of the dot will be large or small depending upon how early or late respectively during development of the seed the mutational event occurred.

The vast majority of mutations are deleterious to the organism and are kept at low frequency in the population by the action of natural selection. Mutant types are generally unable to compete equally with wild type individuals. Even under optimal environmental conditions many mutants appear less frequently than expected. Mendel's laws of heredity assume equality in survival and/or reproductive capacity of different genotypes. Observed deviations from the expected Mendelian ratios would be proportional to the decrease in survival and/or reproductive capacity of the mutant type relative to wild type. The ability of a given mutant type to survive and reproduce in competition with other genotypes is an extremely important phenotypic characteristic from an evolutionary point of view.

> **Example 9.3.** White eyed flies may be only 60% as viable as flies with pigmented eyes. Therefore among 100 zygotes from the cross $w^+w \, ♀$ (wild type) $\times$ $wY \, ♂$ (white), the Mendelian zygotic expectation is 50 wild type : 50 white. If only 60% of white eyed flies survive, then we would observe in the adult progeny
>
> $$50 \times 0.6 = 30 \text{ white} : 50 \text{ wild type}$$

Ionizing radiations such as X-rays are known to increase the mutability of all genes in direct proportion to the radiation dosage. A linear relationship between dosage (in roentgen units) and the induction of sex-linked lethal mutations in *Drosophila* is shown graphically in Fig. 9-8. This indicates that there is no level of dosage which is safe from the genetic standpoint. If a given amount of radiation is received gradually in small amounts over a long period of time (chronic dose) the genetic damage is sometimes less than if the entire amount is received in a short time interval (acute dose). In most cases, dose rate effects are not demonstrable. Ionizing radiations produce their mutagenic effects most frequently by inducing small deletions in the chromosome.

Fig. 9-8. X chromosome lethal mutations in *Drosophila* induced by X-rays

The student's first encounter with the terminology involved in the study of mutations is sometimes a source of confusion. Mutations can be classified on the basis of several criteria. The following outline may be useful in showing the interrelationships of concepts and terms.

A CLASSIFICATION OF MUTATIONS

I. **Size**
  A. Point mutation — a change in a very small segment of DNA; usually considered to involve a single nucleotide or nucleotide pair.
  B. Gross mutations — changes involving more than one nucleotide pair; may involve the entire gene, the entire chromosome, or sets of chromosomes (polyploidy).

II. **Quality**
  A. Structural mutations — changes in the nucleotide content of the gene.
    1. Substitution mutations — substitution of one nucleotide for another.
      (a) *Transition* mutations substitute one purine for another or one pyrimidine for another.
      (b) *Transversion* mutations substitute a purine for a pyrimidine or vice versa.
    2. Deletion mutants — loss of some portion of a gene.
    3. Insertion mutants — addition of one or more extra nucleotides to a gene.
  B. Rearrangement mutations — changing the location of a gene within the genome often leads to "position effects".
    1. Within a gene — two mutations within the same functional gene can produce different effects, depending on whether they occur in the cis or trans position.
    2. Number of genes per chromosome — different phenotypic effects can be produced if the numbers of gene replicas are non-equivalent on the homologous chromosomes.
    3. Moving the gene locus may create new phenotypes, especially when the gene is relocated near heterochromatin.
      (a) Translocations — movement to a non-homologous chromosome.
      (b) Inversions — movement within the same chromosome.

III. **Origin**
  A. Spontaneous mutation — origin is unknown; often called "background mutation".
  B. Genetic control — the mutability of some genes is known to be influenced by other "mutator genes".
    1. Specific mutators — effects limited to one locus.
    2. Non-specific mutators — simultaneously affects many loci.
  C. Induced mutations — through exposure to abnormal environments such as:
    1. Ionizing radiations — changes in chemical valence through the ejection of electrons are produced by protons, neutrons, or by alpha, beta, gamma or X-rays.
    2. Non-ionizing radiations — raise the energy levels of atoms (excitation), rendering them less stable (e.g. ultraviolet radiation, heat); UV often produces thymine dimers, i.e. bonding between thymines on the same strand.
    3. Chemical mutagens — are chemical substances which increase the mutability of genes.
      (a) Copy errors — mutants arising during DNA replication (e.g. base analogue mutagens which are chemically similar to the nucleic acid bases may be incorporated by mistake; acridine causes single base additions or deletions possibly by intercalation between two sequential bases).
      (b) Direct gene change — produced in non-replicating DNA (e.g. nitrous acid by deamination directly converts adenine to hypoxanthine and cytosine to uracil).

IV. **Magnitude of Phenotypic Effect**
  A. Change in mutation rate — some alleles can only be distinguished by the frequency with which they mutate.
  B. Isoalleles — produce identical phenotypes in homozygous or heterozygous combinations with each other, but prove to be distinguishable when in combination with other alleles.

  C. Mutants affecting viability:
      1. Subvitals — relative viability is greater than 10% but less than 100% compared to wild type.
      2. Semi-lethals — cause more than 90% but less than 100% mortality.
      3. Lethals — kill all individuals before adult stage.

V. Direction

  A. Forward mutation — creates a change from wild type to abnormal phenotype.
  B. Reverse or back mutation — produces a change from abnormal phenotype to wild type.
      1. Single site mutation — changes only one nucleotide in the gene
          (e.g. adenine $\xrightarrow{\text{forward}}$ guanine $\xrightarrow{\text{reverse}}$ adenine).
      2. Mutation suppressor — a gene change which occurs at a different site from the primary mutation, yet reverses its effect.
          (a) Extragenic (intergenic) suppressor — occurs in a different gene from that of the mutant.
          (b) Intragenic suppressor — occurs at a different nucleotide within the same gene; shifts the reading frame back into register.
          (c) Photoreactivation — reversal of UV induced thymine dimers by specific enzymes in the presence of visible light waves.

VI. Cell Type

  A. Somatic mutation — occurs in non-reproductive cells of the body, often producing a mutant phenotype in only a sector of the organism (mosaic or chimera).
  B. Gametic mutation — occurs in the sex cells, producing a heritable change.

DEFINING THE GENE

Recall that the elementary concept of linked genes held them to be discrete elements analogous to beads on a string. The structure of DNA now indicates that a gene is one or a sequence of nucleotides. Formerly, a gene was assumed to be a genetic unit by three criteria: (1) the unit of physiological function leading to phenotypic expression, (2) the unit of structure which cannot be subdivided by crossing over, (3) the unit which can be changed by mutation. We now know that these criteria generally do not define the same amount of genetic material. Each of these criteria may be used to define a different genetic element.

A gene can be defined on the basis of its function. For example, the entire structure of an enzyme may be determined by a segment of DNA. The hypothesis that one gene produces an enzyme may hold true for some but not all enzymes. For example, the enzyme typtophan synthetase has been found to consist of two structurally different protein chains (A and B), each chain produced by an adjacent segment of DNA. The "one gene — one enzyme" hypothesis has now been refined to the "one gene — one polypeptide chain" hypothesis. That portion of DNA specifying a single polypeptide chain is termed a *cistron* and is synonymous with the gene of function.

There are many positions or sites within a cistron where mutations can occur. As was shown previously in this chapter in the case of the hemoglobin molecule, a change in a single nucleotide can result in a mutant phenotype. A *muton* is the smallest unit of genetic material that when changed (mutated) produces a phenotypic effect. A muton may thus be delimited to a single nucleotide or some part of a nucleotide. Different forms of a mutationally defined gene are called *homoalleles*.

A mutation within a cistron may render its product defective. A fully active wild type cistron may be produced by recombination between two defective cistrons containing mutations at different sites. The smallest unit of recombination (the *recon*) is believed to involve two adjacent nucleotides. Recombinationally separable forms of a gene within a cistron are referred to as *heteroalleles*.

Example 9.4.   An individual with a mutant phenotype has two mutant sites, m_1 and m_2, within homologous cistrons (diagrammed as boxes). These heteroalleles can recombine and be transmitted to the progeny as a functionally normal cistron.

Two mutants can be assigned to the same or to different cistrons on the basis of the *complementation* or *cis-trans test*. Two mutants in the same cistron will not complement each other to produce wild type (or normal phenotype) when in the trans position. A normal phenotype (indicating complementation) can be produced by two mutants if they belong to different cistrons regardless of their linkage relationships.

Example 9.5.   Two mutants (m_1 and m_2) in the same cistron are functionally allelic.

(*a*) Cis position (both mutant recons on one homologue)

(*b*) Trans position (each homologue has a mutant and a nonmutant recon)

Example 9.6.   Two mutants in different cistrons are functionally non-allelic.

(*a*) Coupling linkage

(*b*) Repulsion linkage

Certain genetic elements associated with duplicated segments of the *Drosophila* chromosome have proven to be separable by recombination (structurally non-allelic), but functionally allelic by the cis-trans test. These very closely linked loci with different, though related, phenotypic effects are called *pseudoalleles*. In some cases, pseudoalleles may actually be heteroalleles, i.e. different mutational sites within the same cistron. In other cases, pseudoallelism may be explained by functional interactions between mutations in different cistrons. Commonly, tens of thousands of offspring must be reared to find a rare crossover individual involving pseudoalleles which are of the magnitude 0.01 to 0.09 map units apart.

> **Example 9.7.** A pair of pseudoalleles in *Drosophila*, called bithorax (*bx*) and post-bithorax (*pbx*), are approximately 0.02 map units apart. Each of these recessive genes when homozygous modify the club-shaped balancers (halteres) into a pair of wing-like structures. The cis form (+ +/*bx pbx*) has normal balancers; the trans form (+ *pbx*/*bx* +) has a slight post-bithorax "position effect". The homozygous genotype, *bx pbx*/*bx pbx*, has a fully developed second pair of wings. The bithorax series is composed of 5 separate pseudoallelic loci and is associated with two doublet bands in the salivary gland chromosomes.

> **Example 9.8.** A dominant mutation called "Star", affecting eye morphology and mapping at locus 1.3 was found in the second chromosome of *Drosophila*. Later, a recessive mutant called "asteroid" which also affects eye morphology was found to map at the same position. When large numbers of progeny from Star × Asteroid parents were raised, about 1 in 5000 showed recombination. Trans heterozygotes (S^+ *ast*/*S ast*$^+$) have reduced eye size whereas cis heterozygotes (S^+ *ast*$^+$/*S ast*) have normal eye size.

All geneticists are not in agreement on the definition of a gene. Perhaps the unit which comes closest to the concept of the classical Mendelian gene is the cistron. The cistron is a relatively large segment of genetic material when compared with the muton or the recon. An attempt to provide for these various segments, defined on the basis of different criteria, is found in the following statement. "The gene of function is that sequence of nucleotides (providing numerous sites for intragenic mutation and/or recombination) which specifies the amino acid sequence of a specific polypeptide chain."

REGULATION OF GENE ACTIVITY

Much of our knowledge of gene structure and gene action has come from the study of microorganisms. A knowledge of the enzyme systems of *E. coli* has been particularly useful in understanding the mechanism of gene regulation. The synthesis of enzymes may be broadly classified into two groups.

(1) Unregulated enzyme production.

  A *constitutive* enzyme is one which is produced continuously by the organism regardless of the presence or absence of its substrate in the environment.

(2) Regulated enzyme production.

  (*a*) An *inducible* enzyme is produced only when its substrate (inducer) is present in the environment. Most enzymes in this category are catabolic in their activity.

  (*b*) A *repressible* enzyme is normally present in the cell, but ceases to be synthesized when high concentrations of its end product are present. The end product is called *corepressor*. A regulator gene produces a substance called *aporepressor* which unites with corepressor to form a functional *repressor* molecule. The repressor inhibits synthesis of mRNA by all genes specifying enzymes in the synthetic pathway. Most repressible enzymes are found in anabolic pathways. Hormones may exert their phenotypic effects by derepressing genes previously repressed.

> **Example 9.9.** High concentrations of histidine in *Salmonella typhimurium* cause that amino acid to act as corepressor, thereby terminating synthesis of all 10 enzymes in the pathway to histidine (coordinate repression).

Feedback inhibition (or end-product inhibition) is a regulatory mechanism which does not affect enzyme synthesis, but rather inhibits enzyme activity. The end product of a synthetic pathway may combine loosely (if in high concentration) with the first enzyme in the pathway. This union does not occur at the catalytic site, but it does modify the tertiary structure of the enzyme and hence inactivates the catalytic site. This *allosteric transition* of protein blocks its enzymatic activity and prevents overproduction of end products and their intermediate metabolites.

Example 9.10   The end product isoleucine in *E. coli*, when present in high concentration, unites with the first enzyme in its synthetic pathway and thus inhibits the entire pathway until isoleucine returns to normal levels through cellular consumption.

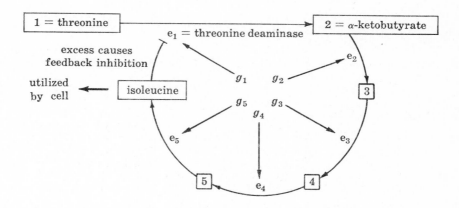

Genes may be broadly classified into two types: (1) genes for structure, (2) genes for function. *Structural* genes encode the specifications for the synthesis of some type of chemical substance. The substance may be (*a*) an enzyme, (*b*) a non-enzymatic structural protein (e.g. actin or myosin filaments of muscle cells, hemoglobin of red blood cells, etc.), (*c*) a protein called *repressor* which prevents the activity of some other gene. Genes which produce repressor substance are called *regulatory* genes. *Operator* genes, which are closely linked to one or more structural genes, produce no detectable substance. An operator controls the synthetic activity of the immediately adjacent structural genes by a mechanism not yet fully understood. An operator plus the structural genes under its control is called an *operon*. Perhaps the operator locus initiates transcription of adjacent DNA cistrons into mRNA molecules coding for one or more polypeptides. An active operator allows transcription to occur. If repressor substance is present, it may combine with the operator site, thereby preventing transcription of the structural genes of the operon into mRNA.

An example of the way an inductive enzyme system is presumed to function is provided by the lactose system of *E. coli*. Catabolism of the sugar lactose requires the cooperation of two enzymes: β-galactoside permease, which makes the cell permeable to the substrate (lactose), and β-galactosidase, an intracellular enzyme which splits the disaccharide into the simple sugars glucose and galactose. The operon consists of the operator (o), the gene for galactosidase (z) and the gene for permease (y). A regulator gene (i) is located near this operon. Some of the alleles which have been found at each of these loci and their functions are listed below.

Operator Alleles.

o^+ = this operator "turns on" the structural genes in its own operon, i.e. the y^+ and z^+ alleles in the same segment of DNA (cis position) can produce enzyme. This operator is sinsitive to repressor substance, i.e. it will "turn off" the synthetic activity of the structural genes in its operon if repressor is present.

o^c = a constitutive operator which is insensitive to repressor substance and permanently "turns on" the structural genes in its own operon.

o^o = a "defective" operator which permanently "turns off" the structural genes in its own operon (now known to be a lesion in a closely linked region of the galactosidase cistron).

Galactosidase Alleles.

z^+ = makes β-galactosidase if its operon is "turned on".

z^- = makes a modified enzymatically inactive substance called Cz protein.

Permease Alleles.

y^+ = makes β-galactoside permease if its operon is "turned on".

y^- = no detectable product is formed regardless of the state of the operator.

Regulator Alleles.

i^+ = makes a diffusible repressor substance which inhibits synthetic activity in any o^+ operon in the absence of lactose; in the presence of lactose, repressor substance is inactivated.

i^- = a defective regulator unable to produce active repressor substance.

i^s = superrepressor which is insensitive to the presence of lactose and inactivates any o^+ operon.

Example 9.11. Bacteria of genotype $i^+o^+z^+y^+$ grown on media devoid of lactose will produce neither galactosidase nor permease because i^+ makes repressor substance which inactivates the o^+ operator and "turns off" the synthetic activity of structural genes y^+ and z^+ in its own operon.

Example 9.12. Partial diploids can be produced in bacteria for this region of the chromosome. Cells of the genotype $\frac{i^-o^+z^+y^-}{i^+o^cz^-y^+}$ will produce Cz protein and permease constitutively (i.e. either with or without the presence of lactose inducer) because the allele o^c permanently "turns on" the genes in its operon (i.e. those in cis position with o^c). Galactosidase will be produced only inductively because in the presence of lactose (inducer) the diffusible repressor substance from i^+ will be inactivated and allow the structural gene z^+ in cis position with the o^+ operator to produce enzyme.

Solved Problems

9.1. How many of the 64 triplet permutations can be made from the four nucleotides A, U, G and C containing (a) no uracils, (b) one or more uracils?

Solution:

(a) Since uracil represents 1 among 4 nucleotides, the probability that uracil will be the first letter of the codon is 1/4; and the probability that U will not be the first letter is 3/4. The same reasoning holds true for the second and third letters of the codon. The probability that none of the three letters of the codon are uracils is $(3/4)^3 = 27/64$.

(b) The number of codons containing at least one uracil is $1 - 27/64 = 37/64$.

9.2. A synthetic polyribotide is produced from a mixture containing U and C in the relative frequencies of 5:1 respectively. Assuming that the ribotides form in a random linear array, predict the relative frequencies in which the various triplets are expected to be formed.

Solution:

The frequencies with which the different triplets are expected to be formed by chance associations can be predicted by combining independent probabilities through multiplication as follows:

UUU should occur with a frequency of $(5/6)(5/6)(5/6) = 125/216$.

Codons with 2U and 1C $= (5/6)^2(1/6) = 25/216$ each (UUC, UCU, CUU).

Codons with 1U and 2C $= (5/6)(1/6)^2 = 5/216$ each (UCC, CUC, CCU).

CCC $= (1/6)^3 = 1/216$.

9.3. Suppose that synthetic RNA's were made from a solution which contained 80% adenine and 20% uracil. The proteins produced in a bacterial cell-free system under direction of these mRNA's were found to contain amino acids in the following relative proportions: 4 times as many isoleucine as tyrosine residues, 16 times as many isoleucine as phenylalanine residues, 16 times as many lysine as tyrosine residues. What triplet codons were probably specifying each of the above amino acids?

Solution:

	Codon			Ratio	Amino Acid
AAA $=$	$(0.8)^3$	$=$	0.512	64	lysine
Some permutation of 2A and 1U $=$	$(0.8)^2(0.2)$	$=$	0.128	16	isoleucine
Some permutation of 1A and 2U $=$	$(0.8)(0.2)^2$	$=$	0.032	4	tyrosine
UUU $=$	$(0.2)^3$	$=$	0.008	1	phenylalanine

phe —4x→ tyr —4x→ ileu —4x→ lys

—— 16x ——

—— 16x ——

9.4. Phage MS2 is a single-stranded RNA virus of *E. coli*. When infected into a bacterium, the phage RNA (the "plus" strand) is made into a double-stranded replicative intermediate form ("plus–minus") from which "plus" RNA is synthesized. The "minus" strands when isolated are not infective. Phage X174 is a single-stranded DNA virus of *E. coli*. When infected into a bacterium, the same events as described for MS2 occur, but the "minus" strands when isolated are infective. Devise a reasonable hypothesis to account for these observations.

Solution:

The DNA "minus" strand can serve as a template and can utilize the bacterial enzyme DNA-polymerase for replication. The "minus" strand of RNA does not code for the enzyme which replicates RNA (RNA synthetase), and this enzyme is absent in uninfected bacteria. The "plus" strand of RNA carries the coded instructions for this enzyme and acts first as mRNA for enzyme synthesis. In the presence of the enzyme, single stranded RNA can form a complementary strand and becomes a double helix replicative form.

9.5.   H. J. Muller developed a system (*ClB* technique) for detecting recessive sex-linked lethal mutations induced by X-ray treatment in *Drosophila*. He used a heterozygous stock which had the dominant sex-linked gene "bar eye" (*B*) linked to a known recessive lethal gene (*l*). The segment of chromosome containing *B* and *l* was within an inversion (represented by the symbol *C*) which effectively prevented crossing over between the *B* and *l* loci. He began by mating these dihybrid bar eye females to wild type males which had been exposed to X-rays. He selected the F_1 bar eyed females and crossed them to unirradiated wild type males in small vials, one female per vial. The incidence of sex-linked recessive lethals induced by the X-ray treatment was determined from inspection of the F_2. What criterion did he use for this determination?

Solution:

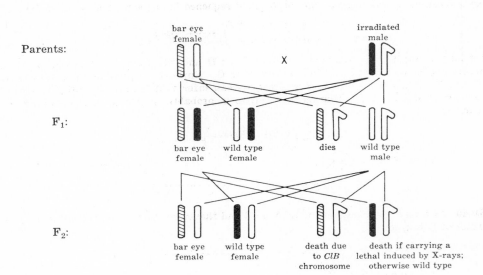

Any vials of the F_2 generation which are devoid of males can be scored as an X-ray induced sex-linked lethal as long as spontaneous mutations are considered negligible. The same procedure could be followed without irradiation treatment of the parental males to obtain an estimate of the rate of spontaneous sex-linked lethals. The reason that the F_1 bar eyed females can survive even though carrying two recessive lethals is that the X-ray induced lethal is, in all probability, at some locus other than the one in the *ClB* chromosome.

9.6.   If 54 mutations are detected among 723 progeny of males which received 2500 r (roentgens) and 78 mutations among 649 progeny of males which received 4000 r, how many mutants would be expected to appear among 1000 progeny of males which received 6000 r?

Solution:

The number of mutations induced by ionizing radiation is directly proportional to the dosage.

$$78/649 \;=\; 12.02\% \text{ mutations at } 4000 \text{ r}$$
$$54/723 \;=\; 7.47\% \text{ mutations at } 2500 \text{ r}$$
$$\text{Difference} \;=\; 4.55\% \text{ mutations for } 1500 \text{ r}$$

Among 1000 progeny at 6000 r we expect $1000(6000/1500)(0.0455) = 182$ mutants.

9.7. Four single mutant strains of *Neurospora* are unable to grow on minimal medium unless supplemented by one or more of the substances A through F. In the following table, growth is indicated by + and no growth by 0. Both strains 2 and 4 grow if E and F or C and F are added to minimal medium. Diagram a biochemical pathway consistent with the data involving all six metabolites, indicating where the mutant block occurs in each of the four strains.

Strain	A	B	C	D	E	F
1	+	0	0	0	0	0
2	+	0	0	+	0	0
3	+	0	+	0	0	0
4	+	0	0	0	0	0

Solution:

Strain 1 will grow only if given substance A. Therefore the defective enzyme produced by the mutant gene in this strain must act sometime prior to the formation of substance A and after the formation of substances B, C, D, E and F. In other words, this mutation is probably causing a metabolic block in the last step of the biochemical sequence in the synthesis of substance A.

$$\left(\begin{array}{c} \text{B, C, D, E, F} \\ \text{order unknown} \end{array} \right) \xrightarrow{\quad 1 \quad} A$$

Strain 2 grows if supplemented by either A or D and therefore its metabolic block must act somewhere earlier in the pathway than either A or D. Since the dual addition of substances E and F or C and F can also cause strain 2 to grow, we can infer that D may be split into two fractions E and F or C and F. The mutation in strain 2 is probably unable to convert substance B into substance D.

$$B \xrightarrow{\ 2\ } D \left\{ \begin{array}{l} \left(\begin{array}{c} \text{order unknown} \\ \text{E, C} \end{array} \right) \\ F \end{array} \right\} \xrightarrow{\ 1\ } A$$

Strain 3 grows if supplemented with A or C and therefore its metabolic block must precede the formation of C but not E.

$$B \xrightarrow{\ 2\ } D \left\{ \begin{array}{l} E \xrightarrow{\ 3\ } C \\ F \end{array} \right\} \xrightarrow{\ 1\ } A$$

Strain 4 can grow if given dual supplementation of E and F or C and F but not if given D alone. The mutation in strain 4 apparently cannot split D into E and F.

$$B \xrightarrow{\ 2\ } D \xrightarrow{\ 4\ } \left\{ \begin{array}{l} E \xrightarrow{\ 3\ } C \\ F \end{array} \right\} \xrightarrow{\ 1\ } A$$

9.8. The two hypothetical biosynthetic pathways shown below are available to an organism. At any one time, only product C or Z is being made. When the intermediate substance B reaches a threshold concentration, it inhibits enzyme 3 (E_3) by allosteric transition. Similarly substance Y inhibits E_1. (*a*) Propose some factors which might determine how one or the other reaction sequence could be "turned on" initially. (*b*) How is this system different from the operon models?

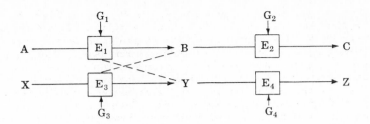

Solution:

(a) During the normal developmental process, substance A might become available to the organism before substance X, in which case only product C will be made. On the other hand, product B might later become a metabolite in some other reaction sequence thereby lowering its concentration below the threshold level necessary to inhibit E_3. In this case product Z would be made and synthesis of B and C would terminate. If the organism was making product Z normally and then came into an environment where substance B was present in relatively high concentration, synthesis of Y and Z would terminate and that of B and C would commence. Perhaps the enzymes of one sequence would be more sensitive to variations in temperature than those of the other sequence. Perhaps at high temperatures E_1 would become inactivated but E_3 would still be functional. The phenotype could thus be modified through manipulation of the environment, either by controlling the temperature or by the concentration of intermediates in one of the reaction sequences.

(b) Operon circuits are presumed to function at the "chromosomal" level and involve the sensitivity of an operator locus to the product of a regulator gene (repressor substance). In the model proposed in this problem, all of the interactions are removed from the gene; an intermediate metabolite in one reaction sequence directly inhibits the enzymatic activity in another sequence.

Supplementary Problems

DNA AND PROTEIN SYNTHESIS

9.9. Given a single strand of DNA $...^{3'}$TACCGAGTAC$^{5'}...$, construct (a) the complementary DNA chain, (b) the mRNA chain which would be made from this strand.

9.10. Suppose a bacterium is grown for many generations in a medium where the only nitrogen source is radioactive "heavy" nitrogen (N^{15}). In the resulting clone, both strands of the DNA will thereby come to be composed of heavy nitrogen. Some of the bacteria are then transferred to medium containing only light nitrogen (N^{14}). (a) We allow one generation of reproduction to occur in N^{14} and then analyze the DNA of this first generation by density gradient centrifugation. What kinds of DNA are expected to be found? (b) What is the density of the first generation DNA expected to be relative to N^{14} and N^{15}? (c) If we allow a second generation of replication to occur in N^{14}, what DNA composition is expected in the population? (d) Now we allow a third generation of replication to occur in N^{14}. What DNA composition is expected in the population?

9.11. The size of a hemoglobin gene in man is estimated to consist of approximately 450 nucleotide pairs. The protein product of the gene is estimated to consist of about 150 amino acid residues. Estimate the size of the codon.

9.12. Using the information in Table 9.1, page 178, convert the following mRNA segments into their polypeptide equivalents (a) $...^{5'}$GAAAUGGCAGUUUAC$^{3'}...$, (b) $...^{3'}$UUUUCGAGAUGUCAA$^{5'}...$, (c) $...^{5'}$AAAACCUAGAACCCA$^{3'}...$.

9.13. In a system containing 70% U and 30% C and an enzyme that links ribotides at random into a synthetic mRNA, determine the relative frequencies with which all possible triplet codons would be expected to be formed.

9.14. Acridine dyes can apparently cause a mutation in the bacteriophage T4 by the addition or subtraction (deletion) of a base in the DNA chain. A number of such mutants have been found in the rII region of T4 to be single base addition type (+) or deletion type (−) mutants. A normal or wild type rII region produces a normal lytic period (small plaque size) in the host bacterium *E. coli* strain B. Phage T4 mutant in the rII region rapidly lyses strain B, producing a larger plaque. Several multiple mutant strains of T4 have been developed. Suppose the mutant sites are close together and also in a region of the chromosome which is not essential to the normal functioning of the protein specified by this gene. Determine the lytic phenotypes (large plaque or small plaque) produced by the following rII single base mutations in *E. coli* B assuming a triplet codon: (*a*) (+), (*b*) (+)(−), (*c*) (+)(+), (*d*) (−)(−), (*e*) (+)(−)(+), (*f*) (+)(+)(+), (*g*) (−)(−)(+), (*h*) (−)(−)(−), (*i*) (+)(+)(+)(+), (*j*) (+)(−)(+)(+)(+).

9.15. A single base addition and a single base deletion approximately 15 bases apart in the mRNA specifying the protein lysozyme from the bacterial virus T4 caused a change in the protein from its normal composition ...lys-ser-pro-ser-leu-asn-ala-ala-lys... to the abnormal form ...lys-val-his-his-leu-met-ala-ala-lys.... (*a*) From the mRNA codons listed in Table 9.1, decipher the segment of mRNA for both the original protein and the double mutant. (*b*) Which base was added? Which was deleted?

9.16. In polynucleotides containing uracil and cytosine produced from a mixture of ribotides where uracil is in excess, more serine is incorporated into polypeptides than proline. However, when cytosine is in excess more proline is incorporated than serine. (*a*) Without reference to Table 9.1, list the codons containing uracil and cytosine which could possibly be coding for serine and for proline. (*b*) Using Table 9.1, page 178, determine the percentage of the various amino acids expected to be incorporated into polypeptides by a synthetic polynucleotide in which uracil constitutes 60% and cytosine 40% of the U-C mixture. (*c*) How much more phenylalanine is expected to be incorporated into protein than proline?

9.17. If the DNA of an *E. coli* has 4.2×10^6 nucleotide pairs in its DNA, and if an average cistron contains 1500 nucleotide pairs, how many cistrons does it possess?

9.18. The following experiment was performed: a short pulse of radioactive isotopes of the 20 amino acids is given to rabbit reticulocytes as they are synthesizing hemoglobin. The introduction of radioactive label occurs when some hemoglobin molecules are partly completed but unlabeled. Shortly after the pulse, completely finished hemoglobin molecules are isolated and analyzed for the location of the radioactive label. Where would you expect to find the label, and why?

9.19. The DNA of phage *lambda* has 1.2×10^5 nucleotides. How many proteins of molecular weight 40,000 could be coded by this DNA? Assume a molecular weight of 100 for the average amino acid.

9.20. In phage T4, deletion 1589 lacks part of the A and B cistrons of the rII region and shows no A but partial B activity in *E. coli* strain B. When a single defect (deletion or addition) is induced in the A cistron by acridine, the B cistron activity is suppressed. What hypothesis is supported by these observations?

MUTATIONS

9.21. The "dotted" gene in maize (*Dt*) is a "mutator" gene influencing the rate at which the gene for colorless aleurone (*a*) mutates to its dominant allele (*A*) for colored aleurone. An average of 7.2 colored dots (mutations) per kernel was observed when the seed parent was *dt/dt, a/a* and the pollen parent was *Dt/Dt, a/a*. An average of 22.2 dots per kernel was observed in the reciprocal cross. How can these results be explained?

9.22. Assuming no intensity effect is operative, which individual would carry fewer mutations; an individual who receives 25 roentgens in 5 hours or an individual who receives only 0.5 roentgens per year for his normal lifetime (60 years)? In terms of percentage, how many more mutations would be expected in the individual with the higher total dosage?

9.23. If the mutation rate of a certain gene is directly proportional to the radiation dosage and the mutation rate of *Drosophila* is observed to increase from 3% at 1000 r to 6% at 2000 r, what percentage of mutations would be expected at 3500 r?

9.24. The frequency of spontaneous mutation at the *R* (plant color) locus in maize is very high (492 per 10^6 gametes). The gene for red aleurone (*Pr*) is estimated to mutate in 11 out of 10^6 gametes. How many plants must be investigated on the basis of probability to find one with mutations at both loci?

9.25. A strain of *Drosophila* called Muller-5 contains the dominant sex-linked mutation for bar eye (B) and the apricot allele of the sex-linked white eye locus (w^{ap}) together with an inversion to prevent crossing over between them. Homozygous bar-apricot females are crossed to X-irradiated wild type males. Each F_1 female is placed in a separate vial together with one or two unirradiated wild type males. Upon inspection of the F_2, what criterion can be used for scoring induced sex-linked lethals?

9.26. Single wild type female *Drosophila* possessing attached-X chromosomes ($\widehat{XX}Y$) is mated to an irradiated wild type male. (*a*) In which generation can a sex-linked mutation be detected? (*b*) What criterion is used to detect a sex-linked viable mutation? (*c*) What criterion is used to detect a sex-linked lethal mutation? (*d*) What percentage death loss is anticipated among the F_1 zygotes due to causes other than lethal mutations?

9.27. A method is known for rendering chromosome 2 of *Drosophila* homozygous so that all recessive mutants induced in that chromosome by irradiation can be detected. This method uses a balanced lethal system involving three genes on the second chromosome: curly wings (Cy), plum eye color (Pm) and lobe eye shape (L). A ($Cy + L/+ Pm +$) female fly is mated to an X-rayed wild type male. A curly, lobed F_1 male is then backcrossed to a curly, plum, lobed female. From the backcross progeny, select and intercross curly-lobe flies. Predict the phenotypic ratios among the offspring when (*a*) no mutant was induced, (*b*) a viable recessive mutant was induced, (*c*) a semilethal or subvital was induced, (*d*) a lethal was induced.

9.28. The number of sex-linked lethals in *Drosophila* as detected by the *ClB* and Muller-5 techniques (Problems 9.5 and 9.25) increases in direct proportion to the amount of radiation at low dosage levels. However, at high dosage levels the amount of detectable lethal mutations falls below the linear expectations. How can this phenomenon be explained?

9.29. If the production of chromosomal rearrangements such as inversions or reciprocal translocations requires two hits on chromosomes within the same nucleus, then one might expect the number of such rearrangements to increase more nearly as the square of the radiation dosage rather than in direct proportion to the dosage. If 100 r produces 2.5% single-hit mutations, what percentage of double-hits would be expected at 150 r (neglecting background mutations)?

9.30. Assume that the rate of induced mutations is directly proportional to the radiation dosage. Further suppose that 372 individuals out of 6000 incur a mutation at 2000 r, and that 610 out of 5000 individuals incur a mutation at 4000 r. Estimate the spontaneous mutation rate.

9.31. Concerning a single nucleotide pair, list all possible (*a*) transitions, (*b*) transversions. (*c*) If purines and pyrimidines become replaced at random during evolution, what ratio of transversions to transitions is expected? (*d*) A comparison of homologous residues in the polypeptide chains of hemoglobins and myoglobins from various species indicates that 293 transitions and 548 transversions have probably occurred during evolution. Are these figures consistent with the hypothesis that transitions and transversions occur in a $1:2$ ratio respectively? Test the hypothesis by chi-square.

9.32. A number of nutritional mutant strains was isolated from wild type *Neurospora* which responded to the addition of certain supplements in the culture medium by growth (+) or no growth (0). Given the following responses for single gene mutants, diagram a metabolic pathway which could exist in the wild type strain consistent with the data, indicating where the chain is blocked in each mutant strain.

(*a*)

Mutant Strain	Supplements added to minimal culture medium				
	Citrulline	Glutamic semi-aldehyde	Arginine	Ornithine	Glutamic acid
1	+	0	+	0	0
2	+	+	+	+	0
3	+	0	+	+	0
4	0	0	+	0	0

(b)

Strain	Growth Factors			
	A	B	C	D
1	0	0	+	+
2	0	0	0	+
3	+	0	+	+
4	0	+	+	+

(c)

Strain	Nutrients			
	E	F	G	H
1	+	0	0	+
2	0	0	+	+
3	0	0	0	+
4	0	+	0	+

REGULATION OF GENE ACTIVITY

9.33. In addition to the i^+ allele, producing repressor for the lactose system in *E. coli* and the constitutive i^- allele, a third allele i^s has been found, the product of which is unable to combine with the inducer (lactose). Hence the repressor ("superrepressor") made by i^s remains unbound and free to influence the operator locus. In addition to the repressor-sensitive o^+ operator and its constitutive o^c allele, an inactive or "null" allele o^o is known which permanently turns off or inactivates the operon under both induced and non-induced conditions. (*a*) Order the three alleles of the *i*-locus in descending order of dominance according to their ability to influence the lactose operator. (*b*) Order the three alleles of the *o*-locus in descending order of dominance according to their ability to "turn on" their operon. (*c*) Using + for production and 0 for non-production of the enzymes permease (P) and β-galactosidase (β-gal), complete the following table.

Genotype	Inducer Absent		Inducer Present	
	P	β-gal	P	β-gal
(1) $i^+o^+y^+z^+$				
(2) $i^-o^+y^+z^+$				
(3) $i^s o^+y^+z^+$				
(4) $i^+o^c y^+z^+$				
(5) $i^+o^o y^+z^+$				
(6) $i^-o^c y^+z^+$				
(7) $i^-o^o y^+z^+$				
(8) $i^s o^c y^+z^+$				
(9) $i^s o^o y^+z^+$				

9.34. For each of the following partial diploids, determine if enzyme formation is constitutive or inductive: (*a*) $i^+/i^+, o^+/o^+$, (*b*) $i^+/i^+, o^+/o^c$, (*c*) $i^+/i^+, o^c/o^c$, (*d*) $i^+/i^-, o^+/o^+$, (*e*) $i^-/i^-, o^+/o^+$.

9.35. In the lactose system of *E. coli*, y^+ makes permease, an enzyme essential for the rapid transportation of galactosides from the medium to the interior of the cell. Its allele y^- makes no permease. The galactoside lactose must enter the cell in order to induce the z^+ gene to produce the enzyme β-galactosidase. The allele z^- makes a related but enzymatically inactive protein called Cz. Predict the production or non-production of each of these products with a normal operator o^+ by placing a + or 0 respectively in the table below.

Genotype	Inducer Absent			Inducer Present		
	P	β-gal	Cz	P	β-gal	Cz
(*a*) $i^+y^+z^-$						
(*b*) $i^+y^+z^+$						
(*c*) $i^-y^+z^+$						
(*d*) $i^+y^-z^+$						
(*e*) $i^-y^-z^-$						
(*f*) $i^-y^-z^+$						

9.36. The i^- allele allows constitutive enzyme production by the y^+ and z^+ factors in an operon with a normal operator gene o^+. The action of i^- might be explained by one of two alternatives: (1) i^- produces an internal *inducer*, thus eliminating the need for lactose in the medium to induce enzyme synthesis; i^+ produces no inducer or (2) i^+ produces a *repressor* substance which, in the absence of lactose inducer, blocks enzyme formation, but in the presence of lactose inducer becomes inactivated and allows enzyme synthesis; i^- produces no repressor. (a) Assuming dominance of the i^- allele under the first alternative in an *E. coli* partial heterozygote of the constitution i^+/i^-, would internal inducer be produced? (b) Would enzymes be produced constitutively or inductively? (c) Assuming dominance of the i^+ allele under the second alternative in a partial heterozygote of the constitution i^+/i^-, would repressor be produced? (d) Would enzymes be produced constitutively or inductively? (e) From the pattern of reactions exhibited by different heterozygotes in the following table, determine which of the two assumptions is correct.

Genotypes	Lactose Absent		Lactose Present	
	P	β-gal	P	β-gal
(1) $o^+y^-z^-i^-/o^+y^+z^+i^-$	+	+	+	+
(2) $o^+y^+z^+i^-/o^+y^-z^-i^-$	+	+	+	+
(3) $o^+y^-z^-i^-/o^+y^+z^+i^+$	0	0	+	+
(4) $o^+y^-z^-i^+/o^+y^+z^+i^-$	0	0	+	+

(f) Is the repressor substance diffusible, or can it only act on loci in cis position with the i-locus? How can this be determined from the information in the table of part (e)?

Answers to Supplementary Problems

9.9. (a) $^{5'}$ATGGCTCATG$^{3'}$ (b) $^{5'}$AUGGCUCAUG$^{3'}$

9.10. (a) All hybrid molecules with one strand containing N^{15} and the other strand containing N^{14} (b) intermediate between N^{15} and N^{14} (c) $\frac{1}{2}$ hybrid DNA molecules : $\frac{1}{2}$ light DNA molecules (both strands N^{14}) (d) 25% hybrid DNA : 75% light DNA

9.11. Approximately 3 nucleotides code for each amino acid

9.12. (a) - glu - met - ala - val - tyr -   (b) - phe - ala - arg - cys - asn -   (c) - lys - thr - (nonsense), chain terminates prematurely

9.13. $3U = 0.343$, $2U + 1C = 0.441$, $1U + 2C = 0.189$, $3C = 0.027$

9.14. (a), (c), (d), (e), (g), (i) = large; (b), (f), (h), (j) = small

9.15. (a)

	lys	ser	pro	ser	leu	asn	ala
normal mRNA	AA?	A GU	CCA	UCA	CUU	AAU	GC?
mutant mRNA	AA?	GUC	CAU	CAC	UUA	AUG	G C?
	lys	val	his	his	leu	met	ala

(b) G was added, A was deleted (at shaded positions)

9.16. (a) serine: UUC, UCU, CUU; proline: CCU, CUC, UCC. (b) phenylalanine = 0.36, leucine = 0.24, proline = 0.16, serine = 0.24. (c) $2\frac{1}{4}$

9.17. 2800 cistrons

9.18. Most molecules would be labeled more in the COOH end because synthesis is unidirectional starting at the NH_2 end.

9.19. 50 proteins, assuming only one chain of the DNA is transcribed into mRNA.

9.20. Codons of the rII region are read unidirectionally beginning at the A end.

9.21. Seed parent contributes two sets of chromosomes to triploid endosperm; one *Dt* gene gives 7.2 mutations/kernel, two *Dt* genes increase mutations to 22.2/kernel

9.22. 20% more mutations in the individual receiving 0.5 r/yr.

9.23. $10\frac{1}{2}\%$

9.24. 1.848×10^8 (approx.)

9.25. Any vial which does not contain wild type male progeny is the result of a sex-linked lethal induced by X-ray treatment.

9.26. (*a*) F_1 (*b*) The appearance of the mutant trait in all F_1 males in a vial. (*c*) The absence of F_1 males in any vial. (*d*) 50%; superfemales ($\overset{\wedge}{\mathbf{XXX}}$) are usually inviable; all zygotes without an X chromosome die.

9.27. (*a*) 2/3 curly, lobe : 1/3 wild type (*b*) 2/3 curly, lobe : 1/3 recessive mutant (*c*) greater than 2/3 curly, lobe : less than 1/3 wild type (*d*) all curly, lobe

9.28. A single ionization ("hit") of a genetic element may destroy the functioning of a vital gene and result in death. Multiple hits at high dosage levels score as a single lethal event.

9.29. 14.0625%

9.30. 0.2%

9.31. (*a*)

Original DNA	A : T	T : A	G : C	C : G
Transition DNA	G : C	C : G	A : T	T : A

(*b*)

Original DNA	A : T	A : T	T : A	T : A	G : C	G : C	C : G	C : G
Transversion DNA	T : A	C : G	A : T	G : C	T : A	C : G	A : T	G : C

(*c*) **2 transversions : 1 transition**

(*d*) Yes. $\chi^2 = 0.86$, P = 0.3-0.5

9.32. (*a*)

(*b*)

(*c*)

9.33. (a) i^s, i^+, i^- (b) o^c, o^+, o^o

(c)

	Inducer Absent		Inducer Present	
	P	β-gal	P	β-gal
(1)	0	0	+	+
(2, 4, 6, 8)	+	+	+	+
(3, 5, 7, 9)	0	0	0	0

9.34. (a), (d) = inductive;   (b), (c), (e) = constitutive

9.35.

	Inducer Absent			Inducer Present		
	P	β-gal	Cz	P	β-gal	Cz
(a)	0	0	0	+	0	+
(b)	0	0	0	+	+	0
(c)	+	+	0	+	+	0
(d)	0	0	0	0	+	0
(e)	0	0	+	0	0	+
(f)	0	+	0	0	+	0

9.36. (a) Yes (b) Constitutively (c) Yes (d) Inductively (e) Note that in (3) and (4) the i^- allele fails to produce enzymes in the absence of the external inducer (lactose). It fails to exhibit dominance. Therefore the first assumption is incorrect. Under the second assumption, i^+ is dominant and produces repressor which, in the absence of lactose inducer, blocks enzyme synthesis as seen in (3) and (4). (f) Heterozygote (4) has y^+ and z^+ on one DNA segment and the i^+ allele on the other. Yet in the absence of lactose inducer, the repressor made by i^+ still prevents the production of enzymes by y^+ and z^+. Therefore repressor must be able to act at a distance (diffusible).

Chapter 10

Genetics of Microorganisms

MATERIAL FOR GENETIC STUDY

There are several advantages in the genetic study of microorganisms such as viruses and bacteria. Most microorganisms have only one set of chromosomes or one set of genetic instructions, as is characteristic of the haploid gamete of a diploid organism. The genes of a haploid organism are neither dominant nor recessive, since these terms are without meaning where only one allele is present in an individual. In this respect, the study of microorganisms is relatively simple because, barring interaction, every gene which the individual possesses can be expressed in its phenotype. Moreover, the study of rare events such as mutations is facilitated by the ease with which very large populations of microorganisms (e.g. 10^6 to 10^9 individuals) can be raised within the confines of a petri dish or a test tube. Use of selective media can easily isolate one mutant individual cell in a million. The relative simplicity of microorganisms such as viruses offers the best opportunity for studying gene structure and function at the molecular level. Most microorganisms have short generation times. For example, some bacteria divide about once every 30 minutes. Beginning with a single cell, thirty generations can elapse within fifteen hours, producing approximately a billion progeny cells. All of the asexual descendants of a single bacterium are genetically identical (barring mutation) and are referred to as a *clone* or colony visible to the naked eye when grown on solid medium such as an agar plate.

One of the disadvantages of using some microorganisms for genetic studies is the relative dearth of regular recombinational events. Asexual (vegetative) reproduction is by *amitosis*, a direct nuclear division without formation of condensed chromosomes or spindle fibers. Some sexual mechanisms are known to exist and these will be described in this chapter. Another disadvantage is the relative lack of morphological variation in microorganisms. Study of the gross phenotypic characteristics of an individual is generally unfruitful because of its very small size. The morphology of a clone grown on an agar plate, however, may exhibit variation in size per unit time, shape of perimeter or growth habit, texture, color, etc. Genetically different clones may respond differentially to nutrients, dyes, drugs, or pathogens in the culture medium. Wild type strains are able to grow on minimal medium (*prototrophic*), whereas some mutant strains require supplementation (*auxotrophic*). Though they are called haploid, most bacteria are actually multinucleate. A delay in phenotypic expression of some mutants is to be anticipated until nuclear and bacterial divisions can segregate out the mutated nuclei from the others to form a pure clone. The more nuclei per cell the longer the delay is expected to be. Even viruses, too small to be seen with the light microscope, can show variation in the type of cell they will parasitize (host range), in the rapidity with which they cause rupturing of its host cell (lysis), and in the shape of the "hole" (*plaque*) which appears in a confluent growth of host cells on solid media. These variations may become apparent to the investigator only after several recombinational events or "rounds of matings" have occurred, so that population dynamics may become a source of confusion in genetic analysis. Bacteria and viruses do not possess easily visible chromosomes comparable to those of higher organisms, thus precluding cytological study at that level. But even the morphology of viruses can now be studied through the electron microscope.

BACTERIA

1. Asexual Reproduction.

Most reproduction in bacteria is asexually accomplished by amitosis, a process often referred to as "binary fission". A large population of bacteria (10^8-10^9 cells) can be grown in liquid media (broth) and then distributed evenly over an agar plate so that a solid mass of cells, called a "lawn", covers the surface of the agar. If one mutant cell in a million is present in this lawn it can be detected by the use of selective media. For example, if a mutation to streptomycin resistance has occurred in a sensitive strain, we could plate the bacteria on agar containing streptomycin. All cells without the mutation would be sensitive to this antibiotic and unable to grow; only the streptomycin resistant mutant would form a colony. Furthermore, the spontaneous mutation to streptomycin resistance would be produced regardless of the presence or absence of streptomycin in the environment. Some kinds of spontaneous mutations are *preadaptive,* i.e. they would be advantageous to the organism in a different environment. This can be demonstrated by a technique called *replica plating*. A sterile piece of velvet is impressed onto a lawn of bacteria grown on agar without streptomycin (master plate) and transferred to any number of agar plates containing streptomycin (replica plates). The nap of the velvet picks up representatives of each clone from the master plate and inoculates them onto each replica plate. The position of the clones which grow on each replica plate is always the same, indicating that the mutation to streptomycin resistance occurred in the master plate prior to any contact with streptomycin, i.e. the mutation is preadapted to surviving in a different environment, namely in the presence of streptomycin.

Example 10.1.   Master Plate   Replica Plates
Without Streptomycin   Containing Streptomycin

Lawn of 10^8 bacteria

2. Genetic Recombination.

Several mechanisms exist in bacteria which can effect recombination.

(a) *Transformation* — naked DNA molecules from one bacterial strain can be "absorbed" by another strain and utilized in the production of a new (recombinant) phenotype.

(b) *Conjugation* — the unidirectional transfer of genetic information through the formation of a cytoplasmic bridge from one cell to another.

(c) *Transduction* — gene transfer from one bacterium to another mediated by a virus. Bacterial viruses are called *bacteriophage* or simply *phage*, symbolized ϕ.

(d) *Sexduction* — bacterial genes carried from one cell to another on a molecule of DNA which acts as a "sex factor" called F. This sex gene can reside in a bacterial chromosome or it may exist as an autonomous unit extrachromosomally. Genetic elements which possess the dual capacity to exist either as a chromosomal or an extrachromosomal entity are called *episomes*. Sexduction is sometimes referred to as "F-mediated transduction" or "F-duction".

(a) *Transformation.*

When pneumococci are surrounded by polysaccharide capsules, they are *virulent* (capable of producing disease) and form colonies with a smooth border on solid medium. Unencapsulated pneumococci are *avirulent* and plate as rough shaped colonies. When a rough strain is exposed to a purified DNA extract from a smooth strain, some rough cells are *transformed* into smooth cells. This is one line of evidence in the proof that DNA is genetic material. Transformation may occur in some species with frequencies as high as 25% but more commonly occurs at very low frequencies. Aging cultures of some bacteria spontaneously incur cell rupture (autolysis) which releases DNA into the environment with other cells, and thereby offers the opportunity for transformation to occur. A cell must be in a physiologically receptive state, called *competence,* which occurs only during a fraction of its growth cycle. During competence, DNA is transiently bound to the cell surface. Each cell has a number of sites at which DNA can attach. These receptor sites can be saturated with nontransforming DNA (e.g. DNA from an unrelated organism), thus preventing the appearance of transformants. Only relatively large DNA fragments can penetrate the competent cell, but once inside, the DNA is permanently bound. One explanation of the integration process assumes that DNA penetrates only at two sites corresponding to the two replication sites located internally on the cell membrane. As transforming DNA rotates past the stationary replication fork, the synthesis of host DNA is interrupted at the homologous region and transforming DNA becomes integrated into the host chromosome. Usually only a small segment of transforming DNA becomes integrated. Transforming DNA is never found free in the cytoplasm, and is capable of producing a phenotypic effect only after integration. The frequency of transformation increases with the concentration of DNA up to the saturation level. If two markers are closely linked on the same transforming piece of DNA, they may both attain phenotypic expression. Such *double transformation* events are rare and their frequency is a function of the degree of linkage.

(b) *Conjugation.*

The genetic material of bacteria and viruses is organized into a single circular structure rather than into several linear structures as in higher organisms. *Conjugation* is a one way transfer of DNA from a donor cell (male) to a recipient cell (female). In *Escherichia coli* strain K-12, the male possesses many replicas of the sex factor F and is symbolized F^+ when the sex factor is in its extrachromosomal phase. Females do not have the sex factor and are symbolized F^-. When F^+ cells conjugate with F^- cells, one or more sex factors are transmitted across the cytoplasmic bridge to infect the F^- recipients and convert them into F^+ (male) cells. No other genetic material is transferred in $F^+ \times F^-$ conjugations.

A few of the F^+ cells in a culture may integrate one of the sex particles into its bacterial "chromosome". These cells are then called Hfr (high frequency of recombination) cells with potential for genetic transfer. Extrachromosomal F particles soon disintegrate and disappear in newly formed Hfr cells. When an F particle takes up residence in the chromosome, it breaks the ring at that point. The end of the chromosome distal to the F factor is the first to be transferred during conjugation. The F factor at the terminal end of the Hfr chromosome is seldom transferred, since the cytoplasmic bridge is maintained for only a short period of time. Rupture of the bridge stops the transfer of donor genetic material into the recipient cell. Thus unless the entire chromosome is transferred (with F particle at its terminal end) the exconjugant (recipient cell after conjugation is completed) of Hfr $\times$ F^- is always F^-. Each Hfr strain transfers its markers in a particular order.

For a few generations after conjugation the exconjugant will be a partial diploid (*merozygote*) for that portion of the chromosome it received from the Hfr. Unless the extra piece (*exogenote* or *merogenote*) becomes integrated into the host chromosome, it is eventually lost and the merozygote again becomes haploid.

Example 10.2.

This Hfr strain transfers its markers in the order BCDEGAF.

This Hfr strain transfers its markers in the order GABCDEF.

This Hfr strain transfers its markers in the order DEGABCF.

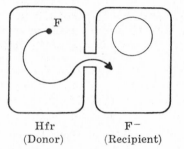

Hfr
(Donor)

F⁻
(Recipient)

(c) *Transduction.*

In order to understand transduction, we must first become familiar with the life cycle of bacteriophage. The best known of the transducing systems is the lambda (λ) phage in its host *E. coli* and phage P22 in its host *Salmonella typhimurium*. The lytic cycle of the virulent T-even phages (2, 4, 6) which infect *E. coli* is represented in Fig. 10-1.

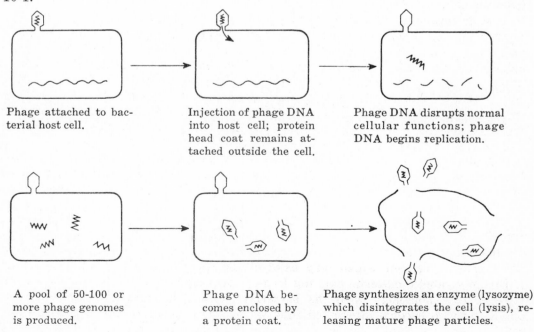

Phage attached to bacterial host cell.

Injection of phage DNA into host cell; protein head coat remains attached outside the cell.

Phage DNA disrupts normal cellular functions; phage DNA begins replication.

A pool of 50-100 or more phage genomes is produced.

Phage DNA becomes enclosed by a protein coat.

Phage synthesizes an enzyme (lysozyme) which disintegrates the cell (lysis), releasing mature phage particles.

Fig. 10-1.   Life cycle of T-even phages

When a virus infects a cell, it has two mutually exclusive choices: (1) it can act as a *virulent* phage and enter the vegetative (lytic) cycle or (2) it can act as a nonvirulent (temperate) phage, becoming integrated into the host chromosome as a *prophage* and replicating in synchrony with the bacterial chromosome. A cell which harbors a prophage is said to be *lysogenic* because the prophage DNA may, under appropriate conditions, be released or *induced* from the bacterial chromosome (*deintegration*) and returned to the lytic phase. Lysogenic bacteria usually cannot be distinguished from normal bacterial cells with the exception that lysogenic cells are immune to infection by other phage of the same species. Some lysogenic bacteria can be induced to release their prophage from the host chromosome by treatment with ultraviolet light (UV induction) or by the process of conjugation (zygotic induction).

When a prophage deintegrates from the bacterial chromosome, it may take with it a small adjacent segment of host DNA, loosing some of its own genome in the process. Such a phage particle can mediate the transfer of a bacterial gene or a portion of a bacterial gene from one cell to another in a process called *transduction*. All transducing phages are defective for a portion of their own genome. There are two major types of transducing phages: (1) generalized transducers and (2) restricted transducers.

Generalized transducers do not have a specific site of attachment to the chromosome; they may attach anywhere, and thus have an equal probability of transducing any gene. If the exogenote of a generalized transducing phage is incorporated into the genome of the recipient, a clone of recombinant haploid cells is produced. This is termed *complete transduction*. If the exogenote fails to be integrated, but is maintained as a non-replicating particle, it will exist as a merozygote in only one cell of a clone (*abortive transduction*).

Restricted transduction occurs only in cells which possess a prophage integrated into the chromosome at a specific locus called the "prophage site." Only the locus immediately adjacent to the prophage site can be transduced. The best example is the phage λ (lambda) in *E. coli* strain K12. The prophage site of λ is adjacent to the bacterial gene for galactose fermentation (gal^+). When a gal^+ strain lysogenic for λ is induced to lyse by means of ultraviolet light a few of the λ particles will carry the gal^+ gene. A transducing λ, having "traded" part of its own genome for the gal^+ marker, is called λdg (defective lambda galactose) and therefore can neither lyse nor lysogenize a host cell by itself. If a lysogenic gal^- bacterial strain (containing a normal λ pro-phage) is exposed to a solution containing λdg, the few resulting gal^+ transductants become unstable heterogenotes gal^+/gal^- ("double lysogenization"). The exogenote in restricted transduction is not integrated into the host chromosome, but may replicate with the host to form a clone of heterogenotes. When these heterogenotes are induced to lyse (by the activity of the normal "helper" phage) nearly every λ particle carries *gal* genes, resulting in a high frequency of transduction (Hft). Lysogenization and transduction are mutually exclusive properties of a single phage particle.

(d) Sexduction.

Recall from the discussion of conjugation that the sex factor (F) is an episome, i.e. a genetic element which may exist either chromosomally or extrachromosomally. If the only genetic material existing in an F particle is the sex gene, it would probably possess little homology with the bacterial chromosome and hence would have little opportunity to become integrated into the host chromosome (converting it into a Hfr cell). When an F particle in an Hfr cell deintegrates, it may include a portion of adjacent host chromosome. Such an F particle is said to possess *chromosomal memory* and would be expected, upon infection, to become integrated into the F$^-$ chromosome with relatively high frequency. Occasionally the memory piece of an F particle is long enough to allow the sex factor to autonomously replicate as an infectious particle and it may also be capable of producing a phenotypic effect if it carries a complete cistron. This process is called *sexduction* and may produce phenotypic effects in merozygotes by complementation or by becoming integrated into the host chromosome.

Example 10.3.

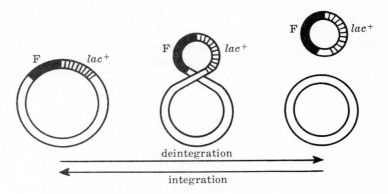

If the lactose locus is adjacent to the F locus, an F-*lac*$^+$ particle can be formed by deintegration (breakage and reunion).

MAPPING THE BACTERIAL CHROMOSOME
1. Interrupted Conjugation.

When Hfr and F$^-$ cultures are mixed, conjugation can be stopped at any desired time by subjecting the mixture to the shearing forces of a Waring blender which artificially disrupts the conjugation bridge. The sample is diluted immediately and plated on selective media, incubated, and then scored for recombinants. In addition to the selected marker, an Hfr strain must also carry a distal auxotrophic or sensitivity marker which prevents the growth of Hfr cells on the selective medium and thereby allows only recombinant cells to appear. This technique is called *contraselection*. Because of the polarity with which the Hfr chromosome is transferred, the time at which various genetic markers appear in the recipient indicates their linear organization in the donor chromosome. At a given temperature, the transfer of the first half of the Hfr chromosome proceeds at a relatively uniform rate. Therefore the time of entry of different markers into a recipient (F$^-$) cell is a function of the physical distance between them. Because of errors introduced by experimental manipulations, this method is best suited for markers which are more than two minutes apart.

Example 10.4.   An Hfr strain carrying the prototrophic markers a^+, b^+, c^+ is mixed with a F$^-$ strain carrying the auxotrophic alleles a, b, c. Conjugation was interrupted at 5 minute intervals and plated on media which revealed the presence of recombinants.

Time (minutes)	Recombinants
5	ab^+c
10	ab^+c^+
15	$a^+b^+c^+$

The order of the genes in the Hfr donor strain is b^+-c^+-a^+; b is less than 5 time units from the origin; c is less than 10 time units from b; a is less than 10 time units from c.

2. Uninterrupted Conjugation.

When conjugation is allowed to proceed without artificial interruption, the time of rupture of the cytoplasmic bridge is apparently randomized among the mating pairs. The nearer a marker is to the origin (leading end of donor chromosome) the greater its chances of appearing as a recombinant in a recipient cell. Donor and recipient cells are mixed for about an hour in broth and then plated on selective media which only allows growth of F⁻ recombinants for a specific marker. Contraselection against Hfr must also be part of the experimental design. The contraselective marker should be located as distally as possible from the selected marker so that unselected recombinants will not be lost by its inclusion. The frequencies with which unselected markers appear in selected recombinants are inversely related to their distances from the selected marker, provided they lie distal to it. Obviously, any unselected marker between the selected marker and the origin of the chromosome will always be transferred ahead of the selected marker. Proximal markers more than three time units apart exhibit approximately 50% recombination, indicating that the average number of exchanges between them is greater than one. Just at the point where gross mapping by conjugation becomes ineffective, i.e. for markers less than two time units apart, recombination mapping becomes very effective, permitting estimation of distances between closely linked genes or between mutant sites within the same gene. Distances between genes can be expressed in three types of units: (1) time units, (2) recombination units, or (3) chemical units.

> **Example 10.5.** If 1 minute of conjugation is equivalent to 20 recombination units in *E. coli*, and the entire chromosome is transferred in 100 minutes, then the total map length is 2000 recombination units. If 10^7 nucleotide pairs exist in the chromosome, then 1 recombination unit represents $10^7/2000 = 5000$ nucleotide pairs.

3. Recombination Mapping.

Virtually all of the opportunities for recombination in bacteria involve only a partial transfer of genetic material (*meromyxis*) and not the entire chromosome. One or more genes have an opportunity to become integrated into the host chromosome by conjugation, depending upon the length of the donor piece received. Exogenotes usually must become integrated if they are to be replicated and distributed to all of the cells in a clone. Only a small segment of DNA is usually integrated during transformation or transduction. Thus if a cell becomes transformed for two genetic markers by the same transforming piece of DNA (double transformation) the two loci must be closely linked. Similarly, if a cell is simultaneously transduced for two genes by a single transducing phage DNA (*cotransduction*) the two markers must be closely linked. The degree of linkage between different functional genes (intercistronic) or between mutations within the same functional gene (intracistronic) may then be estimated from the results of specific crosses.

In merozygotic systems where the genetic contribution of the donor parent is incomplete, an even number of crossovers is required to integrate the exogenote into the host chromosome (*endogenote*).

> **Example 10.6.**

> Prototrophic recombinants must integrate the exogenote from somewhere left of the *a* locus to right of the *b* locus. Two crossovers (an even number) are required for this integration.

Example 10.7.

A prototrophic recombinant in this example requires a quadruple (even number) crossover for integration of all wild type genes.

The total number of progeny is unknown in merozygotic systems so that recombination frequency cannot be expressed relative to this base. Therefore recombination frequencies must be made relative to some standard which is common to all crosses. For example, the number of prototrophic recombinants produced by crossing two mutant strains can be compared to the number emerging from crossing wild type by mutant type. However, many sources of error are unavoidable when comparing the results of different crosses. This problem can be circumvented by comparing the number of prototrophic recombinants to some other class of recombinants arising from the same cross.

Example 10.8. Ratio test for different functional genes. Suppose we have two mutant strains, a and b, where the donor strain (a^+b) can grow on minimal medium supplemented with substance B, but the recipient strain (ab^+) cannot do so.

Crossing over in regions (1) and (2) produces prototrophic recombinants (a^+b^+) able to grow on unsupplemented medium. If the medium is supplemented with substance B, then a^+b recombinants arising by crossing over in regions (1) and (3) can grow in addition to the prototrophs.

$$\text{Standardized recombination ratio} = \frac{\text{number of prototrophs}}{\text{number of recombinants}}$$

Example 10.9. Intracistronic ratio test. Consider two intracistronic mutations, b_1 and b_2, unable to grow in medium without substance B. The recipient strain contains a mutation in another functionally different gene (a), either linked or unlinked to b, which cannot grow unless supplemented by substances A and B.

On unsupplemented medium, only prototrophs arising through crossovers in regions (1) and (3) appear. On medium supplemented only by substance B, recombinants involving region (1) and any of the other three regions can survive.

$$\text{Standardized recombination ratio} = \frac{\text{number of colonies on unsupplemented medium}}{\text{number of colonies on B-supplemented medium}}$$

4. Establishing Gene Order.

Mapping small regions in microorganisms has revealed that multiple crossovers often occur with much greater than random frequency, a phenomenon called "localized negative interference". The only unambiguous method for determining the order of very closely linked sites is by means of three factor reciprocal crosses. Suppose that the location of gene a is known to be to the left of gene b but that the order of two mutants within the adjacent b

cistron is unknown.　Reciprocal crosses will yield different results, depending upon the **order** of the mutant sites.

Example 10.10. Assume the order of sites is a-b_1-b_2.

In the original cross, prototrophs ($+\,+\,+$) can be produced by crossovers in regions (1) and (3).　In the reciprocal cross, prototrophs arise by crossovers in regions (3) and (4).　The numbers of prototrophs should be approximately equivalent in the two crosses.

Example 10.11. Assume the order of sites is a-b_2-b_1.

Original Cross:

Reciprocal Cross:

In the original cross, the production of prototrophs requires four crossovers, one in each of the regions (1), (2), (3) and (4).　Only two crossovers (in regions (2) and (3)) in the reciprocal cross are needed to produce prototrophs.　Therefore many more prototrophic recombinants are expected from the reciprocal cross than from the original cross.

5. Complementation Mapping.

An F particle which carries another bacterial gene other than the sex factor produces a relatively stable F^+ merozygote.　These partial diploids can be used for complementation tests of mutants affecting the same trait.

Example 10.12. An Hfr strain of *E. coli* is unable to ferment lactose (z_1^-) and can transfer the z_1^- gene through sexduction to a mutant (z_2^-) recipient, forming the heterogenote $z_2^-/(F\text{-}z_1^-)$.　If z_1 and z_2 belong to the same cistron (functional alleles), then complementation does not occur and only mutant phenotypes are produced.　If z_1 and z_2 are mutants in different cistrons, complementation could produce wild types able to ferment lactose.

Intracistronic complementation may sometimes be possible when the enzyme product is composed of two or more identical polypeptide chains.　Experimental evidence has shown that an *in vitro* mixture of inactive enzymes from some complementing mutants can "hybridize" to produce an enzyme with up to 25% normal activity.　Mutants that fail to complement with some but not all other mutants are assumed to overlap in function.　A complementation map can be constructed from the experimental results of testing all possible pairs of mutants for complementary action in bacterial merozygotes or in fungal heterokaryons. A complementation map cannot be equated in any way with a crossover map, since the gene is defined by different criteria. A complementation map tells us nothing of the structure or location of the mutations involved. Complementation maps are deduced from merozygotes or heterokaryons; crossover maps from recombination experiments.

Example 10.13. Three mutants map by complementation as follows:

$$\begin{array}{cc} \underline{1} & \underline{2} \\ \multicolumn{2}{c}{\underline{3}} \end{array}$$

This indicates that mutants 1 and 2 are complementary and do not overlap in function. Hence 1 and 2 are nonallelic mutations by this criterion. Mutant 3 fails to complement with either 1 or 2 and hence must overlap (to some degree) with both 1 and 2. Hence 3 is functionally allelic with both 1 and 2.

6. Mapping by Deletion Mutants.

A deletion in some segment of a functional gene cannot recombine with point mutations in that same region even though two point mutations at different sites within this region may recombine to produce wild type. Another distinctive property of deletion mutants is their stability, being unable to mutate back to wild type. The use of overlapping deletions can considerably reduce the work in fine structure analysis of a gene.

Example 10.14. Determining the limits of a deletion. Suppose that a series of single mutants (1, 2, 3, 4) has already been mapped as shown below:

$$\begin{array}{cccc} 1 & 2 & 3 & 4 \\ \underline{X} & & \underline{Y} \\ \multicolumn{4}{c}{\underline{Z}} \end{array}$$

A deletion that fails to recombine with point mutants 1 and 2 but does produce wild type with 3 and 4 extends over region X. A deletion that yields no recombinants with 3 and 4 has the boundaries diagrammed as Y. A deletion mutant which produces wild type only with point mutants 1 or 4 has the limits of Z.

Example 10.15. Assigning point mutations to deletion regions.

$$\begin{array}{cccc} 1 & 2 & 3 & 4 \\ \multicolumn{4}{c}{\underline{R}} \\ & & S & \\ & & \underline{T} \end{array}$$

Given the deletions R, S and T as shown above, the point mutation which recombines to give wild type with deletions S and T, but not with R, is 1. Number 3 is the only one of the four mutants which fails to recombine with one of the three deletions.

VIRUSES

The bulk of our knowledge about viruses has come from a study of those which infect bacterial hosts, the "bacteriophage". The life cycle of the virulent T-even phages was presented in the discussion concerning transduction.

During replication of phage DNA, a pool of perhaps 100 or more phage genomes may be present within the host cell. There is an opportunity for each DNA molecule to encounter several recombinational events, called "rounds of matings". This aspect of its life cycle renders the interpretation of recombination data considerably more difficult than in most higher organisms. Compensation can be made for some of these difficulties by appropriate experimental design and the acceptance of their concurrent assumptions. By these techniques, analysis of the phage genome has approached the nucleotide level of resolution.

Perhaps the most definitive fine structure analysis ever performed on a gene was Benzer's study of the r_{II} region in phage T4. When wild type (r^+) T4 infects its host *E. coli*, it produces relatively small plaques with fuzzy edges. Many mutations in the r region have been found, all of which produce more rapid lysis of their host than wild type, yielding larger plaques with relatively smooth edges. These r mutants may be classified into three phenotypic groups, depending on their ability to lyse three strains of *E. coli*.

Strain of Phage	Plaque type on *E. coli* strains		
	B	S	K
r^+	wild	wild	wild
r_I	large	large	large
r_{II}	large	wild	no plaques
r_{III}	large	wild	wild

The sites of r_I, r_{II} and r_{III} map at distinctly different noncontiguous locations. The r_{II} region is about 8 recombination units long, representing approximately 1% of the phage chromosome. By means of complementation tests, the r_{II} region is shown to consist of two adjacent and contiguous cistrons, A and B.

When two different r_{II} strains (containing mutations in different cistrons) are added to strain K12 in sufficiently large numbers to insure that each cell is infected with at least one representative of each mutant, all of the cells will rapidly lyse, releasing a normal number of progeny phage (most of which are defective like the parental strains). If the two phage strains contain mutations in the same r_{II} cistron, only the rare wild type recombinants will be capable of causing lysis and the number of cells so affected will be very small. Thus, the results of complementation are easily distinguished from those of recombination.

Overlapping deletions have been used to delimit a number of mutant sites to a small segment of a cistron. Benzer did not attempt to order the mutant sites within each of these small segments, but he did subject them to recombination tests to ascertain identity or nonidentity. This was accomplished by doubly infecting strain B with a pair of r_{II} mutants (r_{IIa} and r_{IIb}) in broth and allowing them to lyse the culture. The total number of progeny phage is estimated by plating dilutions of this lysate on *coli* B and counting the resulting plaques. Wild type recombinants are scored by plating the lysate on *coli* K. For every wild type ($r_{IIa}^+ r_{IIb}^+$) plaque counted on K, we assume that an undetected double mutant ($r_{IIa} r_{IIb}$) reciprocal recombinant was also formed.

$$\text{Recombination Percentage} \quad = \quad \frac{200 \text{ (number of plaques on K)}}{\text{number of plaques on B}}$$

The smallest reproducible recombination frequency observed between two sites in the r_{II} region is about 0.02%, corresponding to approximately 1/400 of a gene whose total length is only 8 recombination units!

Solved Problems

10.1. Two triple auxotrophic strains of *E. coli* are mixed in liquid medium and plated on complete medium which then serves as a master for replica plating onto 6 kinds of media. From the position of the clones on the plates and the ingredients in the media, determine the genotype for each of the 6 clones. The gene order is as shown.

$$T^-L^-B_1^-\ B^+Pa^+C^+\ \times\ T^+L^+B_1^+\ B^-Pa^-C^-$$

Nutritional supplements are abbreviated as follows:

T = threonine	B = biotin
L = leucine	Pa = phenylalanine
B_1 = thiamin	C = cystine

Master Plate
(complete medium)

Replica plates: Each dish contains minimal medium plus the supplements listed below each dish.

      T, L   L, B_1 B, Pa

     Pa, C   T, B_1 B, C

Solution:

    #1 grows when supplemented with T and L or T and B_1, but not with L and B_1. Therefore this is auxotrophic for T alone ($T^-L^+B_1^+\ B^+Pa^+C^+$).

    #2 appears only on the plate supplemented with Pa and C. This is a double auxotrophic clone of genotype $T^+L^+B_1^+\ B^+Pa^-C^-$.

    #3 appears on all replica plates and therefore must be prototrophic ($T^+L^+B_1^+\ B^+Pa^+C^+$).

    #4 grows only when supplemented with T and L and must be a double auxotroph of genotype $T^-L^-B_1^+\ B^+Pa^+C^+$.

    #5 and #1 always appear together on the replica plates and therefore have the same genotype.

    #6 can grow in the presence of Pa and C or B and C. The common factor is C for which this strain is singly auxotrophic ($T^+L^+B_1^+\ B^+Pa^+C^-$).

10.2. Under optimal conditions, some bacteria can divide every 20 minutes. Suppose each cell has a mass of 2×10^{-9} milligrams. The mass of the earth is approximately 5.97×10^{27} grams. Determine the time (in hours) required for the progeny of a single cell dividing without restriction at the above rate to equal the weight of the earth.

Solution:

    At time zero we have 1 cell; 20 minutes later we have 2 cells; at 40 minutes there are 4 cells; at 60 minutes there are 8 cells; etc. The number of cells at any hour, t, is obviously 2^{3t}. The number of cells equivalent to the weight of the earth is

$$(5.97 \times 10^{27})/(2 \times 10^{-12}) \ = \ 2.98 \times 10^{39} \ = \ 2^{3t}$$

from which $3t \log 2 \ = \ \log 2.98 + \log 10^{39}, \quad t \ = \ \dfrac{\log 2.98 + 39}{3 \log 2} \ = \ \dfrac{39.475}{3(0.301)} \ = \ 43.7 \text{ hours.}$

10.3. A strain of *E. coli* unable to ferment the carbohydrate arabinose (ara^-) and unable to synthesize the amino acids leucine (leu^-) and threonine (thr^-) is transduced by a wild type strain ($ara^+ \, leu^+ \, thr^+$).   Recombinants for leucine are detected by plating on minimal medium supplemented with threonine.   Colonies from the transduction plates were replicated or streaked onto plates containing arabinose.   Out of 270 colonies which grew on the threonine supplemented plates, 148 could also ferment arabinose.   Calculate the amount of recombination between *leu* and *ara*.

Solution:

In order for a transductant to be $leu^+ \, ara^+$, crossing over in regions (1) and (3) must occur; for $leu^+ \, ara^-$ to arise, crossing over in regions (1) and (2) must occur.

$$\text{Standardized recombination ratio} \ = \ \frac{\text{no. of } leu^+ \, ara^-}{\text{no. of } leu^+ \, ara^+} \ = \ \frac{(270 - 148)}{270} \ = \ 0.45 \text{ or } 45\%$$

10.4. Several z^- mutants, all lacking the ability to synthesize β-galactosidase, have been isolated.   A cross is made between Hfr ($z_1^- \, Ad^+ \, S^s$) $\times$ F$^-$ ($z_2^- \, Ad^- \, S^r$) where $Ad^- =$ adenine requirement, S^s and $S^r =$ streptomycin sensitivity and resistance respectively.   After about an hour, the mixture is diluted and plated on minimal medium containing streptomycin.   Many of the Ad^+ clones were able to ferment lactose, indicating β-galactosidase activity.   Only a few Ad^+ clones from the reciprocal cross Hfr ($z_2^- \, Ad^+ \, S^s$) $\times$ F$^-$ ($z_1^- \, Ad^- \, S^r$) were able to ferment lactose.   What is the order of the markers relative to the Ad locus?

Solution:

Assume that the order is z_2-z_1-Ad. In the first mating, four crossovers are required to produce a streptomycin resistant prototroph able to ferment lactose ($z_2^+ \, z_1^+ \, Ad^+ \, S^r$).

The reciprocal mating requires only two crossovers to produce a prototroph able to ferment lactose.

Double crossovers are expected to be much more frequent than quadruple crossovers. The above scheme does not fit the data because the first mating was more frequent than the reciprocal mating. Our assumption must be wrong.

Let us assume that the order is z_1-z_2-Ad. The first cross now requires a double crossover.

The reciprocal cross requires four crossover events.

The reciprocal cross is expected to be much less frequent under this assumption and is in agreement with the observations.

10.5. Six mutations are known to belong to three cistrons. From the results of the complementation tests, determine which mutants are in the same cistron.

	1	2	3	4	5	6	
	0	+	+				1
		0		+	+		2
			0	+	0		3
				0		+	4
					0	+	5
						0	6

+ = complementation
0 = non-complementation
blank = not tested

Solution:

Obviously mutations 3 and 5 are in the same cistron, since they fail to complement each other. Mutations 1 and 3 are in different cistrons, since they do complement each other. We will arbitrarily assign these to cistrons A and B.

(3, 5)	1	
Cistron A	Cistron B	Cistron C

1 and 2 are in different cistrons, but we do not know whether 2 is in A or C. However, 5 and 2 complement and therefore 2 cannot be either in cistron A or B and thus must be in C.

3 and 4 complement; thus 4 must be in either B or C. But 2 and 4 also complement; thus 4 cannot be in C and must reside in B.

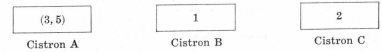

6 cannot be in A since it complements with 5. Thus 6 is either in B or C. Since 6 and 4 comple-ment, they are in different cistrons. If 6 cannot be in A or B, it must be in C. The mutants are grouped into cistrons as shown below.

| (3, 5) | (1, 4) | (2, 6) |
| Cistron A | Cistron B | Cistron C |

VIRUSES

10.6. In an attempt to determine the amount of recombination between two mutations in the rII region of phage T4, strain B of *E. coli* is doubly infected with both kinds of mutants. A dilution of $1:10^9$ is made of the lysate and plated on strain B. A dilution of $1:10^7$ is also plated on strain K. Two plaques are found on K, 20 plaques on B. Calculate the amount of recombination.

Solution:

In order to compare the numbers of plaques on B and K, the data must be corrected for the dilution factor. If 20 plaques are produced by a 10^9 dilution, the lesser dilution (10^7) would be expected to produce 100 times as many plaques.

$$\text{Recombination percentage} = \frac{200(\text{no. of plaques on K})}{\text{no. of plaques on B}} = \frac{200(2)}{20(100)} = 0.2\%$$

10.7. Seven deletion mutants within the A cistron of the rII region of phage T4 were tested in all pairwise combina-tions for wild type recombinants. In the adjacent table of results, $+ = $ re-combination, $0 = $ no recombination. Construct a topological map for these deletions.

	1	2	3	4	5	6	7
1	0	+	0	0	+	0	0
2		0	0	0	+	+	0
3			0	0	+	+	0
4				0	+	0	0
5					0	0	0
6						0	0
7							0

Solution:

If two deletions overlap to any extent, no wild type recombinants can be formed.

(1) Deletion #1 overlaps with 3, 4, 6 and 7 but not with 2 or 5.

```
        1                2, 5
   ├────────┤       ├────────┤
      3, 4, 6, 7
   ├──────────┤
```

(2) Deletion #2 overlaps with 3, 4 and 7 but not with 1, 5 or 6.

```
        1              2          5
   ├────────┤     ├──────┤    ├──────┤
        3, 4, 7
   ├────────────┤
        6
   ├──────┤
```

(3) Deletion #3 overlaps with 1, 2, 4 and 7 but not with 5 or 6.

```
         1             2         5
    ├────────┤     ├──────┤   ├──────┤
    6              3
 ├──────┤     ├──────────┤
         4, 7
    ├──────────┤
```

(4) Deletion #4 overlaps with 1, 2, 3, 6 and 7 but not with 5.

(5) Deletion #5 overlaps with 6 and 7 but not with 1, 2, 3 or 4. To satisfy these conditions we will shift 5 to the left of 1 and extend 7 into part of region 5 so that the overlaps in step (4) have not changed. Now segment 5 can overlap 6 and 7 without overlapping 1, 2, 3 or 4.

(6) Deletion #6 overlaps 1, 4, 5 and 7 but not 2 or 3. No change is required.

(7) Deletion #7 overlaps all other regions, just as it was temporarily diagrammed in step (5). This completes the topological map. Although the overlaps satisfy the conditions in the table, we have no information on the actual lengths of the individual deletions.

10.8. Five point mutations (*a* through *e*) were tested for wild type recombinants with each of the seven deletion mutants in the above problem. Determine the order of the point mutations and modify the topological map accordingly.

	1	2	3	4	5	6	7
a	0	+	0	0	+	+	0
b	+	+	+	0	+	0	0
c	+	+	+	+	0	0	0
d	0	+	+	0	+	0	0
e	+	0	0	0	+	+	0

Solution:

A deletion mutation cannot recombine to give wild type with a point mutant which lies within its boundaries. The topological map was developed in Problem 10.7.

(1) Mutant *a* does not recombine with 1, 3, 4 and 7 and therefore must be in a region common to all of these deletions.

(2) Mutant *b* does not recombine with 4, 6 and 7 and thus lies in a region common to these three deletions. As the topological map stands in step (1), a point mutant could not be in regions 4, 6 and 7 without also being in region 1. Therefore this information allows us to modify the

topological map by shortening deletion 1, but still overlapping deletion 6. This now gives us a region in which *b* can exist.

(3) Mutant *c* lies in a region common to deletions 5, 6 and 7. Mutant *d* lies in a region common to deletions 1, 4, 6 and 7. Mutant *e* lies in a region common to deletions 2, 3, 4 and 7.

Thus the order of these point mutations is *c-b-d-a-e* and the topological map is modified as shown in step 2.

Supplementary Problems

BACTERIA

10.9. Approximately 10^8 *E. coli* cells of a mutant strain are plated on complete medium forming a bacterial lawn. Replica plates are prepared containing minimal medium supplemented by the amino acids arginine, lysine and serine. (*a*) From the results, determine the genotype of the mutant strain. (*b*) Explain the colonies which appear on the replica plates.

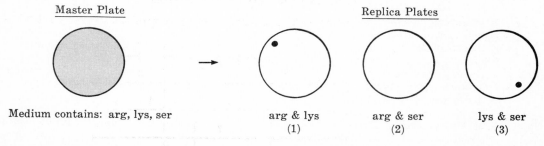

Master Plate

Replica Plates

Medium contains: arg, lys, ser

arg & lys
(1)

arg & ser
(2)

lys & ser
(3)

10.10. Two triple auxotrophic bacterial strains are conjugated in broth, diluted and plated onto complete agar (master plate). Replica plates containing various supplements are then made from the master. From the position of each clone and the type of media on which it is found, determine its genotype.

$$met^- thr^- pan^- pro^+ bio^+ his^+ \quad \times \quad met^+ thr^+ pan^+ pro^- bio^- his^-$$

Symbols

met = methionine
thr = threonine
pan = pantothenic acid
pro = proline
bio = biotin
his = histidine

Master Plate

Replica plates: Each dish contains minimal medium plus the supplements shown at the bottom.

met, thr

met, pan

thr, pan

pro, bio

pro, his

bio, his

10.11. A bacterial strain unable to synthesize methionine (met^-) is transduced by a strain unable to synthesize isoleucine ($ileu^-$). The broth culture is diluted and plated on minimal medium supplemented with isoleucine. An equivalent amount of diluted broth culture is plated on minimal medium. Eighteen clones appeared on the minimal plates and 360 on the isoleucine plates. Calculate the standardized recombination ratio.

10.12. Calculate the standardized recombination ratio between two mutants of the arginine locus, using the following information. A bacterial strain which is doubly auxotrophic for thymine and arginine ($thy^-\ arg_{E1}^-$) is transformed by using a high concentration of DNA from a single auxotrophic strain ($thy^+\ arg_{E2}^-$). Identical dilutions are plated on minimal medium and on minimal plus arginine. For every colony which appears on the unsupplemented plates there are about 120 colonies on the serine-supplemented plates.

10.13. Two mutants at the tryptophan locus, try_A^- and try_B^-, are known to be to the right of a cysteine locus (cys). A bacterial strain of genotype $cys^+\ try_A^-$ is transduced by phage from a strain which is $cys^-\ try_B^-$. The reciprocal cross is also made wherein the strain $cys^-\ try_B^-$ is transduced by phage from a strain which is $cys^+\ try_A^-$. In both cases the number of prototrophic recombinants are equivalent. Determine the order of the tryptophan mutants relative to the cysteine marker.

10.14. A cross is made between the streptomycin resistant (S^r) F^- strain marked with the characters $Gal^-T^-Az^rLac^-T1^rMal^-Xyl^-L^-$ and the prototrophic Hfr strain having opposite characters. After 60 minutes of contact, samples are transferred to plates with minimal medium plus streptomycin. The original mixture is in the ratio of 2×10^7 Hfr to 4×10^8 F^-. The frequencies (percentages) of the Hfr characters recovered in the $T^+L^+S^r$ recombinants are as follows: 72% $T1^s$, 0% Mal^+, 27% Gal^+, 91% Az^s, 0% Xyl^+, 48% Lac^+. (a) How many F^- cells exist in the original mixture for every Hfr cell? (b) What is the counterselective agent which prevents the Hfr individuals from obscuring the detection of recombinants? (c) In what order are these genes probably being transmitted by the Hfr?

10.15. Four Hfr strains of *E. coli* are known to transfer their genetic material during conjugation in different sequences. Given the time of entry of the markers into the F^- recipient, construct a genetic map which includes all of these markers and label the time distance between adjacent gene pairs.

     Strain 1.   Markers: *arg - thy - met - thr*

                  Time in minutes: 15   21   32   48

Strain 2.	Markers:	*mal - met - thi - thr - try*
	Time in minutes:	10 17 22 33 57
Strain 3.	Markers:	*phe - his - bio - azi - thr - thi*
	Time in minutes:	6 11 33 48 49 60
Strain 4.	Markers:	*his - phe - arg - mal*
	Time in minutes:	18 23 35 45

10.16. Abortive transductants are relatively stable merozygotes which can be used for complementation tests. Six mutants were tested in all pairwise combinations, yielding the results shown in the table (+ = complementation, 0 = non-complementation). Construct a complementation map consistent with the data.

1	2	3	4	5	6	
0	+	0	+	+	+	1
	0	0	+	+	+	2
		0	+	+	+	3
			0	0	+	4
				0	0	5
					0	6

10.17. Six point mutants are known to reside in three cistrons. Complete the following table where + = complementation and 0 = non-complementation.

	1	2	3	4	5	6
1	0	+		+	+	+
2		0	+			+
3			0	0		
4				0		
5					0	+
6						0

10.18. Given the topological map of 6 deletion mutants shown below, predict the results of recombination experiments involving the 5 point mutants (*a* thru *e*) with each of the 6 deletions (1 thru 6). Complete the accompanying table of results by using + for recombination and 0 for no recombination.

	Deletions					
	1	2	3	4	5	6
a						
b						
c						
d						
e						

10.19. Five point mutations (*a* thru *e*) were tested for wild type recombinants with each of the five deletions shown in the topological map below. The results are listed in the table below (+ = recombination, 0 = no recombination). Determine the order of the point mutations.

Deletions

	1	2	3	4	5
a	0	0	+	+	+
b	+	+	+	0	+
c	0	0	+	+	0
d	0	+	0	0	0
e	0	+	0	0	+

VIRUSES

10.20. Six deletion mutants within the A cistron of the *r*II region of phage T4 were tested in all pairwise combinations for wild type recombinants. In the following table, + = recombination, 0 = no recombination. Construct a topological map for these deletions.

	1	2	3	4	5	6
1	0	0	0	0	0	0
2		0	0	0	0	+
3			0	+	0	0
4				0	+	+
5					0	+
6						0

10.21. Five deletion mutants within the B cistron of the *r*II region of phage T4 were tested in all pairwise combinations for wild type recombinants. In the following table of results, + = recombination, 0 = no recombination. Construct a topological map for these deletions.

	1	2	3	4	5
1	0	+	+	0	0
2		0	+	0	+
3			0	+	0
4				0	0
5					0

10.22. The DNA of bacteriophage T4 contains approximately 200,000 nucleotide pairs. The *r*II region of the T4 genome occupies about 1% of its total genetic length. Benzer has found about 300 sites are separable by recombination within the *r*II region. Determine the average number of nucleotides in each recon.

10.23. The molecular weight of DNA in phage T4 is estimated to be 160×10^6. The average molecular weight of each nucleotide is approximately 400. The total genetic map of T4 is calculated to be approximately 2500 recombination units long. With what frequency are r^+ recombinants expected to be formed when two different *r* mutants (with mutations at adjacent nucleotides) are crossed?

10.24. A number of mutations were found in the *r*II region of phage T4. From the recombination data shown in the table on the right, determine whether each mutant is a point defect or a deletion (+ = recombination, 0 = no recombination). Two of the four mutants have been known to undergo back mutation; the other two have never been observed to backmutate. Draw a topological map to represent your interpretation.

	1	2	3	4
1	0	0	0	+
2		0	+	0
3			0	+
4				0

10.25. *E. coli* strain B is doubly infected with two *r*II mutants of phage T4. A 6×10^7 dilution of the lysate is plated on *coli* B. A 2×10^5 dilution is plated on *coli* K. Twelve plaques appeared on strain K, 16 on strain B. Calculate the amount of recombination between these two mutants.

Answers to Supplementary Problems

10.9.   (a) $arg^- lys^- ser^-$ (triple auxotroph) (b) plate (1) contains a mutation to ser^+, plate (3) contains a mutation to arg^+.

10.10.

Clone	Genotype of Clone					
	met	*thr*	*pan*	*pro*	*bio*	*his*
1	+	+	+	+	+	+
2	+	−	−	+	+	+
3	−	+	−	+	+	+
4	+	+	+	+	+	−
5	+	+	+	−	+	+
6	+	−	+	+	+	+

10.11.   20% recombination

10.12.   0.83% recombination

10.13. cys - try_B - try_A

10.14.   (a) 20 (b) streptomycin; Hfr is streptomycin sensitive (S^s) (c) origin - $(T^+ L^+)$ - Az^s - $T1^s$ - Lac^+ - Gal^+ - S^s - $(Mal^+ Xyl^+)$. *Note*: The order of markers within parentheses cannot be determined from the data.

10.15. arg - thy - mal - met - thi - thr - azi - bio - try - his - phe - arg
                6   4   7   5   11   1   15   8   14   5   12

10.16.

10.17.

Cistron A	Cistron B	Cistron C
2, 5	1	3, 4, 6

	1	2	3	4	5	6
1	0	+	+	+	+	+
2		0	+	+	0	+
3			0	0	+	0
4				0	+	0
5					0	+
6						0

Note: Name of cistron is arbitrary.

10.18.

Point Mutations	Deletions					
	1	2	3	4	5	6
a	0	+	+	0	0	+
b	+	+	0	+	+	0
c	+	0	0	+	+	+
d	0	0	+	+	0	+
e	+	0	0	+	+	0

10.19. $a - c - d - e - b$

10.20.

10.21.

10.22.   Approximately 7 nucleotides per recon

10.23.   0.00625% of all progeny are expected to be r^+ recombinants.

10.24. m_1 and m_2 are deletions, m_3 and m_4 are point mutations.

10.25.   0.5% recombination

Chapter 11

Quantitative Genetics

QUALITATIVE VS. QUANTITATIVE TRAITS

The classical Mendelian traits encountered in the previous chapters have been qualitative in nature, i.e. traits which are easily classified into distinct phenotypic categories. These discrete phenotypes are under the genetic control of only one or a very few genes with little or no environmental modifications to obscure the gene effects. In contrast to this, the variability exhibited by many agriculturally important traits fails to fit into separate phenotypic classes (discontinuous variability), but instead forms a spectrum of phenotypes which blend imperceptively from one type to another (continuous variability). Economically important traits such as body weight gains, mature plant heights, egg or milk production records, yield of grain per acre, etc., are *quantitative* or *metric* traits with continuous variability. The basic difference between qualitative and quantitative traits involves the number of genes contributing to the phenotypic variability and the degree to which the phenotype can be modified by environmental factors. Quantitative traits are usually governed by many genes (perhaps 10 to 100 or more), each contributing such a small amount to the phenotype that their individual effects cannot be detected by Mendelian methods. Genes of this nature are called *polygenes*. In addition, the phenotypic variability expressed in most quantitative traits has a relatively large environmental component, and a correspondingly small genetic component. It is the task of the geneticist to determine the magnitude of the genetic and environmental components of the total phenotypic variability of each quantitative trait in a population. In order to accomplish this task, use is made of some rather sophisticated mathematics, especially of statistics. Only some of the more easily understood rudiments of this branch of genetics will be presented in this chapter. Below are summarized some of the major differences between quantitative and qualitative genetics.

Qualitative Genetics	Quantitative Genetics
1. Characters of *kind*.	1. Characters of *degree*.
2. *Discontinuous* variation; discrete phenotypic classes.	2. *Continuous* variation; phenotypic measurements form a spectrum.
3. *Single gene* effects discernible.	3. *Polygenic* control; effects of single genes too slight to be detected.
4. Concerned with *individual matings* and their progeny.	4. Concerned with a *population* of organisms consisting of all possible kinds of matings.
5. Analyzed by making *counts and ratios*.	5. Statistical analyses give estimates of *population parameters* such as the mean and standard deviation.

QUASI-QUANTITATIVE TRAITS

In the early days of Mendelian genetics it was thought that there was a fundamental difference in the essence of qualitative and quantitative traits. One of the classical examples which helped to bridge the gap between these two kinds of traits is the multiple gene model developed about 1910 by the Swedish geneticist Nilsson-Ehle to explain kernel color in wheat. When he crossed a certain dark-red strain to a white strain he observed that the F_1 was all medium red and that approximately $\frac{1}{16}$ of the F_2 was as extreme as the parents, i.e. $\frac{1}{16}$ were white and $\frac{1}{16}$ were dark red. He interpreted these results in terms of two genes, each with a pair of alleles exhibiting cumulative effects.

P: $R_1R_1R_2R_2$ $\times$ $r_1r_1r_2r_2$
            dark red   white

F_1: $R_1r_1R_2r_2$
                       medium red

F_2:

$$\frac{1}{16} = R_1R_1R_2R_2 \quad : \quad \frac{4}{16} = \begin{cases} R_1R_1R_2r_2 \\ R_1r_1R_2R_2 \end{cases} \quad : \quad \frac{6}{16} = \begin{cases} R_1R_1r_2r_2 \\ R_1r_1R_2r_2 \\ r_1r_1R_2R_2 \end{cases} \quad : \quad \frac{4}{16} = \begin{cases} R_1r_1r_2r_2 \\ r_1r_1R_2r_2 \end{cases} \quad : \quad \frac{1}{16} = r_1r_1r_2r_2$$

    dark red   red   medium red   light red   white

Each of the "active" alleles R_1 or R_2 adds some red to the phenotype, so that the genotype of whites contains neither of these alleles and a dark red genotype contains only R_1 and R_2 alleles. These results are plotted as histograms in Fig. 11-1. Note that the phenotype of the F_1 is intermediate between the two parental types and that the average phenotype of the F_2 is the same as that of the F_1 but is a much more variable population, i.e. the F_2 contains many more phenotypes (and genotypes) than in the F_1. The student should recognize the F_2 distribution as an expansion of the binomial $(a + b)^4$, where $a = b = \frac{1}{2}$.

Fig. 11-1. Wheat color as an example of a quasi-quantitative trait

Certain other strains of wheat with dark red kernels when crossed to whites exhibit an F_1 phenotype intermediate between the two parental types, but only $\frac{1}{64}$ of the F_2 are white. In this case the F_1 is probably segregating for three pairs of genes and only the genotype $r_1r_1r_2r_2r_3r_3$ produces white. Of course there would be many more shades of red exhibited in the F_2 than in the previous case where only two genes are segregating. Even if the environment does not modify these color phenotypes (which it probably does to some extent), the ability of the eye to measure subtle differences in shading would probably be difficult with this many phenotypes and would become impossible if 4 or 5 genes were each contributing to kernel color.

Thus these multiple gene models, which are adequate to explain certain examples wherein discontinuous variation is still evident, may (by conceptual extension to include more genes plus environmental modifications) be useful in understanding the origin of continuous variation characterizing truly quantitative traits.

A rough estimate of the number of gene loci contributing to a quasi-quantitative trait can be obtained by determining the fraction of the F_2 (resulting from selfing the F_1 hybrid between two pure varieties) which is as extreme in its phenotype as that of one of the pure parental strains.

Number of gene loci	1	2	3	...	n
Fraction of F_2 as extreme as one parent	1/4	1/16	1/64	...	$(1/4)^n$

THE NORMAL DISTRIBUTION

The study of a quantitative trait in a large population usually reveals that very few individuals possess the extreme phenotypes and that progressively more individuals are found nearer the average value for that population. This type of symmetrical distribution is characteristically bell-shaped as shown in Fig. 11-2 and is called a *normal distribution*. It is approximated by the binomial distribution $(p + q)^n$ introduced in Chapter 7 when the power of the binomial is very large and p and q are both $1/n$ or greater.

Fig. 11-2.   A normal distribution

1. Average Measurements.

The average phenotypic value for a normally distributed trait is expressed as the arithmetic mean ($\bar{X}$, read "X bar"). The arithmetic mean is the sum of the individual measurements (ΣX) divided by the number of individuals measured (N). The Greek letter "sigma" (Σ) directs the statistician to sum what follows.

$$\bar{X} \;=\; \frac{\sum_{i=1}^{N} X_i}{N} \;=\; \frac{X_1 + X_2 + X_3 + \cdots + X_N}{N} \tag{11.1}$$

It is usually not feasible to measure every individual in a population and therefore measurements are usually made on a sample from that population in order to estimate the population value (parameter). If the sample is truly representative of the larger population of which it is a part, then $\bar{X}$ will be an accurate estimate of the mean of the entire population (μ). Note that letters from the English alphabet are used to represent *statistics*, i.e. measurements derived from a sample, whereas Greek letters are used to represent *parameters*, i.e. attributes of the population from which the sample was drawn. Parameters are seldom known and must be estimated from results gained by sampling. Obviously, the larger the sample size, the more accurately the statistic estimates the parameter.

2. Measurement of Variability.

In comparing two populations for the same quantitative trait, it is not sufficient to know only their means, because mean values tell us nothing of how variable the two populations are. Consider the two populations shown below. The means are identical ($\mu_1 = \mu_2$), but population (a) is obviously much more variable than (b). Perhaps the most useful measure of the amount of variability in a population is the *standard deviation*, symbolized by the small Greek letter "sigma" (σ). A sample drawn from this population will have a sample standard deviation (s). To calculate s, the sample mean ($\bar{X}$) is subtracted from each individual measurement (X) and the deviation $(X - \bar{X})$ is squared $(X - \bar{X})^2$, summed for all individuals in the sample $\left(\sum (X - \bar{X})^2\right)$ and divided by $N - 1$, where N is the sample size. The calculation is completed by taking the square root of this value.

$$s = \sqrt{\frac{\sum (X - \bar{X})^2}{N - 1}} \qquad\qquad (11.2)$$

Again, if the sample adequately reflects the variability present in the larger population, then the statistic s estimates the parameter σ.

It is the property of every normal distribution that approximately $\frac{2}{3}$ of the measurements (68%) will lie within plus or minus one standard deviation from the mean $(\mu \pm \sigma)$. Approximately $\frac{19}{20}$ of the measurements (95%) will lie within two standard deviations of the mean $(\mu \pm 2\sigma)$. More than 99% of the measurements will be found within plus or minus three standard deviations of the mean $(\mu \pm 3\sigma)$.

> **Example 11.1.** The mean height of a sample from a plant population is 56 inches; the sample standard deviation is 6 inches. This indicates that approximately $\frac{2}{3}$ of the sample will be found between the values $56 \pm 6 = 50$ inches to 62 inches. Approximately $2\frac{1}{2}$% of all plants in this sample will measure smaller than $56 - (2 \times 6) = 56 - 12 = 44$ inches and $2\frac{1}{2}$% will measure larger than $56 + (2 \times 6) = 68$ inches.

The standard deviation can be plotted on a normal distribution by locating the point of inflection of the curve (point of maximum slope). A perpendicular constructed from the baseline which intersects the curve at this point is one standard deviation from the mean (Fig. 11-2).

Coefficient of Variation. Traits with relatively large average metric values generally are expected to have correspondingly larger standard deviations than traits with relatively small average metric values. Furthermore, since different traits may be measured in different units, the *coefficients of variation* are useful for comparing their relative variabilities. Dividing the standard deviation by the mean renders the coefficient of variation independent of the units of measurement.

$$\text{Coefficient of Variation} = \sigma/\mu \text{ for a population}$$
$$= s/\bar{X} \text{ for a sample} \qquad\qquad (11.3)$$

3. Variance.

The square of the standard deviation is called *variance* (σ^2). Unlike the standard deviation, however, variance cannot be plotted on the normal curve and can only be represented mathematically. Variance is widely used as an expression of variability because of the additive nature of its components. By a technique called "analysis of variance", the total phenotypic variance (σ_P^2) expressed by a given trait in a population can be statistically fragmented or partitioned into components of genetic variance (σ_G^2), nongenetic (or environmental) variance (σ_E^2), and variance due to genotype-environment interactions (σ_{GE}^2). Thus

$$\sigma_P^2 = \sigma_G^2 + \sigma_E^2 + \sigma_{GE}^2 \qquad\qquad (11.4)$$

It is beyond the scope of this text to present the analysis of variance, but a knowledge of variance components is essential to a discussion of breeding theory. Both the genetic variance and environmental variance can be further partitioned by this technique, so that the relative contributions of a number of factors influencing a metric trait can be ascertained. In order to simplify discussion, we shall ignore the interaction component.

Example 11.2. An analysis of variance performed on the birth weights of humans produced the following results:

Variance Component	Percent of Total Phenotypic Variance
Offspring genotype	16
Sex	2
Maternal genotype	20
Maternal environment	24
Chronological order of child	7
Maternal age	1
Unaccountable variations (error)	30
	100

Variance Method of Estimating the Number of Genes.

A population such as a line, a breed, a variety, a strain, a subspecies, etc., is composed of individuals which are more nearly alike in their genetic composition than those in the species as a whole. Phenotypic variability will usually be expressed even in a group of organisms which are genetically identical. All such variability within pure lines is obviously environmental in origin. Crosses between two pure lines produce a genetically uniform hybrid F_1. Phenotypic variability in the F_1 is likewise non-genetic in origin. In the formation of the F_2 generation, gene combinations are reshuffled and dealt out in new combinations to the F_2 individuals. It is a common observation that the F_2 generation is much more variable than the F_1 from which it was derived.

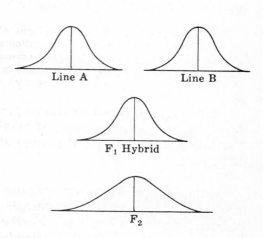

In a normally distributed trait, the means of the F_1 and F_2 populations tend to be intermediate between the means of the two parental lines. If there is no change in the environment from one generation to the next, then the environmental variation of the F_2 should be approximately the same as that of the F_1. An increase in phenotypic variance of the F_2 over that of the F_1 may then be attributed to genetic causes. Thus the genotypic variance of the F_2 (σ^2_{GF2}) is equal to the phenotypic variance of the F_2 (σ^2_{PF2}) minus the phenotypic variance of the F_1 (σ^2_{PF1}):

$$\sigma^2_{GF2} \;=\; \sigma^2_{PF2} \;-\; \sigma^2_{PF1}$$

The genetic variance of the F_2 is expressed by the formula $\sigma^2_{GF2} = (a^2N)/2$, where a is the contribution of each active allele and N is the number of *pairs* of genes involved in the metric trait. An estimate of a is obtained from the formula $a = D/2N$, where D is the numerical difference between the two parental means. Making substitutions and solving for N,

$$\sigma^2_{PF2} \;-\; \sigma^2_{PF1} \;=\; \sigma^2_{GF2} \;=\; a^2N/2 \;=\; D^2/8N$$

from which
$$N \;=\; \frac{D^2}{8(\sigma^2_{PF2} - \sigma^2_{PF1})} \tag{11.5}$$

This formula is an obvious over-simplification since it assumes all genes are contributing cumulatively the same amount to the phenotype, no dominance, no linkage and no interaction. Much more sophisticated formulas have been developed to take such factors into consideration, but these are beyond the scope of a first genetics course.

TYPES OF GENE ACTION

Alleles may interact with one another in a number of ways to produce variability in their phenotypic expression. The following models may help us understand various modes of gene action.

(1) With dominance lacking, i.e. additive genes, each A^1 allele is assumed to contribute nothing to the phenotype (null allele), whereas each A^2 allele contributes one unit to the phenotype (active allele).

Scale of phenotypic value:
```
         0              1              2
         |_____|_____|
Genotype:  A¹A¹          A¹A²          A²A²
```

(2) With partial or incomplete dominance the heterozygote is almost as valuable as the A^2A^2 homozygote.

Scale of phenotypic value:
```
         0                        1.5    2
         |_____|_____|
Genotype:  A¹A¹                   A¹A²  A²A²
```

(3) In complete dominance identical phenotypes are produced by the heterozygote and A^2A^2 homozygote.

Scale of phenotypic value:
```
         0                               2
         |_____|
Genotype:  A¹A¹                          A¹A²
                                         A²A²
```

(4) In *overdominance* the heterozygote is more valuable than either homozygous genotype.

Scale of phenotypic value:
```
         0                        2    2.5
         |_____|_____|
Genotype:  A¹A¹                  A²A²  A¹A²
```

If allelic interaction is completely additive, a linear phenotypic effect is produced. In Fig. 11-3, a constant increment (i) is added to the phenotype for each A^2 allele in the genotype.

Fig. 11-3.   Additive gene action

Fig. 11-4.   Dominant gene action

Even if complete dominance is operative, an underlying component of additivity (linearity) is still present (solid line in Fig. 11-4). The deviations from the additive scheme (dotted lines) due to many such genes with partial or complete dominance can be statistically estimated from appropriately designed experiments. The genetic contributions from such effects appear in the dominance component of variance (σ_D^2).

In a much more complicated way, deviations from an underlying additive scheme could be shown to exist for the interactions between genes at different loci (epistatic relationships). The contribution to the total genetic variance (σ_G^2) made by these genetic elements can be partitioned into a component called the epistatic or interaction variance (σ_I^2).

The sum of the additive gene effects produced by genes lacking dominance (additive genes) and by the additive contribution of genes with dominance or epistatic effects appears in the additive component of genetic variance (σ_A^2).

Thus the total genetic variance can be partitioned into three fractions:

$$\sigma_G^2 = \sigma_A^2 + \sigma_D^2 + \sigma_I^2 \qquad\qquad (11.6)$$

Additive vs. Multiplicative Gene Action.

Additive gene action produces an arithmetic series of phenotypic values such as 2, 4, 6, 8, ... representing the contributions of 1, 2, 3, 4, ... active alleles respectively. Additive gene action tends to produce a normal phenotypic distribution with the mean of the F_1 intermediate between means of the two parental populations. However, not all genes act additively. Some exhibit multiplicative gene action forming a geometric series such as 2, 4, 8, 16, ... representing the contributions of 1, 2, 3, 4, ... active alleles respectively. Traits governed by multiplicative gene action tend to be skewed into an asymmetrical curve such as that shown for the F_2 in Fig. 11-5. The means of the F_1 and F_2 are nearer to one of the parental means because the geometric mean of two numbers is the square root of their product.

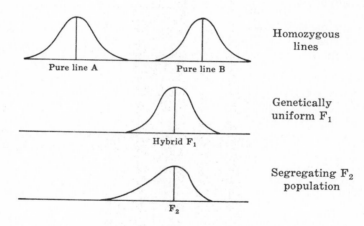

Fig. 11-5.   Multiplicative gene action

Example 11.3.   (a) The geometric mean of 2 and 8 in the geometric series 2, 4, 8, which is increasing by a multiplicative increment of 2, is $\sqrt{2 \times 8} = 4$. The arithmetic mean of 2 and 8 is $(2+8)/2 = 5$.

(b) The geometric mean between 1.2 and 2.7 is $\sqrt{1.2 \times 2.7} = 1.8$, forming the geometric series 1.2, 1.8, 2.7, ... which is increasing by a multiplicative increment of 0.5. The arithmetic mean of 1.2 and 2.7 is $(1.2 + 2.7)/2 = 1.95$.

If a skewed distribution can be converted to a normal distribution by merely transforming the data to a logarithmic scale, this is evidence for multiplicative gene action.

Example 11.4.   If the geometric series 1, 10, 100, 1000, ... (increasing by a multiplicative increment of 10) is converted to logarithms, we have the arithmetic series 0, 1, 2, 3, ... (increasing by an additive increment of one unit).

The variance and the mean are independent parameters in a normal distribution. That is, if the population mean is increased we cannot predict in advance to what degree the variance will be increased. In the case of multiplicative gene action, however, the variance is dependent upon the mean so that as the mean increases the variance increases proportionately. The coefficients of variation in segregating populations thereby remain constant.

The concepts of heritability and selection theory discussed in the following sections will deal only with normal distributions.

HERITABILITY

One of the most important factors in the formulation of effective breeding plans is a knowledge of the relative contribution which genes make to the trait under consideration. *Heritability* (symbolized h^2) is the proportion of the total phenotypic variance due to gene effects.

$$h^2 = \sigma_G^2/\sigma_P^2 \qquad (11.7)$$

The heritability of a given trait may be any fraction from zero to one.

Example 11.5. If all of the phenotypic variability is genetic in nature, then heritability equals one, i.e. if $\sigma_G^2 = \sigma_P^2$, then $h^2 = 1$.

Example 11.6. If all of the phenotypic variability is environmental in nature, then heritability is zero, i.e. if $\sigma_E^2 = \sigma_P^2$, then $\sigma_G^2 = 0$ and $h^2 = 0/\sigma_P^2 = 0$.

Example 11.7. If half of the phenotypic variability is due to gene effects, then heritability is 50%, i.e. if $\sigma_G^2 = \frac{1}{2}\sigma_P^2$, then $2\sigma_G^2 = \sigma_P^2$ and so $h^2 = \frac{1}{2} = 50\%$.

Example 11.8. If the environmental component of variance is three times as large as the genetic component, heritability is 25%, i.e. if $\sigma_E^2 = 3\sigma_G^2$, then

$$h^2 = \frac{\sigma_G^2}{\sigma_G^2 + \sigma_E^2} = \frac{\sigma_G^2}{\sigma_G^2 + 3\sigma_G^2} = \frac{1}{4} = 25\%$$

The parameter of heritability involves all types of gene action and thus forms a broad estimate of heritability. In the case of complete dominance, when a gamete bearing the active dominant allele A^2 unites with a gamete bearing the null allele A^1 the resulting phenotype might be two units. When two A^2 gametes unite, the phenotypic result would still be two units. On the other hand if genes lacking dominance (additive genes) are involved, then the A^2 gamete will add one unit to the phenotype of the resulting zygote regardless of the allelic contribution of the gamete with which it unites. Thus only the additive genetic component of variance has the quality of predictability necessary in the formulation of breeding plans. Heritability in this narrower sense is the ratio of the additive genetic variance to the phenotypic variance:

$$h^2 = \sigma_A^2/\sigma_P^2 \qquad (11.8)$$

Unless otherwise specified in the problems of this book, heritability in the narrow sense is to be employed.

1. Response to Selection.

Let us assume we wished to increase the birth weight of beef cattle by selecting parents who themselves were relatively heavy at birth. Assume our initial population ($\bar{P}_1$) has a mean birth weight of 80 pounds with a 10 pound standard deviation (Fig. 11-6(a) below). Further suppose that we will save all animals for breeding purposes which weigh over 95 pounds at birth. The mean of these animals which have been selected to be parents of the next generation ($\bar{P}_p$) is 100 pounds. The difference $\bar{P}_p - \bar{P}_1$ is called the *selection differential* symbolized ΔP (read "delta P") and sometimes referred to as "reach". Some individuals with an inferior genotype are expected to have high birth weights largely because of a favorable intrauterine environment. Others with a superior genotype may possess a low birth weight because of an unfavorable environment. In a large, normally distributed population, however, the plus and minus effects produced by good and poor environments are assumed to cancel each other so that the average phenotype ($\bar{P}_1$) reflects the effects of the average genotype ($\bar{G}_1$). Random mating among the selected group produces an offspring generation (Fig. 11-6(b)) with its phenotypic mean ($\bar{P}_2$) also reflecting its average genotypic mean ($\bar{G}_2$). Furthermore, the mean genotype of the parents ($\bar{G}_p$) will be indicated in the mean phenotype of their offspring ($\bar{P}_2$) because only genes are transmitted from one generation to the next.

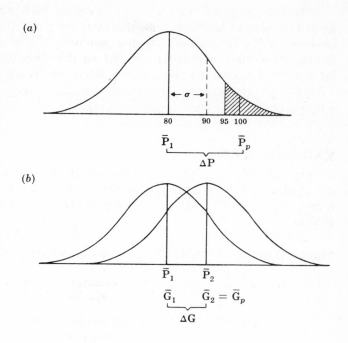

Fig. 11-6.   Selection for birth weight in beef cattle

Assuming the environmental effects remain constant from one generation to the next, we can attribute the difference $\bar{G}_2 - \bar{G}_1$ to the selection of genes for high birth weight in the individuals that we chose to use as parents for the next generation. This difference ($\bar{G}_2 - \bar{G}_1$) is called "genetic gain", symbolized ΔG. If all of the variability in birth weight exhibited by a population was due solely to additive gene effects, and the environment was contributing nothing at all, then by selecting individuals on the basis of their birth weight records we would actually be selecting the genes which are responsible for high birth weight. That is, we will not be confused by the effects which a favorable environment can produce with a mediocre genotype or by the favorable interaction ("nick") of a certain combination of genes which will be broken up in subsequent generations. Realized heritability is defined as the ratio of the genetic gain to the selection differential:

$$h^2 \; = \; \Delta G / \Delta P \qquad\qquad\qquad (11.9)$$

Example 11.9.   If we gained in the offspring all that we "reached" for in the parents, then heritability is unity, i.e. if $\bar{P}_2 - \bar{P}_1 = 100 - 80 = 20$, and $\Delta P = \bar{P}_p - \bar{P}_1 = 100 - 80 = 20$, then $h^2 = \Delta G / \Delta P = 20/20 = 1$.

Example 11.10.   If selection of parents with high birth weights fails to increase the mean birth weight of their offspring over that of the mean in the previous generation, then heritability is zero, i.e. if $\bar{P}_2$ and $\bar{P}_1 = 80$, then $\Delta G = \bar{P}_2 - \bar{P}_1 = 0$ and $h^2 = \Delta G / \Delta P = 0/20 = 0$.

Example 11.11.   If the mean weight of the offspring is increased by half the selection differential, then heritability of birth weight is 50%, i.e. if $\Delta G = \frac{1}{2}\Delta P$, $\Delta P = 2\Delta G$, $h^2 = 0.5 = 50\%$. This is approximately the heritability estimate actually found for birth weight in beef cattle (Fig. 11-6(b)).

Most metric traits are not highly heritable. What is meant by high or low heritability is not rigidly defined, but the following values are generally accepted.

High heritability	> 0.5
Medium heritability	$= 0.2\text{-}0.5$
Low heritability	< 0.2

Notice that when heritability is less than one the mean of the offspring in relationship to the mean of the parents tends to move back or "regress" toward the mean of the previous generation. The amount of this regression is directly related to the heritability of the trait. When heritability is 0.5, the mean of the offspring regresses 50% toward the mean of the previous generation. When heritability is 0.25, the mean of the offspring regresses 75% toward the mean of the previous generation. Thus *Heritability = 100% − Regression percentage.* The foregoing is not to be confused with the "statistical regression coefficient" (symbolized b) which indicates the amount one variable can be expected to change per unit change in some other variable. When one variable is the phenotype of the offspring and the other variable is the average phenotype of the two parents (midparent) then $b = h^2$.

Example 11.12. If $b = h^2 = 1$, then the offspring should have the same phenotypic value as the midparent value. That is, for each unit of increase in the phenotype of midparent, the offspring are expected to increase by the same amount.

Example 11.13. If $b = h^2 = 0.5$, for each unit of phenotypic increase in the midparent only $\frac{1}{2}$ unit increase is expected to appear in the offspring.

Example 11.14. If $b = h^2 = 0$, then the offspring are not expected to produce any better than the average of the population regardless of the midparent value.

2. Selection Index.

Selection is seldom made on the basis of one characteristic alone. Breeders usually desire to practice selection on several criteria simultaneously. However, the more traits selected for, the less selection "pressure" can be exerted on each trait. Selection should thus be limited to the two or three traits which the breeder considers to be the most important economically. It is probable that individuals scoring high in trait A will be mediocre or even poor in trait B (unless the two traits have a positive genetic correlation, i.e. some of the genes increasing trait A are also contributing positively to trait B). The breeder therefore must make compromises, selecting some individuals on a "total merit" basis which would probably not be saved for breeding if selection was being practiced on the basis of only a single trait.

The model used to illustrate the concept of genetic gain, wherein only individuals which score above a certain minimum value for a single trait would be saved for breeding, must now be modified to represent the more probable situation in which selection is based on the total merit of two or more traits (Fig. 11-7).

In selecting breeding animals on a "total merit" basis, it is desirable to reduce the records of performance on the important traits to a single score called the *selection index.*

Selection on the basis of a single trait (shaded area represents selected individuals).

Selection applied to the same trait when the criterion is total merit.

Fig. 11-7.   Selection on single trait vs. total merit

The index number has no meaning by itself, but is valuable in comparing several individuals on a *relative* basis. The methods used in constructing an index may be quite diverse, but they usually take into consideration the heritability and the relative economic importance of each trait in addition to the genetic and phenotypic correlations between the traits.   An index (I) for three traits may have the general form

$$I = aA' + bB' + cC'$$

where a, b and c are coefficients correcting for the relative heritability and the relative economic importance for traits A, B and C respectively and where A', B' and C' are the numerical values of traits A, B and C expressed in "standardized form".   A *standardized variable* (X') is computed by the formula

$$X' = \frac{X - \bar{X}}{\sigma_X} \qquad\qquad (11.10)$$

where X is the record of performance made by an individual, $\bar{X}$ is the average performance of the population, and σ_X is the standard deviation of the trait.   In comparing different traits, one is confronted by the fact that the mean and variability of each trait is different and often the traits are not even expressed in the same units.

> **Example 11.15.** An index for poultry might use egg production (expressed in numbers of eggs per laying season), egg quality (expressed in terms of grades such as AA, A, B, etc.), and egg size (expressed in ounces per dozen).

> **Example 11.16.** An index for swine might consider backfat thickness (in inches), feed conversion (pounds of feed per pound of gain), and conformation score (expressing the appearance of the individual in terms of points from a standard grading system).

The standardized variable, however, is a pure number (i.e. independent of the units used) based on the mean and standard deviation.   Therefore any production record or score of a quantitative nature can be added to any other such trait if they are expressed in standardized form.

3. Progeny Test.

A *progeny test* is a method of estimating the breeding value of an animal by the performance or phenotype of its offspring.   It has its greatest utility for those traits which (1) can only be expressed in one sex (e.g. estimating the genes for milk production possessed by a bull), (2) cannot be measured until after slaughter (e.g. carcass characteristics), (3) have low heritabilities so that individual selection is apt to be highly inaccurate.

Progeny testing cannot be practiced until after the animal reaches sexual maturity. In order to progeny test a male, he must be mated to several females.   If the sex ratio is 1:1, then obviously every male in a flock or herd cannot be tested.   Therefore males which have been saved for a progeny test have already been selected by some other criteria earlier in life.   The more progeny each male is allowed to produce the more accurate the estimate of his "transmitting ability" (breeding value), but in so doing, fewer males can be progeny tested.   If more animals could be tested, the breeder would be assured that he was saving only the very best for widespread use in his herd or flock.   Thus a compromise must be made, in that he fails to test as many animals as he would like because of the increased accuracy that can be gained by allotting more females to each male under test.

The information from a progeny test can be used in the calculation of the "equal parent index" (sometimes referred to as the "midparent index").   If the progeny receive a sample half of each of their parents' genotypes and the plus and minus effects of Mendelian errors and errors of appraisal tend to cancel each other in averages of the progeny and dams, then Average of progeny = sire/2 + (average of dams)/2 or

$$\text{Sire} = 2(\text{average of progeny}) - (\text{average of dams}) \qquad\qquad (11.11)$$

INBREEDING

Inbreeding is the mating of individuals more closely related than the average of the population to which they belong. Fig. 11-8(*a*) shows a pedigree in which no inbreeding is evident because there is no common ancestral pathway from B to C (D, E, F and G all being unrelated). In the inbred pedigree of Fig. 11-8(*b*), B and C have the same parents and thus are full sibs (brothers and/or sisters). In the standard pedigree form shown in Fig. 11-8(*b*), sires appear on the upper lines and dams on the lower lines. Thus B and D are males; C and E are females. It is desirable to convert a standard pedigree into an arrow diagram for analysis (Fig. 11-8(*c*)). The *coefficient of relationship* (R) estimates the percentage of genes held in common by two individuals because of their common ancestry. Since each individual transmits only a sample half of his genotype to his offspring, each arrow in the diagram represents a probability of $\frac{1}{2}$. The sum (Σ) of all pathways between two individuals through common ancestors is the coefficient of relationship.

(*a*)

(*b*)

(*c*)

Fig. 11-8. Pedigree diagrams

Example 11.17. In the arrow diagram of Fig. 11-8(*c*), there are two pathways connecting B and C. $R_{BC} = \Sigma (\frac{1}{2})^s$, where s is the number of steps (arrows) from B to the common ancestor and back to C.

B and C probably contain $(\frac{1}{2})(\frac{1}{2}) = \frac{1}{4}$ of their genes in common through ancestor D.

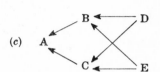

Similarly, B and C probably contain $\frac{1}{4}$ of their genes in common through ancestor E.

The sum of these two pathways is the coefficient of relationship between the full sibs B and C; $R_{BC} = \frac{1}{4} + \frac{1}{4} = \frac{1}{2}$ or 50%.

When matings occur only between closely related individuals (inbreeding) the genetic effect is an increase in homozygosity. The most intense form of inbreeding is self fertilization. If we start with a population containing 100 heterozygous individuals (*Aa*) as shown in Table 11.1, the expected number of homozygous genotypes is increased by 50% due to selfing in each generation.

Table 11.1. Expected Increase in Homozygosity Due to Selfing

Generation	Genotypes			Percent Heterozygosity	Percent Homozygosity
	AA	*Aa*	*aa*		
0		100		100	0
1	25	50	25	50	50
2	25 12.5	25	12.5 25	25	75
3	37.5 6.25	12.5	6.25 37.5	12.5	87.5
4	43.75 3.125	6.25	3.125 43.75	6.25	93.75

Other less intense forms of inbreeding produce a less rapid approach to homozygosity, shown graphically in Fig. 11-9. As homozygosity increases in a population, either due to inbreeding or selection, the genetic variability of the population decreases. Since heritability depends upon the relative amount of genetic variability, it also decreases so that in the limiting case (pure line) heritability becomes zero.

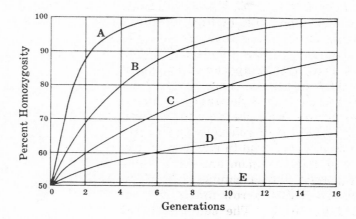

Fig. 11-9.   Increase in percentage of homozygosity under various systems of inbreeding. (A) self fertilization, (B) full sibs, (C) double first cousins, (D) single first cousins, (E) second cousins.

When population size is reduced to a small isolated unit containing less than about 50 individuals, inbreeding very likely will result in a detectable increase in genetic uniformity. The *coefficient of inbreeding* (symbolized by F) is a useful indicator of the probable effect which inbreeding has had at two levels.

(1) On an *individual basis,* the coefficient of inbreeding indicates the probability that the two alleles at any locus are identical by descent, i.e. they are both replication products of a gene present in a common ancestor.

(2) On a *population basis,* the coefficient of inbreeding indicates the percentage of all loci which were heterozygous in the base population that now have probably become homozygous due to the effects of inbreeding. The base population is that point in the history of the population from which we desire to begin a calculation of the effects of inbreeding. Many loci are probably homozygous at the time we establish our base population. The inbreeding coefficient then measures the *additional* increase in homozygosity due to matings between closely related individuals.

The coefficient of inbreeding (F) can be determined for an individual in a pedigree by several similar methods.

(1) If the common ancestor is not inbred, the inbreeding coefficient of an individual (F_x) is half the coefficient of relationship between his sire and dam (R_{SD}):

$$F_x = \tfrac{1}{2}R_{SD} \tag{11.12}$$

(2) If the common ancestors are not inbred, the inbreeding coefficient is given by

$$F_x = \sum (\tfrac{1}{2})^{p_1 + p_2 + 1} \tag{11.13}$$

where p_1 is the number of generations (arrows) from one parent back to the common ancestor and p_2 is the number of generations from the other parent back to the same ancestor.

(3) If the common ancestors are inbred (F_A), the inbreeding coefficient of the individual must be corrected for this factor:

$$F_x = \sum \left[(\tfrac{1}{2})^{p_1 + p_2 + 1} (1 + F_A) \right] \qquad (11.14)$$

(4) The coefficient of inbreeding of an individual may be calculated by counting the number of arrows (n) which connect the individual through one parent back to the common ancestor and back again to his other parent, and applying the formula

$$F_x = \sum (\tfrac{1}{2})^n (1 + F_A) \qquad (11.15)$$

The following table will be helpful in calculating F.

n	1	2	3	4	5	6	7	8	9
$(\tfrac{1}{2})^n$	0.5000	0.2500	0.1250	0.0625	0.0312	0.0156	0.0078	0.0039	0.0019

Linebreeding is a special form of inbreeding utilized for the purpose of maintaining a high genetic relationship to a desirable ancestor. Fig. 11-10 shows a pedigree in which close linebreeding to B has been practiced so that A possesses more than 50% of B's genes. D possesses 50% of B's genes and transmits 25% to C. B also contributes 50% of his genes to C. Hence C contains $50\% + 25\% = 75\%$ B genes and transmits half of them (37.5%) to A. B also contributes 50% of his genes to A. Therefore A has $50\% + 37.5\% = 87.5\%$ of B's genes.

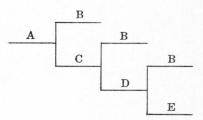

Fig. 11-10. Pedigree exemplifying close linebreeding

HYBRID VIGOR

Many recessives remain hidden in heterozygous conditions in non-inbred populations, but as homozygosity increases in an inbred population there is a greater probability that recessive traits, many of which are deleterious, will begin to appear. One of the consequences of inbreeding is a loss in vigor (i.e. less productive vegetatively and reproductively) which commonly accompanies an increase in homozygosity (*inbreeding depression*). Crosses between inbred lines usually produce a vigorous hybrid F_1 generation. This increased "fitness" of heterozygous individuals has been termed *heterosis*. The genetic basis of heterosis is still a subject of controversy, largely centered about two theories.

(1) The *dominance theory* of heterosis. Hybrid vigor is presumed to result from the action and interaction of dominant growth or fitness factors.

> **Example 11.18.** Assume that four loci are contributing to a quantitative trait. Each recessive genotype contributes one unit to the phenotype and each dominant genotype contributes two units to the phenotype. A cross between two inbred lines could produce a more highly productive (heterotic) F_1 than either parental line.
>
> P: *AA bb CC dd*   ×   *aa BB cc DD*
>
> Phenotypic Value: $2 + 1 + 2 + 1 = 6$ $1 + 2 + 1 + 2 = 6$
>
> F_1:   *Aa Bb Cc Dd*
>
> $2 + 2 + 2 + 2 = 8$

(2) The *overdominance theory* of heterosis. Heterozygosity *per se* is assumed to produce hybrid vigor.

Example 11.19. Assume that four loci are contributing to a quantitative trait, recessive genotypes contribute 1 unit to the phenotype, heterozygous genotypes contribute 2 units, and homozygous dominant genotypes contribute $1\frac{1}{2}$ units.

$$P: \qquad aa\ bb\ CC\ DD \qquad \times \qquad AA\ BB\ cc\ dd$$

Phenotypic Value: $\qquad 1 + 1 + 1\frac{1}{2} + 1\frac{1}{2} = 5 \qquad\qquad 1\frac{1}{2} + 1\frac{1}{2} + 1 + 1 = 5$

$$F_1: \qquad\qquad Aa\ Bb\ Cc\ Dd$$

$$2 + 2 + 2 + 2 = 8$$

Phenotypic variability in the hybrid generation is generally much less than that exhibited by the inbred parental lines (Fig. 11-11). This indicates that the heterozygotes are less subject to environmental influences than the homozygotes. Geneticists use the term "buffering" to indicate that the organism's development is highly regulated genetically ("canalized"). Another term often used in this connection is *homeostasis* which signifies the maintenance of a "steady state" in the development and physiology of the organism within the normal range of environmental fluctuations.

A rough guide to the estimation of heterotic effects (H) is obtained by noting the average excess in vigor which F_1 hybrids exhibit over the midpoint between the means of the inbred parental lines (Fig. 11-11).

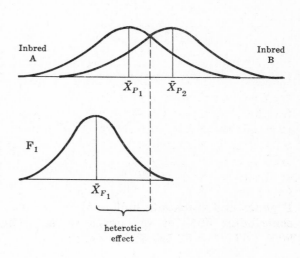

Fig. 11-11. Heterosis in the progeny from crossing inbred lines.

$$\mathrm{H}_{F_1} = \bar{X}_{F_1} - \tfrac{1}{2}(\bar{X}_{P_1} + \bar{X}_{P_2}) \qquad\qquad (11.16)$$

The heterosis exhibited by an F_2 population is commonly observed to be half of that manifested by the F_1 hybrids.

Solved Problems

QUASI-QUANTITATIVE TRAITS

11.1. The mean internode length of the Abed Binder variety of barley was found to be 3.20 mm. The mean length in the Asplund variety was 2.10 mm. Crossing these two varieties produced an F_1 and F_2 with average internode lengths of 2.65 mm. About 6% of the F_2 had an internode length of 3.2 mm and another 6% had a length of 2.1 mm. Determine the most probable number of gene pairs involved in internode length and the approximate contribution each gene makes to the phenotype.

Solution:

With one pair of genes we expect about $\frac{1}{4}$ or 25% of the F_2 to be as extreme as one of the parents. With two pairs of genes we expect approximately $\frac{1}{16}$ or 6.25% as extreme as one parent. Thus we may postulate two pairs of genes. Let A and B represent growth factors and a and b represent null genes.

P: $AA\,BB$ × $aa\,bb$
                Abed Binder   Asplund
        4 growth genes = 3.2 mm   No growth genes = 2.1 mm

F_1: $Aa\,Bb$
                        2 growth genes = 2.65 mm

The difference $2.65 - 2.10 = 0.55$ mm is the result of two growth genes. Therefore each growth gene contributes 0.275 mm to the phenotype.

F_2:

No. of Growth Genes	Mean Internode Length (mm)	Frequency	Genotypes
4	3.200	1/16	$AABB$
3	2.925	1/4	$AaBB$, $AABb$
2	2.650	3/8	$AAbb$, $AaBb$, $aaBB$
1	2.375	1/4	$aaBb$, $Aabb$
0	2.100	1/16	$aabb$ (physiological minimum due to residual genotype)

11.2. A large breed of chicken, the Golden Hamburg, was crossed to small Sebright Bantams. The F_1 was intermediate in size. The mean size of the F_2 was about the same as that of the F_1, but the variability of the F_2 was so great that a few individuals were found to exceed the size of either parental type (*transgressive variation*). If all of the alleles contributing to size act with equal and cumulative effects, and if the parents are considered to be homozygous, how can these results be explained?

Solution:

Let capital letters stand for growth genes (active alleles) and small letters stand for alleles which do not contribute to growth (null alleles). For simplicity we will consider only four loci.

P: $aa\,BB\,CC\,DD$ × $AA\,bb\,cc\,dd$
        large Golden Hamburg   small Sebright Bantam
            6 active alleles   2 active alleles

F_1: $Aa\,Bb\,Cc\,Dd$
                        intermediate sized hybrid
                            4 active alleles

F_2:   Some genotypes could segregate out in the F_2 with phenotypic values which exceed that of the parents. For example:

$AA\,BB\,CC\,DD$ 8 active alleles   ⎫ larger than
$Aa\,BB\,CC\,DD$ 7 active alleles   ⎭ Golden Hamburg

$Aa\,bb\,cc\,dd$ 1 active allele   ⎫ smaller than
$aa\,bb\,cc\,dd$ no active alleles ⎭ Sebright Bantams
                   (physiological
                   minimum)

THE NORMAL DISTRIBUTION

11.3. A representative sample of lamb weaning weights is shown below. Determine the weight limits within which 95% of all lambs from this population are expected to be found at weaning time.

81	81	83	101	86
65	68	77	66	92
94	85	105	60	90
94	90	81	63	58

Solution:

The standard deviation is calculated as follows.

$$\bar{X} = \frac{\Sigma X}{N} = \frac{1620}{20} = 81.0$$

X	$X - \bar{X}$	$(X - \bar{X})^2$
81	0	0
65	−16	256
94	+13	169
94	+13	169
81	0	0
68	−13	169
85	+4	16
90	+9	81
83	+2	4
77	−4	16
105	+24	576
81	0	0
101	+20	400
66	−15	225
60	−21	441
63	−18	324
86	+5	25
92	+11	121
90	+9	81
58	−23	529
$\Sigma X = 1620$	$\Sigma (X - \bar{X}) = 0$	$\Sigma (X - \bar{X})^2 = 3602$

$$s = \sqrt{\frac{\Sigma (X - \bar{X})^2}{N - 1}} = \sqrt{\frac{3602}{19}} = 13.77$$

95% of all weaning weights are expected to lie within $\pm 2s$ of the mean. Thus $\bar{X} \pm 2s = 81.0 \pm 2(13.77) = 81.0 \pm 27.54$. The upper limit is 108.54 and the lower limit is 53.46.

11.4. The average fleece weight in a large band of sheep together with its standard deviation was calculated to be 10.3 ± 1.5 lb. The statistics for fleece grade (on a scale from 0 to 10) was 5.1 ± 0.7 units. Which trait is relatively more variable?

Solution:

Relative variability may be determined from a comparison of their coefficients of variation.

C.V. (fleece weight) $= s/\bar{X} = 1.5/10.3 = 0.146$

C.V. (fleece grade) $= 0.7/5.1 = 0.137$

Fleece weight has a slightly higher coefficient of variation and thus is relatively more variable than fleece grade.

11.5. The Flemish breed of rabbits has an average body weight of 3600 grams. The Himalayan breed has a mean of 1875 grams. Matings between these two breeds produce an intermediate F_1 with a standard deviation of ± 162 grams. The variability of the F_2 is greater as indicated by a standard deviation of ± 230 grams. (a) Estimate the number of pairs of factors contributing to mature body weight in rabbits. (b) Estimate the average metric contribution of each active allele.

Solution:

(a) From equation (11.5), page 225,

$$N = \frac{D^2}{8(\sigma_{PF2}^2 - \sigma_{PF1}^2)} = \frac{(3600 - 1875)^2}{8(230^2 - 162^2)} = 13.95 \text{ or approximately 14 pairs}$$

(b) The difference $3600 - 1875 = 1725$ grams is attributed to 14 *pairs* of factors or 28 active alleles. The average contribution of each active allele is $1725/28 = 61.61$ grams.

11.6. In a population having a phenotypic mean of 55 units, a total genetic variance for the trait of 35 units², and an environmental variance of 14 units², between what two phenotypic values will approximately 68% of the population be found?

Solution:

$\sigma_P^2 = \sigma_G^2 + \sigma_E^2 = 35 + 14 = 49, \quad \sigma_P = 7.$

68% of a normally distributed population is expected to be found within the limits $\mu \pm \sigma = 55 \pm 7$, or between 48 units and 62 units.

TYPES OF GENE ACTION

11.7. The F_1 produced by crossing two varieties of tomatoes has a mean fruit weight of 50 grams and a phenotypic variance of 225 gm². The F_1 is backcrossed to one of the parental varieties having a mean of 150 grams. Assuming that tomato fruit weight is governed by multiplicative gene action, predict the variance of the backcross progeny.

Solution:

The expected mean of the backcross progeny is the geometric mean of 150 and 50, or $\sqrt{150 \times 50} = \sqrt{7500} = 86.6$. If multiplicative gene action is operative the variance is dependent upon the mean, thus producing a constant coefficient of variation in segregating populations.

F_1 coefficient of variation $= s/\bar{X} = \sqrt{225}/50 = 0.3$, and so the coefficient of variation in the backcross generation is also expected to be 0.3.

Standard deviation of backcross $= 0.3(86.6) = 25.98$.

Variance of backcross $= (25.98)^2 = 675$ gm².

HERITABILITY

11.8. The total genetic variance of 180 day body weight in a population of swine is 250 lb². The variance due to dominance effects is 50 lb². The variance due to epistatic effects is 20 lb². The environmental variance is 350 lb². What is the heritability estimate (narrow sense) of this trait?

Solution:

$\sigma_P^2 = \sigma_G^2 + \sigma_E^2 = 250 + 350 = 600.$

$\sigma_G^2 = \sigma_A^2 + \sigma_D^2 + \sigma_I^2, \quad 250 = \sigma_A^2 + 50 + 20, \quad \sigma_A^2 = 180.$

$h^2 = \sigma_A^2/\sigma_P^2 = 180/600 = 0.3.$

11.9. The heritability of feedlot rate of gain in beef cattle is 0.6. The average rate of gain in the population is 1.7 lb/day. The average rate of gain of the individuals selected from this population to be the parents of the next generation is 2.8 lb/day. What is the expected average daily gain of the progeny in the next generation?

Solution:

$\Delta P = \bar{P}_p - \bar{P}_1 = 2.8 - 1.7 = 1.1. \quad \Delta G = h^2(\Delta P) = 0.6(1.1) = 0.66. \quad \bar{P}_2 = \bar{P}_1 + \Delta G = 2.36$ lb/day.

11.10. Fifty gilts (female pigs) born each year in a given herd can be used for proving sires. Average litter size at birth is 10 with 10% mortality to maturity. Only the five boars (males) with the highest sire index will be saved for further use in the herd. If each test requires 18 mature progeny, how much culling can be practiced among the progeny tested boars, i.e. what proportion of those tested will not be saved?

Solution:

Each gilt will produce an average of $10 - (0.1)(10) = 9$ progeny raised to maturity. If 18 mature progeny are required to prove a sire, then each boar should be mated to two gilts. (50 gilts)/(2 gilts per boar) = 25 boars can be proved. $20/25 = 4/5 = 80\%$ of these boars will be culled.

11.11. Given the following pedigree with butterfat records on the cows and equal-parent indices on the bulls, estimate the index for young bull X (*a*) using information from A and B, (*b*) when the record made by B is only one lactation, and that made in another herd.

X ─── A (750 lb index)
   └── B (604 lb record) ─── C (820 lb index)
                          └── D (492 lb record)

Solution:

(*a*) The midparent index (estimate of transmitting ability) for X is $(750 + 604)/2 = 677$.

(*b*) Since we cannot rely on B's record, we should use information from C and D, recalling that X is separated by two Mendelian segregations from his grandparents. Then $X = 750/2 + 820/4 + 492/4 = 703$.

INBREEDING

11.12. Calculate the inbreeding coefficient for A in the following pedigree.

A ─── B ─── E ─── G ─── I
              │   └── J
              │   └── H ─── I
              │   └── J
              └── D
   └── C ─── E ─── G ─── I
              │   └── J
              │   └── H ─── I
              │   └── J
              └── F

Solution:

First we must convert the pedigree to an arrow diagram.

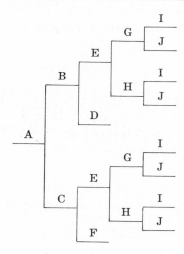

There is only one pathway from B to C and that goes through ancestor E. However, ancestor E is himself inbred. Note that the parents of E are full sibs, i.e. G and H are 50% related (see Example 11.17). By (11.12),

$$F_E = \tfrac{1}{2}R_{GH} = \tfrac{1}{2}(0.5) = 0.25$$

The inbreeding coefficient of A is given by equation (11.15),

$$F_A = \sum (\tfrac{1}{2})^n (1 + F_{ancestor}) = (\tfrac{1}{2})^3 (1 + 0.25) = 0.156$$

where n is the number of arrows connecting the individual (A) through one parent (B) back to the common ancestor (E) and back again to his other parent (C).

HYBRID VIGOR

11.13. The average plant heights of two inbred tobacco varieties and their hybrids have been measured with the following results: Inbred parent (P_1) = 47.8 inches, Inbred parent (P_2) = 28.7 inches, F_1 hybrid ($P_1 \times P_2$) = 43.2 inches. (*a*) Calculate the amount of heterosis exhibited by the F_1. (*b*) Predict the average height of the F_2.

Solution:

(*a*) The amount of heterosis is expressed by the excess of the F_1 average over the midpoint between the two parental means.

$$\text{Heterosis of } F_1 = \bar{X}_{F_1} - \tfrac{1}{2}(\bar{X}_{P_1} + \bar{X}_{P_2}) = 43.2 - \tfrac{1}{2}(47.8 + 28.7) = 43.2 - 38.25 = 4.95 \text{ inches.}$$

(*b*) As a general rule the F_2 shows only about half the heterosis of the F_1: $\tfrac{1}{2}(4.95) = 2.48$. Hence the expected height of F_2 plants = $38.25 + 2.48 = 40.73$ inches.

Supplementary Problems

QUASI-QUANTITATIVE TRAITS

11.14. Beginning at some arbitrary date, two varieties of wheat were scored for the length of time (in days) to heading, from which the following means were obtained: variety X = 13.0 days, variety Y = 27.6 days. From a survey of 5,504,000 F_2 progeny, 86 were found to head out in 13 days or less. How many pairs of factors are probably contributing to early flowering?

11.15. Suppose that 5 pairs of genes with equal and cumulative effects are contributing to body weight in laboratory albino rats. Two highly inbred strains (homozygous) have the extreme high and low mature weights respectively. A hybrid F_1 generation is produced by crossing these two lines. The average cost of raising a rat to maturity is $2.00. What will it probably cost the breeder to recover in the F_2 a rat which is as extreme as the high parental line?

THE NORMAL DISTRIBUTION

11.16. From a sample of 10 pig body weights determine (*a*) mean body weight, (*b*) sample standard deviation (s), (*c*) the weight which will probably be exceeded by $2\tfrac{1}{2}\%$ of this population. Pig weights: 210, 215, 220, 225, 215, 205, 220, 210, 215, 225.

VARIANCE

11.17. Suppose 6 pairs of genes were contributing to a metric trait in a cultivated crop. Two parental lines with averages of 13,000 lb/acre and 7,000 lb/acre produced an intermediate hybrid F_1 with a variance of 250,000 lb². Estimate the standard deviation of the F_2 by (11.5), page 225.

11.18. Two strains of mice were tested for susceptibility to a carcinogenic drug. The susceptible strain had an average of 75.4 tumorous lung nodules, whereas the resistant strain failed to develop nodules. The F_1 from crossing these two strains had an average of 12.5 nodules with a standard deviation of ±5.3; the F_2 had 10.0 ± 14.1 nodules. Estimate the number of gene pairs contributing to tumor susceptibility by use of (11.5), page 225.

TYPES OF GENE ACTION

11.19. Calculate the metric values of the parents and their F_1 hybrids in the cross $AA\,B'B'\,CC\,D'D' \times A'A'\,BB\,C'C'\,DD$ assuming (a) additive gene action where unprimed alleles contribute 3 units each to the phenotype and primed alleles contribute 6 units each, (b) primed alleles are fully dominant to unprimed alleles; at a given locus, genotypes with one or two primed alleles produce 12 units and the recessive genotype produces 6 units.

11.20. Several generations of selection and inbreeding in a laboratory strain of mice produced a giant strain with a mean of 40 grams at two months of age and a midget strain with an average of 12 grams. The phenotypic variance of the giant strain is 26.01 and of the midget strain is 2.92. (a) Calculate the coefficient of variation for the giant and the midget strains. (b) On the basis of your findings in part (a), calculate the expected mean of the F_1 produced by crossing these two lines.

11.21. Several examples of multiplicative gene action are known in crosses between tomato varieties. Calculate the arithmetic mean and geometric mean for each F_1 and compare each of their absolute deviations from the F_1 mean. The mean fruit weight in grams for each group is given in parentheses.

	Variety #1	Variety #2	F_1
(a)	Yellow Pear (12.4)	Honor Bright (150.0)	(47.5)
(b)	Yellow Pear (12.4)	Peach (42.6)	(23.1)
(c)	Dwarf Aristocrat (112.4)	Peach (42.6)	(67.1)
(d)	Tangerine (173.6)	Red Currant (1.1)	(8.3)

HERITABILITY

11.22. A flock of chickens has an average mature body weight of 6.6 lb. Individuals saved for breeding purposes have a mean of 7.2 lb. The offspring generation has a mean of 6.81 lb. Estimate the heritability of mature body weight in this flock.

11.23. Yearly wool records (in pounds) are taken from a sample of 10 sheep: 11.8, 8.4, 9.5, 10.0, 10.9, 7.8, 10.8, 8.5, 11.8, 10.5. (a) Calculate the range within which approximately 95% of the sheep in this population are expected to be found. (b) If the additive genetic variance is 0.60, what is the heritability estimate of wool production in this breed?

11.24. Determine (a) the dominance variance and (b) the environmental variance from the following information: heritability (Formula (11.8)) = 0.3, phenotypic variance = 200 lb^2, total genetic variance = 100 lb^2, and epistatic variance is absent.

11.25. Thickness of backfat in a certain breed of swine has been estimated to have a heritability of 80%. Suppose the average backfat thickness of this breed is 1.2 inches and the average of individuals selected from this population to be the parents of the next generation is 0.8 inches. What is the expected average of the next generation?

11.26. The average yearly milk production of a herd of cows is 18,000 lb. The average milk production of the individuals selected to be parents of the next generation is 20,000 lb. The average milk production of the offspring generation is 18,440 lb. (a) Estimate the heritability of milk production in this population. (b) If the phenotypic variance of this population is 4,000,000 lb^2, estimate the additive genetic variance. (c) Between what values is 68% of this population expected to be found?

11.27. The average weight at 140 days in a swine population is 180 lb. The average weight of individuals selected from this population for breeding purposes is 195 lb. Heritability of 140 day weight in swine is 30%. Calculate (a) selection differential, (b) expected genetic gain in the progeny, (c) predicted average 140 day weight of the progeny.

11.28. About 1903 Johannsen, a Danish botanist, measured the weight of seeds in the Princess Variety of bean. Beans are self fertilizing and therefore this variety is a pure line. The weights in centigrams of a small but representative sample of beans are listed below.

19	31	18	24	27	28	25	30	29
22	29	26	23	20	24	21	25	29

(a) Calculate the mean and standard deviation for bean weight in this sample. (b) Calculate the environmental variance. (c) Estimate the heritability of bean weight in this variety. (d) If the average bean weight of individuals selected to be parents from this population is 30 cg, predict the average bean weight of the next generation.

11.29. The length of an individual beetle is 10.3 mm or 0.5 when expressed in "standardized" form. The average measurement for this trait in the beetle population is 10.0 mm. What is the variance of this trait?

11.30. Given the swine selection index $I = 0.14W - 0.27S$, where W is the pig's own 180 day weight and S is its market score. (a) Rank the following three animals according to index merit:

Animal	Weight	Score
X	220	48
Y	240	38
Z	200	30

(b) If differences in index score are 20% heritable, and parents score 3.55 points higher than the average of the population, how much increase in the average score of the progeny is expected?

11.31. A beef cattle index (I) for selecting replacement heifers takes the form $I = 6 + 2WW' + WG'$, where WW' is weaning weight in standardized form and WG' is weaning grade in standardized form. The average weaning weight of the herd = 505 lb with a standard deviation of ± 34.5 lb. The average weaning grade (a numerical score) is 88.6 with a standard deviation of ± 2.1. Which of the following animals has the best overall merit?

Animal	Actual Weaning Weight	Actual Weaning Grade
A	519	88
B	486	91

11.32. Suppose 360 ewes (female sheep) are available for proving sires. All ewes lamb; fifty percent of ewes lambing have twins. The ten rams with the highest progeny test scores will be kept as flock sires. How much selection can be practiced among the progeny tested individuals, i.e. what proportion of those tested can be saved if a test requires (a) 18 progeny, (b) 12 progeny, (c) 6 progeny?

11.33. During the same year three dairy bulls were each mated to a random group of cows. The number of pounds of butterfat produced by the dams and their daughters (corrected to a 305 day lactation at maturity with twice daily milking) was recorded as shown below.

Bull	Dam	Dam's Record	Daughter's Record
A	1	600	605
	2	595	640
	3	615	625
	4	610	600
B	5	585	610
	6	590	620
	7	620	605
	8	605	595
C	9	590	590
	10	590	595
	11	610	600
	12	600	605

(a) Calculate the sire index for each of the three sires. (b) Which sire would you save for extensive use in your herd?

INBREEDING

11.34. A is linebred to B in the following pedigree. Calculate the inbreeding coefficient of A.

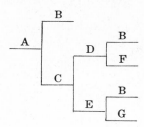

11.35. Given the following arrow diagram, calculate the inbreeding coefficient of A.

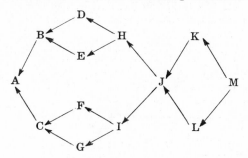

11.36. Calculate the inbreeding of A in the following. *Hint.* There are 9 pathways between B and C.

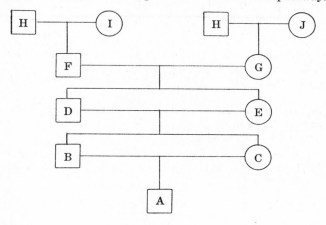

HYBRID VIGOR

11.37. The yield of seed (in bushels per acre) and plant height (in centimeters) was measured on several generations of corn. Calculate by equation (*11.16*), page 235, (*a*) the amount of heterosis in the F$_1$ resulting from crossing the parental varieties with the inbreds, (*b*) the yield and height expectations of the F$_2$.

	Seed Yield	Plant Height
Parental varieties	73.3	265
Inbreds	25.0	193
F$_1$ hybrids	71.4	257

Answers to Supplementary Problems

11.14. 8 pairs of factors

11.15. $2048

11.16. (a) 216 lb   (b) ±6.58 lb   (c) 229.16 lb

11.17. ±1000 lb/acre

11.18. 4.16 or approximately 4 gene pairs

11.19. (a) Both parents, $F_1 = 36$ units   (b) Both parents = 36 units, $F_1 = 48$ units

11.20. (a) Giant strain = 0.13, midget strain = 0.14   (b) Multiplicative gene action is indicated by the similarity of the two coefficients of variation; $\bar{X}_{F_1} = 21.9$ grams.

11.21.

	Arithmetic mean	Absolute deviation from F_1 mean	Geometric mean	Absolute deviation from F_1 mean
(a)	81.2	33.7	43.1	4.4
(b)	27.5	4.4	23.0	0.1
(c)	77.5	10.4	69.2	2.1
(d)	87.3	79.0	13.8	5.5

11.22. 0.35

11.23. (a) 7.16 to 12.84 lb   (b) 0.3

11.24. (a) 40 lb^2 (b) 100 lb^2

11.25. 0.88 inches

11.26. (a) 0.22   (b) 880,000 lb^2 (c) 16,000 to 20,000 lb

11.27. (a) 15 lb   (b) 4.5 lb   (c) 184.5 lb

11.28. (a) $\bar{X} = 25$ cg, $s = \pm 3.94$ cg   (b) 15.53 cg^2; note that this is the square of the phenotypic standard deviation in part (a). In pure lines, all of the variance is environmentally induced.   (c) $h^2 = 0$, since a pure line is homozygous; there is no genetic variability.   (d) $\bar{X} = 25$ cg; no genetic gain can be made by selecting in the absence of genetic variability.

11.29. 0.36 mm^2

11.30. (a) Y = 23.34, Z = 19.90, X = 17.84   (b) 0.71 point

11.31. $I_A = 6.526$, $I_B = 6.041$; A excels in overall merit.

11.32. (a) 1/3   (b) 22.2%   (c) 1/9

11.33. (a) A = 630.0, B = 615.0, C = 597.5   (b) Sire A

11.34. 0.25

11.35. 0.0351

11.36. 0.4375

11.37. (a) Heterosis for seed yield = 22.2 bu/A, for plant height = 28 cm   (b) 60.3 bu/A, 243 cm

Chapter 12

Population Genetics

HARDY-WEINBERG EQUILIBRIUM

A *Mendelian population* may be considered to be a group of sexually reproducing organisms with a relatively close degree of genetic relationship (such as a species, subspecies, breed, variety, strain, etc.) residing within defined geographical boundaries wherein inter-breeding occurs. If all the gametes produced by a Mendelian population are considered as a hypothetical mixture of genetic units from which the next generation will arise, we have the concept of a *gene pool*.

If we consider a pair of alleles (*A* and *a*), we will find that the percentage of gametes in the gene pool bearing *A* or *a* will depend upon the genotypic frequencies of the parental generation whose gametes form the pool. For example, if most of the population was of the recessive genotype *aa* then the frequency of the recessive allele in the gene pool would be relatively high, and the percentage of gametes bearing the dominant (*A*) allele would be correspondingly low.

When matings between members of a population are completely at random, i.e. when every male gamete in the gene pool has an equal opportunity of uniting with every female gamete, then the zygotic frequencies expected in the next generation may be predicted from a knowledge of the gene (allelic) frequencies in the gene pool of the parental population. That is, given the relative frequencies of *A* and *a* gametes in the gene pool, we can calculate (on the basis of the chance union of gametes) the expected frequencies of progeny genotypes and phenotypes. If p = percentage of *A* alleles in the gene pool and q = percentage of *a* alleles, then we can use the checkerboard method to produce all the possible chance combinations of these gametes.

♀ \ ♂	p (A)	q (a)
p (A)	p^2 AA	pq Aa
q (a)	pq Aa	q^2 aa

Note that $p + q = 1$, i.e. the percentage of A and a gametes must add to 100% in order to account for all of the gametes in the gene pool. The expected genotypic (zygotic) frequencies in the next generation then may be summarized as follows:

$$(p + q)^2 \;=\; p^2 + 2pq + q^2 \;=\; 1.0$$
$$AA \quad Aa \quad aa$$

Thus p^2 is the fraction of the next generation expected to be homozygous dominant (AA), $2pq$ is the fraction expected to be heterozygous (Aa), and q^2 is the fraction expected to be recessive (aa). All of these genotypic fractions must add to unity to account for all genotypes in the progeny population.

This formula, expressing the genotypic expectations of progeny in terms of the gametic (allelic) frequencies of the parental gene pool, is called the *Hardy-Weinberg law*. If a population conforms to the conditions on which this formula is based, there should be no change in the gametic or the zygotic frequencies from generation to generation. Should a population initially be in disequilibrium, one generation of random mating is sufficient to bring it into genetic equilibrium and thereafter the population will remain in equilibrium (unchanging in gametic and zygotic frequencies) as long as the Hardy-Weinberg conditions persist.

1. Equilibrium Conditions.

Several assumptions underlie the attainment of genetic equilibrium as expressed in the Hardy-Weinberg equation.

(1) The population is infinitely large and mates at random (*panmictic*).

(2) No selection is operative, i.e. each genotype under consideration can survive just as well as any other (no differential mortality), and each genotype is equally efficient in the production of progeny (no differential reproduction).

(3) The population is closed, i.e. no immigration of individuals from another population into nor emigration from the population under consideration is allowed.

(4) There is no mutation from one allelic state to another. Mutation may be allowed if the forward and back mutation rates are equivalent, i.e. A mutates to a with the same frequency that a mutates to A.

(5) Meiosis is normal so that chance is the only factor operative in gametogenesis.

2. Evolution.

If we define *evolution* as any change in a population from the equilibrium conditions, then a violation of one or more of the Hardy-Weinberg restrictions could cause the population to move away from the gametic and zygotic equilibrium frequencies. Changes in gene frequencies can be produced by a reduction in population size, by selection, migration or mutation pressures, or by *meiotic drive* (nonrandom assortment of chromosomes). No population is infinitely large, spontaneous mutations cannot be prevented, selection and migration pressures usually exist in most natural populations, etc., so it may be surprising to learn that despite these violations of Hardy-Weinberg restrictions many genes do conform, within statistically acceptable limits, to equilibrium conditions between two successive generations. Changes too small to be statistically significant deviations from equilibrium expectations between any two generations can nonetheless accumulate over many generations to produce considerable alterations in the genetic structure of a population.

For two populations to diverge genetically on different evolutionary paths, which will eventually lead to *speciation* (the formation of new species), they must first become geographically isolated from each other. If a large population is fragmented into two or more units which are geographically isolated from one another, the independent units may follow different evolutionary paths for several reasons: (1) different mutations appear in separated groups of organisms, providing the raw materials of organic diversity; (2) the mutations and gene combinations which appear in separate populations will have different adaptive values in the new environments; (3) organisms which originally colonize a certain geographical area and form an isolated population may not be representative of the group from which they came so that different gene frequencies exist from the beginning (founder principle); (4) the size of the new population may become quite small at various times so that a genetic "bottleneck" is formed from which all subsequent organisms will arise. Gene frequencies will fluctuate in unpredictable directions during periods of small population size (*genetic drift*).

When migration is eliminated between two populations in different geographical areas, their gene pools become the isolated entities which are prerequisite to the accumulation of genetic differences. If the two gene pools of what was originally one population can remain isolated for a sufficient length of time, these differences can become so great that members of one population will no longer interbreed with or can no longer produce viable and fertile offspring by a member of the other population even when they are no longer geographically isolated from one another. The two populations have become *reproductively isolated* from each other and can then be said to represent different *biological species*. Much evolution (genetic change) can occur in a population without its transformation into different species. Speciation, being a special aspect of evolution, is beyond the scope of this book.

CALCULATING GENE FREQUENCIES

1. Autosomal Loci With Two Alleles.

(a) Codominant Autosomal Alleles.

When codominant alleles are present in a two-allele system, each genotype has a distinctive phenotype. The numbers of each allele in both homozygous and heterozygous conditions may be counted in a sample of individuals from the population and expressed as a percentage of the total number of alleles in the sample. If the sample is representative of the entire population (containing proportionately the same numbers of genotypes as found in the entire population) then we can obtain an estimate of the allelic frequencies in the gene pool. Given a sample of N individuals of which D are homozygous for one allele (A^1A^1), H are heterozygous (A^1A^2), and R are homozygous for the other allele (A^2A^2), then $N = D + H + R$. Since each of the N individuals are diploid at this locus, there are 2N alleles represented in the sample. Each A^1A^1 genotype has two A^1 alleles. Heterozygotes have only one A^1 allele. Letting p represent the frequency of the A^1 allele and q the frequency of the A^2 allele, we have

$$p = \frac{2D + H}{2N} = \frac{D + \frac{1}{2}H}{N}, \qquad q = \frac{H + 2R}{2N} = \frac{\frac{1}{2}H + R}{N}$$

(b) Dominant and Recessive Autosomal Alleles.

Determining the gene frequencies for alleles which exhibit dominance and recessive relationships requires a different approach from that used with codominant alleles. A dominant phenotype may have either of two genotypes, AA or Aa, but we have no way (other than by laboriously testcrossing each dominant phenotype) of distinguishing how many are homozygous or heterozygous in our sample. The only phenotype whose genotype is known for certain is the recessive (aa). If the population is in equilibrium, then we can obtain an estimate of q (the frequency of the recessive allele) from q^2 (the frequency of the recessive genotype or phenotype).

Example 12.1. If 75% of a population was of the dominant phenotype (A-), then 25% would have the recessive phenotype (aa). If the population is in equilibrium with respect to this locus, we expect $q^2 = $ frequency of aa.

Then $q^2 = 0.25$, $q = 0.5$, $p = 1 - q = 0.5$.

(c) Sex-Influenced Traits.

The expression of dominance and recessive relationships may be markedly changed in some genes when exposed to different environmental conditions, most notable of which are the sex hormones. In sex-influenced traits (Chapter 5), the heterozygous genotype usually will produce different phenotypes in the two sexes, making the dominance and recessive relationships of the alleles appear to reverse themselves. We shall consider only those sex-influenced traits whose controlling genes are on autosomes. Determination of allelic frequencies must be indirectly made in one sex by taking the square root of the frequency of the recessive phenotype ($q = \sqrt{q^2}$). A similar approach in the opposite sex should give an estimate of p. Corroboration of sex-influence is obtained if these estimates of p and q made in different sexes add close to unity.

2. Autosomal Loci With Multiple Alleles.

If we consider three alleles, A, a' and a, with the dominance hierarchy $A > a' > a$, occurring in the gene pool with respective frequencies p, q and r, then random mating will generate zygotes with the following frequencies:

$$(p + q + r)^2 \quad = \quad p^2 + 2pq + 2pr + q^2 + 2qr + r^2 \quad = \quad 1$$

Genotypes: $\underbrace{AA \quad Aa' \quad Aa}$ $\underbrace{a'a' \quad a'a}$ $\underbrace{aa}$

Phenotypes: $\quad\quad\quad A$ $\quad\quad a'$ $\quad a$

For ease in calculation of a given allelic frequency, it may be possible to group the phenotypes of the population into just two types.

Example 12.2. In a multiple allelic system where $A > a' > a$, we could calculate the frequency of the top dominant allele A by considering the dominant phenotype (A) in contrast to all other phenotypes produced by alleles at this locus. The latter group may be considered to be produced by an allele a^x, which is recessive to A.

Let $p = $ frequency of allele A, $q = $ frequency of allele a^x.

$q^2 = $ frequency of phenotypes other than A

$q = \sqrt{q^2}$

$p = 1 - q = $ frequency of gene A.

Many multiple allelic series involve codominant relationships such as $(A^1 = A^2) > a$, with respective frequencies p, q and r. More genotypes can be phenotypically recognized in codominant systems than in systems without codominance.

$$(p + q + r)^2 \quad = \quad p^2 + 2pr + 2pq + q^2 + 2qr + r^2 \quad = \quad 1$$

Genotypes: $\underbrace{A^1A^1 \quad A^1a}$ $\underbrace{A^1A^2}$ $\underbrace{A^2A^2 \quad A^2a}$ $\underbrace{aa}$

Phenotypes: $\quad\quad A^1$ $\quad A^1A^2$ $\quad\quad A^2$ $\quad a$

The use of this formula in calculating multiple allelic frequencies is presented in Problems 12.8 and 12.9. Similar methods may be utilized to derive other formulas for calculating gene frequencies in multiple allelic systems with more than three alleles, but their computation becomes too involved for our purposes at the introductory level. Therefore multiple allelic problems in this chapter will be mainly concerned with three alleles.

3. Sex-Linked Loci.

(a) Codominant Sex-Linked Alleles.

Data from both males and females can be used in the direct computation of sex-linked codominant allelic frequencies. Bear in mind that in organisms with an X-Y mechanism of sex determination, the heterozygous condition can only appear in females. Males are hemizygous for sex-linked genes.

Example 12.3. In domestic cats, coat colors are determined by a pair of sex-linked codominant alleles, C^b and C^y.

	Phenotypes		
	Black	Tortoise-shell	Yellow
Females	$C^b C^b$	$C^b C^y$	$C^y C^y$
Males	$C^b Y$	—	$C^y Y$

Let p = frequency of C^b, q = frequency of C^y.

$$p = \frac{2\left(\begin{array}{c}\text{no. of black} \\ \text{females}\end{array}\right) + \left(\begin{array}{c}\text{no. of tortoise-} \\ \text{shell females}\end{array}\right) + \left(\begin{array}{c}\text{no. of black} \\ \text{males}\end{array}\right)}{2(\text{no. females}) + \text{no. males}}$$

$$q = \frac{2\left(\begin{array}{c}\text{no. of yellow} \\ \text{females}\end{array}\right) + \left(\begin{array}{c}\text{no. of tortoise-} \\ \text{shell females}\end{array}\right) + \left(\begin{array}{c}\text{no. of yellow} \\ \text{males}\end{array}\right)}{2(\text{no. females}) + \text{no. males}}$$

(b) Dominant and Recessive Sex-Linked Alleles.

Since each male possesses only one sex-linked allele, the frequency of a sex-linked trait among males is a direct measure of the allelic frequency in the population, assuming of course that the allelic frequencies thus determined are representative of the allelic frequencies among females as well.

TESTING A LOCUS FOR EQUILIBRIUM

In cases where dominance is involved, the heterozygous class is indistinguishable phenotypically from the homozygous dominant class. Hence there is no way of checking the Hardy-Weinberg expectations against observed sample data unless the dominant phenotypes have been genetically analyzed by observation of their progeny from test-crosses. Only when codominant alleles are involved can we easily check our observations against the expected equilibrium values through the chi-square test (Chapter 7).

Degrees of Freedom.

The number of variables in chi-square tests of Hardy-Weinberg equilibrium is not simply the number of phenotypes minus one (as in chi-square tests of classical Mendelian ratios, page 141). The number of observed variables (number of phenotypes = k) is further restricted by testing their conformity to an expected Hardy-Weinberg frequency ratio generated by a number of additional variables (number of alleles, or allelic frequencies = r). We have $k - 1$ degrees of freedom in the number of phenotypes, $(r - 1)$ degrees of freedom in establishing the frequencies for the r alleles. The combined number of degrees of freedom is $(k - 1) - (r - 1) = k - r$. Even in most chi-square tests for equilibrium involving multiple alleles, the number of degrees of freedom is the number of phenotypes minus the number of alleles.

Solved Problems

HARDY-WEINBERG EQUILIBRIUM

12.1. In a population gene pool, the alleles A and a are at initial frequencies p and q respectively. Prove that the gene frequencies and the zygotic frequencies do not change from generation to generation as long as the Hardy-Weinberg conditions are maintained.

Solution:
Zygotic frequencies generated by random mating are

$$p^2(AA) + 2pq(Aa) + q^2(aa) = 1$$

All of the gametes of AA individuals and half of the gametes of heterozygotes will bear the dominant allele (A). Then the frequency of A in the gene pool of the next generation is

$$p^2 + pq = p^2 + p(1-p) = p^2 + p - p^2 = p$$

Thus each generation of random mating under Hardy-Weinberg conditions fails to change either the allelic or zygotic frequencies.

12.2. Prove the Hardy-Weinberg law by finding the frequencies of all possible kinds of matings and from these generating the frequencies of genotypes among the progeny using the symbols shown below.

	Alleles		Genotypes		
	A	a	AA	Aa	aa
Frequency:	p	q	p^2	$2pq$	q^2

Solution:
There are six kinds of matings (ignoring male-female differences) which are easily generated in a mating table.

		Male Parent		
		AA p^2	Aa $2pq$	aa q^2
Female Parent	AA p^2	p^4	$2p^3q$	p^2q^2
	Aa $2pq$	$2p^3q$	$4p^2q^2$	$2pq^3$
	aa q^2	p^2q^2	$2pq^3$	q^4

The matings $AA \times Aa$ occur with the frequency $4p^3q$. Half the offspring from this mating are expected to be AA $[\frac{1}{2}(4p^3q) = 2p^3q]$, and half are expected to be Aa (again with the frequency $2p^3q$). Similar reasoning generates the frequencies of genotypes among the progeny shown in the following table.

	Mating	Frequency	Genotypic Frequencies Among Progeny		
			AA	Aa	aa
(1)	$AA \times AA$	p^4	p^4	—	—
(2)	$AA \times Aa$	$4p^3q$	$2p^3q$	$2p^3q$	—
(3)	$AA \times aa$	$2p^2q^2$	—	$2p^2q^2$	—
(4)	$Aa \times Aa$	$4p^2q^2$	p^2q^2	$2p^2q^2$	p^2q^2
(5)	$Aa \times aa$	$4pq^3$	—	$2pq^3$	$2pq^3$
(6)	$aa \times aa$	q^4	—	—	q^4

Sums:
$$(AA) = p^4 + 2p^3q + p^2q^2 = p^2(p^2 + 2pq + q^2) = p^2$$
$$(Aa) = 2p^3q + 4p^2q^2 + 2pq^3 = 2pq(p^2 + 2pq + q^2) = 2pq$$
$$(aa) = p^2q^2 + 2pq^3 + q^4 = q^2(p^2 + 2pq + q^2) = q^2$$
$$\text{Total} = 1.00$$

CALCULATING GENE FREQUENCIES
Autosomal Loci With Two Alleles.
Codominant Autosomal Alleles.

12.3. In Shorthorn cattle, the genotype C^RC^R is phenotypically red, C^RC^W is roan (a mixture of red and white) and C^WC^W is white. (a) If 108 red, 48 white and 144 roan animals were found in a sample of Shorthorns from the central valley of California, calculate the estimated frequencies of the C^R allele and the C^W allele in the gene pool of the population. (b) If this population is completely panmictic, what zygotic frequencies would be expected in the next generation? (c) How does the sample data in part (a) compare with the expectations for the next generation in part (b)? Is the population represented in part (a) in equilibrium?

Solution:

(a)

Numbers	Phenotypes	Genotypes
108	red	C^RC^R
144	roan	C^RC^W
48	white	C^WC^W
300		

First, let us calculate the frequency of the C^R allele. There are 108 red individuals each carrying two C^R alleles; $2 \times 108 = 216$ C^R alleles. There are 144 roan individuals each carrying only one C^R allele; $1 \times 144 = 144$ C^R alleles. Thus the total number of C^R alleles in our sample is $216 + 144 = 360$. Since each individual is a diploid (possessing two sets of chromosomes, each bearing one of the alleles at the locus under consideration), the total number of alleles represented in this sample is $300 \times 2 = 600$. The fraction of all alleles in our sample of type C^R becomes $360/600 = 0.6$ or 60%. The other 40% of the alleles in the gene pool must be of type C^W. We can arrive at this estimate for C^W by following the same procedure as above. There are $48 \times 2 = 96$ C^W alleles represented in the homozygotes and 144 in the heterozygotes; $96 + 144 = 240$; $240/600 = 0.4$ or 40% C^W alleles.

(b) Recall that panmixis is synonymous with random mating. We will let the frequency of the C^R allele be represented by $p = 0.6$, and the frequency of the C^W allele be represented by $q = 0.4$. Then according to the Hardy-Weinberg law, we would expect as genotypic frequencies in the next generation

$$p^2 = (0.6)^2 = 0.36\ C^RC^R \ : \ 2pq = 2(0.6)(0.4) = 0.48\ C^RC^W \ : \ q^2 = (0.4)^2 = 0.16\ C^WC^W$$

(c) In a sample of size 300 we would expect $0.36(300) = 108\ C^RC^R$ (red), $0.48(300) = 144\ C^RC^W$ (roan), and $0.16(300) = 48\ C^WC^W$ (white). Note that these figures correspond exactly to those of our sample. Since the genotypic and gametic frequencies are not expected to change in the next generation, the original population must already be in equilibrium.

Dominant and Recessive Autosomal Alleles.

12.4. White wool is dependent upon a dominant allele B and black wool upon its recessive allele b. Suppose that a sample of 900 sheep of the Rambouillet breed in Idaho gave the following data: 891 white and 9 black. Estimate the allelic frequencies.

Solution:

$$p^2(BB) + 2pq(Bb) + q^2(bb) = 1.0$$

If we assume the population is in equilibrium, we can take the square root of that percentage of the population which is of the recessive genotype (phenotype) as our estimator for the frequency of the recessive allele.

$$q = \sqrt{q^2} = \sqrt{9/900} = 0.1 = \text{frequency of allele } b.$$

Since $p + q = 1$, the frequency of the allele B is 0.9.

12.5. It is suspected that the excretion of the strongly odorous substance methanethiol is controlled by a recessive gene m in man; nonexcretion is governed by the dominant allele M. If the frequency of m is 0.4 in Iceland, what is the probability of finding two nonexcretor boys and one excretor girl in Icelandic families of size three where both parents are nonexcretors?

Solution:

In order that two nonexcretor parents produce an excretor child, they must both be heterozygous Mm, in which case $\frac{1}{4}$ of their children would be expected to be excretors (mm). Girls are expected with a frequency of 0.5. Therefore the probability of $Mm \times Mm$ parents producing an excretor girl is $(\frac{1}{4})(\frac{1}{2}) = \frac{1}{8}$. The probability of having a nonexcretor bcy $= (\frac{3}{4})(\frac{1}{2}) = \frac{3}{8}$. The probability of a nonexcretor individual in this population being heterozygous can be estimated from the equilibrium expectations. Let $q = 0.4$, then $p = 0.6$.

$$
\begin{array}{ccccccc}
p^2\,MM & + & 2pq\,Mm & + & q^2\,mm & = & 1.0 \\
(0.6)^2 & + & 2(0.6)(0.4) & + & (0.4)^2 & = & 1.0 \\
\underbrace{0.36 \quad + \quad 0.48}_{\text{nonexcretor}} & & & + & \underbrace{0.16}_{\text{excretor}} & = & 1.0
\end{array}
$$

The probability of a nonexcretor individual being heterozygous is $48/(36+48) = 0.57$. The probability of both parents being heterozygous $= (0.57)^2 = 0.325$.

Let $a = $ probability of heterozygous parents producing a nonexcretor boy $= \frac{3}{8}$,

$b = $ probability of heterozygous parents producing an excretor girl $= \frac{1}{8}$.

The probability of heterozygous parents producing two nonexcretor boys and one excretor girl is found in the second term of the expansion $(a+b)^3 = a^3 + 3a^2b + \cdots$; thus $3(\frac{3}{8})^2(\frac{1}{8}) = 0.053$. The probability that both nonexcretor parents are heterozygous *and* produce 2 nonexcretor boys and 1 excretor girl is $(0.325)(0.053) = 0.017$ or 1.7%.

12.6. Two independently assorting recessive genes govern production of salmon silks (sm) and shrunken endosperm (sh) of maize. A sample from a population which is mating at random yielded the following data: 6 shrunken : 10 salmon, shrunken : 30 wild type : 54 salmon. Determine the frequencies of the salmon allele q and shrunken allele t.

Solution:

6	$Sm\text{-}sh\,sh$	shrunken
10	$sm\,sm\,sh\,sh$	salmon, shrunken
30	$Sm\text{-}Sh\text{-}$	wild type
54	$sm\,sm\,Sh\text{-}$	salmon
100		

Let $q^2 = $ frequency of the recessive trait, salmon silks $= (10+54)/100 = 0.64$; $q = 0.8$.

Let $t^2 = $ frequency of the recessive trait, shrunken endosperm $= (6+10)/100 = 0.16$; $t = 0.4$.

Sex-Influenced Traits.

12.7. In the human population, an index finger shorter than the ring finger is governed by a sex-influenced gene which appears to be dominant in males and recessive in females. A sample of the males in this population was found to contain 120 short and 210 long index fingers. Calculate the expected frequencies of long and short index fingers in females of this population.

Solution:

Since the dominance relationships are reversed in the two sexes, let us use all lower case letters with superscripts to avoid confusion with either dominance or codominance symbolism.

Genotype	Phenotypes	
	Males	Females
s^1s^1	short	short
s^1s^2	short	long
s^2s^2	long	long

Let p = frequency of s^1 allele, q = frequency of s^2 allele. $p^2(s^1s^1) + 2pq(s^1s^2) + q^2(s^2s^2) = 1.0$.

In males, the allele for long finger s^2 is recessive. Then $q = \sqrt{q^2} = \sqrt{210/(120 + 210)} = \sqrt{0.64} = 0.8$; $p = 1 - 0.8 = 0.2$.

In females, short index finger is recessive. Then $p^2 = (0.2)^2 = 0.04$ or 4% of the females of this population will probably be short fingered. The other 96% should possess long index fingers.

Autosomal Loci With Multiple Alleles.

12.8. A multiple allelic system governs the coat colors of rabbits; C = full color, c^h = Himalayan, c = albino, with dominance expressed as $C > c^h > c$ and occurring with the frequencies p, q and r respectively. (a) If a population of rabbits containing full colored individuals, Himalayans and albinos, is mating at random, what is the expected genotypic ratio in the next generation in terms of p, q and r? (b) Derive a formula for the calculation of allelic frequencies from the expected phenotypic frequencies. (c) A sample from a rabbit population contains 168 full color, 30 Himalayan and 2 albino. Calculate the allelic frequencies p, q and r. (d) Given the allelic frequencies $p = 0.5$, $q = 0.1$ and $r = 0.4$, calculate the expected genotypic ratios among the full colored rabbits.

Solution:

(a) The zygotic expectations from a population mating at random with allelic frequencies p, q and r can be found by expanding $(p + q + r)^2$.

	p (C)	q (c^h)	r (c)
p (C)	$p^2\,CC$	$pq\,Cc^h$	$pr\,Cc$
q (c^h)	$pq\,Cc^h$	$q^2\,c^hc^h$	$qr\,c^hc$
r (c)	$pr\,Cc$	$qr\,c^hc$	$r^2\,cc$

Summary:

Genotypic Frequencies	Genotypes	Phenotypes
p^2	CC	
$2pq$	Cc^h	full color
$2pr$	Cc	
q^2	c^hc^h	
$2qr$	c^hc	Himalayan
r^2	cc	albino

(b) r = frequency of allele c = $\sqrt{\text{frequency of albinos}}$ = $\sqrt{r^2}$

q = frequency of allele c^h; let H = frequency of the Himalayan phenotype.

$$q^2 + 2qr = \text{H}$$

Completing the square,

$$q^2 + 2qr + r^2 = \text{H} + r^2, \quad (q+r)^2 = \text{H} + r^2, \quad q + r = \sqrt{\text{H} + r^2}, \quad q = \sqrt{\text{H} + r^2} - r$$

p = frequency of allele C = $1 - q - r$.

(c) The frequency of allele $c = r = \sqrt{2/(168 + 30 + 2)} = \sqrt{2/200} = 0.1$. To calculate the frequency of the allele c^h, let H represent the frequency of the Himalayan phenotype in the population; then $q = \sqrt{\text{H} + r^2} - r = \sqrt{30/200 + 0.01} - 0.1 = 0.3$. The frequency of the allele $C = p = 1 - q - r = 1 - 0.1 - 0.3 = 0.6$.

(d)
$$\left.\begin{array}{lll} p^2\,CC &= (0.5)^2 &= 0.25 \\ 2pq\,Cc^h &= 2(0.5)(0.1) &= 0.10 \\ 2pr\,Cc &= 2(0.5)(0.4) &= 0.40 \end{array}\right\} \text{full color}$$
$$\overline{0.75}$$

Therefore considering only the full colored rabbits, we expect

$$\begin{array}{ll} 25/75\ CC &= 33\tfrac{1}{3}\% \\ 10/75\ Cc^h &= 13\tfrac{1}{3}\% \\ 40/75\ Cc &= 53\tfrac{1}{3}\% \end{array}$$
$$\overline{100\% \text{ of the full colored rabbits}}$$

12.9. The ABO blood group system is governed by a multiple allelic system in which some codominant relationships exist. Three alleles, I^A, I^B and i form the dominance hierarchy $(I^A = I^B) > i$. (a) Determine the genotypic and phenotypic expectations for this blood group locus from a population in genetic equilibrium. (b) Derive a formula for use in finding the allelic frequencies at the ABO blood group locus. (c) Among New York Caucasians, the frequencies of the ABO blood groups were found to be approximately 49% type O, 36% type A, 12% type B and 3% type AB. What are the allelic frequencies in this population? (d) Given the population in part (c) above, what percentage of type A individuals is probably homozygous?

Solution:

(a) Let p = frequency of I^A allele, q = frequency of I^B allele, r = frequency of i allele. The expansion of $(p + q + r)^2$ yields the zygotic ratio expected under random mating.

Genotypic Frequencies	Genotypes	Phenotypes (Blood Groups)
p^2	$I^A I^A$	A
$2pr$	$I^A i$	A
q^2	$I^B I^B$	B
$2qr$	$I^B i$	B
$2pq$	$I^A I^B$	AB
r^2	ii	O

(b) Let $\bar{\text{A}}$, $\bar{\text{B}}$ and $\bar{\text{O}}$ represent the *phenotypic* frequencies of blood groups A, B and O respectively. Solving for the frequency of the recessive allele i, $r = \sqrt{r^2} = \sqrt{\bar{\text{O}}}$.

Solving for the frequency of the I^A allele,

$$p^2 + 2pr + r^2 = \bar{\text{A}} + \bar{\text{O}}, \quad (p+r)^2 = \bar{\text{A}} + \bar{\text{O}}, \quad p = \sqrt{\bar{\text{A}} + \bar{\text{O}}} - r = \sqrt{\bar{\text{A}} + \bar{\text{O}}} - \sqrt{\bar{\text{O}}}$$

Solving for the frequency of the I^B allele, $q = 1 - p - r$. Or, following the method for obtaining the frequency of the I^A allele, $q = \sqrt{\bar{\text{B}} + \bar{\text{O}}} - \sqrt{\bar{\text{O}}}$.

Presenting the solutions in a slightly different form,

$$\underbrace{\sqrt{\bar{A}+\bar{O}}-\sqrt{\bar{O}}}_{p} + \underbrace{\sqrt{\bar{B}+\bar{O}}-\sqrt{\bar{O}}}_{q} + \underbrace{\sqrt{\bar{O}}}_{r} = 1.0$$

$$p = 1 - \sqrt{\bar{B}+\bar{O}}, \quad q = 1 - \sqrt{\bar{A}+\bar{O}}, \quad r = \sqrt{\bar{O}}$$

(c) Frequency of allele $i = \sqrt{\bar{O}} = \sqrt{0.49} = 0.70 = r$

Frequency of I^B allele $= 1 - \sqrt{\bar{A}+\bar{O}} = 1 - \sqrt{0.36 + 0.49} = 0.08 = q$

Frequency of allele $I^A = 1 - \sqrt{\bar{B}+\bar{O}} = 1 - \sqrt{0.12 + 0.49} = 0.22 = p$

Check: $p + q + r = 0.22 + 0.08 + 0.70 = 1.00$

(d) $p^2 = I^A I^A = (0.22)^2 = 0.048$
     $2pr = I^A i = 2(0.22)(0.7) = \underline{0.308}$
     $ \overline{0.356} = $ total group A individuals

Thus $48/356 = 0.135$ or $13\frac{1}{2}\%$ of all group A individuals in this population is expected to be homozygous.

Sex-Linked Loci.

Codominant Sex-Linked Alleles.

12.10. The genetics of coat colors in cats was presented in Example 12.3: $C^B C^B$ ♀♀ or $C^B Y$ ♂♂ are black, $C^Y C^Y$ ♀♀ or $C^Y Y$ ♂♂ are yellow, $C^B C^Y$ ♀♀ are tortoise-shell (blotches of yellow, white and black). A population of cats in London was found to consist of the following phenotypes:

	Black	Yellow	Tortoise-Shell	Totals
Males	311	42	0	353
Females	277	7	54	338

Determine the allelic frequencies using all of the available information.

Solution:

The total number of C^B alleles in this sample is $311 + 2(277) + 54 = 919$. The total number of alleles (X chromosomes) in this sample is $353 + 2(338) = 1029$. Therefore the frequency of the C^B allele is $919/1029 = 0.893$. The frequency of the C^Y allele would then be $1 - 0.893 = 0.107$.

Dominant and Recessive Sex-Linked Alleles.

12.11. White eye color in *Drosophila* is due to a sex-linked recessive gene w, and wild type (red) eye color to its dominant allele w^+. A laboratory population of *Drosophila* was found to contain 170 red eyed males and 30 white eyed males. (a) Estimate the frequency of the w^+ allele and the w allele in the gene pool. (b) What percentage of the females in this population would be expected to be white eyed?

Solution:

(a)

Observed No. of Males	Genotypes of Males	Phenotypes of Males
170	w^+Y	wild type (red eye)
30	wY	white eye
$\overline{200}$		

Thus 30 of the 200 X chromosomes in this sample carry the recessive allele w.

$q = 30/200 = 0.15$ or 15% w alleles.

$p = 1 - q = 1 - 0.15 = 0.85$ or 85% w^+ alleles.

(b) Since females possess two **X** chromosomes (hence two alleles), their expectations may be calculated in the same manner as that used for autosomal genes.

$$p^2(w^+w^+) + 2pq(w^+w) + q^2(ww) = 1.0 \text{ or } 100\% \text{ of the females.}$$

$$q^2 = (0.15)^2 = 0.0225 \text{ or } 2.25\% \text{ of all females in the population is expected to be white eyed.}$$

TESTING A LOCUS FOR EQUILIBRIUM

12.12. An anemic condition in man called thalassemia is known to be governed by a pair of codominant alleles. The homozygous genotype T^mT^m results in severe anemia (thalassemia major) and the heterozygous genotype T^mT^n results in a mild anemia (thalassemia minor). Normal individuals are homozygous T^nT^n. The distribution of this disease among the Italian population was found to be approximately 4 major, 400 minor and 9596 normal. Does this population sample conform within statistically acceptable limits to the equilibrium expectations?

Solution:

We must first find the allelic frequencies in this population.

Let p = frequency of T^m allele = $\dfrac{2(4) + 400}{2(10,000)} = 0.02$

q = frequency of T^n allele = $1 - 0.02 = 0.98$.

Next, determine the equilibrium genotypic frequencies and then convert the frequencies to numbers on the basis of 10,000 individuals.

Genotypes	Equilibrium Frequencies	Calculations			Expected Numbers
T^mT^m	p^2	$(0.02)^2$	=	$0.0004(10,000)$ =	4
T^mT^n	$2pq$	$2(0.02)(0.98)$	=	$0.0392(10,000)$ =	392
T^nT^n	q^2	$(0.98)^2$	=	$0.9604(10,000)$ =	9,604
					10,000

Finally, check the observed numbers against the expected numbers by chi-square test.

Phenotypes	o	e	$(o-e)$	$(o-e)^2$	$(o-e)^2/e$
thalassemia major	4	4	0	0	0
thalassemia minor	400	392	8	64	0.163
normal	9596	9604	−8	64	0.007
					$\chi^2 = 0.170$

df = k phenotypes − r alleles = $3 - 2 = 1$,   P = 0.5-0.7 (Table 7.1)

This is not a significant χ^2 value and we may accept the hypothesis that this population is conforming to the equilibrium distribution of genotypes.

12.13. One of the "breeds" of poultry has been largely built on a single gene locus, that for "frizzled" feathers. The frizzled phenotype is produced by the heterozygous genotype M^NM^F. One homozygote M^FM^F produces extremely frizzled birds called "woolies". The other homozygous genotype M^NM^N has normal plumage. A sample of 1000 individuals of this "breed" in the United States contained 800 frizzled, 150 normal and 50 wooly birds. Is this population in equilibrium?

Solution:

Let p = frequency of the M^F allele = $\dfrac{2(50) + 800}{2(1000)} = 0.45$

q = frequency of M^N allele = $1 - 0.45 = 0.55$

Genotypes	Equilibrium Frequencies	Calculations			Expected Numbers
$M^F M^F$	p^2	$(0.45)^2$	=	$0.2025(1000)$ =	202.5
$M^F M^N$	$2pq$	$2(0.45)(0.55)$	=	$0.4950(1000)$ =	495.0
$M^N M^N$	q^2	$(0.55)^2$	=	$0.3025(1000)$ =	302.5

Chi-square test for conformity to equilibrium expectations.

Phenotypes	o	e	$(o-e)$	$(o-e)^2$	$(o-e)^2/e$
wooly	50	202.5	-152.5	23,256	114.8
frizzle	800	495.0	$+305.0$	93,025	187.9
normal	150	302.5	-152.5	23,256	76.9
					$\chi^2 = 379.6$

$$df = 1, \qquad P < 0.01 \quad (\text{Table 7.1})$$

This highly significant chi-square value will not allow us to accept the hypothesis of conformity with equilibrium expectations. The explanation for the large deviation from the equilibrium expectations is two-fold. Much *artificial selection* (by man) is being practiced. The frizzled heterozygotes represent the "breed" type and are kept for show purposes as well as for breeding by bird fanciers. They dispose of (cull) many normal and wooly types. *Natural selection* is also operative on the wooly types because they tend to lose their feathers (loss of insulation) and eat more feed just to maintain themselves, are slower to reach sexual maturity, and lay fewer eggs than do the normal birds.

Supplementary Problems

CALCULATING GENE FREQUENCIES
Autosomal Loci With Two Alleles
Codominant Autosomal Alleles

12.14. A population of soybeans is segregating for the colors golden, light green, and dark green produced by the codominant genotypes $C^G C^G$, $C^G C^D$, $C^D C^D$ respectively. A sample from this population contained 2 golden, 36 light green and 162 dark green. Determine the frequencies of the alleles C^G and C^D.

12.15. The M-N blood group system in man is governed by a pair of codominant alleles (L^M and L^N). A sample of 208 Bedouins in the Syrian Desert was tested for the presence of the M and N antigens and found to contain 119 group M ($L^M L^M$), 76 group MN ($L^M L^N$) and 13 group N ($L^N L^N$). (a) Calculate the gene frequencies of L^M and L^N. (b) If the frequency of $L^M = 0.3$, how many individuals in a sample of size 500 would be expected to belong to group MN?

Dominant and Recessive Autosomal Alleles

12.16. The ability of certain people to taste a chemical called PTC is governed by a dominant allele T, and the inability to taste PTC by its recessive allele t. If 24% of a population is homozygous taster and 40% is heterozygous taster, what is the frequency of t? *Hint.* Use the same method as that employed for codominant alleles for greatest accuracy.

12.17. Gene A governs purple stem and its recessive allele a produces green stem in tomatoes; C governs cut-leaf and c produces potato-leaf. If the observations of phenotypes in a sample from a tomato population were 204 purple, cut : 194 purple, potato : 102 green, cut : 100 green, potato, determine the frequency of (a) the cut allele, (b) the allele for green stem.

12.18. An isolated field of corn was found to be segregating for yellow and white endosperm. Yellow is governed by a dominant allele and white by its recessive allele. A random sample of 1000 kernels revealed that 910 were yellow. Find the allelic frequency estimates for this population.

12.19. The R locus controls the production of one system of antigens on the red blood cells of humans. The dominant allele results in Rh-positive individuals, whereas the homozygous recessive condition results in Rh-negative individuals. Consider a population in which 85% of the people are Rh-positive. Assuming the population to be at equilibrium, what is the gene frequency of alleles at this locus?

12.20. What is the highest frequency possible for a recessive lethal which kills 100% of its bearers when homozygous? What is the genetic constitution of the population when the lethal allele reaches its maximum?

12.21. Dwarf corn is homozygous recessive for gene d which constitutes 20% of the gene pool of a population. If two tall corn plants are crossed in this population, what is the probability of a dwarf offspring being produced?

12.22. A dominant gene in rabbits allows the breakdown of the yellowish xanthophyll pigments found in plants so that white fat is produced. The recessive genotype yy is unable to make this conversion, thus producing yellow fat. If a heterozygous buck (male) is mated to a group of white fat does (females) from a population in which the frequency of Y is $\frac{2}{3}$, how many offspring with yellow fat would be expected among 32 progeny?

12.23. A metabolic disease of man called "phenylketonuria" is the result of a recessive gene. If the frequency of phenylketonurics is 1/10,000 what is the probability that marriages between normal individuals will produce a diseased child?

12.24. Two recessive genes in *Drosophila*, h and b, producing hairy and black phenotypes respectively, assort independently of one another. Data from a large population mating at random follows: 9.69% wild type, 9.31% hairy, 41.31% black, 39.69% hairy and black. Calculate the frequencies for the hairy and the black alleles.

Sex-Influenced Traits

12.25. Baldness is governed by a sex-influenced trait which is dominant in men and recessive in women. In a sample of 10,000 men, 7225 were found to be non-bald. In a sample of women of equivalent size, how many non-bald women are expected?

12.26. The presence of horns in some breeds of sheep is governed by a sex-influenced gene which is dominant in males and recessive in females. If a sample of 300 female sheep is found to contain 75 horned individuals, (*a*) what percentage of the females is expected to be heterozygous, (*b*) what percentage of the males is expected to be horned?

Autosomal Loci With Multiple Alleles

12.27. The genetics of the ABO human blood groups is presented in Problem 12.9. (*a*) A sample of a human population was blood grouped and found to contain 23 group AB, 441 group O, 371 group B and 65 group A. Calculate the allelic frequencies of I^A, I^B and i. (*b*) Given the gene frequencies $I^A = 0.36$, $I^B = 0.20$ and $i = 0.44$, calculate the percentage of the population expected to be of groups A, B, AB and O.

12.28. The color of screech owls is under the control of a multiple allelic series: G^r (red) $> g^i$ (intermediate) $> g$ (gray). A sample from a population was analyzed and found to contain 38 red, 144 intermediate and 18 gray owls. Calculate the allelic frequencies.

12.29. Several genes of the horse are known to control coat colors. The A locus apparently governs the distribution of pigment in the coat. If the dominant alleles of the other color genes are present, the multiple alleles of the A locus produce the following results: A^+ = wild type (Prejvalski) horse (bay with zebra markings), A = dark or mealy bay (black mane and tail), a^t = seal brown (almost black with lighter areas), a = recessive black (solid color). The order of dominance is $A^+ > A > a^t > a$. If the frequency of $A^+ = 0.4$, $A = 0.2$, $a^t = 0.1$ and $a = 0.3$, calculate the equilibrium phenotypic expectations.

Sex-Linked Loci

12.30. A genetic disease of man called hemophilia (excessive bleeding) is governed by a sex-linked recessive gene which constitutes 1% of the gametes in the gene pool of a certain population. (*a*) What is the expected frequency of hemophilia among men of this population? (*b*) What is the expected frequency of hemophilia among women?

12.31. Color blindness in man is due to a sex-linked recessive gene. A survey of 500 men from a local population revealed that 20 were color blind. (*a*) What is the gene frequency of the normal allele in the population? (*b*) What percentage of the females in this population would be expected to be normal?

12.32. The white eyes of *Drosophila* are due to a sex-linked recessive gene and wild type (red eyes) to its dominant allele. In a *Drosophila* population the following data were collected: 15 white eyed females, 52 white eyed males, 208 wild type males, 365 wild type females (112 of which carried the white allele). Using all the data, calculate the frequency of the white allele.

TESTING A LOCUS FOR EQUILIBRIUM

12.33. A pair of codominant alleles governs coat colors in Shorthorn cattle: $C^R C^R$ is red, $C^R C^W$ is roan and $C^W C^W$ is white. A sample of a cattle population revealed the following phenotypes: 180 red, 240 roan and 80 white. (*a*) What is the frequency of the C^R allele? (*b*) What is the frequency of the C^W allele? (*c*) Does the sample indicate that the population is in equilibrium? (*d*) What is the chi-square value? (*e*) How many degrees of freedom exist? (*f*) What is the probability that the deviation of the observed from the expected values is due to chance?

12.34. A blood group system in sheep, known as the X-Z system, is governed by a pair of codominant alleles (X and X^z). A large flock of Rambouillet sheep was blood grouped and found to contain 113 X/X, 68 X/X^z and 14 X^z/X^z. (*a*) What are the allelic frequencies? (*b*) Is this population conforming to the equilibrium expectations? (*c*) What is the chi-square value? (*d*) How many degrees of freedom exist? (*e*) What is the probability of the observed deviation being due to chance?

12.35. The frequency of the T allele in a human population $= 0.8$, and a sample of 200 yields 90% tasters (T-) and 10% non-tasters (tt). (*a*) Does the sample conform to the equilibrium expectations? (*b*) What is the chi-square value? (*c*) How many degrees of freedom exist? (*d*) What is the probability that the observed deviation is due to chance?

12.36. In poultry, the autosomal gene F^B produces black feather color and its codominant allele F^W produces splashed-white. The heterozygous condition produces Blue Andalusian. A splashed-white hen is mated to a black rooster and the F_2 was found to contain 95 black, 220 blue and 85 splashed-white. (*a*) What F_2 ratio is expected? (*b*) What is the chi-square value? (*c*) How many degrees of freedom exist? (*d*) What is the probability that the observed deviation is due to chance? (*e*) May the observations be considered to conform to the equilibrium expectations?

Answers to Supplementary Problems

12.14. $C^D = 0.9$, $C^G = 0.1$

12.15. (*a*) $L^M = 75.5\%$, $L^N = 24.5\%$ (*b*) 210

12.16. $t = 0.56$

12.17. (*a*) $C = 0.30$ (*b*) $a = 0.58$

12.18. $Y = 0.7$, $y = 0.3$

12.19. $R = 0.613$, $r = 0.387$

12.20.   0.5; all individuals are heterozygous carriers of the lethal allele.

12.21.   1/36

12.22.   4

12.23. $\left(\dfrac{2(0.99)(0.01)}{(0.99)^2 + 2(0.99)(0.01)} \right)^2 (0.25) = 0.01\%$

12.24. $h = 0.7, \quad b = 0.9$

12.25.   9775

12.26.   (a) 50%   (b) 75%

12.27.   (a) $I^A = 0.05, I^B = 0.25, i = 0.70$ (b) A = 44.6%, B = 21.6%, AB = 14.4%, O = 19.4%

12.28. $G^r = 0.1, \ g^i = 0.6, \ g = 0.3$

12.29.   64% wild type, 20% dark bay, 7% seal brown, 9% black

12.30.   (a) 1/100   (b) 1/10,000

12.31.   (a) 0.96   (b) 99.84%

12.32. $w = 0.19$

12.33.   (a) 0.6   (b) 0.4   (c) Yes   (d) 0   (e) 1   (f) 1

12.34.   (a) $X = 0.75, \ X^z = 0.25$ (b) Yes   (c) 0.7   (d) 1   (e) 0.3-0.5

12.35.   (a) No   (b) 18.75   (c) 1   (d) < 0.001

12.36.   (a) $\frac{1}{4}$ black : $\frac{1}{2}$ blue : $\frac{1}{4}$ splashed-white   (b) 4.50   (c) 1   (d) 0.01-0.05   (e) No

Chapter 13

Cytoplasmic Factors

MATERNAL EFFECTS

Some attributes of progeny are not expressions of their own genes, but rather those of the maternal parent. Such effects may be ephemeral or may persist throughout the lifespan of the individual. The substances which produce maternal effects are not self-perpetuating, but must be synthesized anew for each generation of progeny by the appropriate maternal genotype.

Example 13.1. A dominant gene K in the meal moth *Ephestia* produces a hormone-like substance called *kynurenine* which is involved in pigment synthesis. The recessive genotype kk is kynurenineless and cannot synthesize pigment. Females with K produce eggs containing a small amount of kynurenine. For a short time during early development, a larva may use this supply of kynurenine to develop pigment even though its own genotype is kk. The color fades as the larvae grow older because the maternally supplied kynurenine becomes depleted.

Example 13.2. The direction in which the shell coils in the snail *Limnaea* can be *dextral* like a right hand screw or *sinistral* like a left hand screw. The maternal genotype organizes the cytoplasm of the egg in such a way that cleavage of the zygote will follow either of these two patterns regardless of the genotype of the zygote. If the mother has the dominant gene s^+, all her progeny will coil dextrally; if she is of genotype ss, all her progeny will coil sinistrally. This coiling pattern persists for the life of the individual.

PLASMAGENES

The behavior of some genetic elements indicates that they are not located on chromosomes. The smallest heritable extrachromosomal unit is called a *plasmagene*. All of the plasmagenes of a cell constitute the *plasmon*. Cytoplasm contains several organelles which may have physical continuity from one generation to the next. It is assumed that they do not arise *de novo* (i.e. manufactured by the cell from elementary particles), but are produced by replication of a preexisting organelle. The centrioles, which organize the polar regions during division, probably reproduce themselves as do the basal granules (sometimes called blepharoplasts or kinetosomes) associated with cilia or flagella. Mitochondria and plastids probably develop from undifferentiated structures such as proplastids. The fact that DNA has been found in mitochondria and plastids is one line of evidence which indicates that these organelles could carry genetic information. Other organelles such as microsomes, lysosomes, Golgi bodies, etc., may also be the residence of plasmagenes, but evidence at the present does not delimit the site of extranuclear genetic factors to these structures.

Traits with an extranuclear basis are identified by the accumulated evidence from a number of diagnostic criteria, as exemplified in the following cases.

(1) Differences in reciprocal crosses which cannot be attributed to sex-linkage or some other chromosomal basis tend to implicate extranuclear factors.

    (a) When progeny shows only the characteristics of the female parent, *maternal inheritance* is operative. If this can be attributed to unequal cytoplasmic contributions of male and female parents, then plasmagenic inheritance is suspect.

Example 13.3. In higher plants, pollen usually contributes very little, if any, cytoplasm to the zygote. Most of the cytoplasmic elements are transmitted through the maternal parent. In the plant called "four-o'clock" (*Mirabilis jalapa*), there may be normal green, pale green, and variegated branches due to two types of chloroplasts. Plants grown from seeds which developed on normal green branches (with all normal chloroplasts) will all be normal green; those which developed on pale green branches (with abnormal chloroplasts) will all be pale green; those on variegated branches (with both normal and abnormal chloroplasts) will segregate green, pale green, and variegated in irregular ratios. The type of pollen used has no effect in this system. The irregularity of transmission from variegated branches is understandable if plasmagenes exist in the chloroplasts, because there is no mechanism to insure the regular distribution of chloroplasts to daughter cells as there is for chromosomes.

(*b*) The unidirectional inheritance of a trait which cannot be attributed to unequal cytoplasmic contributions from parental gametes may nonetheless involve cytoplasmic factors.

Example 13.4. The uniting gametes of the single celled alga *Chlamydomonas reinhardi* (Fig. 1-11) are morphologically indistinguishable. One strain of the alga which is streptomycin resistant (*sr*) and of the "plus" mating type (mt^+) is crossed to a cell of "negative" mating type (mt^-) which is streptomycin sensitive (*ss*). All progeny are resistant, but the nuclear genes for mating type segregate as expected: $\frac{1}{2}mt^+, \frac{1}{2}mt^-$. The reciprocal cross $ss\,mt^+ \times sr\,mt^-$, again shows the expected segregation for mating type, but all progeny are sensitive. Repeated backcrossings of $sr\,mt^+$ to $ss\,mt^-$ fail to show segregation for resistance. It appears as though the plasmagenes of the mt^- strain become lost in a zygote of mt^+. The mechanism which inactivates the plasmagenes of mt^- in the zygote is unknown.

(2) Extranuclear factors may be detected by either the absence of segregation at meiosis (Example 13.5) or by segregation which fails to follow Mendelian laws (Example 13.6).

Example 13.5. Slow-growing yeast cells called *petites* lack normal activity of the respiratory enzyme cytochrome oxidase associated with the mitochondria. Petites can be maintained indefinitely in vegetative cultures through budding, but can sporulate only if crossed to wild type. When a haploid neutral petite cell fuses with a haploid wild type cell of opposite mating type, a fertile wild type diploid cell is produced. Under appropriate conditions, the diploid cell reproduces sexually (sporulates). The four ascospores of the ascus (Fig. 1-12) germinate into cells with a 1 : 1 mating type ratio (as expected for nuclear genes), but they are all wild type. The petite trait never appears again, even after repeated backcrossings of both mating types to petite. The mitochondrial factors for petite are able to perpetuate themselves vegetatively, but are "swamped", lost or permanently altered in the presence of wild type factors. Neutral petite behaves the same in reciprocal crosses regardless of mating type, and in this respect is different from the streptomycin resistance factors in *Chlamydomonas* (Example 13.4).

Example 13.6. Another type of petite in yeast called *supressive* may segregate, but in a manner different from chromosomal genes. When haploid supressive petites are crossed to wild types and each zygote is grown vegetatively as a diploid strain, both petites and wild types may appear, but in frequencies which are hardly Mendelian, varying from 1% to 99% petites. Diploid wild type cells may sporulate producing only wild type ascospores. By special treatment, all diploid zygotes can be made to sporulate. The majority of the ascospores thus induced germinates into petite clones. Some asci have 4, 3, 2, 1 or 0 petite ascospores, suggesting that environmental factors may alter their segregation pattern. Nuclear genes, such as mating type, maintain a 1 : 1 ratio in all asci.

(3) Repeated backcrossing of progeny to one of the parental types for several generations causes their chromosomal genetic endowment to rapidly approach 100% that of the parental line. The persistence of a trait in the progeny, when the backcross parent exhibits an alternative character, may be considered evidence for cytoplasmic factors.

Example 13.7.   The protoperithecial parent in *Neurospora* (Fig. 1-13) supplies the bulk of the extrachromosomal material of the sexually produced ascospores. Very slow spore germination characterizes one strain of this fungus. The trait exhibits differences in reciprocal crosses, maternal inheritance, and fails to segregate at meiosis. When the slow strain acts as protoperithecial parent and the conidial strain has normal spore germination, all the progeny are slow, but possess 50% of the nuclear genes of the conidial parent. Each generation is then backcrossed to the conidial parent, so that the F_2 contains 75%, F_3 contains 87.5%, etc., of nuclear genes of the conidial parent. After the fifth or sixth backcross, the nuclear genes are almost wholly those of the conidial parent, but the slow germination trait persists in all of the progeny.

(4) Many substances are known which cause nuclear genes to mutate, but these *mutagens* are non-specific, i.e. they increase the frequency of mutations at many loci, and only a minority of the survivors of the treatment will have mutated. Extra-nuclear genetic elements, however, may not exhibit these mutational characteristics.

Example 13.8.   Petite yeast arise spontaneously at low frequency in most cultures. If yeast are grown in media containing a small amount of acriflavine, all of the cells survive, and up to 100% of them will show only the petite trait. The specific induction by this mutagen and the high rate of recovery of petite mutants suggests changes in cytoplasmic factors rather than in nuclear genes.

SPECIFIC INDUCTION OF PHENOTYPIC CHANGE

A specifically induced change in the phenotype need not emanate from a permanent heritable change in either the nuclear or extranuclear genetic systems. All of these changes collectively represent a broad spectrum of stabilities. An induced phenotypic change may persist for the life of the individual (Example 13.9); it may persist in subsequent generations or it may be induced to change at any time during the life cycle (Example 13.10); or it may gradually disappear in subsequent generations of progeny (Example 13.11).

Example 13.9.   An environmentally induced change which resembles the effects of a gene mutation is called a *phenocopy*. By injecting boric acid into chick eggs at the appropriate stage of development, birds with shortened limbs are produced resembling the "creeper" trait attributed to chromosomal genes. The effect of the treatment which produces any phenocopy does not extend beyond the life of the individual. All of the sexually produced offspring will be normal. The inducing agent presumably interferes with the function of genes and/or plasmagenes during critical stages of development, but does not induce permanent changes in the hereditary material.

Example 13.10.   The antigens of *Paramecium* are under the control of nuclear genes. An individual of a certain strain may have several loci, each specifying a different antigen, but only one locus is active at a given time, and thus only one antigen can be detected. In strain 90, low temperatures activate the locus which specifies antigen S, all other loci being inactivated; at intermediate temperatures, only the locus for antigen G becomes active; at high temperatures only antigen D appears. If the environment remains constant, the induced antigenic change persists through subsequent generations of progeny. At any time during the life cycle (Fig. 1-10) however, a change in temperature could cause a transformation in the serotype. In the absence of cytoplasmic exchange, reciprocal crosses give different results. Even though the nuclei are genetically identical, the serotype of each exconjugant is the same as that prior to conjugation. It appears that temperature can predictably modify the organization of the cytoplasm. The state of the cytoplasm then determines which locus can become active.

Example 13.11.   *Dauermodifications* are transient, environmentally induced changes in plasmagenes, decreasing in penetrance and expressivity in succeeding generations in the absence of the inducing stimulus. Treatment of *Phaseolus vulgaris* with a 0.75% solution of chloral hydrate results in abnormal leaf development. Only abnormal plants are used as parents in each generation. The first generation of sexual progeny reared in a normal environment may have about 75% abnormal plants. As late as the fourth generation nearly 50% of the plants may still be abnormal. By the seventh generation only normal plants may be found. The reversion of a dauer-modification to normal phenotype might be due to backmutation of altered plasmagenes or to the cumulative selection of normal cytoplasmic components which have survived the treatment.

SYMBIONTS

Organisms which live together are called *symbionts*. Some symbionts live at the expense of their hosts, as parasites. Some symbionts help each other as exemplified by the association of algae and fungi in lichens. An intracellular symbiont such as a bacterium or a virus may produce a novel phenotype in its host. The distinction between a living and a non-living organism becomes tenuous when we consider a virus and the various phases in which it may exist. A virus may exist in an autonomous and infective state or its genetic material may be so similar to a portion of its host that it becomes a part of the host chromosome. The virus may be induced to return to an autonomous state under the appropriate environmental stimulus. Other genetic elements are known to have the option of a chromosomal or extrachromosomal existence. All such elements are non-essential to the life of the host cell and are called *episomes*. Symbionts may exhibit an infection-like transmission with a hereditary continuity of their own. Letters of the Greek alphabet (*kappa, lambda, mu*, etc.) are commonly used to name intracellular symbionts.

> **Example 13.12.** *Killer* paramecia harbor parasitic or symbiotic particles called *kappa* in their cytoplasm. These particles are about the size of a large virus or small bacterium and contain some DNA. Kappa produce a poison, *paramecin*, which kills individuals lacking kappa (*sensitives*). A dominant nuclear gene K must be present for the maintenance and replication of kappa. Cells of genotype kk that have acquired kappa are *unstable*, will loose these particles, and eventually become sensitives. Kappa can be regained by conjugation with a killer in which cytoplasmic exchange occurs. Kappa cannot be generated *de novo* in sensitives of genotypes KK or Kk. Sensitive cells are resistant to the effects of paramecin during conjugation with killer cells.

Solved Problems

MATERNAL EFFECTS

13.1. The hermaphroditic snail *Limnaea peregra* can reproduce either by crossing or by self-fertilization. The direction in which the shell coils is a maternal effect as explained in Example 13.2, page 261. A homozygous dextral snail is fertilized with sperm from a homozygous sinistral snail. The heterozygous F_1 undergoes two generations of self-fertilization. (*a*) What are the phenotypes of the parental individuals? (*b*) Diagram the parents, F_1, and two selfing generations, showing phenotypes and genotypes and their expected ratios.

Solution:

(*a*) Although we know the genotypes of the parents, we have no information concerning the genotype of the immediate maternal ancestor which was responsible for the organization of the egg cytoplasm from which our parental individuals developed. Therefore we are unable to determine what phenotypes these individuals exhibit. Let us assume for the purpose of diagramming part (*b*) that the maternal parent is dextral and the paternal parent is sinistral.

(b) Let D = dextrally organized cytoplasm, S = sinistrally organized cytoplasm.

Parents:

dextral egg
parent

×

sinistral sperm
parent

F_1:

dextral F_1

First Selfing Generation:

dextral
$\frac{1}{4}$

dextral
$\frac{1}{2}$

dextral
$\frac{1}{4}$

Second Selfing Generation:

dextral
$\frac{1}{4}$

dextral
$\frac{1}{2}$

dextral
$\frac{1}{4}$

sinistral

Notice that the F_1 is coiled dextrally, not because its own genotype is s^+/s, but because the maternal parent possessed the dominant dextral gene s^+. Likewise in the first selfing generation, all are phenotypically dextral regardless of their own genotype because the F_1 was s^+/s. In the second selfing generation, we expect the following:

First Selfing Generation		Second Selfing Generation			Summary Genotypes				Phenotypes	
$\frac{1}{4}$ s^+s^+	×	all s^+s^+	=	$\frac{1}{4}$ s^+s^+	s^+s^+	=	$\frac{1}{4}+\frac{1}{8}$	=	$\frac{3}{8}$	$\Big\}\frac{5}{8}$ dextral
		$\begin{cases}\frac{1}{4}\ s^+s^+ \\ \frac{1}{2}\ s^+s \\ \frac{1}{4}\ ss\end{cases}$	$\begin{matrix}= \\ = \\ =\end{matrix}$	$\begin{matrix}\frac{1}{8}\ s^+s^+ \\ \frac{1}{4}\ s^+s \\ \frac{1}{8}\ ss\end{matrix}$	s^+s	=	$\frac{1}{4}$	=	$\frac{2}{8}$	
$\frac{1}{2}$ s^+s	×									
$\frac{1}{4}$ ss	×	all ss	=	$\frac{1}{4}$ ss	ss	=	$\frac{1}{8}+\frac{1}{4}$	=	$\frac{3}{8}$	sinistral

PLASMAGENES

13.2. Assume that a neutral petite yeast (Example 13.5, page 262) has the chromosomal genes for normally functioning mitochondria, but has structurally defective mitochondria. Another kind of yeast is known, called *segregational petite,* which has structurally normal mitochondria which cannot function because of inhibition due to a recessive mutant chromosomal gene. What results would be expected among the sexual progeny when the neutral petite crosses with the segregational petite?

Solution:

The diploid zygote receives structurally normal mitochondria from the segregational petite parent which should be able to function normally in the presence of the dominant nuclear gene from the neutral petite parent. Sporulation would probably distribute at least some structurally normal mitochondria to each ascospore. The nuclear genes would segregate 1 normal : 1 segregational petite. Let shaded cytoplasm contain defective mitochondria. See figure below.

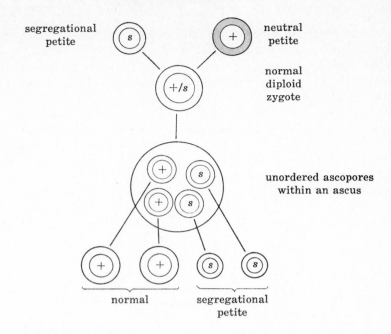

13.3. A condition called "poky" in *Neurospora* is characterized by slow growth due to an abnormal respiratory enzyme system similar to that of petite yeast. The poky trait is transmitted through the maternal (protoperithecial) parent. A chromosomal gene *F* interacts with poky cytoplasm to produce a faster growing culture called "fast-poky" even though the enzyme system is still abnormal. Poky cytoplasm is not permanently modified by transient contact with an *F* genotype in the zygote. It returns to the poky state when the genotype bears the alternative allele *F'*. Gene *F* has no phenotypic expression in the presence of a normal cytoplasm. If the maternal parent is fast-poky and the paternal (conidial) parent is normal, predict the genotypes and phenotypes of the resulting ascospores.

Solution:

Let shaded cytoplasm contain poky mitochondria. The chromosomal alleles segregate in a 1:1 ratio, but poky cytoplasm follows the maternal (protoperithecial) line. The recovery of poky progeny indicates that poky cytoplasm has not been altered by its exposure to the *F* gene in the diploid zygotic stage.

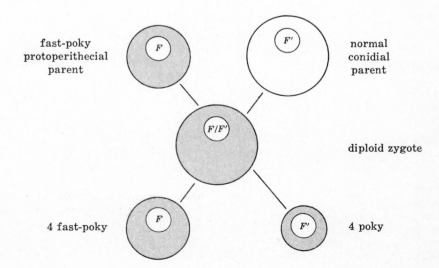

13.4. Commercial corn results from a "double-cross". Starting with four inbred lines (A, B, C, D), a single cross is made between A and B by growing the two lines together and removing the tassels from line A so that A cannot self-fertilize, and thus receives only B pollen. In another locality the same procedure is followed for lines C and D. The yield of single cross hybrid seed is usually low because the inbred parent lacks vigor and produces small cobs. Plants that germinate from single-cross seed are usually vigorous hybrids with large cobs and many kernels. It is undesirable for the single-cross hybrid to self-fertilize, as this inbreeding process commonly produces less vigorous progeny. Therefore a double-cross is made by using only pollen from the CD hybrid on the AB hybrid. Detasseling is a laborious and expensive process. A cytoplasmic factor which prevents the production of pollen (male-sterile) is known. There also exists a dominant nuclear gene R which can restore fertility in a plant with male sterile cytoplasm. Propose a method for eliminating hand detasseling in the production of double-cross hybrid commercial seed.

Solution:

Let S = male sterile cytoplasm, F = male fertile cytoplasm. The ABCD double cross hybrid seed develops on the large ears of the vigorous AB hybrid. When these seeds are planted they will grow into plants, half of which carry the gene for restoring fertility so that ample pollen will be shed to fertilize every plant.

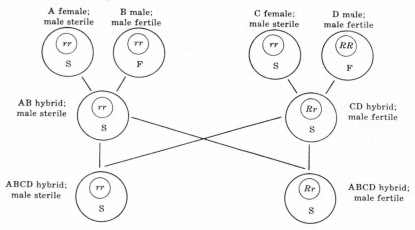

13.5. A recessive chromosomal gene produces green and white stripes in the leaves of maize, a condition called "japonica". This gene behaves normally in monohybrid crosses giving a 3 green : 1 striped ratio. Another striped phenotype was discovered in Iowa, named "iojap" (a contraction of Iowa and japonica), which is produced by a recessive gene ij when homozygous. If a plant with iojap striping serves as the seed parent, then the progeny will segregate green, striped and white in irregular ratios regardless of the genotype of the pollen parent. Backcrossing striped progeny of genotype Ij/ij to a green pollinator of genotype Ij/Ij produces progeny which continue to segregate green, striped and white in irregular ratios. White plants die due to lack of functional chloroplasts. Green plants produce only green progeny except when the genotype of the progeny is ij/ij; striping then reappears. Interpret this information to explain the inheritance of iojap.

Solution:

It appears that the chromosomal gene ij when homozygous induces irreversible changes in normal plastids. The plastids exhibit autonomy in subsequent generations, being insensitive to the presence of Ij in single or double dose. Random distribution of plastids to daughter cells could give all normal plastids to some, all defective plastids to others, and a mixture of normal and defective plastids to still others. All plastids are not rendered defective in the presence of ij/ij as this would produce only white (lethal) seedlings.

SYMBIONTS

13.6. If a woman contracts German measles during the first trimester of pregnancy, the child may be seriously affected even though the mother herself suffers no permanent physical effects. Such anomalies as heart and liver defects, deafness, cataracts and blindness often occur in the affected children at birth. Can these phenotypic results be considered hereditary abnormalities?

Solution:

It is important to distinguish between *congenital* defects (recognizable at birth) which are acquired from the environment during embryonic development and genetic defects which are produced in response to the baby's own genotype. The former may be produced by infective agents such as the virus of German measles, which is not really a part of the baby's genotype but is acquired through agents external to the developing individual. An active case of this disease usually produces immunity so that subsequent children of this mother should not be susceptible to the crippling influences of this virus. A hereditary disease is one which is produced in response to instructions of an abnormal gene belonging to the diseased individual and which can be transmitted in Mendelian fashion from generation to generation.

13.7. The killer trait in *Paramecium* was explained in Example 13.12, page 264. A killer paramecium of genotype Kk conjugates with a sensitive paramecium of the same genotype without cytoplasmic transfer. One of the exconjugants is killer, the other is sensitive. Each of those exconjugants undergoes autogamy. Predict the genotypes and phenotypes of the autogamous products.

Solution:

Reciprocal fertilization in paramecia produces identical genotypes in the exconjugants. In the micronuclear heterozygotes Kk, which of the four haploid nuclei produced by meiosis (K, K, k, k) will survive depends on chance. Thus whether cytoplasmic mixing occurs or not, both exconjugants are expected to be KK 25% of the time, Kk 50% of the time, and kk 25% of the time. Autogamy of the exconjugants cannot produce any genotypic change in the homozygotes, but does produce homozygosity in heterozygotes. Half of the autogamous products of the monohybrid Kk are expected to be KK and half kk.

$$
\begin{array}{cc}
\text{Exconjugants with} & \\
\text{Kappa (Killers)} & \text{Autogamous Products} \\
\frac{1}{4}\,KK & = \frac{1}{4}\,KK \\
& \frac{1}{2}\,KK = \frac{1}{4}\,KK \quad\Big\} \quad \frac{1}{2}\,KK \text{ (killer)} \\
\frac{1}{2}\,Kk & \\
& \frac{1}{2}\,kk = \frac{1}{4}\,kk \\
\frac{1}{4}\,kk & = \frac{1}{4}\,kk \quad\Big\} \quad \frac{1}{2}\,kk \text{ (unstable)}
\end{array}
$$

The same genotypic ratios would be expected in the autogamous products of exconjugants without kappa, but phenotypically they would all be sensitive.

13.8. The conjugation of paramecia occasionally results in the fusion of the two cells into a single animal with two gullets and other sets of organelles. Fission of doublets produces only more doublets. The genetic determinants for the doublet trait apparently reside neither in the nucleus nor the cytoplasm, but exclusively in the rigid outer envelope or cortex. A killer doublet of genotype KK conjugates with a sensitive singlet of genotype kk, in one case with and in another without cytoplasmic transfer. Predict the genotypic and phenotypic results of (*a*) fission in the exconjugants, (*b*) autogamy in the exconjugants.

Solution:

(*a*) Let us diagram this cross using shaded cytoplasm to represent the presence of kappa as shown below.

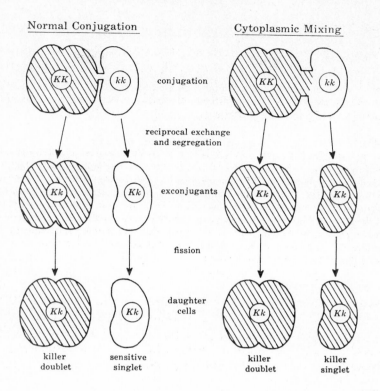

(b) Autogamy of the exconjugants produces homozygosity for its nuclear genes. There is a 50% chance that autogamy in a heterozygote (Kk) will produce homozygous KK, and a 50% chance for kk. Unstable individuals usually loose kappa within 8 or 10 fissions.

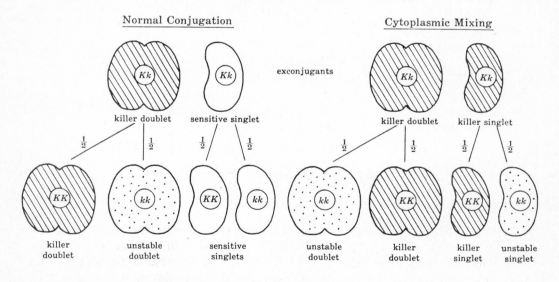

Notice in parts (a) and (b) that the predetermined structure of a doublet in its immobile ectoplasm does not segregate either with the nuclear gene K or the cytoplasmic marker kappa.

Supplementary Problems

MATERNAL EFFECTS

13.9. Continued use of certain drugs can lead to addiction. Addicted mothers by non-addicted fathers give birth to babies which are addicted. The children of addicted fathers by non-addicted mothers are normal. This difference in reciprocal crosses is not due to extranuclear genetic elements. Suggest a mechanism to account for the results.

13.10. *Eythroblastosis fetalis* or hemolytic disease of the newborn is caused by a blood group incompatibility between a mother and her child. The blood group antigen most frequently involved is D, governed by a dominant gene, *R*. Individuals who do not possess the D antigen are called Rh negative and may be considered homozygous recessive *rr*. When an Rh positive child develops in the uterus of an Rh negative woman, some of the baby's cells pass into the maternal circulation. The mother's body reacts to this foreign antigen (D) by producing Rh antibodies. The maternal antibodies pass across the placenta into the baby's circulation and react with the baby's blood cells, resulting in their destruction. A jaundiced condition and anemia are symptomatic of the disease. About 85% of the U.S. population is Rh positive. (*a*) Erythroblastotic children may appear from the cross $RR \male \times rr \female$. Can the reciprocal cross produce Rh hemolytic disease? (*b*) What is the probability of a husband and wife having incompatible Rh bloodtypes that could lead to erythroblastosis in some of their children?

13.11. A snail produced by a cross between two individuals has a shell with right hand twist (dextral). This snail produces only left hand (sinistral) progeny by selfing. Determine the genotype of this snail and its parents. See Example 13.2, page 261, and Problem 13.1, page 264.

13.12. The genetic control of eye and skin color in larvae of the meal moth *Ephestia* is outlined in Example 13.1, page 261. (*a*) Determine the larval and adult phenotypes (colored or white) in the F_1 and F_2 from the mating $KK \female \times kk \male$. (*b*) Do the same for the reciprocal cross.

13.13. A male and female *Ephestia* moth, both colored as larvae, were crossed. About half of the adult progeny were colored, half were white. What color did the male and female parents possess as adults?

PLASMAGENES

13.14. Most strains of *Chlamydomonas* are sensitive to streptomycin. A strain is found which requires streptomycin in the culture medium for its survival. How could it be determined whether streptomycin-dependence is due to a chromosomal gene or to a cytoplasmic element?

13.15. Exposing a culture of white yeast to the mutagenic action of mustard gas produced some red individuals. When the red mutants were propagated vegetatively, some white cells frequently reappeared. How can these results be explained?

13.16. A yeast culture, when grown on medium containing acriflavine, produces numerous minute cells which grow very slowly. How could it be determined whether the slow growth was due to a cytoplasmic factor or to a nuclear gene?

13.17. The nuclear gene *F* in the presence of poky cytoplasm produces a fast-poky phenotype (Problem 13.3). In the presence of normal cytoplasm it has no phenotypic expression. How could a strain of *Neurospora* with normal growth be tested for the presence of *F* or its allele, *F'*?

13.18. Determine the genotypes and phenotypes of sexual progeny in *Neurospora* from the following crosses: (*a*) fast-poky male × normal female of genotype *F'*, (*b*) poky female × fast-poky male, (*c*) fast-poky female × poky male.

13.19. The cells of a *Neurospora* mycelium are usually multinucleate. Fusion of hyphae from different strains results in the exchange of nuclei. A mycelium which has genetically different nuclei in a common cytoplasm is called a *heterokaryon*. Moreover, the union results in a mixture of two different cytoplasmic systems called a *heteroplasmon* or a *heterocytosome*. The mycelia of two slow growing strains, each with an aberrant cytochrome spectrum, fuse to form a heteroplasmon that exhibits normal growth. Abnormal cytochromes *a* and *b* are still produced by the heteroplasmon. Offer an explanation for this phenomenon.

13.20. A striped phenotype in maize can be produced by either of two independently assorting recessive genes, japonica (j) or iojap (ij) (see Problem 13.5). Suppose that stocks of all the various genotypes for these two traits are available and you are given a striped plant which is either japonica or iojap. (a) What cross would you make to discover the genotype of this striped plant? (b) Give the genotype and phenotype expected in the F_1 if the plant was japonica. (c) List the phenotypes expected in the F_1 if the plant was iojap.

13.21. Male sterile plants in corn may be produced either by a chromosomal gene or by a cytoplasmic factor. (a) At least 20 different male sterile genes are known in maize, all of which are recessive. Why? Predict the F_1 and F_2 results of pollinating (b) a genetic male sterile by a normal, (c) a cytoplasmic male sterile by a normal.

13.22. Given seed from a male sterile line of corn, how would you determine if the sterility was genic or cytoplasmic?

13.23. Fireweed or the willow herb belongs to the genus *Epilobium*. Interspecific crosses of *E. luteum* ♀ × *E. hirsutum* ♂ gives a fertile F_1, but the reciprocal cross gives a pollen-sterile F_1. It has been suggested that *luteum* plastids function normally in combination with the hybrid genotype but *hirsutum* plastids function abnormally with adverse effects on fertility. To test this hypothesis it would be desirable to observe the effects of *hirsutum* plastids in *luteum* cytoplasm and of *luteum* plastids in *hirsutum* cytoplasm. Can you discern any biological impediment in the implementation of these experiments?

SYMBIONTS

13.24. Determine which of the three paramecial phenotypes (killer, unstable, or sensitive) is produced by the following combinations of genotype and cytoplasmic state. *Hint.* See Example 13.12, page 264.

	Genotype	Cytoplasm
(a)	*KK*	kappa
(b)	*Kk*	no kappa
(c)	*kk*	kappa
(d)	*KK*	no kappa
(e)	*Kk*	kappa
(f)	*kk*	no kappa

13.25. When a killer strain of paramecia conjugates without cytoplasmic transfer with a sensitive strain, half of the exconjugants are sensitives and half are killers. Autogamy of the killer exconjugants produces only killers; autogamy of the sensitive exconjugants produces only sensitives. What are the genotypes of (a) the two original strains, (b) the exconjugants, (c) the autogamous products?

13.26. When two paramecia, each of genotype *Kk*, conjugate, with what frequencies are the following genotypes expected in the two exconjugants?

	Exconjugant #1	Exconjugant #2
(a)	*KK*	*KK*
(b)	*KK*	*Kk*
(c)	*KK*	*kk*
(d)	*Kk*	*Kk*
(e)	*Kk*	*kk*
(f)	*kk*	*kk*

13.27. When paramecia of genotype *Kk* possessing kappa conjugate with sensitive cells of genotype *kk*, and the exconjugants undergo autogamy, what percentage of the autogamous products are expected to possess and be able to maintain kappa through subsequent fissions if (a) conjugation is normal, (b) cytoplasmic mixing occurs?

13.28. From the following paramecial matings, predict the phenotypic ratios among the exconjugants under normal conditions and under conditions of cytoplasmic mixing.

| | \multicolumn{4}{c}{Conjugating Paramecia} | \multicolumn{2}{c}{Exconjugant Phenotypes} |
	Genotype	Cytoplasm	× Genotype	Cytoplasm	Normal Conjugation	Cytoplasmic Mixing
(a)	KK	kappa	KK	no kappa		
(b)	KK	no kappa	KK	no kappa		
(c)	KK	kappa	kk	no kappa		
(d)	Kk	kappa	kk	no kappa		

13.29. What percentage of exconjugants from the following paramecial matings will possess and be able to maintain kappa through subsequent asexual divisions?

| | \multicolumn{3}{c}{Mating Type} | \multicolumn{2}{c}{Exconjugants Produced By:} |
	Kappa Present	× Kappa Absent	Normal Conjugation	Cytoplasmic Mixing
(a)	KK	KK		
(b)	KK	Kk		
(c)	KK	kk		
(d)	Kk	Kk		
(e)	Kk	kk		
(f)	kk	kk		

13.30. With reference to the doublet trait described in Problem 13.8, where conjugations occur both with and without cytoplasmic mixing between sensitive doublets of genotype *kk* and killer singlets of genotype *KK*, predict the genotypic and phenotypic results of (*a*) fission in the exconjugants, (*b*) autogamy in the exconjugants.

13.31. Some *Drosophila* flies are known to be very sensitive to carbon dioxide gas, rapidly becoming anesthetized under its influence. Sensitive individuals possess a cytoplasmic particle called *sigma* which has many of the attributes of a virus. Resistant individuals do not have *sigma*. This trait shows strictly maternal inheritance. Predict the results of a cross between (*a*) sensitive female × resistant male, (*b*) sensitive male × resistant female.

13.32. Injection of body fluids or implantation of organs from a carbon dioxide sensitive fly (see Problem 13.31) into a normal resistant fly can render the recipient sensitive to CO_2. What kind of progeny would an inoculated female be likely to produce? Why?

13.33. A virus is suspected to be involved in the development of breast cancer in certain strains of mice. The virus is transmitted through the milk to the offspring. In crosses where the female carries the "milk factor" and the male is from a strain free of the factor, about 90% of the female progeny develop breast cancer prior to 18 months of age. The virus usually does not initiate cancer development in the infected mouse until she enters the nursing stage, and then only in conjunction with a hormone (estrone) from the ovaries. Males from a virus infected strain are crossed with females from a virus-free strain. (*a*) Predict the proportion of the offspring from this cross which, if individually isolated from weaning to 18 months of age, will probably exhibit breast cancer. (*b*) Predict the proportion of offspring from this cross which will probably exhibit breast cancer if housed in a group from weaning to 18 months of age. (*c*) Answer part (*a*) when the reciprocal cross is made. (*d*) Answer part (*b*) when the reciprocal cross is made.

13.34. Another case in which a disease is acquired through the milk (see Problem 13.33) is hemolytic anemia in newborn horses. A mare may produce two or three normal offspring by the same stallion and the next foal may develop severe jaundice within about 96 hours after birth and die. Subsequent matings to the same stallion often produces the same effect. Subsequent matings to another stallion could produce normal offspring. It has been found that if nursed for the first few days on a foster mother the foal will not become ill and develops normally. Evidently something is in the early milk (colostrum) which is responsible for this syndrome. If the foal should become ill, and subsequently recovers, the incompatibility is not transmitted to later generations. (*a*) How might this disease be generated? (*b*) How is the acquisition of this disease different from that of breast cancer in mice?

13.35. A bacterial spirochaete which is passed to the progeny only from the maternal parent has been found in *Drosophila willistoni*. This microorganism usually kills males during embryonic development but not females. The trait is called "sex ratio" (SR) for obvious reasons. Occasionally, a son of an SR female will survive. This allows reciprocal crosses to be made. The SR condition can be transferred between *D. equinoxialis* and *D. willistoni*. The spirochaete is sensitive to high temperatures which inactivates them, forming "cured" strains with a normal sex ratio. (*a*) What would you anticipate to be the consequence of repeated backcrossing of SR females to normal males? (*b*) A "cured" female is crossed to a rare male from an SR culture. Would the sex ratio be normal? Explain.

Answers to Supplementary Problems

13.9. Small molecular weight molecules are continually diffusing across the placenta from the maternal circulation to that of the fetus and vice versa. Drugs taken by the mother enter the fetus in this manner.

13.10. (*a*) No. If the mother has the D factor she will not make antibodies against her own antigens. (*b*) $0.85 \times 0.15 = 0.13$

13.11. Parents: $s^+s\,♀ \times s/?\,♂$; F_1: ss

13.12. (*a*) F_1: larvae and adults colored (Kk); F_2: $\frac{3}{4}$ colored larvae and adults (K-) : $\frac{1}{4}$ colored larvae, white adults (kk). (*b*) same as part (*a*)

13.13. Colored female (Kk); white male (kk)

13.14. Cross $ss\,mt^-$ (male) $\times$ $sd\,mt^+$ (female); if chromosomal, 25% of the sexual progeny should be $ss\,mt^-$, 25% $ss\,mt^+$, 25% $sd\,mt^-$, 25% $sd\,mt^+$; if cytoplasmic, almost all of the progeny should follow the maternal line (streptomycin dependent) as in Example 13.5, page 262, while mating type segregates $1\,mt^-$: $1\,mt^+$.

13.15. Asexual reproduction cannot produce segregation of nuclear genes, but cytoplasmic constitutents can be differentially distributed to fission products.

13.16. From a cross of minute $\times$ normal, a nuclear gene will segregate in the spores in a $1:1$ ratio (e.g. segregational petite in Problem 13.2). If an extranuclear gene is involved, segregation will not be evident and all spores will be normal (e.g. neutral petite in Example 13.5, page 262).

13.17. Use the unknown as conidial parent on a standard poky strain. If the unknown carries F, half of the ascospores will be poky and half fast-poky. If the unknown carries F', all of the sexual progeny will be poky.

13.18. (*a*) all phenotypically normal; $\frac{1}{2}F'$ (normal cytoplasm) : $\frac{1}{2}F$ (normal cytoplasm). (*b*) and (*c*) $\frac{1}{2}$ fast-poky; F (poky cytoplasm) : $\frac{1}{2}$ poky; F' (poky cytoplasm)

13.19. One strain may have an abnormal cytochrome-a but a normal cytochrome-b. The other strain might have an abnormal cytochrome-b but a normal cytochrome-a. The normal cytochromes in the heteroplasmon complement each other to produce rapid growth.

13.20. (*a*) Use the striped plant as seed parent; use pollen from a japonica plant of genotype $Ij/Ij, j/j$. (*b*) all japonica striped (j/j). (*c*) green, striped and white in unpredictable ratios.

13.21. (*a*) A plant in which a dominant genic male sterile gene arose by mutation of a normal gene would be unable to fertilize itself and would be lost unless cross-pollinated by a fertile plant. The gene would be rapidly eliminated from heterozygotes within a few generations by continuous back crossing to normal pollen parents. (*b*) F_1: $+/ms$, fertile; F_2: $\frac{1}{4}+/+$, $\frac{1}{2}+/ms$, $\frac{1}{4}ms/ms$; $\frac{3}{4}$ fertile, $\frac{1}{4}$ male sterile. (*c*) male sterile cytoplasm is transmitted to all F_1 progeny; a selfed F_2 cannot be produced because none of the F_1 plants can make fertile pollen.

13.22. Plant the seeds and pollinate the resulting plants with normal pollen from a strain devoid of male sterility. If the F_1 is sterile, then it is cytoplasmic; if the F_1 is fertile, it is genic.

13.23. Plastids are rarely transmitted through the pollen. For this reason it is not possible to get *hirsutum* plastids in *luteum* cytoplasm or vice versa.

13.24. Killer = $(a), (e)$; unstable = (c); sensitive = $(b), (d), (f)$

13.25. $(a) (b) (c)$ All killers are *KK* with kappa; all sensitives are *KK* without kappa.

13.26. $(b) (c) (e) = 0\%$; $(a) (f) = 25\%$; $(d) = 50\%$

13.27. (a) 12.5% (b) 25%

13.28.

	Normal Conjugation	Cytoplasmic Mixing
$(a) (c)$	1 killer : 1 sensitive	both killers
		both sensitive
(b)	both sensitive	both sensitive
(d)	1 killer : 1 unstable : 2 sensitive	1 killer : 1 unstable

13.29.

	Normal Conjugation	Cytoplasmic Mixing
$(a) (b) (c)$	50%	100%
(d)	37.5%	75%
(e)	25%	50%
(f)	0%	0%

13.30.

	Normal Conjugation		Cytoplasmic Mixing	
	Doublet	Singlet	Doublet	Singlet
(a)	*Kk* sensitive	*Kk* killer	*Kk* killer	*Kk* killer
(b)	$\frac{1}{2}KK$ sensitive	$\frac{1}{2}KK$ killer	$\frac{1}{2}KK$ killer	$\frac{1}{2}KK$ killer
	$\frac{1}{2}kk$ sensitive	$\frac{1}{2}kk$ unstable	$\frac{1}{2}kk$ unstable	$\frac{1}{2}kk$ unstable

13.31. (a) all progeny sensitive (b) all progeny resistant

13.32. Only sensitive progeny would probably be produced because *sigma* is an infective agent which would invade the ooplasm.

13.33. $(a) (b)$ None of the progeny is expected to develop breast cancer because non-infected females have nursed them. (c) None of the progeny is expected to develop breast cancer because in isolation the infected females could never produce a litter and subsequently enter a lactation period, a prerequisite for expression of the milk factor. (d) 50% females $\times$ 90% of females develop breast cancer = approximately 45%.

13.34. (a) This disease is similar to the Rh blood group system incompatibility between a human mother and her baby in Problem 13.10. In this case, antibodies are transferred to the offspring through the milk rather than across the placenta. (b) The particular stallion that is used has an immediate effect on the character. This is not true in the acquisition of breast cancer in mice. The incompatibility disease in horses cannot be transmitted to later generations, so there is no evidence of a specifically self-duplicating particle like the infective agent which causes mice cancer.

13.35. (a) If interspecific crosses can transmit the spirochaete, it is probably relatively insensitive to the chromosomal gene complement. Backcrossing would cause no change in the SR trait; indeed this is how the culture is maintained. (b) The sex ratio would probably be normal. It is unlikely that the spirochaete would be included in the minute amount of cytoplasm which surrounds the sperm nucleus.

INDEX

Catalog

If you are interested in a list of SCHAUM'S OUTLINE SERIES in Science, Mathematics, Engineering and other subjects, send your name and address, requesting your free catalog, to:

SCHAUM'S OUTLINE SERIES, Dept. C
McGRAW-HILL BOOK COMPANY
1221 Avenue of Americas
New York, N.Y. 10020